Late Fragments

CHARLES BAUDELAIRE

Late
Fragments

FLARES, MY HEART LAID BARE,
PROSE POEMS, BELGIUM DISROBED

Translated from the French and Edited by Richard Sieburth

A MARGELLOS
WORLD REPUBLIC OF LETTERS BOOK

Yale UNIVERSITY PRESS | NEW HAVEN & LONDON

Yale University Press books may be purchased in quantity for
educational, business, or promotional use. For information,
please e-mail sales.press@yale.edu (US office) or sales@yaleup
.co.uk (UK office).

Set in Source Serif Pro type by Motto Publishing Services.
Printed in the United States of America.

Library of Congress Control Number: 2021946537
ISBN 978-0-300-18518-8 (hardcover : alk. paper)

A catalogue record for this book is available from the British
Library.

This paper meets the requirements of ANSI/NISO Z39.48-1992
(Permanence of Paper).

10 9 8 7 6 5 4 3 2 1

Contents

PART THREE · *Belgium Disrobed*

Appendixes

Preface

I first began seriously reading Baudelaire as an undergraduate at the University of Chicago in the late nineteen sixties, under the tutelage of art critic Harold Rosenberg, author of *The Tradition of the New*. In the fall of my senior year, Walter Benjamin's *Illuminations* appeared in English: its essays "On Some Motifs in Baudelaire" and "On the Task of the Translator" were revelations. My very first publication, a translation of the black humor bits of Baudelaire's *Poor Belgium*, appeared in the college's undergraduate literary magazine in the spring of 1970. My second venture into print, shortly thereafter, was a (pirate) translation of Benjamin's "Hashish in Marseilles."

Over the years Benjamin's work continued to inform my reading and teaching of Baudelaire. In 2013, I was awarded a Guggenheim Fellowship to complete the English edition of Baudelaire's *Late Fragments*, a sample of which was first published in the "Exiles" issue of *Conjunctions* in the spring of 2014. Various previous commitments (compounded by the mimetic contagion of Baudelaire's own habits of procrastination) delayed the timely completion of this book—which, like my other editions of French or German authors, conjoins the art of the introductory essay with the crafts of philology and translation.

The past few decades have seen an extraordinary flowering of Baudelaire scholarship. Let me here record my debt (in alphabetical order) to those critics who have most shaped my conceptualization of this project over the years: Leo Bersani (*Baudelaire and Freud*, 1977), Yves Bonnefoy (*Sous le signe de Baudelaire*, 2011), Richard D. E. Burton (*Baudelaire and the Second Republic: Writing and Revolution*, 1991), Roberto Calasso (*La*

Folie Baudelaire, 2012), Ross Chambers (*Mélancolie et opposition,* 1987), T. J. Clark (*The Absolute Bourgeois: Artists and Politics in France, 1848–1851,* 1973), Antoine Compagnon (*Les Antimodernes de Joseph de Maistre à Roland Barthes,* 2005; *Baudelaire l'irréductible,* 2014), Barbara Johnson (*Défigurations du langage poétique: La Seconde Révolution baudelairienne,* 1987), Françoise Meltzer (*Seeing Double: Baudelaire's Modernity,* 2011), Steve Murphy (*Logiques du dernier Baudelaire,* 2007), Philippe Muray (*Le 19e Siècle à travers les âges,* 1984), Jean Starobinski (*Portrait de l'artiste en saltimbanque,* 1970; *La Mélancolie au miroir,* 1989), Jérome Thélot (*Baudelaire: Violence et poésie,* 1993), and Cornelia Wild (*Später Baudelaire: Praxis poetischer Zustände,* 2008).

To these names should of course be added that of the late Claude Pichois, editor and annotator of the Pléiade volumes of Baudelaire's *Oeuvres complètes* (1975–76) and of his *Correspondance* (1973), as well as that of his successor, André Guyaux, whose Folio edition of *Fusées, Mon Coeur mis à nu, La Belgique déshabillée* (1986) has proved seminal. My understanding of the notion of the fragment reaches back to my first readings of Jean-Luc Nancy's and Philippe Lacoue-Labarthe's *L'Absolu littéraire: Théories le littérature du romantisme allemand* (1978); my apprehension of *la bêtise* was quickened by Avital Ronell's *Stupidity* (2001); Edward Said's *Late Style: Music and Literature Against the Grain* (2006) provided further instigation.

All references to Pichois's Pléiade volumes are indicated as follows: OC1 and OC2 for Baudelaire's *Oeuvres complètes,* and C1 and C2 for his *Correspondance.*

Unless otherwise indicated, all translations are my own.

Late Fragments

Introduction

In his influential essay "Late Style in Beethoven," Theodor Adorno observed:

> The maturity of the late works of significant artists does not resemble the kind one finds in fruit. These late works are, for the most part, not round, but furrowed, even ravaged. Devoid of sweetness, bitter and prickly, they do not surrender themselves to mere delectation. They lack all the harmony that the classicist aesthetic is in the habit of demanding from works of art, and they show more traces of history than of growth. . . . In the history of art late works are the catastrophes.[1]

Baudelaire's late writings of the 1860s—*Flares, My Heart Laid Bare, Belgium Disrobed,* and the final prose poems of *Paris Spleen*—seem especially to invite Adorno's imagery of desiccation and discord, presenting as they do a bitter harvest of anger and outrage, prickly to the palate and virtually impossible to swallow, as the mounting pile of rejection slips toward the end of his career proved. Unpublishable and unfinishable, these late works of Baudelaire never made it beyond manuscript form, existing merely as *feuilles volantes*—stray leaves of scrap paper or stationery afloat in that state of permanent indecision, akin to idleness, unemployment, or boredom, that Maurice Blanchot called *désoeuvrement.* If they can be deemed works at all, it is only in Blanchot's special sense that they are *oeuvres de l'absence de l'oeuvre,* works of (or in) the absence of that great prospective Oeuvre-to-come of which Baudelaire would dream until his final days—namely, a uniform edition of his

Works that would include his verse, his prose poems, his literary essays, and his art criticism, and whose publication would finally assure him a steady literary income and, more important, guarantee his immortality as he contemplated his fast-approaching death. Absent the realized, working capital of such an Oeuvre, ever harried by creditors, ever falling deeper into debt, Baudelaire gradually withdrew himself from circulation and instead chose exile in Brussels (a place he positively loathed), where he henceforth devoted himself to the production of fragments destined for a series of unmarketable and unrealizable books—the scattered shards of a totality that continued to escape him.

In his influential 1966 study, *Le Dernier Baudelaire*, the French psychocritic Charles Mauron was the first to provide a detailed literary diagnosis of the Late Baudelaire, a figure whose emergence—or whose catastrophe—he roughly dated to 1861.[2] Indeed, after the appearance of the second, expanded edition of his *Flowers of Evil* that same year, Baudelaire would publish no further major book of poetry or prose. During his two-year residence in Brussels from 1864 to 1866, the final installments of his five-volume translation of Poe appeared in Paris, but since he had already sold back all his eventual royalties to their publisher, Michel Lévy, to raise much-needed cash, he made strictly nothing on the deal—further testimony of his ill-advised squandering of his literary assets. In March of 1866, a mere month before he was felled by the stroke that would reduce him to terminal aphasia, Baudelaire brought out his final, broken volume of verse, fittingly entitled *Les Épaves* (variously translated as *Wrecks* or *Scraps* or *Flotsam*). Assembled with the help of his longtime friend the Belgium-based publisher of erotica and esoterica, Auguste Poulet-Malassis, this limited edition of 260 copies, purportedly published in Amsterdam "At the Sign of the Cock," collected the flotsam and jetsam of his poetic career. At the core of this late project lay Baudelaire's desire to showcase the six notorious poems (or "Pièces condamnées") that, as a result of the trial of *The Flowers of Evil* in 1857, had been excised from all subsequent editions on the grounds of their obscenity. Belgium was laxer when it came to the censorship of literature, but imperial France proved unforgiving. Two years after its publication—and with Baudelaire already in his grave—a judge in Lille, happening upon an illegally imported copy of *Les Épaves*, decreed that the entire edition be destroyed, sentencing Malassis (still well beyond the reach of the law in Brussels) to a year's imprisonment and a hefty fine of 500 francs. Not until 1949, more than ninety years after their initial publication, would the ban on these six poems be officially lifted by the French courts—a posthumous life of crime beyond Baudelaire's wildest dreams.

The frontispiece to this 1866 volume of *Les Épaves* was provided by Félicien Rops, a young Belgian artist whom Baudelaire had met through Malassis.[3] The engraving is a *memento mori* whose allegorical motifs imitate a sixteenth-century woodcut featuring Adam and Eve standing to the sides of a large skeleton whose upper portion, its arms outstretched in crucifixion, gradually turns into the trunk and sprouting leaves of a tree. In Rops's gonzo rendition, the top of the frame is occupied by a comic medallion portrait of Baudelaire's head, carried off by a chimera into a sky cluttered with fetuslike putti. Below the arborescent skeleton lie small banners of the seven deadly sins, strewn among a field of charnel bones and decaying vegetation. At the bottom, there is another balloon-like medallion containing the image of an ostrich eating a horseshoe, surrounded by the Latin motto "Virtus Durissima Coquit" ("virtue nourishes itself on the vilest things"). Despite the crude, cartoonish quality of Rops's frontispiece, it served to call attention to Baudelaire's rediscovery of the baroque during his exile in Belgium—a late style that he described (in an insight not lost on Walter Benjamin) as proposing a "new antiquity" on which a new poetics of modernity might build.

In publishing this late wreckage site of *Épaves*—littered with the *disjecta membra* of the *Flowers of Evil*, bits of rococo kitsch, allegorical grotesquerie, and doggerel satirizing Belgium—Baudelaire signaled the dusk of his poetic career or "Le Coucher du soleil romantique" ("The Sunset of Romanticism"), as the title of the sonnet that prefaced *Les Épaves* put it.[4] The publisher's note that prefaced the volume (very likely composed by the poet himself) speaks bleakly of its potential readership: "The author will be duly informed of the publication of this book, as will the two hundred and sixty likely readers who more or less make up what its kindly publisher considers to be the literary public in France, now that the speech of humans, over there, has obviously been arrogated by the beasts" ("depuis que les bêtes y ont décidemment usurpé la parole sur les hommes"). *Les bêtes*: not simply animals at their lowest or most frightening but, in French, those people who, like beasts, are (inhumanly or subhumanly) *stupid*, that is, who incarnate *la bêtise*—Baudelaire's chief object of opprobrium toward the end of his life (as it was the late Flaubert's and the late Nietzsche's). Having chosen to commit a slow suicide in Brussels, finding his morose delectation in the unerring *bêtise* (or *Dummheit*) of its brutish populace, Baudelaire was in a sense fulfilling the imperative of one of his early alexandrines: "Ne cherchez plus mon coeur, les bêtes l'ont mangé." Stop looking for my heart, it's been eaten by the beasts. Whatever heart he had left in him in Belgium he would now throw entirely—and self-sacrificially—to the dogs.

*   *   *

But when, exactly, can Baudelaire be said to have become *late* (or, for that matter, *bête* or *belge*—those two monosyllabic black holes of his final years)? For Jean-Paul Sartre, in his book-length introduction to the 1946 edition of Baudelaire's *Écrits intimes* (which included *Flares* and *My Heart Laid Bare*), the poet's biography needed to be understood in terms of the foundational crisis that divided his life into a before and after. This crisis, according to Sartre, occurred when Baudelaire was seven. A year after the death at age sixty-eight of her first husband (adored by his young son, Charles), the thirty-four-year-old Caroline Baudelaire (née Dufaÿis) becomes pregnant with the child of the army officer Jacques Aupick. A shotgun marriage is arranged, and three weeks later, she gives birth to a stillborn daughter. In Sartre's existential psychoanalysis, the Oedipal Baudelaire, feeling utterly abandoned, betrayed and disgusted by his mother, is now violently expelled from his infant paradise and makes his "original choice"—that "absolute engagement by which each of us decides in a particular situation what he will be and what he is."[5] From here on in, Baudelaire determines to become *another*—other than his mother, other than Aupick, and, in a supreme act of *mauvaise foi*, or bad faith, other than himself. A Narcissus engaged in the rapt contemplation of his sterile reflection, forever trying to turn himself into a *thing* in his own eyes and those of *autrui*, Baudelaire is constructed by the Marxist Sartre as an emblematic figure of bourgeois self-alienation and self-reification. For such a subject, there can be no progress, no history, no development, no revolution, but merely (as Walter Benjamin says of allegory) an ongoing state of "petrified unrest." As the victim of an original Fall (or false existential "choice") that occurred at age seven, Baudelaire will therefore always experience his life as already or about to be over. "Few existences have been more stagnant than his," Sartre comments. "He fell to pieces rather than evolved. Year after year we find him just the same, simply older, gloomier, his mind less rich and less alert, his body more battered. And for those who have followed him step by step, the final dementia appears less like an accident than the logical outcome of his decline."[6] In other words, if Baudelaire does not change, it is because it will always have been too *late*.

"Baudelaire chose to advance backwards, his face turned toward the past," Sartre adds, in a metaphor that recalls Benjamin's celebrated description of the angel of history in Paul Klee's *Angelus Novus*:

He has his face turned toward the past. What we perceive as a chain of events, he sees as a single catastrophe endlessly heaping ruin upon ruin and hurling the debris at his feet. He would gladly linger on—to wake the dead, to piece together what has been shattered. But a storm is blowing from Paradise, so mighty that it has gotten caught in his wings and made it impossible for the angel to close them. The storm irresistibly buffets him into the future to which his back is turned, while the pile of debris before him mounts skyward. This storm is what we call progress.[7]

To judge from his correspondence, the seminal catastrophe to which Baudelaire reverted back in anger and horror again and again, the irremediable blow that had been fatally dealt both to his liberty and his pride, the judgment that had forever fixed his destiny and guilt, was his family's decision in 1844 to appoint a *conseil judiciaire* (or legal trustee) to oversee his finances. At his majority, Baudelaire had inherited the comfortable sum of 100,000 francs (roughly equivalent to the same amount in dollars), nearly half of which he managed to dilapidate over the next two years, living the high bohemian life of Paris, acquiring a quadroon mistress by the name of Jeanne Duval—and, more disastrously for his subsequent health, apparently catching syphilis from a Jewish whore known as Sara. Despite his family's attempt to correct his extravagant Parisian ways by dispatching him on a slow boat to India (from which he jumped ship at Réunion after three months), Baudelaire's profligacy ran on so uncurbed that his alarmed relatives finally obtained a decree from the Civil Tribunal of the Seine that essentially demoted him to the permanent status of a minor. From the age of twenty-three to the day of Baudelaire's death, Narcisse Désiré Ancelle would act as the administrator of his trust fund, allotting him an allowance of 200 francs a month. Baudelaire experienced this tutelage to his conseil judiciaire (which he hid from even the closest of his friends) as a theological mark of Cain. Here, too, when it came to money matters, he was therefore condemned to being always *late*—chronically behind on his rent, forever in arrears to his creditors, forced to fend off the burden of ever-mounting debt by trying his luck in the literary marketplace, placing his work as best he could in the periodical press, often selling the same pieces over and over again or attempting to cadge advances from magazine editors on the reputation of his name. It is estimated that Baudelaire's lifetime earnings from his literary work amounted to 14,000 francs—9,000 coming from his translations of Edgar Allan Poe and 5,000 from his original works—roughly the equivalent of the salary that a midlevel bureaucrat of the period would have earned over three years of employment.[8] Given his inability to balance his expenses against his income, Baudelaire therefore lives in a world of perpetually deferred obligation where nothing can ever get paid or done *on time*. Gnawed by endless remorse—that deepest moral prick of debt and belatedness, Joyce's "agenbite of inwit"—all Baudelaire can do is to try to make reparations as best he can and hope for eventual forgiveness from above.

According to the grand inquisitorial logic of Sartre, just as Baudelaire had on some level masochistically sought out the humiliation of living under the iron rule of his conseil judiciare, so in his ongoing need for punishment he had also deliberately provoked the French courts into bringing his *Flowers of Evil* to justice in 1857. Having followed the trial of Gustave Flaubert's *Madame Bovary* earlier that same year, Baudelaire was no doubt defiantly playing with fire by publishing poems that prominently featured blasphemy and sapphism, but in the notes that he prepared for his defense counsel he insisted that instead of exclusively focusing on the various offending poems that the prosecution had singled out as sacrilegious or obscene, his book should be judged as a *whole*. Only if read as a totality, he suggested, would the book's terrifying moral vision of Evil fully emerge as a passionate ethical admonition to the modern world. Besides, in holding him legally responsible for his utterances, the court was confusing the speakers of his poetry—who were, after all, mere dramatic characters or personae—with the author behind the book, mistaking the "I" of the poems for the actual Charles Baudelaire, man of letters, who stood accused before Imperial Prosecutor Pierre Ernest Pinard. Finally, and as a further argument in his defense, the formal excellence of the work—as an example of art for art's sake—should have easily trumped whatever objectionable content it might have contained, for the high price and limited distribution of the volume proved that these poems were not intended for the general public and therefore could have no deleterious impact on the religion or morality of the nation. The trial was of course a farce—with Baudelaire being accused among other things of the crime of graphic "realism" (an aesthetic he despised)—but in the end he got off relatively easily. The number of incriminated poems was dropped from twenty-one to six and, after the poet wrote a sycophantic letter to the empress, his fine was reduced from 300 to a more manageable 50 francs.

The 1857 trial of the *Flowers of Evil* made of Baudelaire an instant celebrity—a disreputable and somewhat sulfurous figure to the old classicist guard, but to the young generation of disillusioned postromantics his work represented (in the words of Victor Hugo) *un frisson nouveau*, a new thrill. Baudelaire would later try to dismiss the trial as nothing but a "misunderstanding," though he privately admitted it was a complete "humiliation." His perfectly architected volume of verse, composed exactly of one hundred poems and carefully supported by five thematic columns ("Spleen and Ideal," "Flowers of Evil," "Wine," "Revolt," "Death"), had been, with the violent excision of the six indicted poems, turned into a ruined temple of a work. After the ruling against *The Flowers of Evil* was made public in late August, its publisher, Malassis (also heavily fined but who had ducked his court appearance, given the jail time he had previously served for his left-wing participation in the bloody June days of 1848) remained in Alençon, trying to salvage the two hundred copies that survived from the initial print run of one thousand. The censored poems were torn out, along with other texts that happened to be on the same leaf; replacement stubs were then re-composed to be reinserted at the appropriate place. Baudelaire begged Malassis to stop this "ridiculous surgical operation." There was no way that the wounds inflicted on the body of his poems could be healed. His precious book was now a maimed, truncated fragment of itself.

During the very same month that he learned of the court's decision to mangle his first volume of verse, Baudelaire was consoled by the magazine publication in *Le Présent* of his "Poèmes nocturnes" ("Night poems"), a sequence of six poems written in prose, three of which, significantly enough, were recastings of texts he had initially composed in verse. From the very outset, then, Baudelaire conceived the prose poem as a form that emerges *after* or that belatedly displaces or rhetorically "defigures" (in Barbara Johnson's deconstructive sense) traditional lyric.[9] He had come to the genre through his discovery of Aloysius Bertrand's 1842 *Gaspard de la nuit*, now commonly recognized as the first modern collection of *poèmes en prose* in French. In addition, he had been reading and translating Poe's short stories for more than ten years now, with his recent editions of the American's *Histoires extraordinaires* and *Nouvelles Histoires extraordinaires* doing well in sales. The coincidence in August 1857 of the mutilation of *The Flowers of Evil* and of the first appearance of the germ of the collection he would later call his *Petits Poèmes en prose* or *Le Spleen de Paris* thus defines the precise chiasmus where Baudelaire's verse begins to cross over into unlineated prose. From this point on, his rhymed poetry would become more "prosaic," even as, in a complementary diagonal move, he would continue to explore the rhythmic and phrasal structures of the poème en prose. By 1861, he more or less gives up writing and publishing serious verse on a regular basis altogether: his late work (with the exception of the wreckage of *Les Épaves*) will all take place within the medium of prose—essays, translations, reviews, maxims, reflections, *pensées*, anecdotes, prose poems, unwritten short stories and novels, and finally the ferocious rubble of his unpublished (and unpublishable) "Book on Belgium," initially entitled *Pauvre Belgique* and subsequently named *La Belgique déshabillée* (*Belgium Disrobed,* possibly in allusion to Francisco de Goya's *Maja desnuda*).

Baudelaire's evolution toward the prosaic is most notable in the new section of "Tableaux parisiens" (or "Parisian Views") that he added to the revised and expanded 1861 edition of *The Flowers of Evil,* most of whose significant poems were written during his last intense burst of creativity during the annus mirabilis of 1859, largely spent at his mother's cottage in Honfleur on the Normandy coast. In the three great pieces dedicated to Victor Hugo—"Le Cygne" ("The Swan"), "Les Sept Vieillards" ("The Seven Old Men"), "Les Petites Vieilles" ("Little Old Ladies")—Baudelaire abandoned the strictures of the short lyric for looser, longer narrative forms. Indeed, the concluding piece that he added to this edition, "Le Voyage" ("The Journey"), is a condensed epic, a nihilistic anti-*Odyssey* of sorts. The speaker of many of these new poems resembles less a traditional lyric "I" than a split ego out of Poe, at once the ironic object and subject of his own disintegrating urban consciousness. In addition, Baudelaire breaks down the armature of classical French prosody: enjambments become more frequent, the phrasing more paratactic, median caesurae are weakened, while rhymes on such modern everyday words as "omnibus" and "rebus" add to the cacophony of the ghostly Unreal City that contemporary Paris had now become to him. Paul Claudel famously said of Baudelaire's "Swan" that the poet had managed to combine Racine with Second Empire journalism. Of his poem "The Seven Old Men" (originally entitled "Parisian Phantoms") Baudelaire proudly observed in a letter of 1859 that he had here finally "managed to exceed the limits assigned to poetry." To Malassis he similarly wrote that in their shattering of conventions, this new batch of poems was meant to be "like a gas explosion in a glass factory." Composed with consummate craft, blending the classical with the baroque, the imagistic with the allegorical, the topical with the eternal, here at last was poetry that was as urgent as the latest news. And news, at least insofar as its impact on subsequent history of modernist verse is concerned, that would definitely *stay news.* To his mother he wrote: "For the first time in my life, I am almost content. . . . This is a book that will *last*—as evidence of my disgust and hatred for all things."[10]

Brought out by Malassis in a printing of 1,500 copies in February 1861, the second edition of *The Flowers of Evil* was a *succès d'estime,* despite its lukewarm reception by the press: only Swinburne would dithyrambically greet its appearance in an essay published in England the following year. Immediately after its publication, Baudelaire slipped into postpartum depression. He wrote Malassis in March:

> From some time now, I have been on the verge of suicide, and the only thing holding me back has nothing to do with cowardice or regret. It's out of sheer pride that I don't want to leave all my business matters in a mess. *I shall leave behind whatever needs to be paid.* . . . I am not, as you know, a sniveler or a liar. In the last two months, I have fallen into an alarming state of sluggishness and despair. I have felt myself attacked by a kind of malady à la Gérard [de Nerval], namely the fear of being unable to think anymore, or to write a single line. It was only four or five days ago that I managed to verify that I wasn't dead in that respect. Which is not negligible.[11]

The project that had proved to Baudelaire that his mental faculties were indeed still intact was his ecstatic "improvisation" of a review (composed, so he claimed, at a white heat over three days in a printing shop) of the first performance of Richard Wagner's *Tannhäuser* in Paris—the pioneer appreciation of the German composer to appear in France, as Nietzsche would later discover with astonishment and approval.

By the following month, however, he had again fallen into despondency. His mother, now four years a widow after the death of her beloved General Aupick, had written from Honfleur to say that she had indeed received her son's most recent edition of *Les Fleurs du mal* but that before reading it she had reluctantly felt impelled to show it to her confessor—who had promptly consigned the volume to the flames. Wracked by anguish, her nerves frayed, she told her son she wished she were dead. Baudelaire replied by assuring her that he too had considered taking his own life and that, like her, he felt "lost, absolutely lost." In early May he wrote her a long letter in which, addressing her by the familiar *tu*, he finally laid everything on the line: his passionate love for her in his early childhood, his immense feeling of betrayal when she married Aupick, and, above all, his resentment of her acquiescence in having Ancelle appointed as his conseil judiciaire when he was twenty-three: "In short, the harm is done, done by your imprudent acts and by my errors. We are evidently destined to love one another, to live for one another, to end our lives as properly and smoothly as possible. And yet, in the terrible circumstances in which I am placed, I am convinced that one of us shall kill the other, and that in the end we shall be the mutual cause of each other's demise." "My situation is atrocious," he continued: although his "literary prospects" seemed decent, his "spiritual health" was wretched—and not just his spiritual health, but his very physical well-being. A bombshell followed:

> I don't want to talk about those nervous diseases which are destroying me day by day and which are rendering my willpower void—the vomitings, the insomnias, the nightmares, the fainting fits. I have mentioned these to you too often. But there's no use in being cagey with you. You know that when I was a very young man, I caught a syphilitic infection, of which I later believed I had been completely cured. In Dijon, after 1848, it broke out again—and then again went into remission. Now it has again returned and taken on a new form—patches on my skin and an extraordinary fatigue in all my joints. In the misery into which I have sunken, perhaps my terror is aggravating the disease. But I must put myself on a strict regimen; I can no longer afford to live the life I lead.

He went on to conclude, after this devastating confession, that he now saw his existence as "a continuum of horror" and lived in permanent expectation of an imminent "catastrophe." Despite the appointment of Ancelle as his conseil judiciaire—his mother's fault, of course—he underlined that "*everything is eaten up, and I am old and miserable.*" He wondered whether some sort of "rejuvenation" might be possible but left the question open. He informed his mother that he felt like an ossified "mummy." He had just turned forty.[12]

From mid-1861 onward, his health failing, his finances ever more in disarray, feeling he had outlived himself as a poet, Baudelaire enters into his endgame. In May, deeply into debt to his friend and publisher Malassis, he sells him the exclusive rights to reproduce all of his previously published literary works as well as all those eventually to appear (conveniently forgetting the contract he had previously signed with Lévy for his Poe translations). In July, remembering the extraordinary spurt of creativity he had experienced two years earlier and still holding out hope for his "renewal," he speaks to his mother of moving back to her retirement cottage at Honfleur and sends several trunks of papers on ahead in preparation for what he hopes will be a productive stay. He tells her that he has a long list of projects waiting to be completed: "twenty ideas for novels, two ideas for plays, and a major book about *myself*, my *Confessions*"—the never-to-be completed *My Heart Laid Bare*. But like all the innumerable projects he elaborates toward the end of life, this *nostos* to the *maison joujou* (or "toy house") of Honfleur would be forever deferred. In this same July letter to his mother, he also announced his decision to submit his candidacy for a vacant seat at the august Académie française, a decision which he made official to its permanent secretary Abel Villemain in December of that year— the same month that, in another vain attempt to put his life in order, he broke with Jeanne Duval, his mistress and muse of nearly twenty years.[13]

Baudelaire's quixotic candidacy to the French Academy was in part an endeavor to gain respectability in the eyes of his mother and to erase the humiliating memory of his 1857 trial, four years earlier. It was also a publicity campaign of sorts, in which he presented himself as the stalking horse (or, as he put it, "the sacrificial goat") for the newer school of writers informally gathered under the label of *l'art pour l'art* or "pure literature"—Flaubert, Gautier, Banville, Leconte de Lisle—all of whom were still excluded from official recognition by the Academy. (As Flaubert remarked in his *Dictionary of Received Ideas*: "Académie Française: Denigrate it, but become a member of it if you can"). After embarking on the obligatory rounds to garner votes from the Immortals, Baudelaire quickly realized that his candidacy had been an egregiously stupid move on his part—*une grosse sottise* ("la sottise" happening to be the very first noun in the "Au Lecteur" poem that opens his *Fleurs du mal*). Only the aged Alfred de Vigny had received him courteously, deigning to recognize his talents as a writer while sagely advising him not to venture into the maze of the Academy's byzantine electoral process—and, most important, encouraging him to take himself more seriously as a poet. Baudelaire hinted to Vigny that he had engaged in his campaign only to collect material for a *livre buffon* (or jestbook) that would narrate his visits to the various academicians, providing a series of Daumierlike caricatures of the Immortals in all their neoclassical idiocy.[14] If all else failed, at least his candidacy would have served as a proto-Dadaist stunt that might enable him to take his revenge on the French literary establishment once and for all. The only trace of this livre buffon was found among his papers after his death. Entitled "The Spirit and Style of M. Villemain," it is a twenty-page ad hominem screed against the academy's permanent secretary, a text whose unremitting (and very Célinian) vitriol points forward to his later fulminations against Belgium.

Unable to extricate himself from the very public predicament into which he had placed himself, Baudelaire felt as if he had gone into a dizzying free fall. On a stray piece of paper, later included in the manuscript he called *Flares/Hygiene*, he confided: "Morally and physically I have always had a sensation of the abyss—not only the abyss of sleep, but the abyss of action, of dream, of memory, of desire, of regret, of remorse, of beauty, of number, etc. I have cultivated my hysteria with joy and terror. Now, I am continually beset by vertigo, and today, January 23, 1862, I was given a special warning: I felt *the wind of the wing of imbecility* pass over me."[15] How to interpret this *vent de l'aile de l'imbécillité*? Christopher Isherwood translates it as "the wind of the wing of madness"—poetically seductive, to be sure, but certainly over the mark as a rendering of "imbecility," which has less to do with insanity than with feebleness of mind. Claude Pichois, Baudelaire's premier modern editor and biographer, sees in the word an allusion to a possible cerebral hemorrhage brought on by the "old wound" (as Baudelaire called it) of his syphilis, while however failing to mention that this lesion, real or imagined, would have compounded the poet's growing dread of falling into the kind of terminal writer's block or state of artistic incapacitation that had driven Gérard de Nerval to hang himself in 1855, unable to bring his final masterpiece, *Aurélia,* to completion. In his 1856 study of Poe, Baudelaire had very precisely remembered the date of Nerval's suicide on the rue de La Vieille Lanterne: "Today, January 26, it was just a year ago that an admirably decent, highly intelligent writer, and one who was *forever lucid*, decided discretely and without bothering anyone—in fact so discretely that his discretion resembled contempt—to untether his soul in the darkest alley he could find."[16] The monitory "wind of imbecility" that panicked Baudelaire in late January 1862 thus uncannily coincided, nearly to the day, with the seventh anniversary of

Nerval's death. In "Le Gouffre," published two months later in *L'Artiste,* Baudelaire would transform this moment of horripilation into one of his last, great sonnets:

> Pascal avait son gouffre, avec lui se mouvant.
> —Hélas! tout est abîme, —action, désir, rêve,
> Parole! et sur mon poil qui tout droit se relève
> Mainte fois de la Peur je sens passer le vent.

> (Pascal had his chasm, attending his every move.
> —Alas! Everything is abyss, —action, desire, dream,
> Speech! and in my hairs, bristling on my skin,
> I often feel the passing wind of Fear.)

This Pascalian dread of the abyss was no doubt also deepened by the bottomless pit of bêtise into which Baudelaire's candidacy to the Academy had now sucked him. The very day after he penned the journal entry that recorded his calamitous brush with the wind of imbecility, he came upon the article that Sainte-Beuve, the most influential literary critic of the day (and himself an Immortal of long standing), had just published on the recent elections at the Academy in the official governmental newspaper, *Le Constitutionnel.* Sainte-Beuve's article mixed praise for Baudelaire's work—particularly for two of his recent prose poems, "Le Vieux Saltimbanque" ("The Old Acrobat") and "Les Veuves" ("The Widows")—with an equal measure of dripping condescension:

> Monsieur Baudelaire has found the means of building himself, at the end of a peninsula which is said to be uninhabitable, and beyond the bounds of known romanticism, a bizarre kiosk, very ornate, very overwrought, but elegant and mysterious, in which one grows drunk on abominable drugs in cups of exquisite porcelain. This singular kiosk, confected of marquetry and of a deliberate and composite originality which, for some time, has drawn people's eyes to the furthermost extremity of the romantic Kamchatka, is what I call *the Baudelaire Folly.*[17]

Baudelaire immediately penned a long and fawning letter of gratitude to Sainte-Beuve in which, completing misreading the critic's patronizing tone (as the dismayed Proust later pointed out), he took the article as a sign of encouragement to carry on with his campaign. A fortnight later, finally coming to his senses, Baudelaire wrote a curt and offensively polite letter to M. Villemain, officially withdrawing his candidacy.

During the same months that he was pursuing his sacrificial self-immolation by the French Academy, Baudelaire was negotiating with magazine editor Arsène Houssaye for the publication of a new installment of his poems in prose, tentatively suggesting the series be entitled *Le Rôdeur parisien* (*The Parisian Prowler*) or, in homage to the late reveries of Rousseau, *Le Promeneur solitaire* (*The Solitary Walker*). Houssaye was at that point the editor of the mass-circulation daily *La Presse*, originally founded in 1836 by Émile de Girardin, one of whose major innovations had been the introduction of *feuilletons* (or serials) that were printed on the *rez-de-chausée* (that is, the bottom third) of the first and second pages of the newspaper, occupying pride of place amid the surrounding farrago of political news, stock market reports, advertising, obituaries, lottery results and weather forecasts. It was in this space normally reserved for popular serial novels and memoirs that Baudelaire's *Petits Poèmes en prose*, prefaced by a dedicatory letter to Houssaye, finally began their run over the course of three issues of *La Presse* in August and September 1862—twenty poems in all (or rather "fragments," as Baudelaire always preferred to call them), discontinuous in their disposition, offering their readers not "the endless thread of some superfluous plot" but rather the possibility of reconstructing the severed "stumps" (or *tronçons*) of this serpentine serial poem into an ever-new, ever-recombinant snake. As Baudelaire observed in his dedication: "Remove a vertebra, and the two pieces of this torturous fantasy will easily rejoin. Sever it into numerous fragments, and you will see that each of them can exist apart."[18]

An additional fourth installment had already reached proof stage when the series was suddenly cut short. If published, this would have brought Baudelaire's sequence to twenty-six poems, half the number that would eventually make up the book that has come down to us as *Paris Spleen*. Opinions vary as to what might have happened. Houssaye may have pulled the plug, clearly miffed to discover that Baudelaire had, as was increasingly his wont, recycled (for the third or fourth time) some five poems that had previously appeared in other publica-

tions. Or, more likely, Girardin and his stockholders had simply over-
ruled the editor, unhappy that the valuable feuilleton rubric was be-
ing wasted on a string of snarky texts composed in an unfamiliar prose
genre, whose purpose (as Baudelaire later described it) was to extract
from every object or situation therein registered a "disagreeable moral"
intended to offend the cant of the great dailies and of their *bien-pensant*
bourgeois readership.[19]

The abrupt termination of his feuilleton in *La Presse* only exacerbated
Baudelaire's animus against the reigning newspaper and magazine cul-
ture of the Second Empire. His private notes of the period are (like
Poe's "Marginalia") filled with venomous attacks against such press
magnates as Girardin or against the various arrogant and ignorant edi-
tors who, treating his prose poems as mere copy to be processed rather
than as works of art, took the liberty of correcting (often without prior
consultation) his punctuation, diction, or grammar. In one of the en-
tries of *My Heart Laid Bare*, Baudelaire's vision of the press reaches
apocalyptic proportions, the medium of mass print here pictured as
Satan's handservant in the modern world:

> Every newspaper, from the first line to the last, is a tissue of horrors.
> War, crime, theft, shamelessness, torture, crimes of kings, crimes of
> nations, crimes of individuals, the whole world drunk with atrocities.
> And this is the disgusting aperitif that accompanies the morning repast
> of civilized man every day. Everything in this world positively reeks of
> crime: newspapers, posters, human faces. I cannot understand how a
> clean hand could touch a newspaper without a shudder of disgust.[20]

Nonetheless, dependent as he was on the periodical press for his liter-
ary income, Baudelaire was forced to maintain his pact with the devil,
scattering his prose poems among some twelve different journals over
the next three years—many of which, as his bad luck (or *guignon*) would
have it, tended to disappear from circulation the moment his texts ap-
peared. In February 1864, he finally succeeded at having a sequence of
six prose poems published in *Le Figaro*, at that time the liveliest of the
Parisian *petits journaux* addressed to an audience of waggish bohemi-
ans and boulevardiers. Here, too, the publication faltered after two in-
stallments—largely because, as Baudelaire disconsolately explained to

his mother, "according to the director, my poems were simply proving too boring to everybody."[21]

Given his travails in the literary marketplace—even his 1860 essay on Constantin Guys, "The Painter of Modern Life," perhaps the greatest piece of art criticism of its century, was rejected by eight editors before finally being accepted by *Le Figaro* in late 1863—Baudelaire increasingly dreamed of gathering the scattered Osiris-like limbs of his oeuvre into book form, even though, at this specific period of French publishing history, the periodical press was still far more lucrative and influential than the book industry. In the late summer of 1862, he wrote to Malassis that "in order to abandon once and for all the system of fragmentation in journals that has caused me so much distress," he now wanted to pursue another strategy—that is, to gather his writings into five volumes and market them to a single publisher.[22] Baudelaire included a list of his literary assets: two volumes of his *Reflections on My Contemporaries* (that is, his collected literary and art criticism); a new, third edition of *The Flowers of Evil;* a reedition of his 1860 study of drugs and Thomas De Quincey, *Artificial Paradises;* and, finally, his current work-in-progress, *Poems in Prose.* He hoped that Michel Lévy, who had already published three volumes of his Poe translations and who had previously brought out the writings of Heine and Nerval, would agree to take on the venture and that once the contracts were signed, he could then reimburse Malassis the 5,000 francs he still owed him even after having consigned to his publisher friend all the rights to his works both past and to come. With Lévy showing no interest in the project, Baudelaire proceeded in January 1863 to sell a five-year option on his *Poems in Prose* and his *Flowers of Evil* (with *My Heart Laid Bare* and a volume of short stories thrown in for good measure) to Pierre-Jules Hetzel for the sum of 1,200 francs—in direct violation of the contract he had earlier signed with Malassis, who had in the meantime gone bankrupt and had conveniently ended up in debtors' prison.

Baudelaire first began contemplating a sojourn in Belgium in the summer of 1863. It would be his first journey outside France since sailing the Indian Ocean in his youth (as Sartre quips of Baudelaire's constant changes of Parisian addresses: "A hundred removals and not a single voyage").[23] As usual, the primary reasons were monetary. He was still being pursued by his various creditors in Paris, and now that he had signed away the rights to his *Flowers of Evil* and of its prose poem "pendant" to Hetzel, all that remained to him of his salable literary assets were his literary and art criticism—the various *Salons* that he had published over the years, his essays on caricature and laughter, his forthcoming study of Constantin Guys, "the painter of modernity," and his pathbreaking homage to Wagner, not to mention his various articles on contemporary poets and novelists (which included pieces on Gautier, Hugo, and Flaubert).

This was the publishing project he hoped would allow him to recoup his fortunes in Belgium: 20,000 francs (or so he hoped) for two volumes of his collected criticism and a decent new edition of his *Artificial Paradises*. The publisher he had in mind was Albert Lacroix, of the Brussels firm Lacroix, Verboeckhoven. Given Baudelaire's radically antirepublican and antidemocratic political stance ever since the Eighteenth Brumaire of Louis Napoléon had, in his own words, "physically depoliticized" him in the wake of 1848, he could have not chosen a less likely sponsor for his works, for Lacroix specialized in the publication of *proscrits* who had either sought political asylum in Belgium after the coup d'état or whose works were deemed unpublishable in France—Louis Blanc, Edgar Quinet, Pierre-Joseph Proudhon, Jules Michelet, the young Émile Zola, among others. But there was nonetheless the Hugo connection: like Hetzel, Lacroix had been the exiled Victor Hugo's Brussels publisher, paying the author of *Les Misérables* the unheard-of advance of 300,000 francs in 1862 and then orchestrating the publicity campaign that parleyed the book into the century's first international mass-market best seller. (By a quirk of literary history, in 1869, two years after Baudelaire's death, this same firm of Lacroix and Verboeckhoven would issue, *à compte d'auteur* [for the fee of 1,200 francs], the first edition of Lautréamont's *Les Chants de Maldoror*).

It was therefore to Victor Hugo that Baudelaire turned in December 1863 to request an "enormous favor." Lacroix, he had heard, was to be visiting the great poet in his Olympian retreat on the isle of Guernsey: Would he be so kind as to put in a good word for his publishing proposal? As bad luck would have it, Baudelaire's letter was delayed by storms in the Channel and Lacroix had returned to Brussels by the time it arrived. Hugo, dimly aware of Baudelaire's growing animus against him— his review of *Les Misérables* had damned the populist novel with faint praise—nonetheless reassured him that he would see what he could do. In the meantime, Baudelaire had made the acquaintance of another figure who he felt might help him repair his finances in Belgium. Arthur Stevens was a Belgian art dealer who seemed to know everybody who counted in Brussels: Léon Bérardi, the editor-in-chief of its major newspaper, *L'Indépendance belge* (whose reputation in France rivaled that of the *Times* of London); D. J. L. Vervoort, president of the Chamber of Deputies and director of the Cercle artistique et littéraire, an organization that, inspired by the popular success of Charles Dickens's tour of America, administered a series of well-remunerated readings by authors of distinction; and finally, the wealthy stockbroker Prosper Crabbe, whose handsome collection of contemporary art Stevens had largely assembled.

A plan was now taking shape. To attract the attention of Lacroix and negotiate a lucrative contract, Baudelaire would count on the celebrity generated by his lectures in Brussels—just as his hero Poe had promoted his works in New York and Baltimore by public readings. In addition, he would prepare for print a series of pieces on the great private art collections of Belgium, enhanced by essays on his visits to the country's various museums and architectural monuments. In the summer of 1863, he made several applications to the French Ministries of Education and of the Fine Arts asking for financial support of this worthy endeavor—all of which were turned down. In late August, Delacroix died. Baudelaire was devastated: as he observed in the lengthy obituary that he published later that fall, the death of this great painter had struck him "like a solar eclipse, the momentary imitation of the end of the world," representing as it did the extinction of high romantic art as he knew it. Although he continued to announce his departure for Belgium as imminent, Baudelaire—ever indecisive, ever dilatory—delayed it for months. He needed to complete the prose poems of *Paris Spleen* and the autobiographical *My Heart Laid Bare* that he contractually owed to Hetzel; he was still trying to place "The Painter of Modern Life"; he was overseeing Lévy's publication of Poe's major scientific "Prose Poem" entitled *Eureka* and embarking on the translation of another volume of Poe's short stories, *Histoires grotesques et sérieuses*—totally gratuitous tasks, seeing as he had sold back all his royalty rights to Poe to Lévy in late 1863 for the paltry sum of 2,000 francs. By April

1864, he was finally ready to leave and to follow his publisher friend Malassis to Brussels—but not before committing one last foolhardy act. This involved a long anonymous letter to the *Figaro* in which he denounced the planned celebration of the Shakespeare tercentenary in Paris as nothing more than a conspiracy organized by Hugo's acolytes to promote the cause of socialism (see appendix 3). As a result, the imperial authorities canceled the festivities, with some suspecting that Baudelaire, acting as *mouchard*, or government informer, lay behind the whole affair. Before even arriving in Belgium, he had therefore already managed to burn most of his bridges to Hugo and Lacroix.

Upon debarking in Brussels on April 24, Baudelaire took up residence at the Hôtel du Grand Miroir (Hotel of the Great Mirror), a more or less respectable establishment located catty-corner to the nearby rue du Singe (Monkey Street). The Monkey in the Mirror: this would emerge as Baudelaire's most succinct and savage allegorical stereotype of the Belgian, a creature ontologically incapable of anything other than mindless mimicry and complacent self-regard. Baudelaire had originally planned to stay in the Grand Miroir for a few weeks at most. Instead, he ended up living like a penitent monk in the "white and frigid" confines of its room 39 for the next two years, prisoner of his own reflection in the gross looking glass of Belgium. If the *speculum mundi* of Belgium initially provided Baudelaire with the pleasurable confirmation of his own aristocratic superiority to its egalitarian bêtise, this would soon give way to a kind of deeper terror and disgust upon the realization that he might no longer be observing the simian Other at his mirror but rather confronting a hideously reversed replication of himself. "All literature derives from sin—I mean this quite seriously," he had written Malassis in 1860. This is echoed by a late note for his projected Book on Belgium: "One becomes Belgian for having sinned. A Belgian is a hell unto himself." By moving into the Hôtel du Grand Miroir, he had finally fully entered into the infernal, self-reflexive world of the Fall. By January 1866, he was describing to Ancelle how, alone in his room, ravaged by the symptoms of syphilis, he could literally no longer stand up straight: "Vertigos and repeated vomiting for three days. I was obliged to lie on my back . . . for even when crouching on the floor, I kept falling over, headlong. I think it was an intoxication of bile. . . . A moment ago, I was about to break off this letter and throw myself on my bed, which was quite an effort because I'm always afraid of dragging down the pieces of furniture at which I grab."[24]

*   *   *

Maurice Blanchot writes in *L'Attente l'oubli* (*Awaiting Oblivion*): "Waiting begins when there is nothing more to wait for, not even the end of waiting. Waiting is oblivious and destroys what it waits for. Waiting waits for nothing." Baudelaire's 1864–66 letters from Belgium, which come to some 250 serried pages in the Pléiade edition of his correspondence, enact the solipsistic vigil of a late, failing poet sitting alone in his hotel room in Brussels—waiting.[25] If not exactly *Krapp's Last Tape*, they nonetheless record an ongoing rehearsal of ennui, remorse, financial difficulty, and deteriorating health, occasionally relieved by mordant flashes of black humor. In a daguerreotype taken by the Belgian photographer Charles Neyt shortly after the poet's arrival in Brussels, a thin-lipped Baudelaire, aged forty-three, his hair longish and already silvered, dressed in a slightly frayed black frockcoat but wearing an impeccably laundered white shirt, a folded white pocket square, and a soberly knotted tie, holding the stub of a lit cigar between the forefingers of his left hand, stares back at the lens with an air of beleaguered disdain, at once trapped and defiant in the face of the camera's dumb, intrusive gaze. On a copy of this photograph dedicated to Malassis, Baudelaire inscribed a tag from Horace—"ridentem ferient ruinae" ("ruin shall strike him laughing")—while lauding his friend "as the sole being whose humor brightened my gloom in Belgium."[26] There are glimpses by witnesses of this more buoyant Baudelaire, drinking heavily (Belgian faro beer and brandy), making the rounds of the taverns and dives of Brussels with Malassis and his local painter acquaintances, voyeuristically visiting brothels with Guys and Rops in Antwerp, or celebrating his close friend Nadar's visit to the capital in the fall of 1864 for a demonstration of the third ascent of his new balloon, "The Giant," in honor of Belgian Independence Day—although he declined Nadar's invitation to join the revelers in the *montgolfière* basket or to attend the ensuing festivities at Waterloo.

To amuse Malassis, Baudelaire composed a number of scurrilous "Amoenitates belgicae" (or "Belgian Amenities"), recycling into doggerel verse some of the more off-color anecdotes and lampoons he had gathered for use in his big "Book on Belgium." As a terminal poet—and this becomes most evident in his late *Épaves*—the role he was now playing resembled that of the *vieux saltimbanque* of one of his best-known prose poems: a broken-down mountebank or histrio of letters acrobatically executing the low, ribald jests of burlesque (or *satyre*) for a dwindling male coterie. The era of his major lyrics, at any rate, now lay far behind him. Like the late Lord Byron in Venice, he had renounced high seriousness: the modes he now favored were rancorous irony, outright insult, or provocative farce (*bouffonnerie*). All that he retained of his former mastery of verse was his unerring ear for rhyme, now deployed to comic effect in occasional scraps of epigram or *vers de circonstance*—as in the following untranslatable occasional poem, one of the last that he composed on various envelopes addressed to his friend Malassis:

MONSIEUR AUGUSTE MALASSIS
  Rue de *Mércélis*
 Numéro *trente-cinq* bis
 Dans le faubourg d'*Ixelles*
  Bruxelles.
 (Recommandée à l'Arioste
  De la poste,
 C'est-à-dire à quelque facteur
  Versificateur.)[27]

This playful act of address announces itself as a *rien,* a trifle, a little nothing, a versified readymade. Like Mallarmé's later "Loisirs de la poste" ("Idylls of the Post"), it provides a virtuoso performance of the void, an echo of the shell of a poet Baudelaire had now become.

After his initial months visiting the sights in Brussels and traveling through the other provinces of the country to undertake art historical research for his projected magnum opus on Belgium (part art criticism, part tourist guide, part satirical pamphlet), Baudelaire progressively retreated into the monastic confines of room 39 of the Hôtel du Grand Miroir in search of penitential solitude. There he devoted his hours to a variety of readings—the Roman satirical poets, Lucan's *Pharsalia* or *Civil War*, Joubert's posthumous *Pensées* (as edited by Chateaubriand), Shelley's "Stanzas Written in Dejection near Naples." As a hobby (or *passe-temps*), he culled newspaper clippings for his great *sottisier* in progress, cutting and pasting them into various folders—a Karl Kraus avant la lettre. Regularly medicating himself with the opioids available in local pharmacies—see his great prose poem "La Chambre double" ("The Double Room")—Baudelaire also played host in his hotel lodgings to the fantasies of any number of literary enterprises, many-splendored castles in the air doomed to disappear due to lack of publisher interest or to survive only as runic fragments. The list of his late nonworks (or of his *désoeuvrements*) includes: proposed translations of Petronius's *Satyricon* and Maturin's *Melmoth the Wanderer;* an edition of Ronsard's selected poetry; a close analysis of Laclos's *Dangerous Acquaintances* (for Malassis's pirated collection of libertine authors)*;* an extended sociological and stylistic study of *dandyism* as the death mask of French aristocratic writing (as exemplified by the works of *de* Chateaubriand, *de* Custine, *de* Maistre, *de* Molènes, and *d'*Aurevilly); a refutation of Napoleon III's justifications of dictatorship in the preface to his recent *History of Julius Caesar*; a public letter to influential newspaper critic Jules Janin rebuking his denigration of the poetry of Heine and of modern postromantic verse in general (see appendix 6); a "biography" of *The Flowers of Evil*, narrating the circumstances of its trial; a revised de luxe collector's edition of his translations of Poe—not to mention his various reveries of never-to-be-written novels, short stories, and prose poems (gathered in Part Two of this edition under the title "Projects"). As he procrastinated over his three major stalled works-in-progress, *Poor Belgium, Paris Spleen,* and *My Heart Laid Bare*, he put the final touches on the manuscript of *Reflections on My Contemporaries*, which he sent off to his new literary agent, Jules Lemer, for placement with Parisian publishers—to no result. Even as he shored fragments against his ruins, he continued to dream of somehow redeeming them into the total shape of an Oeuvre, posthumous though this might be—something on the order of his cherished 1850 edition of R. W. Griswold's *Works of the Late Edgar Allan Poe*, which Poe had begun assembling shortly before his untimely death at forty, only to have his associate Griswold adulterate the edition, while adding a slanderous preface and stealing all the proceeds from Poe's rightful heirs.

If Poe's death, as Baudelaire had earlier written, had been "almost a suicide—a suicide long in the making," so he, too, currently tenanted in the "prison" of Brussels, now prepared for his own dénouement, offering himself up, just as his American literary hero had, to the "blind Angel of expiation" in order to become "a new saint in the martyrology of letters"—a pariah or *homo sacer* of sorts, banned from the literary polis yet still the object of its sovereign violence.[28] Like the narrator of Poe's "Premature Burial," he remained lucidly conscious of himself as already posthumous, already late, already done for—a living survivor of his own demise. To Manet he wrote in May 1865 (in the same letter in which he cryptically praised him for being "the first in the decrepitude of your art"): "As for finishing *Poor Belgium* here, I'm incapable; I'm enfeebled, I'm dead." To his mother he confessed that death had become his great solace, his *idée fixe*, but a perilous one at that, threatening as it did all the vast projects that still lay before him. "I am no longer master of my time," he informed her in another letter. In fact, he felt he was merely *killing time* abroad, in exile—a metaphor that returns in his late prose poems—while still in desperate need of its further reassurance. He begged Ancelle (for whom he developed a strange affection during these last failing years) to retrieve the gold repeater watch that he had deposited at a pawnbroker's in Paris, citing his "mania for always wanting to know the time" and his "inability to work without a clock"—given that his hotel/prison chamber in Brussels lacked one. When his watch finally arrived from Paris, he spent long frustrating hours at the Brussels customs office dealing with administrative delays, just *waiting* to recuperate his precious timepiece. "None of my former tribulations equal to this," he quipped in one of his notes for *Poor Belgium*—half-ironically, half-hysterically. In Nietzsche's terms, he was now experiencing himself as a figure who had become increasingly *unzeitgemässig* (untimely)—or, as the French translation has it, *intempestif* (out of season, inopportune). In 1864, he laconically observed in one of the fragments of his Big Belgium Book: "Shall we say that the world has become uninhabitable for me?" The phrase could have just as well been uttered by the unnamed and untimely narrator of Dostoyevsky's *Notes from Underground*, published that very same year.[29]

*   *   *

Malassis was the first to notice Baudelaire's rapid mental deterioration shortly after his return from a flying visit to France in the sum-

mer of 1865, where the poet had briefly stopped over in Paris and in
Honfleur to borrow money from Manet and Mme. Aupick in order to
settle the impending lawsuit that had resulted from the conflicting ad-
vances he had deviously wrangled from both Malassis and Hetzel for a
new edition of *The Flowers of Evil* and other works to come. On August
30 Malasssis wrote to Charles Asselineau (Baudelaire's most loyal asso-
ciate back in Paris, later to become his first editor and biographer) that
"Baudelaire's flaws—his procrastination, his obstinacy, his ramblings
and ravings [*radotage*]—have reached such a proportion that it would
be more than a little tiresome to have him over on a daily basis. He will
have wasted his time in Belgium, as you can well imagine. His stud-
ies consist of making everything fit into his preconceived ideas."[30] A
devastating portrait: a Baudelaire no longer welcome even as a guest
at his closest friend's house because his bigoted idées fixes about Bel-
gium had become so unremittingly tedious—the rants of a ruined in-
telligence. Only two days earlier, Baudelaire had penned a page in
which his intransigence against the "race" of Brussels reached apoca-
lyptic proportions. Remembering both Alfred Rethel's lithograph *Death
the Slayer, or the Appearance of Cholera at a Masked Ball in Paris, 1831,*
and Charles Meryon's etchings of the demon-bestridden skies over the
Seine, Baudelaire gives himself over to a phantasmagoria of genocidal
proportions:

Today, Monday the 28th of August 1865, over the course of a hot and
humid evening, I followed the meanderings of a street fair (*Kermesse*),
and in the streets named *Devil's Corner, Monks' Rampart, Our Lady of
Sleep, Six Tokens,* as well in several others, I discovered, to my great de-
light and surprise, frequent symptoms of cholera suspended in the air.
Have I sufficiently invoked cholera, this monster I adore? Have I stud-
ied the advance signs of his arrival attentively enough? How long shall
I have to wait for him, this horrific favorite of mine, this impartial At-
tila, this divine plague who strikes down his victims at random? Haven't
I sufficiently pleaded with My Lord God to speed his passage over the
stinking banks of the *Senne?* And how much pleasure would I finally
derive as I contemplated the grimacing agony of this hideous people
caught in the coils of its fake Styx, its *Briareus-river,* whose waters carry
off more excrements than the sky above provides sustenance to flies! I

shall take great delight—this is certain—in the terrors and tortures inflicted on this race whose traits are yellow hair, nankeen trousers, and lilac complexions![31]

In this palpably over-the-top (and James Ensorish) passage, later marked as a possible "Epilogue" to his *Belgium Disrobed,* Baudelaire the flâneur-prophet, parodying his hero, Joseph de Maistre, the papist philosopher of punitive Armageddon, gleefully calls down the Exterminating Angel upon the City of the Plain (whose filthy river "Senne" is but a grotesque simulacrum of the Parisian "Seine"). Like Shakespeare's "man-hater" Timon, the doom that Baudelaire here invites extends to all of humankind, himself included: "Lips, let sour words go by and language end: / What is amiss plague and infection mend! / Graves only be men's works and death their gain! / Sun, hide thy beams! Timon hath done his reign."[32]

Four months later, rapidly approaching the end of his own misanthropic reign—one of his latest projects, of which several rancorous paragraphs survive, was entitled *Lettres d'un atrabilaire,* in homage to Molière's Alceste—Baudelaire again reported to Ancelle that he had been beset by a series of attacks (vertigo, vomiting, fainting) that had rendered him *"bête et fou."* His greatest fear was now becoming realized: he was finally *becoming-Belgian* (as Deleuze and Guattari might phrase it), transformed into a slow, clumsy, inert sort of creature, little more than an "oyster" encrusted on his sickbed, exactly like those invertebrate Belgian "mollusks" he so disdained. Living on a diet of opium, digitalis, belladonna, and brandy, he tried to numb himself out as best he could, in search of that same soporous state of suspended animation without *Umwelt*—Agamben's "bare life"—for which he had longed in his early poem "De Profondis clamavi": "Je jalouse le sort des plus vils animaux / Qui peuvent se plonger dans un sommeil stupide" ("I envy the fate of the lowliest of beasts / Who can plunge themselves into a stupor of sleep"). To anyone who cared to hear—Ancelle, Mme. Aupick, Sainte-Beuve, Malassis, Asselineau, even Mme. Hugo—he now (uncharacteristically) put his ailing animal body on display, describing in detail his debilitating attacks of "rheumatism and neuralgia in the head" and his fainting spells. Various doctors were consulted. To a certain Dr. Léon Marcq who had come to examine him in his room at the Hôtel du Grand Miroir on January 20, 1866, Baudelaire handed the following stray leaf documenting his "crises." This is one of his last self-portraits, its late style—noun phrases, few verbs—echoing the depersonalized paratactic jottings of his abortive Belgium Book:

> Sequence of sensations:
> Fuzziness in the head. Fits of suffocation. Horrible headaches. Heaviness; congestion; total dizziness. If standing, I fall; if sitting, I fall. All this quite rapidly.
> After regaining consciousness, the need to vomit. Head heating up. Cold sweats.
> The vomit yellow or watery or slimy or spumy. When there's no vomit, sometimes flatulence or hiccups in its stead. Stupor. Two of these crises coincided with a slight cold —constipation. —All I can remember.[33]

Given that Baudelaire apparently refused to make any mention of his history of syphilis, the medical experts were flummoxed. One of the doctors concluded that he was suffering simply from "hysteria." Hearing this diagnosis, he scoffed to Sainte-Beuve: "Don't you think it's wonderful, this elastic use of portentous words designed to hide our ignorance of all things?" And yet hysteria was a term with which Baudelaire was quite familiar from the medical literature of the day (notably Paul Briquet). Indeed, he had used it to brilliant effect in his 1857 review of Flaubert's *Madame Bovary,* describing its heroine's vaporous addictions to fantasy as those of a (male) "hysterical poet" and suggesting there was a great work to be written that would take this "physiological mystery" as its inspiration. During his early 1862 breakdown Baudelaire had confessed in *Flares*: "I have cultivated my hysteria with joy and terror"—and he strategically deployed the term three times in the prose poems of his *Paris Spleen*, rhyming it with Poe's "imp of the perverse." But by February 1866 Baudelaire realized that he was the victim of something far more irremediable. He informed Asselineau: "The illness persists, and the doctor has pronounced the grand word: hysteria. To put it into plain French: *je jette ma langue aux chiens.*" Word for word, this translates as "I toss my tongue to the dogs," but semantically it suggests something more on the order of "I'm stumped" or "I haven't a clue." Baudelaire had previously used this same French idiomatic expression to translate "The police do not know where to begin to look for the answer" in Poe's "Murders in the Rue Morgue."[34]

Je jette ma langue aux chiens. The metaphorical extensions of this expression (beyond its sense of speechless bafflement) are multiple, for here was Baudelaire in Belgium, this *chien de pays* (this bloody country), exasperated by its scum or *canaille* (from the Italian for dog, *canaglia*), experiencing a *chien de peur* (or bloody panic) about returning to Paris, as well as an equal *peur de chien* inspired by his own new literary disciples such as Mallarmé and Verlaine who, in their recently published critical essays in praise of him, were apparently threatening to establish a new *école Baudelaire* back home, whereas all he now wanted was to be left utterly alone, far from the pack—like an isolated *cynic*.[35] Having formerly been the century's supreme poet of the enigmatic, hieratic beauty of cats, Baudelaire devoted his final prose poem (published in the pages of *L'Indépendance belge*) to the encomium of "Les Bons Chiens" (or in Mark Twain parlance, "Good Ole Dawgs")—the subaltern canines of Brussels, whom he refers to as the stray (escaped, rebel) "maroons" or "negroes" of Belgium, the only truly independent and energetic (and proletarian) creatures left in the vast "zoocracy" of the modern world.

A month later, out of answers, stumped, without a clue, he would truly toss his tongue to the dogs. Felled by a cerebral stroke while visiting the baroque Jesuit Church of Saint-Loup in Namur in the company of Rops and Malassis, Baudelaire slowly sank into the aphasia that would cripple him for the next year and a half. Having first lost the ability to write, then to dictate, then to read, then to speak, he was soon entirely paralyzed on his right side and afflicted by a "softening of the brain," which, as Malassis informed Asselineau, made him "incapable of stringing two ideas together." Transported to a Brussels hospital run by Augustinian nuns—the very same establishment where in 1873 Rimbaud would be treated for the gunshot wound inflicted upon him by his lover Verlaine (described by the Belgian arresting officer as a "tentatiffe d'asacinat")—Baudelaire proved to be a refractory patient, refusing to cross himself before meals and replying to the sisters' various religious ministrations with the only two words left in his vocabulary: the negative syllable *Non!* or the more scandalously blasphemous oath *Crénom!* (sometimes heard by witnesses as *Crénon!*), an abbreviation of *Sacré Nom [or Non?] de Dieu,* the French equivalent of his most ab-horred Flemish swear word, *Gottverdomme!* ("Goddammit!").[36] Having been informed of her son's turn for the worse, the seventy-two-year-old Mme. Aupick hurried to Brussels from Honfleur to arrange for his transfer back to the Hôtel du Grand Miroir, eager to nurse her speech-less infant (*in-fans*) back to health—apparently to Baudelaire's intense exasperation. Meanwhile, having observed that his friend had clearly maintained his mental lucidity although now completely mute, Malas-sis was turning to medical textbooks to research the etiology of aphasia (often associated with syphilis, as he knew well, given that he had also contracted *la vérole* in his earlier years). His readings forced him to con-clude that Baudelaire was indeed a terminal victim of "this apparently absurd disease which allows a man go on comprehending that which he can no longer draw forth from himself and express."[37]

In April, reports of Baudelaire's death in Brussels began circulating in the Parisian press. Having read one of these accounts, the young Stéphane Mallarmé, languishing in provincial Tournon as a high school teacher of English, fell into a suicidal depression. Across the channel, Swinburne immediately dashed off his great elegy "Ave Atque Vale: In Memory of Charles Baudelaire"—"O sleepless heart and somber soul unsleeping / That were athirst for sleep and no more life / And no more love, for peace and no more strife!" But despite his premature burial, Baudelaire remained very much awake, attentive to the conversations that were taking place around him, though bereft of speech—except for his repeated cries of *Crénom! Crénom!* which, like the late Hölderlin's *Pallaksch! Pallaksch!,* he deployed to indicate either eager affirmation or furious disagreement, or sometimes both at once. His illness had reduced his speech to that reiterative "monotone of sound" which Poe had described as the essential poetic function of the *refrain* in his "Phi-losophy of Composition"—the parrotry of the Raven's "Nevermore!" (or, in Baudelaire's translation, "Jamais plus!") now emerging as *Crénom! Crénom!* In this, Baudelaire's palalia had also come to resemble that of Egaeus, the diseased hero of "Berenice" who used "to repeat monoto-nously some common word, until the sound, by dint of frequent repeti-tion, ceased to convey any idea whatever to the mind." In short, Baude-laire had plunged into that abyss of language (as Blanchot would call it) prior to, or subsequent to, all articulate speech—the idiom of a-phasia,

of a-logos, located not in the cortex but in the more primitive basal gan-
glia of the brain.[38]

Over the course of the spring of 1866 further doctors were consulted
by Baudelaire's entourage. One of these was Dr. Emile Blanche, the
alienist who had housed Gérard de Nerval (and, subsequently, Guy de
Maupassant) in his chic Montmartre clinic. But given that Baudelaire
was, as all agreed, in no sense mad but simply radically tongue-tied, it
was decided that he instead be moved in late July 1866 to the "hydro-
therapeutic" establishment of Dr. Duval in Paris, near the place de la
Concorde. It was there that he would live out his days for another full
year, lodged in a garden apartment, decorated with two paintings by
Manet (one of which was a copy of Goya's *Duchess of Alba*) and furnished
with a small library (an English-French dictionary, the *Works of the Late
Edgar Poe*, Sainte-Beuve's early poetry). Also present in this room was
a large trunk, to which Baudelaire alone held the key, containing the
manuscripts he had accumulated in Brussels: *Belgium Disrobed, My
Heart Laid Bare, Flares,* and the *Nachlass* of his various uncompleted
projects for essays, prose poems, short stories, and novels—not to men-
tion the mythical revised third edition of his *Flowers of Evil* (which may
or may not ever have existed).

Madame Aupick's hovering, bustling presence in the Duval clinic
continued to be a major source of irritation to her *in-fans*. She reported
to Malassis:

He has always been gentle and polite with everyone. I alone have had to
suffer his great bursts of anger; no doubt because he has things to tell
me which he does not tell to other people, or else because he restrains
himself less with me and knows my weakness. His book of poems [*Les
Épaves*] has often been the cause of terrible outbursts: he has some-
thing to tell me about this work which I cannot make out. The other day
he picked up this wretched book and thrust it into my face to the point
where I had to recoil. He flew into a furious rage because I didn't under-
stand, and stamped his foot as hard as he could; finally, worn out with
fatigue, he threw himself on his sofa. A few minutes later he began to
bellow again at the top of his voice, waving his legs in the air and howl-
ing like a wild animal.[39]

Witnessing the ongoing (and archaic) psychodrama between mother and son, Dr. Duval wisely recommended that Mme. Aupick retreat to Honfleur, assuring her that he would keep her abreast of any change in his patient's condition. She was informed, to her delight, that her son might be soon on the way to recovery—the poet had supposedly been heard to utter the phrases *la lune est belle* and *passez-moi la moutarde*—but Baudelaire's closest friends knew that his condition was beyond repair. Malassis remained his most eloquent diagnostician: "He has lost his memory of language and figurative signs, and no one can tell to what extent his whole mind has been affected by his partial paralysis. Trousseau's *Clinique médicale* has something very sad to say about his condition: 'Whenever you see an aphasic who appears to be in possession of his mental faculties even though he has lost the ability to express himself, remember how many times you have said of certain animals: *If only they could speak.*'"[40]

During the final year of his life, Baudelaire received a steady stream of visitors at the Duval clinic. Nadar fetched him each week in his carriage and hosted him for dinner with friends, but the demands of camaraderie via sign language proving too strenuous and too disheartening, Baudelaire soon repaired to his *Matratzengruft* (as the dying Heine had famously referred to "mattress-crypt" of his Paris death chamber twenty years earlier)—where, smoking the occasional cigar and admiring the cactus plant in his garden, he was consoled by the solicitude of such visiting luminaries as Sainte-Beuve, Maxime Du Camp, Leconte de Lisle, Théodore Banville, and Champfleury. Édouard Manet and his wife remained faithful to the last, as did their friend Mme. Paul Meurice, who brought along a score of *Tannhäuser* and played it to the perfect Wagnerite on the piano, creating a "vivid impression" on the fading poet.[41]

Mute though he had become, the dream of his Complete Works continued to haunt him. Baudelaire managed to make it very clear to Asselineau (by eye movements and finger pointings to a calendar) that he wanted the house of Michel Lévy to publish them in the near future—but not before he had finally got around to finishing his new revised and expanded edition of *The Flowers of Evil* . . . . After Baudelaire's death (and with Malassis's generous acquiescence), Lévy acquired the rights to the (still unrevised) *Fleurs du mal* and three additional volumes of prose, to be edited by Banville and Asselineau, for a bargain 2,000 francs, the same price he had paid for Baudelaire's complete Poe. By 1870, only three years after the poet's demise, Lévy's uniform seven-volume set of the Late Charles Baudelaire's works, which included all his Poe translations, was fully in print.

Just slightly over forty-six years of age, and having accepted the final sacraments, Baudelaire was buried in the Cimetière du Montparnasse (in the family vault of the detested General Aupick) on September 10, 1867—the same year that saw the publication of the first volume of Marx's *Das Kapital* and the death by firing squad of Emperor Maximilian of Mexico, which would leave his Belgian wife, Charlotte, the daughter of King Leopold I, permanently insane until her death in 1927. Invitations went out late and only approximately sixty people attended the ceremony, including Nadar, Houssaye, Stevens, Verlaine, and Manet. A huge thunderclap and late summer windstorm interrupted the proceedings—the imminent arrival of this tempest still audible in the air and still visible in the leaves of Manet's eyewitness painting *The Burial*, generally considered among the greatest of his unfinished works.[42]

NOTES

1. Theodor W. Adorno, *Essays on Music* (Berkeley: University of California Press, 2002), 564–67. See also Edward Said, *On Late Style: Music and Literature Against the Grain* (New York: Pantheon Books, 2002); Ben Hutchinson, *Lateness and Modern European Literature* (Oxford: Oxford University Press, 2016); and Gordon McMullan and Sam Smiles, eds., *Late Style and Its Discontents: Essays in Art, Literature, and Music* (Oxford: Oxford University Press, 2016).

2. Charles Mauron, *Le Dernier Baudelaire* (Paris: José Corti, 1966). Mauron analyzes Baudelaire's late prose poems as an allegory of the self-sabotaging conflict between the punishing superego of his "social self" and his imperfectly repressed "artistic self."

3. Rops wrote Malassis in the spring of 1864 that he wanted to meet Baudelaire because "we share a strange passion, namely, a love for the skeleton, the first of all crystallographic forms." Quoted in Jean-Baptiste Baronian, *Baudelaire au pays des singes* (Paris: Pierre-Guillaume de Roux, 2017), 93.

4. The tercets of this 1862 sonnet speak of the glory days of French romanticism (the 1830s and 1840s) as a sun god now disappearing into the gathering night of the present: "Mais je poursuis en vain le Dieu qui se retire; / L'irrésistible Nuit établit son empire, / Noire, humide, funeste et pleine de frissons; // Une odeur de tom-

beaux dans les ténèbres nage, / Et mon pied peureux froisse, au bord du marécage, / Des crapauds imprévus et de froids limaçons" ("But in vain I pursue the retreating God; / Irresistible Night is establishing its empire, / Black, damp, dismal, and full of shudders; // The smell of the grave floats in the shadows, / And my foot falters on the borders of the bog, / Stumbling upon cold slugs and unexpected toads"). A note (by Baudelaire) follows the poem: "It is obvious that by *irresistible Night* M. Charles Baudelaire was seeking to characterize the present state of literature, and that the *cold slugs* and *unexpected toads* are writers who are not of his school."

5. Jean-Paul Sartre, *Baudelaire*, trans. Martin Turnell (New York: New Directions, 1950), 18.

6. Sartre, 165.

7. Sartre, 165; "On the Concept of History," in Walter Benjamin, *Selected Writings*, vol. 4, trans. Harry Zohn (Cambridge, MA: Harvard University Press, 2003), 392, translation modified.

8. See "Baudelaire's Financial Situation from 1844 to 1864" in Claude Pichois, *Baudelaire*, trans. Graham Robb (London: Hamish Hamilton, 1989), 379–82.

9. Barbara Johnson, *Défigurations du langage poétique: La Seconde Révolution baude-lairienne* (Paris: Flammarion, 1979).

10. C1: 583; 568; C2: 114.

11. C2: 135.

12. C2: 150. On the overall impact of the literal and allegorical figure of Syphilis on such nineteenth-century French writers as Balzac, Stendhal, Gautier, Baudelaire, Flaubert, Zola, Maupassant, Huysmans, and the Goncourts, see Patrick Wald Loso-wiski's brilliant *Syphilis: Essais sur la littérature française du XIXe siècle* (Paris: Galli-mard, 1982). The most recent English-language study is Steven Wilson, *The Language of Disease: Writing Syphilis in Nineteenth-Century France* (Oxford: Legenda, 2020).

13. C2: 180–83.

14. See Allen S. Weiss, *Le Livre bouffon* (Paris: Seuil, 2009), a spirited experimental novel devoted to Baudelaire's ill-starred candidacy to the French Academy.

15. OC1: 668.

16. OC2: 306.

17. OC2: 190; Sainte-Beuve's characterization of Baudelaire's work as a "folly" (*OED*: "a costly ornamental building with no practical purpose") provides the title for Roberto Calasso's *La Folie Baudelaire* (New York: Farrar, Straus and Giroux, 2008).

18. OC1: 275.

19. See Antoine Compagnon, *Baudelaire l'irréductible* (Paris: Flammarion, 2014), 66–70, for a fuller account of Baudelaire, Houssaye, and *La Presse*.

20. OC1: 705.

21. C2: 350.

22. C2: 256.

23. Sartre, *Baudelaire*, 164.

24. C2: 85; OC2: 954; C2: 570. Baudelaire's agon in Belgium was novelized for *le grand public* by Bernard Henri-Lévi in *Les Derniers Jours de Charles Baudelaire* (Paris: Grasset, 1988).

25. *L'attente l'oubli*, as quoted by Leslie Hill, *Maurice Blanchot and Fragmentary Writing* (London, Continuum, 2012), 111. Blanchot's notion of *attente* extends Mar-tin Heidegger's discussion of *Langweile* in his *Fundamental Concepts of Metaphys-*

ics. See Elizabeth S. Goodstein, *Experience Without Qualities: Boredom and Modernity* (Stanford, CA: Stanford University Press, 2005), 281–333. In his letters from Brussels Baudelaire frequently complains of the *ennui* to which he is prey—which led his friend Gautier to comment: "This Baudelaire is astonishing. How explain this mania of his—extending his stay in a country that only causes him to suffer! As for myself, when I took off for Spain or Venice or Constantinople, I knew that I'd find great pleasures there and that upon my return I would craft them into a beautiful book. But Baudelaire just remains on in Brussels, where he's bored stiff, for the sheer pleasure of telling all of us just how bored he's been." Quoted in Guyaux, *Fusées, Mon Coeur mis à nu, et autres fragments posthumes* (Paris: Gallimard, 2016), 542.

26. The photograph and its inscriptions are reproduced as the frontispiece to Eugène Crépet's edition of Baudelaire's *Oeuvres posthumes* (Paris: Maison Quentin, 1887).

27. C2: 598.

28. OC2: 297, 207.

29. C2: 497, 549; OC2: 864, 821.

30. Pichois, *Baudelaire*, 337.

31. OC2: 95.

32. Shakespeare, *Timon of Athens*, 5.1. In May of the following year, Brussels was indeed struck by an outbreak of cholera that caused some 3,500 deaths. For a more extensive analysis of this epilogue, see Patrick Thériault, "Baudelaire prophète c(h)olérique: La référence au choléra dans *La Belgique déshabillée*," *Études françaises* 56 (2020/2): 7–31; and Richard D. E. Burton, "Baudelaire, Belgians, Jews," *Essays in French Literature* 6 (1998–99): 69–112.

33. C2: 575.

34. C2: 583, 587.

35. See the outstanding readings of Jérôme Thélot, *Baudelaire: Violence et poésie* (Paris: Gallimard, 1993), 227–233; and Anne Emanuelle Berchet, "Raining Cats or Dogs? Baudelaire's Cynicism," *Yale French Studies* 125–26 (204): 149–64.

36. Baudelaire writes in a letter of February 3, 1865, to Mme. Paul Meurice (reproduced in appendix 7 below): "A few months ago, I found myself lost one night in an area of town that was unfamiliar to me; I asked two young women for directions and they replied: *Gott for damn!* (or *domn!*) (I'm transcribing this poorly: no Belgian has ever been able to explain the spelling of this national curse word, but it is the equivalent of *Sacré nom de Dieu!*)." Toby Dammit (with his verbal tic "I'll bet") in Poe's story "Never Bet Your Devil the Head" is also suggestive here.

37. Pichois, *Baudelaire*, 351.

38. Baudelaire's descent into coprolalia (the tendency to swear loudly and involuntarily at inappropriate moments) is a symptom not only of Tourette's syndrome but also of what was traditionally known as Broca's aphasia. The latter is characterized by the damaging of the left hemisphere of the brain (which controls propositional speech); this leaves the right hemisphere to predominate in the emission of nonpropositional exclamations (often swear words), caused by the dysfunction of the basal ganglia and their limbic sector—that is, by the disturbance of those more primitive mammalian parts of the brain that evolved before the cortex. See David Shariatmadari, *Don't Believe a Word: The Surprising Truth About Language* (New York: W. W. Norton, 2020), 92–100.

39. Johanna Richardson, *Baudelaire: The Life of Charles Baudelaire* (New York: St. Martin's Press, 1994), 476.

40. Pichois, *Baudelaire,* 361.

41. The Wagner anecdote (which so moved Nietzsche) is related in the "Étude biographique" included in Crépet's edition of Baudelaire's *Oeuvres posthumes.*

42. See the exhibition catalog to *Unfinished: Thoughts Left Visible* (New York: Metropolitan Museum of Art, 2016), 299.

PART ONE

Flares,
Hygiene,
My Heart
Laid Bare

Introduction

After Baudelaire's funeral, his private trunk was transported from the Duval clinic in Paris to his mother's seaside cottage in Honfleur, where Mme. Aupick allowed his devoted friend Charles Asselineau to inspect its contents—which included the two sheaves of semiphilosophical, semiautobiographical fragments entitled *Fusées* and *Mon Coeur mis à nu*, the folders of his big unfinished book on Belgium, the dossier of the trial of *Les Fleurs du mal*, sketches of unfinished plays, inventories of projected prose poems and novels, and a substantial bundle of correspondence. Asselineau quarried this *Nachlass* to fine effect in his warm and well-documented biography of his old friend, published in 1869, just two years after the poet's death. Meanwhile, Baudelaire's erstwhile publisher Auguste Poulet-Malassis, to whom the curatorship of the contents of this trunk had subsequently devolved, proceeded to organize the loose irregular leaves of the manuscripts of *Fusées* and *Mon Coeur mis à nu* (and *Hygiène*), numbering them as best he could, occasionally jumbling their sequence in the process. Malassis's assemblage of manuscripts—or, more precisely, his mosaic of autograph folio scraps of various dimensions that he pasted onto larger, thicker sheets of standard-size paper and then had bound—was first printed (in a slightly sanitized version) in Eugène Crépet's 1887 edition of Baudelaire's *Oeuvres posthumes,* published twenty years after the poet's death under the general title of *Journaux intimes* (*Private Journals,* or simply *Diaries*)—perhaps a nod on Crépet's part to the recent commercial success of the Swiss writer Amiel's posthumous *Fragments d'un journal intime.*[1] Nowhere in his writings, however, does Baudelaire explicitly refer to these texts as his *Journaux intimes,* nor can they be said to be "diaries" in any specifically chronological sense, even though they do share with the journal or notebook form the swift and often discontinuous rhythms of serial composition. *Journaux intimes*, however, they continued to be called in Claude Pichois's authoritative Pléiade volumes and in all the Baudelaire scholarship that builds on these editions, out of sheer respect for philological tradition. In Christopher Isherwood's inaugural English translation of 1930, these *Journaux intimes* were rendered, rather literally, as *The Intimate Journals of Charles Baudelaire*. But like their most recent editor, André Guyaux, I have chosen to avoid grouping them under a single unifying rubric, preferring instead to provide them here as three plural but mutually imbricated collections of fragments: *Flares* (Isherwood's "Squibs and Crackers") and its supplement, *Hygiene*, followed by *My Heart Laid Bare*.[2]

If instead of the time-honored title *Journaux intimes*, one had to elect a loose heading under which to gather the shared shape and tempo of these feuilles volantes, it might be *Brevities*. This was the title that Edgar Allan Poe chose for the book into which he had hoped to collect his short magazine filler pieces from the 1840s, "Marginalia" and "Suggestions"—both of which, under the general title *The Literati*, were later included in volume three of *The Works of the Late Edgar Allan Poe*, edited by R. W. Griswold in 1850 and one of the most precious items in Baudelaire's personal library.[3] In his 1859 study of Poe, with this particular volume in hand, Baudelaire speaks of "leafing through for the hundredth time his delightful 'Marginalia' which are like the secret chambers of his mind."[4] Over the course of this same essay he cites a number of these squibs in his own translation, most of which are caustically contemptuous of the current American literary and cultural scene—and in which (according to Baudelaire) "scorn rains down like a hard hail of bullets," its ballistic damage delivered "with nonchalance and *hauteur*."[5] Situating his pugnacious "Marginalia" in the context of contemporary "magazine literature," Poe had recourse to a similar metaphor for his *Brevities*: "We now demand the light artillery of the intellect; we need the curt, the condensed, the pointed, the readily diffused—in place of the verbose, the detailed, the voluminous, the inaccessible."[6]

Poe lived by his pen, and carefully wrote out his "Marginalia" and "Suggestions" on strips of paper cut to the exact dimensions of a printed column, for which he was paid by the inch. Though addressing a broad magazine readership in the superior pose of a cosmopolitan scholar and Virginia gentleman disdainful of the (northern) literati of his mid-century America, Poe nonetheless also liked to think of his journalistic piecework as an intimate performance: "In the *marginalia*, we talk only to ourselves; we therefore talk freshly—boldly—originally—with *abandonnement*—without conceit."[7] Rather than being the products of philistine labor, his rapid "pencilings" were instead to be taken as an aristocratic pastime on the order of Montaigne's *Essays* or Burton's *Anatomy of Melancholy*—casually erudite utterances tossed off with elegant and acerbic abandon. Like Poe's "Marginalia" and "Suggestions," Baudelaire's *Flares* and *My Heart Laid Bare* hover between private meditation and public posturing, unsure of any readership other than posthumous. These late brevities are perhaps best understood as Pascalian *divertissements*—the diversions and distractions of a man increasingly abandoned to the solitude of his chambers. It is here, on these random scraps of paper, that Baudelaire entertains himself (in the same sense that T. S. Eliot said of Poe that he could only "entertain" ideas). He is, as always, driven to *épater le bourgeois,* of course, but by the same token he is forever tempted to surprise (and provoke) himself. According to Nadar (who had it from Asselineau), such was Baudelaire's need to induce amazement at all costs that when he came home at night, he would go to sleep beneath his bed, simply to *astonish* himself.[8] His *Flares* and *My Heart Laid Bare*, which blend explosions of misanthropic (and rottenly misogynistic) ugliness with sparks of aphoristic beauty, are best approached as Baudelaire's late experiments in the discipline of dandyism—a perverse ascesis that aspires to reshape the self into sublime object of awe and trepidation as it ceaselessly observes itself in the mirror of the page.

Did Baudelaire subscribe to all the incendiary bombs lobbed in these late pages? The question is perhaps poorly framed. As he noted in a section entitled "Politics" in *My Heart Laid Bare:* "I have no convictions, as men of my century understand the term, because I have no ambitions. . . . Only crooks are convinced—of what? Convinced they must succeed. So succeed they do. Why should I succeed, seeing as I lack the slightest desire to do so? . . . Nonetheless, I do harbor a few convictions, in the higher sense—which exceed the understanding of my contemporaries." Walter Benjamin saw in the *boutades* of Baudelaire's *Journaux intimes* a parodic refraction of the conspiratorial milieu of the (politi-

cal) *bohème* that had spawned the future police-state tactics of the dicta-
tor Napoleon III: "As emperor, Napoleon continued to develop his con-
spiratorial habits. Surprising proclamations and mystery-mongering,
sudden sallies, and impenetrable irony were part of the *raison d'état* of
the Second Empire. The same traits are found in Baudelaire's theoreti-
cal writings. He usually presents his views apodictically. Discussion is
not his style; he avoids it even when the glaring contradictions in the
theses he continually appropriates require discussion."[9]

Baudelaire first began making random entries in the manuscript he
called *Fusées* in 1855–56—that is, while composing his major essays on
Poe and while publishing his very first poems in prose. He apparently
took his title from one of the "Marginalia" in which Poe had mockingly
referred to the *Schwärmerei* (the enthusiastic gushings) of the New En-
gland transcendentalist writers (or "Boston bean-eaters") as a species
of metaphysical (and flatulent) "sky-rocketing"—a term that Baudelaire
then ironically applied to the laconic emergency signals he was now
launching with his solitary fusees or flares.[10] In August 1862, ever in
need of publishable copy, he briefly considered going public with these
brief pensées, writing to Arsène Houssaye, the chief editor of *La Presse*,
that he had two new (Poesque) titles on hand, *Flares and Suggestions*
or *Sixty-Six Suggestions*, which he proposed might be published "piece-
meal" in his paper—this, at the very same moment that the disjointed
"stumps" of his experimental *Petits Poèmes en prose* were appearing in
installments in the feuilleton section of the same journal.

This is the first and only time that the *Fusées-Suggestions* manuscript
is mentioned in Baudelaire's correspondence or in the innumerable
lists of projects he hoped to place with publishers. Like its pendant,
the eight loose leaves gathered under the title *Hygiene* (probably jot-
ted down in 1862 at the height of his crisis of "imbecility" and possi-
bly supplemented in Belgium in 1865), *Flares* would remain the most
secret (and most speculative) of Baudelaire's unfinished works. It is in
these pages that he most comes to resemble his master Joseph Joubert,
whose posthumous *Pensées* he had read in Chateaubriand's 1839 edition
and of whom Blanchot would later write:

> Joubert had this gift. He never wrote a book. He only prepared to write
> one, resolutely seeking the exact conditions that would allow him to
> write it. Then he forgot even this plan. . . . In this he was one of the first

completely modern writers, preferring the center to the sphere, sacrificing results to the discovery of their conditions, and writing not in order to add one book to another but to take command of the point from which it seemed to him all books issued, the point which, once it was found, would relieve him of the need to write any books whatsoever.[11]

By contrast, *Mon Coeur mis à nu,* whose intermittent composition is generally dated from 1859 to 1865, was from the outset conceived as a full-fledged *book,* as the many references throughout its pages to possible chapter headings or essay topics make clear. These include such rubrics as: Dandyism; Male Apparel; Female Types; Theater; Religion; Politics; the Revolution of 1848; the Death Penalty; Portraits and Anecdotes (mostly satirizing the contemporary Parisian literary and journalistic scene); excoriations of the political correctness of the two towering literary celebrities of his time, Victor Hugo and George Sand; a linguistic analysis of the "use of military metaphors in the press" (in which Baudelaire records one of the earliest newspaper usages of the term *"avant-garde"* as applied to art); and biographical background documentation relating to his career as a beleaguered man of letters and *poète maudit* (including "The story of my translation of Poe," "The story of the *Fleurs du mal* affair," and "The story of my relations with all the famous men of my day"). Sensing just how much his hero's entire life-and-work remained enmeshed in the partisan literary and art world politics of the Second Empire, the teenage Communard Arthur Rimbaud was no doubt correct to observe: "Baudelaire is the first visionary [*le premier voyant*], the king of poets, *a true God.* Yet the milieu in which he lived was too *artiste.*"[12]

The title of this never-to-be-finished book, *My Heart Laid Bare,* was also drawn from one of Poe's "Marginalia," in which the author of the "Tell-Tale Heart" had thrown down the following gauntlet:

If any ambitious man have a fancy to revolutionize, at one effort, the universal world of human thought, human opinion, and human sentiment, the opportunity is his own—the road to immortal renown lies straight, open, and unencumbered before him. All that he has to do is to write and publish a very little book. Its title should be simple—a few plain words—"My Heart Laid Bare." But—this little book must be *true to its title.*

Now, it is not very singular that, with the rabid thirst for notoriety which distinguishes so many of mankind—so many, too, who care not a fig what is thought of them after death, there should not be found one man having sufficient hardihood to write this little book?. . . But to write it—*there* is the rub. No man dare write it. No man will dare ever write it. No man *could* write it, even if he dared. The paper would shrivel and blaze at every touch of the fiery pen.[13]

With *Mon Coeur mis à nu*, Baudelaire rose to Poe's bait: he would attempt to undertake an absolutely unwritable, self-incinerating book, fully aware though he was that the pretense to absolute frankness was but another literary mask: "Hypocrite lecteur, —mon semblable, —mon frère!" He liked to quote Joseph de Maistre's observation that if anyone were to adopt the motto of Jean-Jacques Rousseau's *Confessions*, "vitam impendere vero" ("to devote one's life to truth"), this would be a sure indication that the author was a bald-faced liar.

Most of the information we have about *My Heart Laid Bare* comes from Baudelaire's letters to his mother. In April 1861, shortly after the publication of the second edition of *The Flowers of Evil*, he wrote her that among the various other projects he had in mind (which included a play and several novels), there was a "major book" about which he had been dreaming for the last two years: "*My Heart Laid Bare*, into which I shall load all my angers. Ah, if this book ever sees the light, J-J's *Confessions* will pale beside it. As you see, I'm still dreaming." But he added that in order to undertake this "singular" work, he would need to have access to all his correspondence of the past twenty years—most of which he had either given away or burned. Two years later, in June 1863, he wrote to inform her that he had recently signed a multibook contract with Hetzel for a new edition of *The Flowers of Evil*, to be followed by the prose poems of *Paris Spleen* and the autobiographical *My Heart Laid Bare*, but that he would have to return to Honfleur (where he had sent several trunks of papers) to complete the latter project, which had now become "the true passion of my brain, something quite different from Jean-Jacques's celebrated *Confessions*." Two days later he added:

Yes, this book that I have so dreamed about will be a book of grudges [*un livre de rancunes*]. But rest assured that my mother and stepfather will be respected in it. But in recounting my education, the manner in which my ideas and my feelings were fashioned, I want relentlessly to convey just how much I feel myself to be a stranger to the world and all its religious creeds. I shall turn my real talent for impertinence against *all of France*. I stand in need of vengeance as an exhausted man stands in need of a bath. . . . Of course, I shall not publish *My Heart Laid Bare* until I have amassed a fortune suitable enough to place myself out of harm's way, beyond France, if necessary.[14]

Having in the meantime expatriated himself to Belgium (and thus presumably out of harm's way), he wrote Mme. Aupick in January 1865 that he planned to finish up *My Heart Laid Bare* (together with a series of short stories) if and when he returned to her maternal side in Honfleur—a homecoming he continued to delay. The following month, he again mentioned *Mon Coeur mis à nu* ("a great monster, dealing *de omni re*") to his literary agent, Julien Lemer, but by this point his projected baring of his heart had given way to the even more rancorous *mise à nu* of Belgium in his other unfinished (and, in many ways, equally autobiographical and equally monstrous) book, *La Belgique déshabillée*—or Belgium Stripped Bare.[15]

*   *   *

Baudelaire's late turn toward the fragmentary[16]—or toward the form of the unfinished, the abandoned, the aborted, the ruined, or the *à venir*—involved not only a conscious renunciation of his Parnassian aesthetics of perfection and unity but more specifically a desertion of the harmonies of the traditional lyric in favor of the disjunctions of prose. This entailed an abandonment of the formal metrical patternings of *le vers* (or, more precisely, of the poetic *line*) in favor of the grammatical unit of the *sentence*, whose propositions (at least in his late fragments) he increasingly preferred to array as horizontal sequencings of *phrases* rather than as vertical imbrications of *clauses*.[17] In his 1859 essay on Théophile Gautier he had written: "It is the character of true poetry to have a regular flow, like that of great rivers in their approach to the sea, to their death, and to infinity, and to avoid everything that is precipitous and jarring. If lyric poetry soars, it is always with an elastic and undular wingbeat. Everything that is brusque and broken displeases it."[18]

Two years earlier in his essay on Poe he had similarly observed that in his prose works the American had at his disposition "a multitude of tones, of linguistic nuances, the reasoning tone, the sarcastic tone, the humoristic tone—all of which poetry repudiates and which are like dissonances and outrages to the idea of pure beauty."[19] Although still occasionally nostalgic for high poetry's sovereign euphonies, in his late fragments Baudelaire abandons the idea of "pure beauty" to embrace instead a counteraesthetic of dissonance, dispersion, and disjointure, attuned less to the auratic universal analogies of *correspondance* than to the specific ironies of *la discrépance*—an Anglicism that he discovered in Poe ("discrepancy," from the Latin *crepare*, to rattle, creak, or crack) and that he deployed in French to express his increasingly melancholy awareness that the modern world was governed by nothing more than *malentendu*, ever liable to futile misunderstanding, mishearing, and misconstrual. Which was the very diagnosis delivered by the great pessimistic tradition of the seventeenth-century French *moralistes*.

An avid reader in his youth of Pascal and of La Bruyère, La Rochefoucauld, Vauvenargues, as well as of their latter-day *moraliste* descendants Chamfort, Joubert, and Stendhal, Baudelaire in his late prose reprises this entire French inheritance of aphorism, apothegm, epigram, maxim, *réflexion*, *sentence*, and *pensée*.[20] Baudelaire's fondness for this tradition of *brevitas* is already apparent in his earliest work. One of the first texts he published (in April 1846 under the name Baudelaire-Dufays, for the small satirical journal *Le Corsaire-Satan*) was "A Choice of Consoling Maxims on Love," wherein the twenty-five-old syphilitic dandy took his public revenge upon his half-brother, Alphonse (stooge of his stepfather, Aupick, and of his hated *conseil judiciaire*, Ancelle), by addressing a series of semiflirtatious pieces of erotic advice (in the epigrammatic manner of Stendhal's *On Love*) to Alphonse's very straitlaced and provincially stuck-up wife, Félicité—a nasty little exercise in journalistic malice, well calculated to offend and outrage Baudelaire's immediate family circle.[21] Many of his late maxims will similarly be retaliatory in impulse, involving a caustic and often intemperate settling of scores. The same month of 1846 also saw the publication, again in a *petit journal*, of Baudelaire's "Advice to Young Writers," cast into a sequence of Voltairean adages that provided a vade mecum for fledgling authors trying to forge a career in the new capitalist dispensation of the bourgeois July Monarchy. Its Balzacian homiletics advise the novice *littérateur* how to break into the marketplace, how to form advantageous alliances (and enemies), what sort of methods of composition to employ, how to make regular daily work the sister of inspiration, what kind of long-term investment the art and craft of verse might represent (maturing slowly, but paying off handsomely in the end), how to best handle one's creditors and mistresses, and so on. These are the same tactical and economic issues that Baudelaire continues to address in the fragments of *Flares, Hygiene,* and *My Heart Laid Bare,* except that in his later years the question has now become not just how to gain fame and glory as a writer but rather how to survive from day to day, how to go on living, how not to commit suicide (or succumb to addiction), once you have outlived yourself as a lyric poet in the era of high capitalism (to reprise Walter Benjamin's title).

By the time he began composing *Flares, Hygiene,* and *My Heart Laid Bare* in the late fifties and early sixties, Baudelaire had added to his earlier pantheon of French *moraliste* models three major new foreign authors he had recently discovered, two of them American (Poe and Emerson), and the third, Joseph de Maistre, a Jesuit-trained Savoyard writing in French from his diplomatic outpost in St. Petersburg (his theodicy in the form of Platonic dialogues, *Les Soirées de St. Petersbourg,* was posthumously published in 1821). If from Poe's "Marginalia" Baudelaire absorbed an epigrammatic *prose de combat* by turns trenchant and digressive, vitriolic and facetious, in Joseph de Maistre, by contrast, he encountered a figure whom he considered a true visionary (or *voyant*), someone whose "metapolitical" (a term Maistre borrowed from the German) perspective on the entire sweep of human history placed him well beyond the local fray of Poe's internecine literary squabbles. An archconservative propagandist, more ultramontane than the pope, more ancien régime than the restored Bourbons, Maistre was the counter-Enlightenment, antimodern and thoroughly retrograde "prophet of the past" (as Barbey d'Aurevilly had dubbed him) whom Baudelaire needed in the wake of his traumatic "depolitization" after the failure of the 1848 Revolution and the subsequent coup d'état of 1851.[22] From Maistre's politico-theological vantage point (far more extreme than Edmund Burke's), the French Revolution had been nothing short of a providential event, a divine punishment visited upon France (and,

indeed, upon all of the modern world), ushering in the reign of unmiti-
gated Evil attendant upon the extermination of all traditional principles
of truth and order, themselves grounded in the absolute sovereignty of
God. This is the Maistre whose analyses of the crisis of sacrality and sov-
ereignty in postrevolutionary Europe presage not only those of Charles
Maurras but also those of Carl Schmidt, Georges Bataille, the 1930s Pa-
risian Collège de sociologie, René Girard, and Roberto Calasso. In *My
Heart Laid Bare* Baudelaire pays homage to Maistre's denunciations of
the Enlightenment belief in progress (and of its dark satanic mills of
industrialization) while nonetheless admitting the possibility of lost
prelapsarian (Native American) cultures whose warrior dandies he had
so admired in the George Catlin portraits displayed at the Salon of 1846:

> Theory of true civilization.
> It does not entail gas, steam, or table-turning; it entails the diminu-
> tion of the traces of original sin.
> Nomadic peoples, hunters, farmers, and even cannibals, can *all* prove
> superior—by their energy, by their dignity—to our Western races.
> Which shall possibly be destroyed.
> Theocracy and communism.

Writing as he was from czarist Russia (while trying to convert its Eastern
Orthodox aristocracy to his immoderate version of papism), Maistre es-
poused a rigid and authoritarian commitment to theocracy as the sole
cure for the rise of secularism, whereas Baudelaire was still enough of
an ex-forty-eighter to imagine the abolition of private property (as pro-
posed by the French utopian socialists) as an alternate religious solu-
tion to the dehumanizations of modern capitalism.

Compared to Baudelaire's ironic and dyspeptic stoicism, Maistre is
more recognizable as an early nineteenth-century romantic when he
is at his most ferociously apocalyptic: in this respect he far more re-
sembles the prophetic Blake than the traditionalist Burke, for he takes
the discourse of revolutionary Terror and dialectically reverses it into
an Augustinian Catholicism so extreme in its abhorrence for the fallen
material world that it often verges on gnosticism—echoed, for exam-
ple, in *My Heart Laid Bare*: "Theology. What is the fall? If it is unity be-
come duality, then it is God who fell. In other terms, would not cre-

ation entail the fall of God?" In the section of his *Arcades Project* entirely devoted to his never-completed book on Baudelaire, Walter Benjamin quotes an emblematic sentence from Maistre's *Saint Petersburg Evenings* to illustrate the ternary rhythms that drive the vatic cadences of his desolation: "The entire earth, continually soaked in blood, is but an immense altar upon which all that lives must be sacrificed without end, without measure, without respite—until all things are burnt up, until all evil is extinguished, until death itself has died."[23] Baudelaire was much taken by the sanguinary sacrificial violence that courses through this passage—which, like his mentor, he used to impart a religious sense to the bloodbath of the French Revolution: "The Revolution and its cult of Reason prove the idea of sacrifice." Elsewhere, deploying the kind of skewed syllogisms so favored by Maistre, he manages to concatenate the sacred (religious worship) with the profane (prostitution) through their shared links to sacrifice:

What is love?
The need to move beyond the self.
Man is an animal who worships.
To worship is to sacrifice and prostitute oneself.
All love is therefore prostitution.

"Religions are the only interesting things on earth," Baudelaire observes in these same notes—with a nod to the Chateaubriand of *Genius of Christianity* and to Maistre. Praised by Auguste Comte as one of the first modern historians to study the sociology of symbolic practices, admired by Émile Durkheim for his anthropology of the sacred and for his grasp of religion as the crucial force underlying social totalities, Maistre was perhaps most notorious in the early nineteenth century for his virulent defense of capital punishment. The very first dialogue of his *Soirées* is devoted to a darkly Dostoevskian celebration of *le bourreau* (or executioner) as a kind of homo sacer who, at once accursed and sublime, serves "L'histoire avec sa grande hache" (Perec)—be it by ax, guillotine, or *badelaire* (scimitar)—in order to fulfill his ritual function as the spiller of the sacrificial blood necessary to contain (as René Girard might explain it) the mimetic contagion of social violence.[24] Here is Baudelaire at his most Maistrian in *My Heart Laid Bare*:

The death penalty is the outgrowth of a mystical idea, totally mis-understood these days. The purpose of the death penalty is not to *save* society, at least not materially. Its purpose is (spiritually) to *save* society and the guilty one. In order for the sacrifice to be perfect, the vic-tim has to assent to it with joy. To give chloroform to a man condemned to death would be disrespectful, for it would rob him of his awareness of his grandeur as a victim while eliminating his chances of going to heaven.

"It might be pleasant to be by turns victim and executioner," he had ob-served a few pages earlier. This impulse, as he explained in his 1859 essay on Poe, was merely the expression of the "natural perversity of man"—forever fated to act out the scissiparities of the Fall in his recip-rocal identities as homicide and suicide, murderer and headsman.

Baudelaire's Maistrian defenses of capital punishment (often sneer-ingly directed against his rival Hugo's much-publicized campaign for its abolition) will no doubt strike today's readers as the most sulfurous and ill-considered aspect of his reactionary antiliberalism—particu-larly when (in the same essay on Poe) he can blithely compare its abo-lition to the scrapping of spelling standards as "two corollary follies."[25] Maistre's tribute to the bourreau is inscribed in his larger theory of re-versibility, itself an extreme formulation of the sacred logic of the Cru-cifixion—in which the blood of the innocent Christ cleanses the wicked-ness of the guilty and in which the expense of his death pays to redeem the debts of all our sins.[26] Although Baudelaire—chronically in arrears to his creditors and, as a syphilitic and addict, reminded daily of the fallenness of his flesh—will not follow Maistre's evangelistic Christian faith in the power of Redemption, he remains fascinated as a poet by the reversal of things into their opposites—as in his baroque 1853 poem entitled "Reversibility" addressed to Mme. Sabatier, in which the ideal-ized attributes of the muse are chiasmically turned back onto the ab-ject traits of her lover-poet. Antoine Compagnon locates Maistre's most characteristic rhetorical performance of reversibility in his practice of the figure known as *antimetabole* (of which Shakespeare's "I wasted time, but now doth time waste me" provides a perfect Baudelairean example). Antimetabole rotates on an axial ABBA structure—which is also the most frequent rhyme scheme of Baudelaire's quatrains.[27] In the second fragment of his *Flares*, Baudelaire puts the Maistrian trope of antimetabole into play in order to imagine the entirely new, modern-ist poetics of the city whose vortex (or *tourbillon*) he was now exploring in the prose poems of his *Paris Spleen*:

> The religious inebriation of great cities. —Pantheism. I am every-body; Everybody is me.
> Whirlpool.

*   *   *

"Poe and De Maistre taught me how to reason," Baudelaire brags in *Flares*. If Poe provided him with a rationale for his aesthetics, and if Maistre furnished him with a systematic (meta)politics and anthropol-ogy of religion, then it was Emerson who lighted his way into the do-main of ethics.[28] In the transcendentalist's 1860 *Conduct of Life* he dis-covered an offhand sententiousness ("the first wealth is health") that proved highly quotable—as evidenced by all the Emerson citations that reverberate through these late pages, especially in *Hygiene*, where the ethical "drill" of self-reliance and self-husbandry prescribed by the Sage of Concord reaches its most hortatory pitch. Baudelaire adduces Emerson's apothegm "The hero is he who is immovably centered" in his great 1863 obituary essay on Delacroix, pointing out the romantic artist's preference for "concise and concentrated writers, those whose prose, unburdened of ornament, seems to imitate the rapid movement of thought, and whose sentences resemble gestures—Montesquieu, for example." With Stendhal, Baudelaire continued, Delacroix shared a propensity for "simple formulas and brief maxims to ensure the good conduct of life"—the marks of fiery temperaments "in need of a shield and armor to protect themselves against the perpetual battle into which the fatality of their genius has cast them."[29] Such self-weaponization reaches back, as Michel Foucault reminds us, to the Stoic practice of *hypomnemata* (the taking down of memoranda and notes) in the service of a *souci de soi* or "care of self" (or "moral dynamics," as Baudelaire would call it after Maistre), less aimed at the confessional revelation of what lies hidden within the heart and more grounded in the disciplined exteriorization or objectification of the self, the better to subject it to a sane and regulated commerce with its own inner and outer worlds.[30]

It is perhaps in this sense that one should understand Baudelaire's claim that he was doing "something quite different" from Rousseau's *Confessions* in *My Heart Laid Bare*, where he provides us, not with a narrative of origins or of autobiographical cause and effect, but with the fractured, almost cubist shards of a self-portrait, presented in notations that often barely rise to the level of achieved sentences:[31]

> A precocious taste for women. I confused the smell of fur with the scent of woman. I remember. . . . In short, I loved my mother for her elegance. I was therefore a precocious dandy.
> My ancestors—idiots or maniacs—in solemn apartments, all victims of terrible passions.
> . . .
> A sense of *solitude*, from childhood onward. Despite my family—and especially among my schoolmates—a sense that it was my fate to be forever alone.
> Nonetheless, a very keen taste for life and pleasure.
> . . .
> When I've inspired universal horror and disgust, I'll have conquered solitude.
> . . .
> To glorify the cult of images (my great, my single, my earliest passion).
> . . .
> As a child, I by turns wanted to be a pope (but a military pope) or an actor.
> The intense pleasures that I derived from these two hallucinations.
> . . .
> Ever since childhood, a tendency toward mysticism. My conversations with God.
> . . .
> As a child, I felt two contrary emotions pulling at my heart: the horror of life and the ecstasy of life.
> A fair characterization of a lazy nervous type.

Above and beyond their focus on the relationship of self (*autos*) to life (*bios*), Baudelaire's late fragments turn most frequently to the problematic act of writing itself—the *graphein* of autobio*graphy*. Roland Barthes somewhere remarked that his two greatest pleasures in writing lay in the moments of beginning or ending a text. Afflicted as he is by the chronic (and like Coleridge and De Quincey, opium-induced) habit of procrastination, Baudelaire is forever exhorting himself to put pen to paper:

> First get yourself going, and then make use of logic and analysis. Any hypothesis demands a conclusion.
> Work yourself up into a frenzy on a daily basis.
> . . .
> Set to work immediately, even if the work be mediocre. It beats dreaming.
> A series of small acts of the will delivers major results.
> . . .
> By putting off what needs to be done, you run the danger of never being able to do it at all. If you don't convert immediately, you risk damnation.
> . . .
> Beginning a novel: tackle the subject at random, and to whet your desire to complete it, kick things off with a string of gorgeous sentences.
> . . .
> The only lengthy works are those that one dares not to begin. They become nightmares.
> . . .
> (I can begin *My Heart Laid Bare* wherever I want, however I want, and continue on with it day by day, following the inspiration of the day or the occasion—provided the inspiration prove lively enough.)

By choosing the medium of the fragment over the finished work, Baudelaire maintains himself in a state of perpetual inception. Every fragment becomes a new beginning, a new project (or what Friedrich Schlegel called "the subjective seed of a developing object"). Yet, as it breaks off into silence or into the interstitial blank of the page, every fragment also declares itself as an act of termination or closure (like Schlegel's famous hedgehog, "entirely isolated from the surrounding world and complete in itself").[32] Always commencing, always concluding, composed in fits and starts on stray sheets of paper, Baudelaire's late pensées and precepts are like a string of promises or resolutions—

made to be broken. Or like a series of dice throws that will never abolish chance. What's more, the more affirmative, the more dogmatic or apodictic he becomes, the more evident his state of disarray—that same *désarroi* that underlies Pessoa's great unfinished *Livro do desassossego,* that fragmentary Book of Disquiet authored by a poet who, like Baudelaire, was forever inventing new identities to do his writing for him.

"The taste for productive concentration should, in the mature man, replace the taste for wastage [*déperdition*]" runs one of the Emersonian adages of *Flares*. This is complemented by the very first sentence of *My Heart Laid Bare*: "On the centralization and vaporization of the *Self*. It all comes down to this." As Béatrice Didier has observed, the economy of Baudelaire's late fragments is simultaneously centripetal and centrifugal, at once aimed at intensifying the concentrated singularity of the One and at the same time given over to the loss or dissemination of the individual within the Many—an economy she associates with the nineteenth-century laws of thermodynamics (equilibrium and entropy) and with the twin pulls of capitalism (accumulation and expenditure).[33] Like any bourgeois of his class, Baudelaire will often define the act of writing as a form of industry or labor, linked to prudential saving, investment, and the creation of surplus value—the very vehicles of his salvation:

> Every time you receive a letter from a creditor, write fifty lines on some extraterrestrial topic and you will be saved.
>
> . . .
>
> A bit of work, repeated 365 times, will generate a bit of money 365 times—which is to say, an enormous sum. At the same time, *glory is obtained.*
>
> . . .
>
> Work, a progressive and cumulative force; like capital, it yields interest, heightening one's faculties, or one's results.
>
> . . .
>
> Examine in all of its modalities—be it in the works of nature or the works of man—the universal and eternal law of gradation: the *by and by,* the *little by little,* with things growing progressively in force, like compound interest on an investment.
>
> The same thing goes for *artistic and literary achievement,* as well as for the variable funds of *willpower.*

Taking up the Maistrian notion of "dynamics" as the motion of the soul within the force field of the divine, Baudelaire will also associate the act of writing with the efficacy of magic or prayer to tap into this higher reservoir of power. Writing here is associated no longer with the accumulation of capital but with archaic ritual, with witchcraft, with the sorcerer's performative capacity to call up energies and voices at will:[34]

> On language and writing, considered as magical operations, sorcery of evocation . . .
> Enlarge all the faculties.
> Conserve all the faculties.
> A cult (magic, sorcery of evocation).
> Sacrifice and vow are the supreme formulas and symbols of exchange.
> . . .
> Know the joys of a harsh life, and pray, pray, without end. Prayer is a reservoir of strength. *(Altar of the Will. Moral Dynamics. The Sorcery of the Sacraments. Hygiene of the Soul.)*
> . . .
> There is in prayer, a magical operation. Prayer is one of the great forces behind the dynamics of the intellect. It works something like an electrical current.

When it comes to the wastage or *déperdition* of such magic powers, however, Baudelaire often has recourse to obscene or scatological imagery: "And what is not a prayer these days? Shitting is a prayer, according to democrats taking their craps." He attacks the populist "flowing style" and promiscuous appeal of George Sand's prose by comparing her to a "latrine." On a similarly misogynistic note, he delivers himself of the following *mot*: "There are only two places where one pays for the right to spend: public toilets and women." The very act of copulation is perceived as a dangerous diminution of that magic reservoir of force or willpower that the writer must constantly safeguard (shades of Balzac!). Baudelaire takes mischievous pleasure in putting the matter as crudely as possible:

> The more a man cultivates the arts, the fewer hard-ons he gets.
> He makes a marked distinction between mind and beast.
> Only brutes get hard-ons, and fucking is the lyricism of the masses.

To fuck is to aspire to enter into another, and the artist never leaves himself.

This fantasy of total autarky, of the complete centralization (involving both the sacralization *and* mortification) of the self is expressed in these late fragments by the figure of the Dandy living and sleeping in his mirror, narcissistically protecting himself from any contaminating lateral commerce with the other. This centripetal drive toward "self-purification and antihumanity" (as he calls it in English) is, however, inseparable from the centrifugal and entropic vector of what Georges Bataille terms "unproductive expenditure." Baudelaire (like Rimbaud) sometimes calls this pure gift or loss of self "charity" (quoting 1 Corinthians: "Without charity, I am but a tinkling cymbal"). More often, however, he refers to it as "prostitution."

Pichois reports that one of the poet's favorite pastimes in his youth was billiards; in *Flares* and *My Heart Laid Bare*, he cues up the word "prostitution" (in the syllogistic manner of his master Joseph de Maistre) to produce an angular series of caroms and bank shots:

> Love is the taste for prostitution. Indeed, there is no noble pleasure that cannot be referred to prostitution.
> At a theater show, at a ball, the pleasure of one is the pleasure of all. What is art? Prostitution.
> . . .
> Love may arise from a generous impulse: the taste for prostitution.
> But it is soon corrupted by the taste for property.
> Love wants to move outside itself, to merge with its victim like a victor with his vanquished, all the while retaining the privileges of a conqueror.
> . . .
> The overpowering taste for prostitution at the heart of man, hence his horror of solitude. He wants to be *two*. The man of genius wants to be *one*, hence solitary.
> Glory involves remaining *one*, and prostituting oneself in a special way.
> . . .
> The most prostituted of beings is the being par excellence—God.

Every individual considers him his supreme friend. He is the shared and inexhaustible reservoir of love.

. . .

Advice to noncommunists: Everything is common, even God.

For Baudelaire the "communist" (a reader of Babeuf and of the economic treatises of Proudhon but apparently not of Marx), all property or individuality can become vaporized or atomized by the sheer process of free, metamorphic exchange, in which (as his writes in his urban prose poem "Crowds") "multitude and solitude become equal and convertible terms for the active and productive poet"—"What men name love is very small, very limited, very weak when compared to that ineffable orgy, that holy prostitution of the soul which gives itself up entirely—poetry and charity—to the unforeseen that reveals itself, to the stranger who passes by."[35]

Flares and *My Heart Laid Bare* are in a sense Baudelaire's commonplace books, containing quotations, recipes, prayers, sayings, reading notes, marginalia, and samplings of literary and journalistic styles. The prostitutes of Baudelaire's poetry and prose texts such as the *Painter of Modern Life*—public women, at once sacred and defiled—provide him with the strongest allegories of the commodified commonplaces of sexual and economic exchange.[36] But language itself, as he observes in *My Heart Laid Bare*, also provides an opportune site for the experience of the *lieu commun*: "The man of wit—who will never be in agreement with anybody—should make it a point to enjoy the conversation of imbeciles and the reading of worthless books. He will derive bitter pleasures from this, pleasures that will largely compensate him for his efforts." In *Hygiene* he writes: "Always be a poet, even in prose. The grand style (nothing more beautiful than the commonplace, *le lieu commun*)." Or this rather ironic asseveration jotted down in *Flares*, coming as it does from a poet who had always placed the hieratic art of verse at the antipodes of the everyday speech of the *vulgus*: "Immense depths of thought in commonplace turns of phrase, holes hollowed out by generations of ants." This is the sunken, hollow zone of language that belongs to everybody—and to nobody (as in Lautréamont's slogan, much admired by the surrealists: "Poetry should be made by all, not by one"). In a projected preface to his *Flowers of Evil*, Baudelaire had claimed, half in jest, that he could (like Poe) teach anyone "how to achieve, through a determinate series of efforts, a proportional degree of originality"—all it took was "the coupling of this noun to that adjective, analogous or contrary."[37] Now, in *Flares*, he muses on how to go about producing something far more difficult—sheer unoriginality:

> To create a *poncif*, this is genius.
> I need to create a *poncif*.

In nineteenth-century French, a *poncif* is a pouncing pattern or stencil—or, more broadly (as Baudelaire uses the term in his earlier art criticism), it can refer to any trite, worn-out, or stereotypical expression lacking originality. It is virtually synonymous with *cliché*, a technical word in printer's jargon for a stereotype block, with the noun use of the past participle of *clicher* ("to click") presumably echoic of a mold striking molten metal—later in the century, the term *cliché* will come to mean the negative of a photograph.[38] This definition of genius as an invention of anonymous and infinitely reproducible clichés or memes is immediately followed by: "The *concetto* is a masterpiece." Here Baudelaire's use of the Italian word alludes primarily not to the commonplace conceits adorning baroque or metaphysical poetry but rather to the stock punch lines or "asides" learned by the performers of commedia dell'arte for use in improvisational performance. Baudelaire had always dreamed of becoming an actor, and the roles he variously plays in his late fragments (including those in his big *livre bouffon* on Belgium) are never far from those of the traditional comic *buffo*, one of whose distinguishing trademarks was the constant stepping in and out of his role—that "permanent parabasis" of which Schlegel speaks in connection with the "transcendental buffoonery" of Irony.[39] Perusing the pages of Baudelaire's *Journaux intimes*, never quite sure whether to take them at their letter or not, Paul Valéry reproached their author for not having overcome his penchant for *paradoxalism*:

> To tell funny stories with a straight face.
> . . .
> The spirit of buffoonery does not necessarily exclude charity, but this is rare.

. . .

I understand how one might desert a cause merely to discover what it feels like to serve another one.

It might be pleasant to be by turns victim and executioner.

. . .

Let us be suspicious of the masses, of common sense, of the heart, and of the obvious.

This restless (and proto-Wildean) play of affirmation and negation, this buffo performance of banality in the service of originality, this acting out of the *alazon* calling forth his own *eiron*—all these are cognate to what Baudelaire in *Flares* characterized as the "two fundamental literary qualities" of modern writing: "Supernaturalism and irony. The individual cast of the eye, the aspect that things assume as they lie before the author, and then the satanic turn of mind." The subjective glimpse of the "supernatural," as Baudelaire goes on to explain, includes "the overall color and accent, that is, the intensity, sonority, limpidity, vibrancy, depth, and reverberation in space and time in which the sensation of existence is immensely heightened." And it is precisely this psychedelic vision of the immensity and expansibility of the here and now that irony proceeds to disenchant and contract, given that the "satanic turn of mind" tropes any poetic dream of *transcendence* (or immanence) into the prosaic lure of *transdescendence*. The interplay of "supernaturalism" and "irony" as fundamental modern literary qualities parallels Baudelaire's celebrated definition in *My Heart Laid Bare* of the fearful symmetries that divide the *homo duplex*: "There are in every man, at every hour, two simultaneous postulations, one toward God, the other toward Satan. The invocation of God, or spirituality, is the desire to move up a notch; the invocation of Satan, or animality, is the joy of downward descent." Baudelaire, following Maistre, insists on the *simultaneity* of the oppositions that he here rehearses. In this rigorously dualistic world, there may be vacillation or vibration or even reversibility between contending forces, but given the mutually self-canceling (and self-propagating) contradictions that define Baudelaire's binary logic, there can be no question of any teleological forward progress or of ultimate redemption—but only that state of petrified (and oxymoronic) unrest that Benjamin characterized as "dialectics at a standstill" or that Blanchot described as "an equilibrium in perpetual disequilibrium."[40]

* * *

The first systematic reader of Baudelaire's *Journaux intimes* was Friedrich Nietzsche, who purchased Crépet's just-published edition of the *Posthumous Works* in a local bookshop in Nice in late 1887 and then proceeded to copy out passages from *Flares* and *My Heart Laid Bare* onto seventy pages of his private notebooks—more space than he devoted to any other author.[41] Nietzsche had been drawn to the French poet ever since 1883 when, during his first winter on the Riviera, he had obtained Paul Bourget's recent *Essays on Modern Psychology*, which contained chapters on Baudelaire's "Pessimism" and "Theory of Decadence," as well as on Flaubert's "Nihilism," on Renan's "Aristocratic Dream," and on Taine's "Philosophic Sensibility"—all topics that Nietzsche would explore in *Beyond Good and Evil* (1886) and in *On the Genealogy of Morals* (1887). In addition, he had acquired a reprint of the posthumous 1868 edition of *The Flowers of Evil*, introduced by a long biographical essay by Théophile Gautier that dealt, among other matters, with Baudelaire's "style of decadence" ("a language veined with the virescence of decomposition, savoring of the Lower Roman Empire and the complicated refinements of the Byzantine School, the last form of Greek Art fallen into deliquescence").[42] Although Gautier had made no mention of Baudelaire's pathbreaking 1861 essay on Wagner's *Tannhäuser*, Nietzsche intuitively felt (as he ambivalently observed in a notebook entry in the spring of 1885) that Baudelaire was "a kind of Richard Wagner without music"—that is, a *decadent*, bent on "expression" at all costs, and like the late romantic Wagner, "sickly-nervous-tortured, without sun"—not to mention possessed of "a certain hypererotic effeminacy that reeks of Paris."[43] Later that summer, he compared Baudelaire to fellow Parisian Heinrich (or Henri) Heine:

> As for the pessimistic Baudelaire, he belongs among those almost unbelievable amphibians who are as German as they are Parisians; his poetry has something of what the Germans call "soul" or "infinite melody" or sometimes "the hangover of remorse" [*Katzenjammer*]. Baude-

laire is moreover a man of perhaps corrupt but also of very distinct, very acute and self-assured tastes—which accounts for his tyranny over all those who are today without convictions. If during his time he was the first prophet and proponent of Delacroix, perhaps today he might be the premiere "Wagnerite" in Paris. There is a great deal of Wagner in Baudelaire.[44]

These notebook entries prefigure the well-known sections 254 and 256 of *Beyond Good and Evil*, in which Nietzsche speaks admiringly of contemporary French artists, writers, and intellectuals, particularly as they emerge (as did Wagner) out of "the *late French romanticism* of the forties" and "experimentally anticipate the European of the future," for "it fell to them to first teach their century—and it is the century of the *crowd*!—the concept of the higher man":

> Even now France is still the seat of the most spiritual and sophisti-
> cated culture in Europe and the foremost school of taste. . . . One point
> they all have in common: they plug their ears against the raging stu-
> pidity [*rasende Dummheit*] and noisy twaddle of the democratic bour-
> geois. Indeed, the foreground today is taken up by a part of France that
> has become stupid and coarse: recently, at Victor Hugo's funeral [May
> 1885], it celebrated a veritable orgy of bad taste and at the same time of
> self-admiration.[45]

In these pages Nietzsche goes on to comment on the impact of Schopen-hauer's pessimism in France, on the popularity of Heine among its lyric poets, on Taine's appropriations of Hegel, and on the immense vogue for Wagner in Paris. He further celebrates the "devotion to *form*" and the practice of *l'art pour l'art* as indicative of the French capacity for purely "artistic passions," while also noting the persistence of the mor-aliste tradition in its contemporary writing: even "the little *romanciers* of the newspapers and the *boulevardiers de Paris*" display a "psychologi-cal hypersensitivity and curiosity" totally lacking among the barbarian Germans of the north. Above all, he praises the French for being "the first artists steeped in world literature" and as "great discoverers in the realm of the sublime, and also of the ugly and gruesome . . . virtuosos through and through, with uncanny access to everything that seduces, allures, compels, overthrows; born enemies of logic and straight lines, lusting after the foreign, the exotic, the tremendous, the crooked, the self-contradictory."[46]

If Baudelaire is notably absent from these published pages, it was largely because Nietzsche still remained completely unaware of his pioneer championing of Wagner. The eureka moment came when he began carefully reading through Crépet's edition of Baudelaire's *Posthumous Works* in Nice. On February 26, 1888—almost five years to the day after his much-admired (and much-loathed) Wagner had died—he excitedly writes to his friend the composer Peter Gast:

> I had always asked myself . . . "Who was it until now who was best prepared for Wagner? Who was the most naturally and intimately Wagnerian—and this despite or even without Wagner?" For the longest time, I said to myself: no doubt that bizarre, three-quarter fool Baudelaire, the poet of the *Fleurs du mal*. I had regretted that this spirit who was so kindred to Wagner had not discovered him in his own lifetime; I had underlined in his poems those passages that bear witness to a sort of *Wagnerian sensibility* which one finds nowhere else expressed in poetry—Baudelaire is *libertine*, mystic, "satanic," but above all Wagnerian. And what happened to me today! I'm leafing through a recently collected edition of the *Posthumous Works* of this genius who is so profoundly esteemed and even loved in France; and there, among the various priceless psychologics of *décadence* (*Mon Coeur mis à nu*, similar in kind to what, in the case of Schopenhauer and Byron, got *incinerated*),[47] my eyes fall on an unpublished letter by Wagner thanking Baudelaire for the essay he had published about him in the *Revue européenne* in April 1861.

Nietzsche then proceeds to quote to Gast the entirety of this affectionate thank-you note (which he had discovered in the extensive "Biographical Study" that prefaced Crépet's edition of Baudelaire's *Posthumous Works*), observing that Wagner was at that point forty-eight years old and Baudelaire forty. (Nietzsche had himself recently turned forty-three—and, like Baudelaire in Namur, would suffer a complete mental collapse in Turin the following January, from which he would never recover.) Nietzsche goes on to comment: "If I am not utterly mis-

taken, Wagner wrote only another single letter filled with such grat-
itude and indeed enthusiasm—after he received my *Birth of Tragedy*."
Clearly delighted to have discovered in Baudelaire another alter ego,
Nietzsche continues: "In this same book [i.e., the *Posthumous Works*]
one finds sketches in which Baudelaire vehemently defends Heine
against his French critics (Jules Janin) [see appendix 6]. Toward the
very end of his life, when he was half-mad and slowly coming to his
wretched end, they would apply *Wagnerian* music to him as a *medicine*;
and even when Wagner's name was merely mentioned, he would 'smile
with great joy.'"[48]

The Baudelaire whom Nietzsche encountered in the winter of 1887–
88 was, to his eyes, an emblematic figure of European decadence, an
exemplar of that disease of late romanticism which he dubbed *der
grosse Ekel*—a term sometimes translated as disgust or nausea but that
also resonates with Baudelairean *ennui* or *spleen*. If Nietzsche was so at-
tentive to Baudelaire's (syphilitic and aphasic) end, it was because he
also (proudly) recognized this illness within himself. As he observed
in his spiritual autobiography, *Ecce Homo*, written eight months later:

> Need I say after all this that in questions of decadence, I am *experi-
> enced*? I have spelled them forward and backward. . . . Looking from the
> perspective of the sick toward *healthier* concepts and values and, con-
> versely, looking again from the fullness and self-assurance of a *rich* life
> down into the secret work of the instinct of decadence—in this I have
> had the longest training, my truest experience; if in anything, I became
> a master in *this*. Now I know how, have the know-how, to *reverse perspec-
> tives*: the first reason why a "revaluation of values" is perhaps possible
> for me alone.[49]

Baudelaire's *Journaux intimes* offered Nietzsche a similar opportunity
for *reversibility* (a key Maistrian concept for Baudelaire as well), for in
them he saw mirrored the forward-backward spelling of himself—a
sick man (or convalescent) in search of health and "hygiene," yet some-
one whose recovery was always shadowed by the lucid awareness that
he was doomed to decline and disappear as the "last man." In short, in
Baudelaire's lateness (as in his own) Nietzsche discovered the condi-
tions for the revaluation of the old into something entirely early and

entirely new—the negativity [*Neinsagen*] of decadence converted into the affirmation [*Jasagen*] of a modernity in which everything is different, now that it has been ironically understood as the Eternal Return of the Same.[50]

For Paul Bourget, Nietzsche's *maître à penser*, decadence was above all a question of style—a dangerous erosion of the classical proportion of part to whole. Nietzsche cited Bourget in French when pointing out that in Wagner's music "the single turn of phrase [*tournure*] becomes sovereign, subordination and arrangement become arbitrary"—indeed, he would always remain fiercely skeptical of the totalitarian, synthesizing ambitions of the *Gesamtkunstwerk*. To the extent that he remained a decadent, Nietzsche's Wagner would never be more than the author of isolated tropes or *tournures*, "the greatest miniaturist in music."[51] From Bourget's conservative vantage point, decadence was just another alarming symptom of the broader decomposition of the traditional body politic: given the democratic privileging of the "individual cell" over the integrity of the "social organism" as a whole, mere "anarchy" was loosed upon the world. As Bourget put it: "An identical law governs the decadence of this other organism which is language. A style of decadence is one in which the unity of the book decomposes to leave place to the independence of the page, where the page decomposes itself to leave place to the independence of the phrase, and the phrase to leave place to the independence of the word."[52] Here was another definition of decadence that could be radically transvalued. Its negative diagnosis of decomposition could, by a pivot of perspective, provide an opening for the late style of early modernism—a poetics of the fragment that in the hands of the anarchic Nietzsche could be wielded like a hammer (or a stick of dynamite) to explode all previous forms of systematic philosophy—as evidenced by the aphorisms of *The Gay Science* (1882), the "Epigrams and Interludes" of *Beyond Good and Evil* (1886), the "Maxims and Arrows" of *Twilight of the Gods* (1889), and the great unfinished mosaic of *The Will to Power*, posthumously published in 1901.[53]

As he methodically copied his way through the pages of Baudelaire's *Flares* and *My Heart Laid Bare*, Nietzsche incorporated their late—and posthumous—style into his own body of language as a kind of (Derridean) *pharmakon*, at once poison and cure. Reading Baudelaire, Nietzsche was inspired not just to quote him but to *rewrite* him, the seventy pages of his notebooks sometimes reproducing the original French, sometimes refracting it into German, and sometimes oscillating between the two languages within the space of a single sentence or passage. One has the sense that in this process of mimetic introjection, Nietzsche is engaging in an uncanny translation (and *Umwertung*) of himself—just as Baudelaire had spoken of having had the eerie sensation, upon first translating Poe, of reading words and phrases he himself had already conceived. As he samples the pages of the *Journaux intimes,* splicing them into a kind of private breviary or self-portrait, Nietzsche heightens those features of Baudelaire in which he most recognizes himself (or his abject other): the proud and wounded embrace of solitude; the tortured self-analysis; the stoic cult of suicide; the gnostic asceticism; the temptation of martyrdom and sainthood; the ideal of the Dandy (translated by Nietzsche as "der höhere Mensch"); the paralysis of will; the unrealized projects; the call for "hygiene" and prayer; the *ressentiment*; the misogyny; the revulsion occasioned by the physical act of love; the aspiration to charity [*Hingebe*]; the Wagnerian confusion of Beauty with Melancholy; the agonistic battle with the absence of God;[54] the brush with "the wing of imbecility"; the manic-depressive leaps from ecstasy to horror; the absolute contempt for one's compatriots and their "herd" mentality; the abhorrence of commerce; the repudiation of the utilitarian *doxa* of the nineteenth century, in particular its ersatz religion of Progress; and, above all, the loathing for all forms of democratic bêtise [*Dummheit*], especially as embodied by Victor Hugo or George Sand (or, for that matter, Wagner at Bayreuth). For the most part, Nietzsche chooses to mime those passages in the *Journaux intimes* whose rhetorical compaction most recalls that of the two French authors he admired above all—Pascal and Stendhal—and those of Emerson, another idol.[55] But significantly enough, he also transcribes in full (into an amphibian French and German) the longest passage in these late fragments—namely, the meditation on the end of the world that closes *Flares* and in which Baudelaire emerges most palpably as a Nietzschean "pessimist of the future" and foreseer of holocausts to come. This is the passage from the final pages of *Flares* that Proust apparently had in mind when he referred to Baudelaire as "the most desolate prophet since the prophets of Israel":

The world is about to end. . . . But it is not specifically in the political institutions that one will observe the effects of universal ruin, or of universal progress—it hardly matters to me what name it goes by. It will be seen in the degradation of the human heart. Need I mention that whatever remains of politics will have to combat the onslaught of widespread animality, and that governments will be forced—just to maintain themselves and create a phantom of order—to resort to methods that would cause men of today to shudder, callous though they already be?

Here Nietzsche inserts one of his rare editorial exclamations: *Haarsträubend!*—Hair-raising! After tracing Baudelaire's musings on the "last man" for a few more paragraphs, Nietzsche finally retires his Doppelgänger back to the bookshelf and turns to a fresh notebook page—whose first words run: "Ein weinig reine Luft!" For a little fresh air! . . .

In *Ecce Homo*, Nietzsche claims that Baudelaire was the very first and no doubt the very last *"intelligent* adherent of Wagner"—and the same might be said of his own adherence to Baudelaire. Nietzsche was the first and last reader to recopy (and thus to reauthor) *Flares* and *My Heart Laid Bare* in his own split-image and -language, discovering his own posthumousness in the process. As he would proclaim six months later at the outset of *The Twilight of the Idols:* "Posthumous men—I, for example—are understood worse than timely ones, but heard better."[56] In France, by contrast, Baudelaire's posthumous *Journaux intimes* tended to fall on deaf ears. Conservative critic Henri Lemaître immediately dismissed these pensées as "tiresome and pretentious stammerings" while his colleague Ferdinand Brunetière saw in this "pitiful journal of impotence" nothing but mystification and banality—indeed, Brunetière would subsequently spear a campaign to deny Baudelaire a public monument in the 1890s. André Gide observed in his diaries that "there is not a single line of these journals that is not lamentably silly," dismissing Baudelaire as a serious "thinker"—with Walter Benjamin later rejoindering to Gide that he was "a bad philosopher, a good theoretician, but only as a brooder was he incomparable."[57] The *Journaux intimes* were better received among the more fervent Catholics. Shortly after their initial publication in 1887 (a year after he had discovered Rimbaud's *Illuminations*), the newly converted Paul Claudel devoured what he extravagantly called Baudelaire's *Écritures intimes*

(*Private Scriptures*), later remembering how relieved he had been to discover that his favorite French poet had, after a lifetime of anxiety and remorse, finally rediscovered his faith in his final years.[58]

After two scholarly re-editions (1909, 1919) and a 1919 chapbook publication by Blaise Cendrars's avant-garde Éditions de la Sirène, the *Écrits intimes* were again brought out to the broader public in 1930, this time by the newly founded Éditions de la Pléiade, edited by Yves Le Dantec and prefaced by Charles Du Bos, who dedicated the volume to fellow Catholic writer François Mauriac. In Du Bos's essay, the Christianization of Baudelaire's "tragic fate" reaches its high-water mark. He reads the last pages of *My Heart Laid Bare*—that is, the notes of the *Hygiene* section that Le Dantec had printed at the end of the *Journaux intimes*—as "one of the most heart-rending *De Profundis*, harrowing in its very humility, that a soul has ever proffered forth." Addressing a God who he is aware may not even exist, Baudelaire's "insurmountable need for prayer at the very heart of disbelief" provides "signal evidence of a soul marked by Christianity," a latter-day reenactment of Mark 9:24: "Help thee mine unbelief." As for Baudelaire's terrifying experience of "the wind of the wing of imbecility," Du Bos interprets this as a special Pascalian dispensation of grace, an urgent admonition to the poet from on high to urgently tend to the salvation of his soul. Even Baudelaire's final descent into aphasia is seen as providing the ultimate and redemptive portal by which God had finally entered the heart of the repentant sinner. Du Bos closes his essay with Nadar's narration of his last (apocryphal?) visit to Baudelaire at the Duval clinic in 1867:

> We were arguing about the immortality of the soul. I say "'we" because in his eyes I could read what he was saying as though he could speak. "How on earth can you believe in God?" I insisted. Baudelaire moved away from the railing on which we were leaning and showed me the sky. In front of us, above us, lay the splendid pageantry of the setting sun, lighting the clouds on fire and silhouetting the profile of the Arc of Triumph with gold and flames. "Crénom! O crénom," he protested, reproaching me, as he indignantly punched his fists toward the sky.[59]

A scholar of English literature, Du Bos had been in regular correspondence with T. S. Eliot since 1922, shortly after the publication of his first volume of *Approximations* (which had contained an earlier piece on Baudelaire's "abulia"). Eliot's 1930 essay on Baudelaire, which was printed as the introduction to Christopher Isherwood's translation of the *Intimate Journals of Charles Baudelaire* for the small British religious publisher Blackamore Press, is quite Du Bosian in its accents. In mid-1927 Eliot had converted to Anglo-Catholicism and adopted British citizenship; his Baudelaire is therefore very much approached from the literary pulpit of the High Church of England. Eliot is indulgent toward Baudelaire's "theological innocence"—

> His Christianity is rudimentary or embryonic: at best he has the excesses of a Tertullian. . . . His business was not to practice Christianity, but—what was more important for his time—to assert its *necessity*. . . . In the middle nineteenth century, an age of bustle, programmes, platforms, scientific progress, humanitarians and revolutions which improved nothing, an age of progressive degradation, Baudelaire perceived that what really matters is Sin and Redemption. . . . Baudelaire was man enough for damnation. . . . In all his humiliating traffic with other beings, he walked secure in this high vocation, that he was capable of damnation denied to the politicians and newspaper editors of Paris.

More autobiographically, Eliot saw in Baudelaire "one of those who have great strength, but strength merely to *suffer*. He could not escape suffering, and could not transcend it, so he *attracted* pain to himself. But what he could do, with that immense passive strength and sensibilities which no pain could impair, was to study his suffering." Even more revealingly, Eliot discovered in *Flares* the deepest stratum of Baudelaire's dolorism: "la volupté unique et suprême de l'amour gît dans la certitude de faire le mal" ("the sole and supreme pleasure of making love lies in the certitude that one is doing *evil*"): "Having an imperfect, vague romantic conception of Good, he was at least able to understand that the sexual act as evil is more dignified, less boring, than as the natural "life-giving," cheery automatism of the modern world. For Baudelaire, sexual operation is at least not analogous to Krushchen salts." The simile is Eliotic to perfection, Krushchen salts being a well-known British product designed to soothe constipation and generally invigorate the constitution. And equally worthy of the Possum: "Baudelaire is a bungler compared with Dante. . . . The complement, and the correction to the *Journaux intimes,* so far as they deal with the relation of man and woman, is the *Vita nuova,* and the *Divine Comedy.*"[60]

To be fair to the author of *The Waste Land,* however, he concluded his piece by praising the *Intimate Journals* as an exemplary modernist piece of writing—in a paragraph that was subsequently dropped when Eliot's "Baudelaire" was collected into his *Selected Essays, 1917–1932*:

> To translate successfully an imperfect series of notes and jottings like the *Journaux Intimes* is a more difficult task than the whole of Baude-laire's formal prose. There are repetitions (of thoughts which are prob-ably all the more important to the author because of being repeated); there are short phrases and single words which seem to be memoranda for thoughts, unknown to us, to be developed later; and there are many references to Baudelaire's familiars and to personages of the day. There is the opportunity for vast annotation by some French student who can devote much time to the subject. . . . The reader need not, however, be deterred. The most important passages are also the most compre-hensible. We need not stop to guess at meanings in cryptograms, or to enquire the identity of all the persons mentioned. There is enough to be done in pondering the passages which are fully expressed. And the more we study it, the more coherence appears, the more sane and se-vere and clear-sighted we find a view of life which is, I believe, much more modern for us than are most philosophies between Baudelaire's time and our own.[61]

A generous tribute indeed to the young Isherwood's somewhat falter-ing translation, apparently completed in 1929, just before he set off for the fleshpots of Berlin.

After a decade of errancy, Isherwood and his long-time friend W. H. Auden emigrated to the United States in 1939, with Isherwood soon set-tling in southern California. In Hollywood, he made contact with the Marcel Rodd Company, another small religious press that in 1945 pub-lished Thomas à Kempis's *Imitation of Christ,* Isherwood's *Vedanta for the Western World* (prefaced by Aldous Huxley), and his cotranslation with Swami Pranhavanda of *The Bhagavad-Gita.* It was with Rodd that

Isherwood brought out the second edition of his *Intimate Journals of Charles Baudelaire* in 1947, revised with the help of UCLA French professor and Stendhal specialist Myron Parker and introduced by Auden—who in 1940, while living in Brooklyn Heights, had reconverted to the Episcopal Church, embracing the Anglican Communion of his youth and an existential Christianity marked by his reading of Kierkegaard and the works of Protestant theologian Reinhold Niebuhr.[62]

Taking his cue from Baudelaire's meditations on "the heroism of modern life," Auden discovers in his *Intimate Journals* a central, abiding question: "What makes a man a hero, i.e. an individual; or conversely, what makes him a churl, i.e. a mere unit in human society without any real individual significance of his own?" Onto this opposition between individual and churl, Auden grafts a number of other dichotomies—spirit versus nature, being versus becoming, private versus public—before moving into a comparative (Carlylean) typology of heroes: to the side of nature, "the hero of Greek poetry" (Agamemnon, endowed by fate with arete); to the side of spirit, "the hero of Greek philosophy" (who "becomes what he wills"); and, including and transcending both, "the religious hero" as found in the Old Testament (Adam, Abraham, Job) or, even more radically, in the Prophets and the Gospels ("the suffering servant, the despised and rejected of men"). In Auden's conceptual machinery, Baudelaire's Dandy is at once a hero of poetry and a hero of philosophy but at the same time a religious hero turned upside-down ("Lucifer, the rebel, the defiant one who refuses all commands"). The Dandy's opposite is "the churlish mass, Woman, the man of commerce, *l'esprit belge*"—all representative of that audience of "public opinion" which threatens the modern poet's ability, now that he has been severed from tradition, to forge a true individuality for himself.[63]

The greatest danger Baudelaire runs, according to Auden (here sounding like Sartre), is to make the Dandy's mistake, that is, to imagine one could transform oneself into a spiritual individual "not as becoming what one wills, but as becoming what others are not." Auden's Baudelaire discovers a solution to this dilemma in the Christian concept of love as *agapé* (in contrast to the Platonic notion of *eros* held by the Dandy), that is, in the humble giving over of the self to the other—"a change of heart," Auden argues, far more spectacular than Rimbaud's (still very dandyish) decision to abandon poetry for a life of trade in Abyssinia. Given that Isherwood's *Intimate Journals* followed the traditional editorial arrangement (officialized by Le Dantec's 1930 edition in which the pages of *Flares/Hygiene* were printed at the conclusion of *My Heart Laid Bare*), Auden therefore encounters this moment of conversion at the very climax of the book, in the entry dated January 23, 1862: "To-day, I have received a singular warning, I have felt the wind of the wing of madness [Isherwood's translation of *imbécilité*] pass over me." In his peroration, Auden moves from pathos and terror into Christian homily:

> The last few pages of *My Heart Laid Bare* which follow this entry are some of the most terrifying and pathetic passages in literature. They present a man fighting against time to eradicate a lifetime's habits of thought and feeling, and set himself in order and acquire a history. . . . To the eye of nature, he was too late. As he spoke, the bird stooped and struck. But, to the eye of the spirit, we are entitled to believe that he was in time—for, though the spirit needs time, an instant of it is enough.[64]

Sartre's major study of Baudelaire, published a year earlier in 1946, wants to have nothing to do with this kind of discourse of forgiveness and redemption. Written in the postwar climate of *épuration*, his essay paints Baudelaire as an abject figure of failure and defeat [*échec*] and, what's more, as an insidious collaborator with the bourgeoisie of his era, proved by his Vichylike decision to side with *les salauds* (Maistre et al.) against such humanist progressives as George Sand and Sartre's childhood idol Victor Hugo. The year 1946 was also the one in which a committee of writers petitioned the French courts to wipe the 1857 verdict against *The Flowers of Evil* off the books—the Supreme Court of Appeals would finally strike down the decision in 1949. In taking on Baudelaire, Sartre is thus combating on the one hand an avant-garde classic still in need of legal rehabilitation and on the other a figure can-onized by the Catholic, fascist right. In a broader sense, Sartre is also using Baudelaire to purge away all the Second Empire drawing room furniture that provided the ideological stage setting for the Hell of his recent play *No Exit* (1944)—just as he would later pursue his particu-lar animus against the nineteenth-century doctrine of l'art pour l'art in his three-volume biography of Flaubert, *The Family Idiot* (1970–72). Baudelaire also provides the philosopher with a perfect allegory of the mechanisms of Bad Faith already explored in his *Being and Nothing-ness* (1943). Because Baudelaire had refused to come to honest onto-logical terms with Being-for-Itself, he was never able to produce his self-consciousness out of Nothingness, choosing instead to reify him-self into a material object having all the reassuring and inauthentic inertness of Being-in-Itself—in short, he had deluded himself that he could somehow fuse existence with essence, subject with object, and out of this false consciousness he had invented a series of ruinous mis-apprehensions of himself: "Baudelaire's fundamental attitude was that of a man bending over himself—bending over his reflection like Narcis-sus. . . . [He] was the man who never forgot himself. He watched him-self see; he watched in order to observe himself watch. . . . He was the man without 'immediacy' . . . the man who chose to look upon himself as though he were another person; his life is simply the story of the fail-ure of this attempt." In the end, Sartre's stagnant Baudelaire is not that far removed from Paul Bourget's portrait of the decadent: "He refused experience. Nothing came from outside to change him. . . . His story is that of a very slow, very painful decomposition."[65]

Critics were quick to point out that by presenting Baudelaire as a case study in Bad Faith and by etherizing him upon a couch of exis-tential psychoanalysis, Sartre had completely overlooked the poet. Ex-surrealist Michel Leiris attempted to mitigate matters in his 1947 pref-ace to the separate Gallimard edition of Sartre's essay that was now dedicated to Jean Genet—an essay that, originally intended as a pref-ace to a collection of Baudelaire's *Écrits intimes* (including *Fusées, Mon Coeur mis à nu,* the recently rediscovered *Carnet,* and a selection from his private correspondence), had inevitably privileged the humiliating traces of the private life over any real analysis of the poetic work.[66] Leiris was responding to two withering reviews of Sartre's book-length preface that had appeared earlier that year. Writing in *Critique,* Georges Bataille (himself a recovering Catholic) delivered a Nietzschean coun-terblast.[67] Whereas Sartre had condemned as delusional Baudelaire's juvenile attempt to repress the distinction between essence and exis-tence, subject and object, Bataille saw here instead the very model of Lévy-Bruhl's *participation mystique* or of Piaget's notion of the *puerile*—an affirmation of the sacred, a willingness to engage in the gratuitous domain of primitive or childlike play. For Bataille, Baudelaire's grandeur lay precisely in his avoidance of work, in his refusal to produce, in his perpetual dissatisfaction with limits, in his wanting the *impossible* to the bitter end. In addition, according to Bataille, Sartre's Marxist critique had insufficiently situated the poet in *history*: his analysis of Baudelaire as an ideological subject (undertaken with far more finesse, as Bataille was perhaps aware, by Walter Benjamin in the thirties) neglected the base at the expense of superstructure, a base whose capitalist modes of accumulation and expenditure, production and consumption, Baudelaire had, according to Bataille, at once maintained and canceled by a more archaic, more aristocratic economy, founded on radical waste and dispossession [*désaisissement*]. Sartre had argued that Baudelaire could only love that which was dead, or past, or fallen. If his Baudelaire was so adamantly opposed to the Enlightenment vision of Progress, it was because as a congenital defeatist he needed to deny the very possibility of "transcendence"—in existentialist parlance, the determination of the present by the future. For the Nietzschean Bataille, by contrast, Baudelaire's particular malediction (and election) instead lay in his courageous leap into the "paradox of the moment"—a present to which we accede only by fleeing it and that slips from our grasp in our very attempt to seize it, with no future at hand.

Maurice Blanchot offered a more gnomic commentary in his review, "L'Échec de Baudelaire."[68] Whereas Sartre had dismissed the *Journaux intimes* as the late, lamentable recyclings of much that Baudelaire had said earlier and better, for Blanchot these late drafts took on prophetic importance as "tragic signals" of the "poetry of the future"—a Mallarméan messianism more fully developed in Blanchot's *Livre à venir (The Book to Come)* of 1959. If Baudelaire's futurity came to the fore in his fragments, Blanchot argued, it was because he had here abandoned his search for the perfectly "finished" autotelic work à la Poe and instead given himself over to a kind of impromptu writing that registered the very "movement of life"—and, more important, that revealed the (Heideggerian) abyss of incompletion on which any such life was ontologically grounded. For Sartre, Baudelaire was the coward who looked into the *gouffre* and shied away from its depths. For Blanchot instead it was in the sacred terror of this abyss that Baudelaire's most heroic, and most ambiguous, embrace of *expérience* (both "experience" and "experiment" in French) took place.[69] Turning Sartre's pejorative into an honorific, this experience of *groundlessness* (or *Grundlosigkeit*) is defined by Blanchot as *l'échec*—that failure whereby defeat is allegorically released into a promise of hope. Baudelaire's ultimate loss of language to the gouffre—like Hölderlin's—was thus, in Blanchot's reading, the "final sacrifice" in which the poet "was led to get rid of himself in order to realize himself and to make present the poetry that is always-to-come, always-to-be made." Blanchot concludes by looking backward to the poet's future: "Having lost everything, he gained everything. . . . If he was responsible for the *échec* of his life, he was also responsible for the success of his afterlife." *Qui perd gagne.* Loser takes all.

NOTES

1. Charles Baudelaire, *Oeuvres posthumes et Correspondances inédites, précédées d'une étude biographique par Eugène Crépet* (Paris: Maison Quantin, 1887). This three-hundred-page edition of the poet's "reliquiae" includes, as its frontispiece, Neyt's photograph of Baudelaire with its inscription to Malassis, a hundred-page "Biographical Study" by Crépet, and seven major sections: (1) Projets de préfaces pour la seconde édition des *Fleurs du mal*; (2) Théâtre ("Le Marquis du 1er Houzards," "La Fin de don Juan"); (3) Projets et plans de romans et nouvelles; (4) La Belgique vraie ("Fragments d'un livre inachevé sur la Belgique"); (5) Lettre à Jules Janin ("Fragments d'un article de journal inachevé"); (6) Journaux intimes ("Fusées," "Mon Coeur mis à nu"); (6) Correspondances (Baudelaire's letters to Malassis and Sainte-Beuve); (7) Appendice ("Pièces relatives au procès des *Fleurs du mal*" and further correspondence with, e.g., Flaubert). This is the edition Nietzsche read in Nice upon its publication.

2. My translation of these fragments conflates the layout and numbering of the Pichois Pléiade with the Guyaux Folio editions. Following Pichois, I place *Hygiene* as a pendant to *Flares*, whereas Guyaux prints a number of its pages after *My Heart Laid Bare*. The most recent detailed discussion and description of the original manuscripts and their editorial arrangements is contained in Guyaux's revised Folio edition of *Fusées* and *Mon Coeur mis à nu* (Paris: Gallimard, 2016), 284–96. Like both these editors, I have transformed all of Baudelaire's underlinings in these manuscripts into italics. In his notes, Pichois provides the precise dimensions (in centimeters) of the various feuilles volantes on which Baudelaire was writing (which Pichois refers to as *fragments*, whereas Guyaux prefers the term *feuillets*).

3. The full 1850 title was *The Literati: Some Honest Opinions About Autorial Merits and Demerits, with Occasional Words of Personality, Together with Marginalia, Suggestions, and Essays.*

4. OC1: 709.

5. C2: 141.

6. Edgar Allan Poe, *The Brevities: Pinakidia, Marginalia, Fifty Suggestions, and Other Works*, ed. Burton R. Pollin (New York: Gordian, 1985), 248.

7. Poe, 108.

Flares, Hygiene, My Heart Laid Bare | 75

8. Félix Nadar, *Charles Baudelaire intime* (Paris: A. Blaizot, 1911), 122.

9. Walter Benjamin, *The Writer of Modern Life: Essays on Charles Baudelaire* (Cambridge, MA: Harvard University Press, 2006), 47.

10. Poe, *Brevities*, 389. "The German *Schwärmerei*—not exactly 'humbug,' but 'sky-rocketing'—seems to be the only term by which we can conveniently designate that peculiar style of criticism which has lately come into fashion, through the influence of certain members of the *Fabian* family—people who live (upon beans) about Boston."

11. Maurice Blanchot as quoted in Paul Auster's introduction to his translation of *The Notebooks of Joseph Joubert* (San Francisco: North Point, 1983).

12. Arthur Rimbaud to Paul Demeny, May 15, 1871, in *Oeuvres complètes*, ed. André Guyaux (Paris: Gallimard, 2009), 348. In this same letter Rimbaud went on to note that Baudelaire's much-vaunted mastery of traditional verse forms struck him as "mesquine" (i.e., "tacky")—even though, as his *Illuminations* show, he was clearly familiar with the 1869 edition of Baudelaire's prose poems.

13. Poe, *Brevities*, 322.

14. C2: 302, 305.

15. C2: 443.

16. In a letter to his mother of March 9, 1865, Baudelaire pointedly uses the term "fragments" to refer to a number of his unfinished projects—including his pieces on Chateaubriand and Literary Dandyism, on Didactic Painting, and on *Les Fleurs du mal* as judged by their author, as well as his letter to Jules Janin on Heine and his refutation of Napoleon III's preface to his *Life of Julius Caesar*. Baudelaire also refers to his recent translation of two Poe stories ("The Mystery of Marie Roget" and "The Philosophy of Furniture") as "fragments." In the same letter he describes his late prose poems as "little baubles" (elsewhere he commonly refers to them as "fragments") and summarizes all of his recent work as "tripotages littéraires" ("literary dabblings"). C2: 472.

17. Keith Waldrop's experimental translations into prose of *The Flowers of Evil* (Middletown, CT: Wesleyan University Press, 2006) reveal the extent to which the syntax of these poems depends on Baudelaire's elaborate handling of subordinate and coordinate clauses. The same is true of his channeling of the hypotactic labyrinths of De Quincey's sentences in his *Artificial Paradises*—one of the most beautiful books in the French language according to Barthes (in *The Neutral*). See, more generally, Jan Mieszkowski's *Crises of the Sentence* (Chicago: University of Chicago Press, 2019).

18. OC2: 126.

19. OC2: 330.

20. See appendix 2 ("Aphorisms and Album Inscriptions"). In 2010, the Parisian house Arléa published a two-hundred-page paperback selection from Baudelaire's prose writings and correspondence simply entitled *Aphorismes*—a clear indication that he was now being marketed to general readers as a latter-day moraliste on the lines of Lichtenberg or Nietzsche.

21. Barthes writes of La Rochefoucauld in his *New Critical Essays*, trans. Richard Howard (New York: Hill and Wang), 3–23: "The maxim is a hard, shiny—and fragile—object, like an insect's thorax; like an insect, too, the maxim possesses a sting, that hook of sharp-pointed words which conclude and crown it—which close it even as

they arm it." See also Andrew Hui, *A Theory of the Aphorism from Confucius to Twitter* (Princeton, NJ: Princeton University Press, 2019); and J. A. Hiddleston "*Fusée, Maxim, and Commonplace in Baudelaire*," *Modern Language Review* 80 (1985): 563–70. For Baudelaire's early journalism, see Graham Robb, *Le Corsaire-Satan en silhouette* (Nashville, TN: Vanderbilt University Press, 1985).

22. I am indebted to the discussions of Baudelaire and Maistre by Antoine Compagnon, *Les Antimodernes, de Joseph de Maistre à Roland Barthes* (Paris: Gallimard, 2005); and by Françoise Meltzer, *Seeing Double: Baudelaire's Modernity* (Chicago: University of Chicago Press, 2011), 25–57. Jesse Goldhammer's *Headless Republic: Sacrificial Violence in Modern French Thought* (Ithaca, NY: Cornell University Press, 2005) provides a valuable analysis of Maistre and the French Revolution.

23. Walter Benjamin, *The Arcades Project* (Cambridge, MA: Harvard University Press, 1999), 344. In the notes for his late lecture course, *The Neutral*, Roland Barthes (using E. M. Cioran's 1957 selections from Maistre as his sourcebook) cites similar passages in order to demonstrate how Maistre's "bad thinking" (or "the assertive, excessive theater of a mad hypothesis"—Poe!) can nonetheless result in a genuine "daredevil" form of Writing, one based on "a violence of speech (speech as violence, no matter what happens) instead of a violence of thought: violence of the sentence as long as it knows it's a sentence" (*The Neutral*, trans. Rosalind E. Krauss and Denis Hollier (New York: Columbia University Press, 2005), 162.

24. René Girard, *Violence and the Sacred*, trans. Patrick Gregory (Baltimore: Johns Hopkins University Press, 1977).

25. See Ève Morisi, *Capital Letters: Hugo, Baudelaire, Camus, and the Death Penalty* (Evanston, IL: Northwestern University Press, 2020), 67–127, which in turn picks up on Jacques Derrida's *Séminaire: La Peine de mort*, vol. 1, ed. Geoffrey Bennington, Marc Crépon, and Thomas Dutuit (Paris: Galilée, 2012).

26. Meltzer, *Seeing Double*, 33–34.

27. Compagnon, *Les Antimodernes*, 143–45.

28. Baudelaire came into contact with Emerson through Émile Montégut's edition of *Essais de philosophie américaine* (Paris: Charpentier, 1851). The volume included a compendium of Emerson's *Essays, First Series* (1841) and "The Uses of Great Men," the first essay in *Representative Men* (1850). Poe famously found Emerson to be completely "over-rated," while Emerson considered the poet of "The Raven" a mere "jingle man."

29. OC2: 758.

30. See, especially for Foucault's notion of *souci de soi*, Cornelia Wild's *Später Baudelaire: Praxis poetische Zustände* (Munich: Wilhelm Fink, 2008), 42–50. Foucault's discussion of hypomnemata may be found in the essay "Self Writing," included in his *Ethics: Subjectivity and Truth*, ed. Paul Rabinow (New York: New Press, 1997), 207–21.

31. I take the distinction between autobiography and autoportrait from Michel Beaujour's *Miroirs d'encre* (Paris: Seuil, 1980).

32. Friedrich Schlegel, *Philosophical Fragments* (Minneapolis: University of Minnesota Press, 1991), 20, 45. As Andrew Hui reminds us (*Theory of the Aphorism*, 13), *fragment* derives from the Latin verb *frangō*: to break, shatter, or defeat. In Greek, the related *klasma* or *apoklasama* (potsherds or shattered bits of things) evoke the violence of *sparagmos*—convulsion, dislocation, or dismemberment.

33. See Béatrice Didier, "Une Économie de l'écriture: 'Fusées,' 'Mon Coeur mis à

nu,'" *Littérature* 10 (1993): 57–64; and Bernard Howells, "'La Vaporisation du moi': Baudelaire's *Journaux intimes*," *French Studies* 42 (1988): 424–42.

34. On poetry and ritualism, see Jonathan Culler, *Theory of the Lyric* (Cambridge, MA : Harvard University Press, 2015), esp. 122–23.

35. OC1: 291.

36. See Charles Bernheimer, *Figures of Ill-Repute: Representations of Prostitution in Nineteenth-Century France* (Cambridge, MA: Harvard University Press, 1989).

37. OC1: 183.

38. In his "Salon of 1846" Baudelaire identifies the term *poncif* with the term *chic* (automatism involving "a memory of the hand rather than a memory of the brain"). The term *poncif* in painting, as he notes, has to do with conventionalized "expressions of the head and attitudes." He continues: "There are *poncif* angers, *poncif* surprises, for example surprise expressed by a hand extended horizontally with a splayed thumb. . . . Everything that is conventional and traditional derives from the *chic* and the *poncif*. When a singer places his hand on his heart this normally means: 'I'll love her forever!' If he balls his hand into a fist while looking at the prompter's box or the boards, this signifies: 'He'll die, the wretch!' This is the *poncif*." See Ruth Amossy, *Le Discours du cliché* (Paris: CDU/Sedes, 1982); and Marjorie Perloff, *Unoriginal Genius: Poetry by Other Means in the New Century* (Chicago: University of Chicago Press, 2010).

39. See Paul de Man, "The Concept of Irony," in *Aesthetic Ideology* (Minneapolis: University of Minnesota Press, 1996), 163–83. Debarti Sanyal builds on De Man in *The Violence of Modernity: Baudelaire, Irony, and the Politics of Form* (Baltimore: Johns Hopkins University Press, 2006).

40. Walter Benjamin, *The Arcades Project* (Cambridge, MA: Harvard University Press, 1999), 462; Maurice Blanchot, "L'Échec de Baudelaire," *La Part du feu* (Paris: Gallimard, 1949), 143. This is Françoise Meltzer's fine summation: "Contradiction, in other words is not to be resolved in Baudelaire; hence the emphasis of words such as *irrémédiable, irrémissible, irrécouvrable*, and *irréparable*. . . . The prefix *ir-* in Baudelaire is the perpetual re-scarring of memory—of the Fall, of the hopelessness of human life, of the irreversibility of evil. The words themselves contain the contradiction of man's double bind: each word contains the positive aspect (remediable, remissible, recoverable) on which the *ir-* , palimpsest-like, produces an a priori erasure" (*Seeing Double*, 56).

41. For Nietzsche and Baudelaire, see Karl Pestalozzi, "Nietzsche's Baudelaire-Rezeption," *Nietzsche-Studien* 7 (Berlin: de Gruyter, 1978), 158–78; Jacques Le Rider, "Nietzsche et Baudelaire," *Littérature* 86 (1992): 85–101; Andrea Gogröf-Voorhees, *Defining Modernism: Baudelaire and Nietzsche on Romanticism, Modernity, Decadence, and Wagner* (New York: Peter Lang, 1999); and Geoff Waite, "Nietzsche's Baudelaire, or the Sublime Proleptic Spin of His Politico-Economic Thought," *Representations* 50 (1995): 14–52.

42. *Charles Baudelaire: His Life by Théophile Gautier*, trans. Guy Thorne (London: Greening, 1915), 20.

43. Friedrich Nietzsche, *Posthumous Fragments*, quoted in Le Rider, "Nietzsche et Baudelaire," 87. The complete Colli and Montanari edition of Nietzsche's *Nachgelessane Fragmente* is available in German via the Nietzsche Channel, www.thenietzsche channel.com. All translations are mine.

44. Nietzsche, June–July 1885 [38] [5].

45. Walter Kaufmann, trans. and ed., *Basic Writings of Nietzsche* (New York: Modern Library, 1968), 382.

46. Kaufmann, 383, 387.

47. Nietzsche is alluding to Byron's Memoirs, entrusted to his friend the poet Thomas Moore but burnt a month after his death by his publisher, John Murray. Wilhelm von Gwinner, Schopenhauer's executor, similarly incinerated Schopenhauer's autobiographical papers after his death. Nietzsche again alludes to these two auto-da-fes in his *Genealogy of Morals* (3:19).

48. Nietzsche to Peter Gast, February 26, 1888, available in both German and English translation on the Nietzsche Channel.

49. Kaufman, *Basic Writings of Nietzsche*, 679.

50. Walter Benjamin comments: "Eternal occurrence is an attempt to combine the two antinomic principles of happiness: that of eternity and that of the 'yet again'— The idea of eternal recurrence conjures the speculative idea (or phantasmagoria) of happiness from the misery of the times. Nietzsche's heroism has its counterpart in the heroism of Baudelaire, who conjures the phantasmagoria of modernity from the misery of philistinism [i.e., *la bêtise*]" (*Writer of Modern Life*, 161).

51. Gorgröf-Vorhees, 183.

52. Quoted in Le Rider, "Nietzsche et Baudelaire," 86.

53. See Maurice Blanchot's "Nietzsche et l'écriture fragmentaire" in *L'Entretien infini* (Paris: Gallimard, 1969), translated by Susan Hanson as *The Infinite Conversation* (Minneapolis: University of Minnesota Press, 1993), as well as Leslie Hill, *Blanchot and Fragmentary Writing* (London: Continuum, 2012), 31–44.

54. Walter Benjamin: "The heroic bearing of Baudelaire is intimately related to that of Nietzsche. Although Baudelaire adheres to Catholicism, his experience of the universe is in exact accord with the experience comprehended by Nietzsche in the phrase 'God is dead'" (*Writer of Modern Life*, 154).

55. See Benedetta Zavatta, *Individuality and Beyond: Nietzsche Reads Emerson*, trans. Alexander Reynolds (Oxford: Oxford University Press, 2019).

56. Walter Kaufmann, trans. and ed., *The Portable Nietzsche* (New York: Viking, 1954), 468.

57. Benjamin, *Writer of Modern Life*, 147.

58. The comments by Lemaître, Brunetière, Gide, and Claudel are culled from A. E. Carter, *Baudelaire et la critique française, 1868–1917* (Columbia: University of South Carolina Press, 1963).

59. Charles Du Bos, "Introduction" to Baudelaire, *Écrits intimes: Mon Coeur mis à nu, Fusées* (Paris: Éditions de la Pléiade, 1930), 17, 62, 107.

60. T. S. Eliot, "Introduction," *The Intimate Journals of Charles Baudelaire* (London: Blackamore, 1930), 11–12, 20, 13, 22, 24.

61. Eliot, 25–26.

62. Like its first 1930 edition, Isherwood's 1947 *Intimate Journals of Charles Baudelaire* is illustrated with a variety of nineteenth-century drawings and prints of Baudelaire and concludes with his "Selection of Consoling Maxims on Love." The most recent translation of this material is Rainer J. Hanshe's small press edition of *My Heart Laid Bare and Other Texts* (New York: Contra Mundum, 2017), which is basically a recasting of Isherwood's volume, including its illustrations, without annotation.

63. W. H. Auden, "Introduction," *The Intimate Journals of Charles Baudelaire*, trans. Christopher Isherwood (Hollywood, CA: Marcel Rodd, 1947), 13–28.

64. Auden, 28.

65. Jean-Paul Sartre, *Baudelaire*, trans. Martin Turnell (New York: New Directions, 1950), 22–28, 42, 192. E. M. Cioran's *Précis de décomposition* was published in 1949.

66. Baudelaire, *Écrits intimes: Introduction par Jean-Paul Sartre* (Paris: Les Éditions du point du jour, 1946).

67. Bataille's review of Sartre's essay was later republished in *La Littérature et le mal* (Paris: Gallimard, 1957), translated into English by Alistair Hamilton as *Literature and Evil* (London: Marion Boyars, 2001).

68. Blanchot's "L'Échec de Baudelaire" was first published in *L'Arche* in February 1947 and then collected in *La Part du feu* (1949), later translated into English by Charlotte Mandell as *The Work of Fire* (Stanford, CA: Stanford University Press, 1995).

69. Blanchot's reading overlaps with Benjamin Fondane's posthumous *Baudelaire et l'expérience du gouffre* (Paris: Seghers, 1947).

Flares

Even if God were not to exist, Religion would still be Holy and *Divine*.*

God is the sole being who, in order to reign, need not even exist.

What the mind creates is more alive than matter.†

Love is the taste for prostitution. Indeed, there is no pleasure, however noble, that cannot be ascribed to Prostitution.

At a theater show, at a ball, the pleasure of each is the pleasure of all.

What is art? Prostitution.

The pleasure of being in crowds is a mysterious expression of the joy taken in the multiplication of number.

---

* *Divine:* Maistre's favorite adjective, variously applied to the French Revolution, to hereditary monarchy, to the papacy, and to sacrificial violence. In one of the aphorisms collected in appendix 2 below, Baudelaire quips: "Were religion to disappear from the face of the earth, it would be rediscovered in the heart of an atheist."

† *What the mind creates:* Cf. Ralph Waldo Emerson's essay collection *Conduct of Life* (1860): "Thought dissolves the material universe, by carrying the mind up into a sphere where all is plastic." Or William Blake's "Only mental things are real."

Everything is number. Number is in *everything*. Number is in the individual. Drunkenness is a number.*

The taste for productive concentration should, in the mature man, replace the taste for wastage.†

Love may arise from a generous impulse: the taste for prostitution. But it is soon corrupted by the taste for property.

Love wants to move outside of itself, to commingle with its victim like a victor with his vanquished, all the while retaining the privileges of a conqueror.

The sensual pleasures experienced by someone who keeps a mistress are akin to those of an angel and a landlord. Charity and ferocity. These delights do not even depend on her sex, her beauty, or animal species.

The shadowy greens of moist summer evenings.

Immense depths of thought in commonplace turns of phrase, holes hollowed out by generations of ants.

The anecdote about the hunter, illustrative of the intimate bond between love and ferocity.

---

* *Everything is number:* Baudelaire borrows this notion of number—at once prosodic, Pythagorean, and theocratic—from section 8 of Joseph de Maistre's *Saint Petersburg Evenings* (1821): "God gave us number, and it is by number that he proves himself to us, as it is by number that men prove themselves to men who are their likeness. Remove number, and you remove the arts, the sciences, and, as a result, intelligence. Restore number: with it will reappear its two celestial daughters, harmony and beauty; the cry becomes *song*, noise resolves into *rhythm*, the leap becomes *dance*, force is called *dynamics,* and traces are *figures.*"

† *The taste for productive concentration:* From Emerson's *Conduct of Life*, cited in the original at the end of *Hygiene*: "The one prudence in life is concentration; the one evil is dissipation."

2 · FLARES

On the femininity of the Church as the reason for her omnipotence.
On the color violet (love contained, mysterious, veiled, color of a canoness).

————

The priest is vital because he makes the crowd believe astonishing things.
It is a law of the human spirit that the Church do everything, be everything.
The masses adore authority.*
Priests are the servants and zealots of the imagination.
Throne and altar, revolutionary maxim.

————

E.G. or the Seductive Adventuress†

————

The religious inebriation of great cities. —Pantheism. I am everybody; Everybody is me.
Whirlpool.

---

* *The masses adore authority:* Perhaps a refraction of one of Poe's *Marginalia*—"The nose of a mob is its imagination. By this, at any time, it can quietly be led" (*The Brevities,* ed. Burton R. Pollin [New York: Gordian, 1985], 377). Where Poe writes "mob," Baudelaire writes "the crowd" (*la foule*) or "the people" (*le peuple*), which I have generally translated as "the masses." This entire series of notations on the Catholic Church, and on the counterrevolutionary pillars of "throne and altar," is Maistrian in inspiration.

† *E.G. or the Seductive Adventuress:* Perhaps Elisa Gu(i)erri (or Nieri), a friend of Mme. Sabetier's to whom Baudelaire dedicated his poem "Sisina."

3 · FLARES

I think I've already observed in my notes that the act of love greatly
resembles torture or a surgical procedure.* But this idea can be
further developed, in the bitterest fashion. Even if the two lovers are
completely taken with each other and overcome with mutual desire,
one of the two will always be cooler headed and less carried away
than the other. This one, male or female, is the surgeon or torturer;
the other is the patient, the victim. Do you hear these sighs, these
preludes to the shameful tragedy to come, these moans, these cries,
these groans? Who among us has not emitted them? Who among
us has not been relentless in extorting them? Do you think that the
tortures carefully applied by the Inquisition were any worse? These
rolled-back sleepwalker eyes, these limbs whose muscles bunch and
stiffen as if under the jolt of a galvanic battery—certainly drunken-
ness, delirium, opium would not provide you with examples this
horrific, this curious. And the human countenance itself, which Ovid
thought was fashioned to reflect the stars,† here contorts into a frenzy
of ferocity or simply goes slack in a species of death. I would certainly
be committing sacrilege were I to apply the word "ecstasy" to this kind
of decomposition.

—A frightful game in which one of the players is bound to forfeit all
self-control.

I once heard people discussing in my presence what was the great-
est pleasure they took in lovemaking. Someone replied (naturally): to
receive! And another: to give of yourself! This one said: the pleasure
lies in one's sense of pride! And that one: in the sensual delights of
humility! All these pieces of filth were merely reciting lessons drawn
from *The Imitation of Jesus Christ.* —Finally there was the brazen
Utopian who proclaimed that for him the greatest pleasure of making
love lay in begetting future citizens for the state.

---

* *I think I've already observed in my notes:* See section 17 below, which Malassis ap-
parently shuffled out of sequence.

† *Which Ovid thought was fashioned to reflect the stars:* Cf. Ovid, *Metamorphosis* 1.85
and Baudelaire's poem "The Swan."

As for me, I say that the sole and supreme pleasure of making love lies in the certitude that one is doing *evil*. —And both man and woman know from birth that it is in evil that all sensual pleasure resides.

4 · SKETCHES. FLARES. PROJECTS

—A Comedy in the manner of Silvestre.
Barbara and the Sheep.
—Chenevard has created a superhuman type.
The vow I made to Levaillant.*
—Preface, a blend of mysticism and blitheness.
Dreams and dream theory à la Swedenborg.†

Campbell's observation (in *The Conduct of Life*).‡
Concentration.
Power of the *idée fixe*.
—Absolute frankness, a means of originality.
—To tell funny stories with a straight face.

5 · FLARES. SUGGESTIONS

When a man takes ill to bed, nearly all of his friends harbor a secret desire to see him dead; some of them in order to reassure themselves

---

* *Silvestre:* Théophile Silvestre, an art critic who, like Baudelaire, was close to Delacroix. *Barbara:* Charles Barbara, painter friend of Baudelaire's. *Chenevard:* Paul Chenevard, subject of Baudelaire's ca. 1860 essay "Philosophical Art." *Levaillant:* Jean-Jacques Levaillant, whose "naturalist philosophy" Baudelaire praised in an 1860 letter to Malassis.

† *Dreams and dream theory à la Swedenborg:* In his *Artificial Paradises* of 1860, Baudelaire distinguishes, à la Swedenborg, between "natural" and "hieroglyphic" dreams.

‡ *Campbell's observation:* In his *Conduct of Life* Emerson quoted the Scottish poet Thomas Campbell to the effect that "a man accustomed to work was equal to any achievement he resolved on, and that, for himself necessity, not inspiration, was the prompter of his muse."

that his health was far poorer than theirs; others in the disinterested hope of studying someone else in the throes of death.*

The arabesque is the most spiritualistic of designs.†

6 · FLARES. SUGGESTIONS

The man of letters manages his investments and inspires a taste for intellectual gymnastics.

The arabesque is the most ideal of all.

We love women in proportion to their greater foreignness to us. Pederasts take pleasure in the love of intelligent women. Bestiality hence excludes pederasty.

Playing the buffoon does not necessarily exclude charity, but this is rare.

Enthusiasm for anything other than abstractions is a sign of weakness and infirmity.

Scrawniness is more naked, more indecent than flab.

7 · —*Tragic skies.* An abstract epithet applied to a material entity.
—Man drinks in light with the air. Thus the masses are right to say that night air is unhealthy for labor.

—The masses are born fire-worshippers.

* *When a man takes ill to bed:* From Emerson's *Conduct of Life*: "A person seldom falls sick but that the bystanders are animated with a faint hope that he will die."
† *The arabesque:* Cf. Poe's short story collection *Tales of the Grotesque and Arabesque* (1840). Friedrich Schlegel similarly comments in his *Atheaneum Fragments*: "Certainly the arabesque is the oldest and most original form of human imagination."

Fireworks, buildings in flames, arsonists.

Imagine a born fire-worshipper, a *born Parsi*, and you could come up with quite a tale.

8 · Our misrecognitions of faces are due to the eclipse of the real image by the hallucination it has engendered.

Know the joys of a harsh life; and pray, pray, without end. Prayer is a reservoir of strength. (*Altar of the Will. Moral Dynamics.* The Sorcery of the Sacraments. Hygiene of the Soul.*)

Music scoops out the sky.

Jean-Jacques said that he never entered a café without a feeling of trepidation. For someone of a timid disposition, a ticket office can resemble the Tribune of Hades.†

Life possesses but a single true charm—the charm of *Gambling*. But what if we care little whether we win or lose?

9 · SUGGESTIONS. FLARES

It is only despite themselves that nations produce great men—like families. They make immense efforts to have none at all. This is why any great man needs, in order to exist, to possess a striking force far greater than the force of resistance developed by millions of individuals.

As for sleep, this sinister nightly adventure, one might say that men go to bed every day with a temerity that would be entirely unintel-

---

* *Moral dynamics:* Maistre refers to prayer as "the dynamic that has been conferred to man" to allow him to raise himself from the universe of the Fall. Section 17 below also speaks of prayer as a "magical operation."

† *Jean-Jacques said:* Rousseau discusses his timidity in public situations and places in his *Confessions*, books 1, 6, and 9.

ligible were we not aware it was the result of their obliviousness to danger.

10 · There are skins so thick as be immune to the backlash of contempt.*

Many friends, many gloves. Those who have loved me were people who were despised, I would even say despicable, if I wanted to flatter respectable folk.

Girardin speaking Latin! *Pecudesque locutoe.*†

Only a Society with no belief in religion could have dispatched Robert-Houdin to the Arabs to dissuade them from believing in miracles.‡

11 · These great gorgeous ships, imperceptibly rocked (dandled) by placid waters, these sturdy ships, lying there idle and nostalgic, aren't they asking us in a silent tongue: When are we due to set sail for happiness?

Not to forget the whole fairytale aspect of drama—witchcraft and romance.

The milieu, the atmosphere in which an entire tale must be bathed. (See *Usher* and refer to the intense sensations of hashish and opium.)§

---

* *There are skins so thick:* Cf. Poe's *Marginalia:* "'Contempt,' says an eastern proverb, 'pierces even through the shell of the tortoise'; but there are some human skulls which would feel themselves insulted by a comparison, in point of impermeability, with the shell of a Galapago turtle" (in Poe, *Brevities*, 228).

† *Girardin speaking Latin!:* Émile de Girardin, the influential editor of the liberal newspaper *La Presse*, was a frequent object of Baudelaire's satiric barbs. The Latin tag from Virgil's *Georgics* reads: "When the beasts begin to speak."

‡ *Robert-Houdin:* The French government had sent the celebrated illusionist Jean-Eugène Robert-Houdin (from whom Harry Houdini later took his name) on a mission to Algeria in 1856 to combat the local influence of sorcerers and magicians.

§ *See Usher:* Alludes to the first paragraph of Poe's story "The Fall of the House of Usher": "I looked upon the scene before me—upon the mere house, and the simple

12 · Is there such a thing as mathematics gone mad and are there madmen who believe that two and two make three? In other terms, can hallucination (if this is not too much a clash in terms) invade the universe of pure reason? If, when a man has grown accustomed to laziness, to reverie, to inertia, always putting off important things to tomorrow, and another man were to wake him up one morning with several lashes of the whip and were to go on whipping him without mercy until, unable to work out of pleasure, he would now work out of fear, wouldn't this man—the one brandishing the whip—be his true friend and benefactor? Besides, one might even claim that pleasure in work might then ensue, with far more justification than one might assert: love ensues from marriage.

By the same token, in politics the true saint is he who whips and kills the people for the good of the people.

Tuesday May 13, 1856.

Pick up copies at Michel's.*
Write to Mann.
 to Willis
 to *Maria Clemm.*
Send to Mad. Dumay
—find out whether Mirès . . .†

---

landscape features of the domain—upon the bleak walls—upon the vacant eye-like windows—upon a few rank sedges—and upon a few white trunks of decayed trees— with an utter depression of soul which I can compare to no earthly sensation more properly than to the after-dream of the reveler upon opium—the bitter lapse into every-day life—the hideous dropping off of the veil."

* *Pick up copies at Michel's:* Michel Lévy published Baudelaire's first translation of Poe's short stories, *Histoires extraordinaires*, in 1856. The Paris-based William W. Mann had loaned Baudelaire copies of the *Southern Literary Messenger* for his work on Poe. Nathan Parker Willis was an American publisher of Poe. Maria Clemm was Poe's aunt and mother-in law.

† *Find out whether Mirès:* Mirès was the owner of the newspapers *Le Pays* and *Le Constitutionnel*, both of which had rejected Baudelaire's translation of Poe's novel, *The Narrative of Arthur Gordon Pym*. Madame Dumay may have been his secretary.

If something is not slightly deformed, it strikes us as lacking in feeling—from which it follows that irregularity, that is to say, the unexpected, the elements of surprise and astonishment are an essential portion and characteristic of beauty.*

13 · NOTES. FLARES

Théodore de Banville is not exactly a materialist; he is luminous.†
His poetry calls forth happier hours.

Every time you receive a letter from a creditor, write fifty lines on some extraterrestrial subject and you will be saved.

Broad smile across a giant's handsome face.

14 · *On Suicide and Suicidal Madness Considered in the Light of Statistics, Medicine, and Philosophy*
Brierre de Boismont‡

Find the passage:
To live with someone who only feels aversion toward you . . .
The portrait of *Serenus* by *Seneca*, that of *Stagyrus* by *Saint John Chrysostomos.*
Acedia, the disease of monks.
Taedium vitae.

---

* *Surprise and astonishment:* "The beautiful is always *bizarre*," Baudelaire observed in his review of the 1855 Exposition Universelle. Poe had written in "Ligea" (translated by Baudelaire the very same year) that there was no true beauty "without a certain strangeness of proportion."

† *Théodore de Banville:* Well-known French poet whose work Baudelaire reviewed in 1861. With Charles Asselineau he would later edit the posthumous edition of Baudelaire's *Complete Works* published by Michel Lévy.

‡ *On Suicide:* Brierre de Boismont's book was published in 1856. The rest of the fragment refers to topics touched upon in the work.

15 · FLARES

Translation and paraphrase of: *Passion ascribes everything to itself.**
Spiritual and physical delights aroused by storms, electricity,
lightning—alarm signals of all those shadowy, lovelorn memories of
bygone days.

16 · FLARES

I have found the definition of Beauty—of my Beauty. It's something
both ardent and sorrowful, something a bit vague, lending itself to
endless conjecture. Let me (if you will) apply my ideas to a sensible
object, to, say, the object that is of most interest to society—a woman's
face. A head lovely and alluring, namely, the head of a woman, one
that provokes dreams which simultaneously—if confusedly—involve
sensuality and sorrow; one that conveys an idea of melancholy, lassi-
tude, even satiety—or else the contrary idea, that is, an ardor, a desire
for life, ever crowded out by surges of bitterness, products as it were
of deprivation or despair. Mystery and regret are also characteristics
of Beauty.

A handsome man's head need not convey—except perhaps to a
woman's eyes (from a male perspective, to be sure)—this idea of volup-
tuousness, which in a woman's face is all the more provocatively at-
tractive because the face is generally more melancholy. But this man's
head will also have something both ardent and sorrowful about it—
spiritual longings, ambitions darkly swallowed—the idea of a power
that lies there growling, unemployed—sometimes the idea of vengeful
imperviousness (for the ideal type of the Dandy is not to be neglected
here)—and sometimes too the idea of mystery (one of the most inter-
esting characteristics of Beauty)—and finally (gathering my courage to

---

* *Passion ascribes everything to itself:* Baudelaire refers back to his 1851 work "Of
Wine and of Hashish," where he speaks of the "victorious monomania" of the hash-
ish eater: "Shall I explain how, under the sway of this poison, my man soon turns
himself into the center of the universe, how he becomes the living and outlandish ex-
pression of the proverb that says that all passion ascribes everything to itself?"

admit just how modern I feel in matters aesthetic), *Misfortune*. —Far
from me to pretend that Joy cannot be associated with Beauty, but I
claim that Joy is merely one of its most vulgar ornaments; —whereas
Melancholy is its illustrious companion, to such an extent that I can-
not conceive (is my brain a witch's mirror?) of a type of Beauty that
would not include *Misfortune*. Building on (some would say, obsessed
by) these ideas, you can imagine that it would be difficult for me not to
conclude that the most perfect type of manly Beauty is *Satan*—in the
manner of Milton.*

17 · FLARES

Self-idolatry

Political harmony of the character.
Eurhythmy of the character and faculties.
Enlarge all the faculties.
Conserve all the faculties.
A cult (magic, the sorcery of evocation).
Sacrifice and vow are the supreme formulae and symbols of
exchange.

Two fundamental literary qualities: supernaturalism and irony.
The individual cast of the eye, the aspect things assume as they
lie before the author, then the satanic turn of mind. The super-
natural includes the overall color and accent, that is, intensity,
sonority, limpidity, vibrancy, depth, and reverberation in space
and time.
There are moments in existence where the expanses of time and
space grow more profound and the sensation of existence is im-
mensely heightened.

---

* *Satan—in the manner of Milton:* Baudelaire, via Chateaubriand's 1836 translation
of *Paradise Lost,* here rejoins the Blake of *Marriage of Heaven and Hell.* The adjunc-
tion of Melancholy, however, comes from Poe's "Philosophy of Composition"—"Mel-
ancholy is thus the most legitimate of all the poetic tones."

On magic as applied to the summoning up of the notable dead, to the reestablishment and perfection of one's health.

Inspiration always comes when man *wants* it to, but it does not always depart when he so desires.

On language and writing, considered as magical operations, the sorcery of evocation.

On women's airs.

The charming airs that make for beauty are:

The blasé air,	The imperious air,
The bored air,	The willful air,
The scatterbrained air,	The wicked air,
The saucy air,	The sickly air,
The icy air,	The catty air, a mix of childishness,
The introspective air,	nonchalance, and malice.

In certain almost supernatural states, the depth of life is fully revealed by the spectacle, however ordinary it might be, that lies before one's eyes—which becomes its symbol.

As I was crossing the boulevard, rushing forward to avoid the traffic, my halo became detached and fell into the muck of the macadam. Fortunately, I had the time to pick it back up, but immediately thereafter the unhappy idea crossed my mind that this was an evil omen; from that point on the idea would not let go of me; it has allowed me no peace all day.*

On the cult of oneself as a lover, from the point of view of health, hygiene, wardrobe, spiritual nobility, and eloquence.

Self-purification and anti-humanity.†

---

* *As I was crossing the boulevard:* A preliminary draft of the late prose poem "Lost Halo." See p. 187 below.

† *Self-purification and anti-humanity:* In English in the text.

There is, in the act of love, a striking resemblance to torture or to a surgical operation.

There is, in prayer, a magical operation. Prayer is one of the great forces behind the dynamics of the intellect. It works something like an electrical current.

The rosary is a medium, vehicle; it is prayer made available to all.

Work, a progressive and cumulative force; like capital, it yields interest, heightening one's faculties, or one's results.

Gambling, even if conducted scientifically, is an intermittent force; but however profitable it be, it will be conquered by sustained work, however meager the latter might prove.

If a poet demanded of the State the right to keep a few bourgeois in his stable, this would cause general consternation, whereas if a bourgeois were to request a poet roasted on a spit, this would be considered quite natural.

This book could never scandalize my women, my daughters, or my sisters.*

Eventually he asked permission to kiss her leg, and he took advantage of the occasion to position it so that its outline was clearly etched against the setting sun.

My kitten, my kitty-cat, my puss-puss, my wolfkins, my lambkins, my little monkey, my big little monkey, my snake, my melancholy little donkey.
These whimsies of language, too often repeated, these all too frequent animal nicknames provide clear proof that when it comes to

* *This book could never scandalize:* Sketch for Baudelaire's self-justifying 1861 preface to *Les Fleurs du mal.*

love there is a satanic side to things; do not demons take on animal shapes? Cazotte's camel.* His camel—a devil and a woman.

A man goes to a shooting range, accompanied by his woman. —He sets up a doll and says to his woman: I'm imagining this is you. —He closes his eyes and blows away the doll. —Then he says to his companion, kissing her hand: Angel dear, if I'm such a good shot I owe it all to you!†

When I shall have inspired universal disgust and horror, I shall have conquered solitude.

This book is not made for my women, my daughters, and my sisters. —Of which I possess few.

There are carapace skins so thick as to provide no satisfaction to contempt.

Many friends, many gloves—fear of scabies.

Those who have loved me were people who were despised, I would say even despicable, if I wanted to flatter *respectable folk*.

God is a scandal—but a profitable one.

18 · FLARES

Despise nobody's sensibility. Each man's sensibility is his genius.

There are only two places where one pays for the right to spend: public toilets and women.

If you set up house with a woman you passionately love, you begin to understand the joys of young newlyweds.

A precocious taste for women. I confused the smell of fur with the scent of woman.

I remember. . . . In short, I loved my mother for her elegance. I was therefore a precocious dandy.

---

* *Cazotte's camel:* In Jacques Cazotte's proto-fantastic tale *The Devil in Love* (1772), the heroine is transformed into a camel.

† *A man goes to a shooting range:* An outline of the late prose poem "The Gallant Marksman." See p. 185 below.

My ancestors—idiots or maniacs—in solemn apartments, all victims of terrible passions.

Protestant countries lack two elements crucial to the happiness of a well-bred man: gallantry and devotion.

The mingling of the grotesque and the tragic is as agreeable to the mind as discordances to jaded ears.

The exhilarating thing about bad taste is that it allows one the aristocratic pleasure of causing offense.

Reverie is expressed in Germany by the line; in England, by perspective.

When any sublime thought is engendered, the cerebellum registers a nervous jolt.

Spain brings to religion the natural ferocity of sex.

STYLE.
The eternal note, the eternal, cosmopolitan style. Chateaubriand, Alphonse Rabbe, Edgar Poe.*

19 · FLARES. SUGGESTIONS

Why democrats don't like cats—easy to guess. Cats are beautiful, suggesting notions of luxury, cleanliness, voluptuous pleasure, etc.

20 · FLARES

A bit of work, repeated 365 times, will generate a bit of money 365 times—which is to say, an enormous sum. At the same time, *glory is obtained.*

Likewise, happiness is made up of a multitude of tiny delights.

———

* *Alphonse Rabbe:* Minor French romantic writer, author of the posthumously published *Album of a Pessimist* (1835), which contains a defense of suicide.

To create a *poncif*—this is genius.*

I need to create a *poncif*.

The *concetto* is a masterpiece.†

The Alphonse Rabbe tone.

The kept-woman tone (*My lovely sweetheart! O fickle sex!*).

The *eternal* tone.

The coloring, crude; the line, deeply chiseled.

The Prima Donna and the Butcher Boy.‡

My mother is fantastical: to be feared and pleased.

Hildebrand the proud.§

The Caesarism of Napoleon III. (Letter to Edgar Ney.) Pope and Emperor.

21 · FLARES. SUGGESTIONS

To give oneself up to Satan, what might this mean?

What could be more absurd than Progress, given that man (as is proved everyday) is forever identical and equal to man, that is, forever a savage. What are the perils of the forest or the prairie compared to

---

* *To create a poncif*: The French reads, "Créer un poncif, c'est le génie." A *poncif* is a pouncing pattern (or stencil)—or, more broadly, any trite, worn-out, or stereotypical expression lacking originality. See p. 58 above and the accompanying note.

† *The concetto is a masterpiece: Concetto*, a literary conceit, or witticism. In Italian commedia dell'arte, a *concetto* was also a stock punch line learned by performers for use in improvisational performances.

‡ *The Prima Donna and the Butcher Boy:* A minor novel of 1831, telling of how a young opera star was sold into vice by her mother.

§ *Hildebrand the proud:* That is, Pope Gregory VII, who humiliated Holy Roman Emperor Henry IV at Canossa in 1077—here contrasted with the "Caesarist" Prince Napoleon, who in 1849 had written a letter to the Vatican requesting an amnesty for his republican political reforms in exchange for his recognition of the pope's temporal powers.

the daily shocks and conflicts of civilization? Whether a man ensnare his mark on the boulevards or stab his prey in unknown forests, is he not eternally man, that is, the most perfect beast of prey?

—They claim I'm thirty years old; but if I have lived three minutes in one . . . wouldn't that make me ninety?

Work—is this not the salt that preserves mummified souls?

Beginning a novel: tackle the subject at random and, to whet your desire to complete it, kick things off with a string of gorgeous sentences.

22 · FLARES

I think that the infinite and mysterious charm that lies in the contemplation of a ship—and, most especially a ship in motion—derives, first, from its regularity and symmetry, one of the primordial prerequisites of the human mind, to the same degree as complication and harmony. Second, it derives from the successive multiplication of all the imaginary curves and figures generated in space by the actual elements of the object.

The poetic idea that emerges from this mobilization of the line is the hypothesis of an immense being—vast, complex, yet eurhythmic—an animal filled with genius, suffering all of mankind's ambitions, sighing all its sighs.

Civilized peoples, you who always speak so idiotically of *savages* and *barbarians*, very soon (as d'Aurevilly points out) you will no longer even rise to the level of *idol worshippers.**

Stoicism, a religion with a sole sacrament—suicide!

An outline for a low comedy—a lyrical piece or an extravaganza—to be performed in pantomime. Translate this into a serious novel. Bathe

---

* *D'Aurevilly:* Barbey d'Aurevilly, author of "Of Dandyism and George Brummel" (1845).

the whole thing in a weird, dreamlike atmosphere—the atmosphere of *exceptional days*. Let there be something soothing—and even serene— to the passions. —Regions of Pure Poetry.

Aroused by the contact of these physical enjoyments that resembled so many memories, deeply affected by thoughts of a past so poorly fulfilled, conscious of all the mistakes, all the quarrels, all the things they had to hide from each other, he began to weep; and there in the dark, his hot tears flowed onto the naked shoulder of his dear and ever-ravishing mistress. She shuddered; she too was overcome by the same tender emotions. The darkness reassured her, providing a cover for her vanity, for her dandyism as a frigid female. These two fallen creatures, still suffering from whatever remained of their nobility, spontaneously clasped each other in their arms, mingling their streams of tears and kisses with the miseries of their past and their faint hopes for the future. It is very likely that, over the course of this night of melancholy and forgiveness, neither had ever before experienced such sweet physical enjoyment—an enjoyment steeped in sorrow and remorse. Across the blackness of the night, he had looked into the deepening years that lay behind him, then had thrown himself into the arms of his guilty lover in order to discover in them the pardon that he was now granting her.

—Hugo often thinks about Prometheus. He applies an imaginary vulture to his breast, whose wounds are cauterized only by his own vanity. Then this hallucination grows ever more intricate and varied (yet following the progressive course described by doctors) and he ends up believing that by a *fiat* of Providence, Saint Helena has taken the place of Jersey.*

This man is so unelegiac, so unethereal that he would even revolt a notary.

Hugo-the-High-Priest always has his head bowed—so bowed he sees nothing but his navel.

---

* *Saint Helena has taken the place of Jersey:* Victor Hugo mistaking his own current place of exile (as of 1852), the Isle of Jersey, for that of Napoleon on Saint Helena.

Who is not a high priest these days? Even youth is a high priesthood—according to the young.*

And what is not a prayer? —Shitting is a prayer, according to democrats taking their craps.

M. de Pontmartin—a man who always seems to have just arrived from the sticks . . . .†

Man, that is everybody, is so *naturally* depraved that he suffers less from the general degradation of everything than from the establishment of a reasonable hierarchy.

The world is about to end.‡ The sole reason it might continue on is that it exists. How feeble a reason, compared to all those that point to the contrary, particularly the following: where, under heaven, is the earth now heading? —For, even supposing that it might continue

---

* *Who is not a high priest these days?:* The attack on Hugo's populist humanitarianism and the "high priests" of utopian socialism echoes the twenty-eighth of Poe's "Fifty Suggestions": "The world is infested, just now by a new sect of philosophers, who have not yet suspected themselves of forming a sect, and who, consequently, have adapted no name. They are *Believers in every thing Odd.* Their High Priest in the East, is Charles Fourier—in the West, Horace Greeley; and high priests they are to some purpose. The only common bond among the sect, is Credulity:—let us call it Insanity at once, and be done with it. Ask any one of them *why* he believes this or that, and, if he be conscientious, (ignorant people usually are), he will make you very much such a reply as Talleyrand made when asked why he believed in the Bible. 'I believe in it first,' said he, 'because I am Bishop of Autun; and secondly, *because I know nothing about it at all.*' What these philosophers call 'argument,' is a way they have '*de nier ce qui est et d'expliquer ce qui n'est pas.*' (*Nouvelle Héloïse*)" (Poe, *Brevities*, 494).

† *M. de Pontmartin:* A critic who had written a moralistic review of Baudelaire's translation of Poe's *Histoires extraordinaires* (1856).

‡ *The world is about to end:* In a December 1861 letter to Arsène Houssaye, Baudelaire mentions, among the list of prose poems he has on hand, a text entitled "The End of the World." This fragment of *Flares* may indeed be a sketch for that unpublished prose poem. The end of the world also appears as a theme in Baudelaire's projects for eventual prose poems, short stories, and novels. See pp. 175–76 below. It was perhaps with this passage of *Flares* in mind that Proust referred to Baudelaire in a letter as "the most desolate prophet since the prophets of Israel." While teaching German at the École Normale Supérieure in Paris in the late 1960s, Paul Celan would regularly assign this fragment of Baudelaire's as a translation exercise.

to exist materially, would this be an existence worthy of the name or in the dictionary definition of the term? I'm not saying that the world will be reduced to the harebrained schemes and farcical chaos of the South American republics—or that we might even lapse back into a state of savagery, searching for fodder, rifle in hand, amid the overgrown ruins of our civilization. No—because this particular fate and these kinds of adventures would still suppose a certain vital energy, an echo of earlier times. Fresh examples and fresh victims of inexorable moral laws, we shall perish by that which we believed had sustained our life. Machinery will have so Americanized us, progress will have so atrophied our spiritual faculties, that none of the bloody, sacrilegious, anti-natural reveries of the Utopians could be compared to its actual effects. I ask any thinking man to show me what remains of life. Useless to speak of religion or to look for its remains: to bother to deny the existence of God is the only scandal still possible in these matters. Property had virtually disappeared with the abolition of the right of primogeniture. But the time shall come when humanity, like some vengeful ogre, even snatches this last morsel from those who believe that the revolutions had legalized their inheritances. Which, it's true, would not be the worst thing to happen.

The human imagination can conceive of republics or of other communitarian states that would be worthy of some glory—if directed by holy men, by certain aristocrats. But it is not specifically in the political institutions that one will observe the effects of universal ruin, or of universal progress—it hardly matters to me what name it goes by. It will be seen in the degradation of the human heart. Need I mention that whatever remains of politics will have to combat the onslaught of widespread animality and that governments will be forced—just to maintain themselves and to create a phantom of order—to resort to methods that would cause men of today to shudder, callous though they already be? —At that point, the son will flee his family, not at age eighteen but at twelve, emancipated by his precocious greed; he will flee, not to seek out heroic adventures, not to rescue some damsel imprisoned in a tower, not to immortalize his garret with sublime thoughts, but to start a business, to make money, to compete with his vile papa, the founder and shareholder of a newspaper that provides such daily enlightenment as will make *Le Siècle* of those days seem like a regular hotbed of superstition. —At that point, those who stray from the course, those who have fallen from their station, those who have gone through several lovers, those who are sometimes called Angels in recognition of and in gratitude for the absolute insouciance that flares forth like some haphazard flame from lives as logical as evil—at that point, I say, these creatures will be pitilessly well behaved, having acquired a wisdom that will condemn everything, except money— everything, even *errors of the senses!* —At that time, everything that re- sembles virtue, indeed, everything that does not thirst for riches, will be considered merely ridiculous. Justice, if justice still obtains during these fortunate times, will banish all citizens incapable of amass- ing wealth. —Your wife, O Bourgeois, your chaste better half, whose lawful weddedness you find so poetic, will henceforth introduce into your legal arrangement a despicable practice beyond reproach. The loving and watchful guardian of your strongbox, she will be the perfect ideal of the kept woman. Your daughter, mature beyond her years, will dream while still in the cradle that she is selling herself for millions. And you yourself, O Bourgeois—even less a poet than you are today—you will find nothing wrong with this, you will regret nothing. For there are things in man that grow stronger and more prosper- ous as others slacken and go into decline: thanks to the progress of these times, all that will remain of your insides will be your bowels! These times are perhaps quite near; who knows whether they are not already upon us, and whether the coarsening of our nature is not the sole obstacle preventing us from recognizing the atmosphere we breathe.

As for me, who sometimes feel myself laughable as a prophet, I know that in these times I shall never encounter the charity of a doctor. Lost in this wretched world, elbowed by crowds, I am like some weary man whose eyes see, in the deepening years behind him, only bitterness and disappointment, while before him there gathers a storm containing nothing new—no new instruction or pain. In the evening, when this man has snatched a few hours of pleasure from fate, lulled by his digestion, forgetting (as much as possible) the past, content with the present and resigned to the future, intox- icated by his own cool composure and dandyism, proud to be less ignoble than those who pass by, he says to himself, contemplating the smoke of his cigar: What does it matter to me what becomes of these consciences?

I think I may have wandered off into what those in the trade call an *hors-d'oeuvre*. Still, I'll let these pages stand—because I want to attach a date to my anger.

sorrow*

* *anger/sorrow:* Baudelaire initially corrected "anger" by "sorrow" but let both words stand in the end.

[Hygiene]

86 · FLARES. HYGIENE. PROJECTS*

The more one wants, the better one wants.

The more one works, the better one works, and the more one wants to work. The more one produces, the more fertile one becomes.

After a debauchery, one always feels more alone, more abandoned.

Morally and physically, I have always had a sensation of the abyss—not only the abyss of sleep but the abyss of action, of dream, of memory, of desire, of regret, of remorse, of beauty, of number, etc.

I have cultivated my hysteria with joy and terror. Now, I am continually overcome by vertigo, and today, January 23, 1862, I was given a special warning: I felt *the wind of the wing of imbecility* pass over me.

---

* *FLARES. HYGIENE. PROJECTS:* The numbering of the folios in this section (86–93) follows that of its first editor, Malassis, who decided to place *Hygiene* after *My Heart Laid Bare* (folios 1–85)—the order followed by most of the early editions of the *Journaux intimes* (and hence of Isherwood's translation of *Intimate Journals*). I follow Pichois's Pléiade edition, however, in seeing *Hygiene* as a more private corollary to, and continuation of, *Flares*, probably dating from 1862, with further additions made three years later in Belgium. I therefore disagree with Guyaux, who presents *Hygiene* as an altogether separate undertaking and prints it after *My Heart Laid Bare*, observing Malassis's original numbering.

87 · HYGIENE. ETHICS

Off to Honfleur, as soon as possible, before I fall even lower.*
God has already sent so many signs and portents—that it is *at long last time* to act, to consider the present moment as the most crucial of moments, and to extract *eternal delight* from my daily torment, that is to say, from Work.

88 · HYGIENE. CONDUCT. ETHICS

At every moment, we are crushed by the idea and sensation of time. And there are but two ways to escape this nightmare, to put it out of mind: Pleasure and Work. Pleasure wears us down. Work fortifies us. The choice is ours.

The more we follow one of these paths, the more the other one revolts us.

The only way to forget time is to make use of it.
It's only little by little that things get done.

FLARES

De Maistre and Edgar Poe taught me how to reason.†
The only lengthy works are those that one dares not begin. They become nightmares.

---

* *Off to Honfleur:* The return to his mother's Honfleur home on the Normandy coast is a constant theme in Baudelaire's letters from 1860 onward. In the event, he never undertook this salvific *nostos*, choosing exile in Belgium instead.

† *De Maistre and Poe taught me how to reason:* Joseph de Maistre, Savoyard political philosopher and diplomat, best known for his *Saint Petersburg Evenings, or Conversations on the Temporal Government of Providence, Followed by a Treatise on Sacrifices* (1821). In an 1856 letter, Baudelaire referred to him as "the great genius of our time—a visionary." Poe described his detective stories—"The Murders in the Rue Morgue," "The Mystery of Marie Rogêt," and "The Purloined Letter" (all translated by Baudelaire) as "tales of ratiocination."

89 · HYGIENE

By putting off what needs to be done, you run the danger of never being able to do it at all. If you don't convert immediately, you risk damnation.

To be cured of everything—of misery, of malady, of melancholy—the only real thing missing is the *Taste for Work.*

90 · VALUABLE ADVICE

Do every day what duty and prudence commend.
If you worked every day, your life would be more bearable.
Work *six* days without respite.

———

To come up with subjects, γνῶθι σεαυτον . . .* (List of my tastes.)
Always be a poet, even in prose. The grand old style (nothing more beautiful than the commonplace).
First get yourself going, and then make use of logic and analysis.
Any hypothesis demands its conclusion.
Work yourself up into a frenzy on a daily basis.

91 · HYGIENE. CONDUCT. ETHICS

TWO PARTS:
Debts (Ancelle).†
Friends (*my mother, friends, myself*)

---

* γνῶθι σεαυτον: Gnothi seauton, "Know thyself"—inscription on the Temple of Apollo at Delphi.

† *Ancelle:* Narcisse Désiré Ancelle, the much-resented *conseil judiciaire* (legal trustee) who had been appointed early on by Baudelaire's family to oversee the poet's finances.

Thus 1,000 francs should be divided in two parts of 500 francs each, and the second part divided into *three parts*.

At Honfleur.
Go through and organize all my *letters* (2 days).
And the same for all my debts (2 days). (Four categories, *notes, major debts, minor debts, friends.*)
Organize engravings (2 days).
Organize notes (2 days).

92 · HYGIENE. CONDUCT. ETHICS

Jeanne 300, my mother 200, myself 300.* 800 francs per month. Work from 6 in the morning to noon, on an empty stomach. Pushing blindly ahead, without a goal in mind, like a madman. We shall see the results.

I suppose I'm pinning my entire fate on the ability to work uninterruptedly for several hours.

Everything is reparable. There is still time. Who knows whether new pleasures . . . ?

Glory, my Debts paid off. My mother and Jeanne *comfortable*.

I have yet to know the pleasure of a realized project. The power of the *idée fixe*. The power of Hope.

The habit of doing your Duty drives away fear. You have to want to dream and know how to dream. Summon up inspiration. The art of magic. Sit right down and write. I rationalize too much.

Set to work immediately, even if the work be mediocre. It beats dreaming.

A series of small acts of the will delivers major results.

Every weakening of the will entails a fresh loss of its substance. Hesitate not, waste not. Imagine the immense efforts needed to repair all these losses!

The man who prays at bedtime is a captain organizing the night watch. Which allows him to sleep.

* *Jeanne 300:* Apparently written before Baudelaire's break with the ailing Jeanne Duval toward the end of 1861, when he ceased supporting her.

Dreams about Death and omens.

Up to the present, I have been alone in taking pleasure in my memories. The pleasure should be shared by two. Transform the pleasures of the heart into a passion.

Because I understand what it means to achieve glory in one's lifetime, I feel I could do the same myself. O Jean-Jacques!

Work by definition promotes good morals, sobriety, and chastity, hence health, wealth, the successive and progressive enjoyments of genius—and charity. *Age quod agis.**

Fish, cold baths, lichens, the occasional lozenge; and the elimination of all stimulants.

> Iceland lichen . . . . 125 grams
> White sugar . . . . 250 grams

Soak the lichen for 12 or 15 hours in a sufficient amount of cold water, then drain off the water.

Boil the lichen in 2 liters of water over a low continuous flame until the two liters have been reduced to one; give it a single skimming; then add the 250 grams of sugar and let it thicken into the consistency of syrup.

Let it cool. Take *three* large spoonfuls a day, morning, noon, and night. Do not hesitate to increase the dosage if the attacks continue.

93 · HYGIENE. CONDUCT. METHOD

I swear to myself that I shall henceforth take the following rules as the lasting regimen of my life:

Every morning, to *pray to God, the reservoir of all force and all justice,* to my *father,* to *Mariette,* and to *Poe,* as intercessors;† to pray to them to grant me the *necessary force* to fulfill all my duties, and to bestow

---

* *Age quod agis:* "Do what thou must"—or "to the business at hand."

† *To my father, to Mariette and Poe:* Baudelaire was said to have transported a portrait of his father from lodging to lodging throughout his life. Mariette was the beloved servant who had taken care of Baudelaire as a child.

upon my mother *a life long enough* to take pleasure in my transformation; to work all day long, or at least *as long as my forces permit*; to put my faith in God, that is, in Justice itself, for the success of my projects; to renew my prayers every evening, to beseech God to grant life and strength to my mother and myself; to do everything possible to come up with four shares—one for daily expenses, one for my creditors, one for my friends, one for my mother; to observe the strictest principles of sobriety, the first of which is the elimination of all stimulants, whatever they may be.

93bis · HYGIENE. ETHICS. CONDUCT

Too late perhaps!* My mother and Jeanne. —To offer them my health, out of charity, out of duty! —Jeanne's illnesses. My mother's infirmities, solitude.

—To do one's duty every day and place faith in God for the morrow.

—The only way of making money is to work in a disinterested fashion.

—Wisdom, in a nutshell: Personal hygiene, prayer, work.

—Prayer: charity, wisdom, power.

—Without charity, I am but a tinkling cymbal.†

—My humiliations have been the grace of God.

—Is my egoistic phase now over?

—The capacity of responding to the necessity of each moment—this exactitude, in a word—must infallibly be rewarded.

"Unrelenting misery produces the same effect in the soul as old age in the body: one can no longer move about; one takes to bed. . . .

On the other hand, extreme youth also provides one with reasons for procrastination; someone with a great deal of time ahead of himself is easily persuaded that he can wait years before rising to the occasion."

CHATEAUBRIAND‡

---

* *Too late perhaps:* See Baudelaire's poem "A une passante": "Ailleurs, bien loin d'ici! trop tard! *jamais* peut-être!"

† *Without charity, I am but a tinkling cymbal:* 1 Corinthians 13:1.

‡ *Chateaubriand:* From his *Memoirs from Beyond the Grave,* book 42, chap. 9, on the recent death of Charles X of France.

93ter · HYGIENE. CONDUCT. METHOD

(Extracts from Emerson's *Conduct of Life*) [in English in the text]

Great men . . . have been, not boasters and buffoons, but perceivers of *the terrors of life*, and have manned themselves to face it.

"Fate is nothing but the deeds committed in a prior state of existence."

"What we wish for in youth comes in heaps on us in old age," too often cursed with the granting of our prayer; and hence the high caution, that since we are sure of having what we wish we beware to ask only for high things.

The one prudence in life is concentration; the one evil is dissipation.

The poet Campbell said that "a man accustomed to work was equal to any achievement he resolved on, and that, for himself necessity, not inspiration, was the prompter of his muse."

In our flowing affairs a decision must be made, —the best, if you can; but any is better than none.

The second substitute for temperament is drill, the power of use and routine.

"More are made good by exercitation than by nature," said Democritus.

Mirabeau said: "Why should we feel ourselves to be men, unless it be to succeed in everything, everywhere. You must say of nothing: *That is beneath me*, nor feel that anything can be out of your power. Nothing is impossible to the man who can will. *Is that necessary? That shall be*. This is the only *Law of success*."

We acquire the strength we have overcome.

The hero is he who is immovably centered.

The main difference between people seems to be, that one man can come under obligations on which you can rely; and another is not. *As he has not a law within him, there's nothing to tie him to.*

If you would be powerful, pretend to be powerful.

Seeketh thou great things? Seek them not.

*Conduct of life** [in English in the text]
   —Great men have not been . . . for high things.

---

* *Conduct of Life:* All the elided quotations from Emerson's book are given in full in the previous section.

—His heart (was) a throne of will.

—Life is search after power.

—No honest seeking goes unrewarded.

—We must reckon success a constitutional trait.

—The one prudence . . . of his muse.

—A decision . . . said Democritus.

—*Pecunia alter sanguis.*

—Mirabeau said . . . immovably centered.

—Your theories and plans of life are fair and commendable; —but will you stick?

—If you . . . powerful.

My Heart Laid Bare

1 · MY HEART LAID BARE

On the vaporization and centralization of the *Self*. It all comes down to this.*

On that particular thrill of pleasure in the company of profligates.

(I can begin *My Heart Laid Bare* wherever I want, however I want, and continue on with it day by day, following the inspiration of the day or the occasion—provided the inspiration prove lively enough.)

2 · The first comer has the right to talk about himself—provided he be amusing.

3 · MY HEART LAID BARE

I understand how one might desert a cause merely to discover what it feels like to serve another one.

It might be pleasant to be by turns victim and executioner.†

---

* *On the vaporization and centralization of the Self:* Cf. Emerson's *Conduct of Life*, as quoted on folio 93ter of *Flares*: "The one prudence in life is concentration; the one evil is dissipation." "The hero is he who is immovably centered."
† *victim and executioner:* This leaf was written on Hôtel du Grand Miroir stationery and is thus subsequent to Baudelaire's arrival in Belgium.

4 · MY HEART LAID BARE

Girardin's asininities:

"It is our habit to take the bull by its *horns.* So let us take this topic up from the *end.*" (Nov. 7, 1863.)

So Girardin believes that bulls' horns are planted on their rumps. He mistakes horn for tail.

"Before they start imitating the Ptolemies of French journalism, let the journalists of Belgium take the time to reflect on a question that I have been studying from various angles for thirty years now, as will be borne out by my soon-to-be published study, *As Regards the Press.* Let them not treat as *outright ridiculous* (1) an opinion that is as true as the fact that the earth turns and that the sun does not."*

EMILE DE GIRARDIN

(1) "There are those who would claim that it is entirely possible that, the sky being motionless, it is the earth that therefore turns on its axis. But these people are unaware, given what takes place all around us, just how outright ridiculous (πανυ γελοιοτατον) their opinion is."

PTOLEMY, *Almagestus,* Book I, chapter IV

Et habet mea mentrita mentum.†

GIRARDIN

5 · MY HEART LAID BARE

Woman is the contrary of the Dandy.

She should therefore inspire horror.

Woman is hungry? She wants to eat. Thirsty? She wants to drink.

---

* *"Before they start imitating the Ptolemies":* This paragraph and its note are newspaper clippings pasted directly onto the page.

† *Et habet mea metrita mentum:* Mangled Latin appropriate to the pretentious bê-tise of Emile de Girardin, editor of the newspaper *La Presse.* It most likely alludes to Jupiter's words in the prologue to Rabelais's *Fourth Book:* "Et habit tua mentula men-tem" ("And your mind [or male member] has wit").

In rut? She wants to get fucked.

How worthy of her!

Woman is *natural*, that is, abominable.

Moreover, she is always vulgar, that is, the contrary of the Dandy.

———

*Re the Legion of Honor**

The person soliciting the cross seems to be saying: if I am not decorated for having done my duty, I shall cease doing so.

—If a man has merit, why decorate him? If he has none, a decoration might be in order—to add luster to his reputation.

To agree to be decorated is to recognize that the state or the sovereign has the right to judge you, to honor you, etc.

———

Besides, if not pride then Christian humility should preclude the cross.

Calculus in favor of God

Nothing exists without a purpose.

Therefore my existence has a purpose. What purpose? I haven't a clue.

Therefore it was not I who determined it.

It is therefore someone more all-knowing than I.

I should therefore pray to this someone to explain it to me. This is the wisest course.

The Dandy should ceaselessly aspire toward sublimity; he should live and sleep before a mirror.

---

* *The Legion of Honor:* Baudelaire had angled for this decoration in 1858, apparently hoping to erase the public humiliation of the trial of *The Flowers of Evil* the previous year. In the last sentence of Flaubert's *Madame Bovary*, M. Homais receives the Legion of Honor.

6 · MY HEART LAID BARE

Analysis of counter-religions. Example: sacred prostitution.

What is sacred prostitution?*

Nervous excitement.

The mystical aspect of paganism.

Mysticism—the link between paganism and Christianity.

Paganism and Christianity provide reciprocal proofs of each other.

The Revolution and its cult of Reason prove the idea of sacrifice.

Superstition is the reservoir of all truths.

7 · MY HEART LAID BARE

There is something at once sordid and agreeable about any major change, something on the order of infidelity or of moving house. This suffices to explain the French Revolution.

8 · MY HEART LAID BARE

My inebriation in 1848.†

What was the nature of this inebriation?

Thirst for revenge. Taking *natural* pleasure in demolition.

Drunk on literature; memory of books read.

May 15th.‡ The same old impulse to destroy. A legitimate impulse—if everything that is natural is legitimate.

---

* *What is sacred prostitution?:* Baudelaire may have encountered the practice of "sacred prostitution" in Benjamin Constant's *On Religion* (1824–31). The following remarks on paganism, sacrifice, and superstition in turn derive from the writings of Joseph de Maistre.

† *My inebriation in 1848:* Baudelaire participated in the February uprising, reportedly carrying a rifle on the Carrefour de Buci and shouting, "Down with Aupick"—his stepfather being at that time the commander of the major military academy in Paris, L'École Polytechnique.

‡ *May 15th:* The day the left-wing clubs tried (and failed) to overthrow the National Assembly.

———

The horrors of June.* The masses and the bourgeoisie gone mad. Natural delight in crime.

———

My fury at the coup d'état.† How many times I came under fire. Another Bonaparte! Shame!

And nonetheless everything quieted down. Is not the president well within his rights?

What the emperor Napoleon III is. What he is worth. Come up with an explanation of his nature, as an instrument of Providence.‡

9 · MY HEART LAID BARE

The notion of being a useful person has always struck me as quite hideous.

———

The only amusing thing about 1848 was that everybody was constructing utopias like castles in the air.

The only charming thing about 1848 was that it achieved the heights of Ridiculousness.

———

* *The horrors of June:* Workers' uprising to protest the closing of the National Workshops. Ten thousand people were either killed or injured, while four thousand insurgents were deported to Algeria. The bloody Days of June (in which Baudelaire apparently participated on the workers' side) marked the final victory of the liberals over the radical republicans.

† *My fury at the coup d'état:* Of Napoleon III's coup d'état, Baudelaire wrote in a letter: "Dec. 2nd *physically depoliticized* me."

‡ *An instrument of Providence:* In the politico-theological sense of Maistre's vision of the providential course of history, in which the Revolution and the ensuing Terror (like Napoleon III here) served as divine and providential chastisements of France.

Robespierre is only to be esteemed because he came up with a few fine phrases.*

10

Revolution, by its reliance on sacrifice, confirms superstition.

11 · MY HEART LAID BARE

POLITICS

I have no convictions, as men of my century understand the term, because I have no ambitions.

I lack any basis for conviction.

There is a certain cowardliness or rather a certain spinelessness to honest folk.

Only crooks are convinced—of what? Convinced they must succeed. So succeed they do.

Why should I succeed, seeing as I lack the slightest desire to do so?

Glorious empires can be founded on crime, and noble religions on deception.

———

Nonetheless, I do harbor a few convictions, in the higher sense— which exceed the understanding of my contemporaries.

12 · MY HEART LAID BARE

A sense of *solitude,* from childhood onward. Despite my family—and especially among my schoolmates—a sense that it was my fate to be forever alone.

Nonetheless, a very keen taste for life and for pleasure.

* *Robespierre:* In his *Artificial Paradises* (1860), Baudelaire described the style of Robespierre as "fiery ice, recooked and frozen into abstraction." Robespierre is later quoted in section 57.

13 · MY HEART LAID BARE

We spend nearly all our lives indulging our idle curiosity.* Whereas there are things that should excite people's curiosity to the highest degree and which, to judge from their day-to-day lives, inspire none whatsoever.

Where are our deceased friends?

Why are we here?

Do we come from anywhere?

What is freedom?

How reconcile it with the laws of Providence?

Is the number of souls finite or infinite?

And the number of inhabitable lands?

Etc., etc.

14 · MY HEART LAID BARE

Nations produce great men only despite themselves. The great man has therefore reaped a victory over his entire nation.

Ridiculous modern religions.†

Molière.

Béranger.

Garibaldi.

15 · MY HEART LAID BARE

The belief in progress is a lazy man's doctrine, a *Belgian* doctrine. It's the individual counting on his neighbors to do his job for him.

The only true (that is, moral) progress that can take place is in the individual and by the individual.

But the world is made up of people who can only think in common, in herds. Hence all the *Belgian Societies.*‡

---

* *Indulging our idle curiosity:* Here, as elsewhere, the Pascalian theme of *divertissement,* or diversion.

† *Ridiculous modern religions:* Molière and the populist poet Béranger were among the darlings of the liberal press—as was the Italian freedom fighter Garibaldi.

‡ *Hence all the Belgian Societies:* See *Belgium Disrobed,* pp. 277, 320–21.

There are also people who can only entertain themselves in packs. The true hero entertains himself alone.

16 · MY HEART LAID BARE

Eternal superiority of the Dandy.
What is the Dandy?

17 · MY HEART LAID BARE

My views on the theater. The thing I have found most beautiful in a theater, from early childhood to this day, is the *chandelier*—a truly gorgeous object, luminous, crystalline, complicated, circular, symmetrical.

Not that I absolutely deny the value of dramatic literature. Except that I wish that actors were mounted on stilts, that they wore masks more expressive than the human face, and that they spoke through megaphones; and finally, that the women's roles were played by men.

After all, the chandelier has always seemed to me the principal actor, whatever end of the opera glasses you look through.

18 · MY HEART LAID BARE

One must work, if not out of inclination, at least out of despair. All things considered, work is far less boring than entertaining oneself.

19 · MY HEART LAID BARE

There are in every man, at every hour, two simultaneous postulations, one toward God, the other toward Satan. The invocation of God, or spirituality, is the desire move up a notch; the invocation of Satan, or animality, is the joy in downward descent. To the latter may be ascribed the love of women and private conversations with animals, dogs, cats, etc. . . . .

The joys derived from these two kinds of love are adapted to the nature of each.

20 · MY HEART LAID BARE

Besotted Mankind.
Quite a picture to paint:

As regards Charity.
As regards licentiousness.
As regards literature, or the stage actor.

21 · MY HEART LAID BARE

The practice of torture, as a technique of drawing out the truth, is barbarian nonsense. It applies material means to a spiritual end.

———

The death penalty is the outgrowth of a mystical idea, totally misunderstood these days.* The purpose of the death penalty is not to *save* society, at least not materially. Its purpose is (spiritually) to *save* society and the guilty one. In order for the sacrifice to be perfect, the victim has to assent to it with joy. To give chloroform to a man condemned to death would be disrespectful, for it would rob him of his awareness of his grandeur as a victim while eliminating his chances of going to heaven.

———

As for torture, it arises from the basest chamber of the human heart, the one thirsting for sensual gratification. Cruelty and sensual delight—identical sensations, like extreme heat and extreme cold.

* *The death penalty:* Baudelaire draws his defense of the sacrificial logic death penalty from Maistre's "Treatise on Sacrifices" (1821)—while at the same time establishing himself, here and elsewhere, in polemic opposition to Victor Hugo's well-publicized campaign against capital punishment.

22 · MY HEART LAID BARE

My views on voting and electoral rights. On the rights of man.
To exercise any public function whatsoever—how vile.
A Dandy does nothing.
Can you imagine a Dandy addressing the masses, except to scoff
at them?

———

The only reasonable and stable form of government is the aristo-
cratic one.
Democratic monarchies or republics are equally absurd and weak.

———

Posters—immense nausea.

———

There are only three beings worthy of respect:
The priest, the warrior, the poet. To know, to kill, to create.
All other men are mere stable boys doing their master's bidding,
that is, exercising what are known as *professions*.

23 · MY HEART LAID BARE

Observe that those who want to abolish the death penalty must
be doing so because they have some sort of *vested interest* in the
matter.
These persons are often executioners. Which can be reduced to:
"Allow me to cut off your head; but you shall not lay a hand on mine."
Those who wish to abolish the soul (*materialists*) also necessarily
wish to abolish *Hell*. Of course they have their own *vested interests*
in mind.
At the very least, these are all people who are afraid of *life after
death*—lazy souls.

24 · MY HEART LAID BARE

Although a princess, Madame de Metternich neglected to respond to my comments on her and on Wagner.*
Manners and morals of the 19th century.

25 · MY HEART LAID BARE

The story of my translation of *Edgar Poe*.†
The story of *The Flowers of Evil*, of the humiliation of being misunderstood, and of my trial.‡

The story of my relations with all the famous men of my age.

Amusing portraits of various imbeciles:§
Clément de Ris.
Castagnary.
Portraits of magistrates, officials, newspaper directors, etc.

———

Portrait of the artist, in general.

———

* *Madame de Metternich:* Wife of the Austrian ambassador to Paris, to whom Baudelaire had in 1861 offered a copy of his study on *Richard Wagner and Tannhäuser*—which was returned to him with a brief note of thanks, its pages uncut.

† *My translation of Edgar Poe:* Baudelaire's translations of Poe, his major source of literary income, included *Histoires extraordinaires* (1856), *Nouvelles histoires extraordinaires* (1857), *Aventures de Gordon Pym* (1858), *Eureka* (1859), *Histoires grotesques et sérieuses* (1864).

‡ *My trial:* Among the late projects sketched out during his Brussels years was. Baudelaire's personal (and documentary) account of the August 1857 trial of *Les Fleurs du mal*.

§ *Amusing portraits of various imbeciles:* The literary critic Athanase-Louis Clément de Ris had descried the "obscenity" of *The Flowers of Evil* in 1862; the art critic Jules-Antoine Castagnary (a friend of Courbet's) had pronounced art "a civilizing influence."

Of editors-in-chief and classroom proctors. How the French people relishes its proctors and its dictators. In a word: "If I were king!"

Portraits and anecdotes.*

François, —Buloz, —Houssaye, —good old Rouy, —de Calonne, —Charpentier, who corrects his authors' proofs, given the equal rights granted to all men by the immortal principles of '89; —Chevalier, a true editor-in-chief in the Empire style.

26 · MY HEART LAID BARE

On *George Sand*.†

The woman Sand is the Prudhomme of immorality.‡ She has always been a moralist.

---

* *Portraits and anecdotes:* A list of some of the major magazine editors with whom Baudelaire experienced his usual frustrations: Ferdinand François (*La Revue indépendante*), François Buloz (*La Revue des deux mondes*), Arsène Houssaye and Henri Rouy (*La Presse*), Alphonse de Calonne (*La Revue contemporaine),* and Gervais Charpentier (*La Revue nationale*), who "corrected" some of Baudelaire's prose poems before publishing them. Auguste Chevalier (of *Le Pays*) turned down Baudelaire's essay "The Painter of Modern Life" in 1862. In number thirteen of his "Fifty Suggestions" Poe observed: "Newspaper editors seem to have constitutions closely similar to those of deities in 'Walhalla,' who cut each other to pieces every day, and yet get up perfectly sound and fresh every morning" (*The Brevities,* ed. Burton R. Pollin [New York: Gordian, 1985], 483).

† *On George Sand:* In his "Skirmishes of an Untimely Man," included in *Twilight of the Idols* (1889), Nietzsche seems to channel Baudelaire's misogynistic diatribe against George Sand (whom Poe also despised): "George Sand—I read the first *Lettres d'un voyageur:* like everything that is descended from Rousseau, false, fabricated, exaggerated. I cannot stand this motley wallpaper style any more than the mob aspiration for generous feelings. The worst feature, to be sure, is the female's coquetry with male attributes, with the manners of naughty boys. How cold she must have been throughout, this insufferable artist! She wound herself up like a clock—and wrote. Cold, like Hugo, like Balzac, like all the romantics as soon as they took up poetic invention. And how self-satisfied she may have lain there all the while, this fertile writing-cow who had in her something German in the bad sense, like Rousseau himself, her master, and who in any case was possible only during the decline of French taste! But Renan reveres her."

‡ *The Prudhomme of immorality:* Joseph Prudhomme, character invented by Henri Monnier (1852), personification of sententious bourgeois bêtise.

Except that once upon a time she was a counter-moralist. —But she has never been an artist.

She writes in that famous *flowing style*, so dear to the bourgeois.

She's dumb [*bête*], she's clumsy, she can't keep her trap shut; when it comes to moral ideas, she displays the same depth of judgment and the same delicacy of feeling as a concierge or a kept woman.

What she has said about her mother.

What she says about poetry.

Her love for workers.

If several men have managed to develop crushes on this latrine, this only proves how low the men of this century have fallen.

See the preface to *Mademoiselle La Quintinie*, where she claims that true Christians do not believe in Hell.* La Sand promotes the *God of decent folk*, the god of concierges and of thieving household servants. She has her own good reasons for wanting to eliminate Hell.

27 · MY HEART LAID BARE

THE DEVIL AND GEORGE SAND.

Let it not be supposed that the Devil tempts only men of genius. He no doubt despises imbeciles, but he does not disdain their coopera-tion. On the contrary, he places great hopes in them.

Take George Sand. She is above all, and more than anything else, *a big fat idiot* [*une grosse bête*]; but she is *possessed*. It's the Devil who per-suaded her to follow *her good heart* and her *common sense*, so that she might persuade all the other big fat idiots to follow their good hearts and their common sense.

I cannot think of this stupid creature without a certain shudder of horror. If I ran into her, I could not resist tossing a font of holy water on her head.

28 · MY HEART LAID BARE

George Sand is one of those aging *ingénues* who never want to leave the stage.

---

* *Mademoiselle La Quintinie:* Novel by George Sand published in 1863.

I recently read a preface (the preface to *Mademoiselle La Quintinie*) where she claims that a true Christian cannot believe in Hell.

She has her own good reasons for wanting to eliminate Hell.

29 · MY HEART LAID BARE

France annoys me, especially because everybody here resembles Voltaire.

Emerson forgot Voltaire in his *Representative Men*.* He could have written a fine chapter entitled "Voltaire, or the *Antipoet*," the king of the gullible, the prince of the superficial, the anti-artist, the sermonizer of concierges, the granddaddy of the newspaper columnists of *Le Siècle*.

30 · MY HEART LAID BARE

In *The Ears of the Count of Chesterfield*, Voltaire jokes about the immortal soul having resided for nine months between excrement and urine. Voltaire, like all lazy people, hated mystery (1).

Unable to eliminate love, the Church at least wanted to disinfect it— and hence created marriage.

(1) At least he might have recognized in this location a bit of mischief or a satire on the part of Providence against love—and, in the world of progeneration, a sign of original sin. It's a fact: we can only make love with our organs of excretion.

---

* *Emerson:* Emerson's 1850 *Representative Men* contains portraits of Plato ("or, the Philosopher"), Swedenborg ("or, the Mystic"), Montaigne ("or, the Skeptic"), Shakespeare ("or, the Poet"), Napoleon ("Man of the World"), and Goethe ("or, the Writer").

31 · MY HEART LAID BARE

Portrait of the literary rabble.
Doctor Bistrosus Crapulosus Pedantissimus. His portrait painted in
the manner of Praxiteles.
His pipe.
His opinions.
His Hegelianism.
His filth.
His ideas about art.
His gall.
His jealousy.
A fine picture of modern youth.

32 · MY HEART LAID BARE

φαρμακοτριθης ανηρ και τῶν τους οφεις ες τα θαυματα τρεφοντων.*
AELIANUS (?)

33 · MY HEART LAID BARE

Theology.
What is the fall?
If it is unity become duality, then it is God who fell.
In other terms, would not Creation entail the fall of God?†

———

Dandyism.
What is the superior man?
Not the specialist.

* φαρμακοτριθης: "The preparer of medicines is among those who nourish snakes
in order to obtain miracles" (Cornelius Aelianus, "On the Nature of Animals").
† *Would not Creation entail the death of God?:* Baudelaire's gnostic extrapolation of
Maistre's account of the Creation as involving the Fall from Unity into what he calls
"Duity."

The man of leisure and liberal education.
To be rich and love one's work.

34 · MY HEART LAID BARE

Why does the man of wit prefer loose women to society women,
even though both are equally idiotic? —A question to be pondered.

35 · MY HEART LAID BARE

There are certain women who resemble the ribbon of the Legion of
Honor. One no longer wants anything to do with them because they
have been sullied by contact with certain men.

I would for the same reason not wear the trousers of someone with
scabies.

The annoying thing about making love: it's a crime one cannot com-
mit without an accomplice.

36 · MY HEART LAID BARE

A study of a Major Disease: The Horror of Settling Down.* Reasons
for the Disease. Gradual worsening of the Disease.

———

Outrage at the asininity of them all—whatever their class, sex, age.

———

Man so loves his fellow man that when he flees the city he still seeks
out crowds—to recreate the city in the country.

* *The Horror of Settling Down:* During his life, Baudelaire lived at twenty-three sep-
arate addresses in Paris.

37 · MY HEART LAID BARE

Durandeau's remarks about the Japanese. ("I am, first and foremost, a Frenchman.") The Japanese are monkeys. At least according to Darjou.*

The remarks of the doctor—a friend of Mathieu's—on the art of not getting pregnant, on Moses, and on the immortality of the soul.

————

Art as a civilizing influence (Castagnary).

38 · MY HEART LAID BARE

Physiognomy of a wise man and his family, sixth-floor residents, drinking their *café au lait*.

————

Monsieur Nacquart senior and Monsieur Nacquart junior.†
How Nacquart junior was appointed legal counsel at the Court of Appeals.

39 · MY HEART LAID BARE

On the love, on the predilection the French have for military metaphors. Here every metaphor sports a moustache.

Militant literature.
To rush into the breach.

* *The Japanese are monkeys:* May refer to the Shimonoseki Campaign of 1863–64. Émile Durandeau and Alfred Darjou were caricaturists at *Le Boulevard*.

† *Monsieur Nacquart senior:* Balzac's private doctor; his son, Nacquart junior, was among the judges at the 1857 trial of *The Flowers of Evil*.

To fly the flag high.
To show one's true colors.
To plunge into the fray.
One of the veterans.

All these glorious turns of phrase are generally applied to priggish pedants and barstool loafers.

40

French metaphors.

A soldier of the judicial press (Bertin).*
The press militant.

41 · MY HEART LAID BARE

Add to the military metaphors:
Frontline poets.
Avant-garde writers.
These habitual military metaphors bespeak minds that are not militant but rather content to be drilled into conformity, minds born to be servants, Belgian minds only capable of thinking in herds.

42 · MY HEART LAID BARE

The craving of pleasure weds us to the present. The concern for our salvation leaves us dependent on the future.
The man who is wedded to pleasure, that is, to the present, strikes me as someone rolling down a steep slope and who, wanting to grab hold of the bushes, uproots them and drags them along in his fall.
Above all, to be *a great man* and *a Saint* in one's own eyes.

---

* *Bertin:* Henri Bertin, a lawyer and director of the journal *Le Droit,* memorably photographed by Nadar.

43 · MY HEART LAID BARE

The hatred the masses feel toward beauty.
Examples thereof.
Jeanne and Madame Muller.*

44 · MY HEART LAID BARE

POLITICS.

In sum, in the eyes of history and of the French people, the great glory
of Napoleon III will have been to prove that the first comer can, by seiz-
ing the telegraph and the National Printing Press, govern a great nation.

Those who believe that these things can be accomplished without
the permission of the masses are imbeciles—as are those who believe
that glory only issues from virtue.

Dictators are the servants of the masses—nothing more—a rotten
role to play, to be sure—and their glory is the result of their having
accommodated their minds to the general idiocy of the nation.

45 · MY HEART LAID BARE

What is love?
The need to move beyond the self.
Man is an animal who worships.
To worship is to sacrifice and prostitute oneself.
All love is therefore prostitution.

45 bis · MY HEART LAID BARE

The most prostituted of beings is the being *par excellence*—God. Ev-
ery individual considers him his supreme friend. He is the shared and
inexhaustible reservoir of love.

---

* *Jeanne and Madame Muller:* Jeanne Duval and the wife of a Belgian journalist,
respectively.

45 ter

PRAYER

Do not punish me via my mother and do not punish my mother on account of me. —I entrust to your keeping the souls of my father and Mariette.* Grant me the immediate strength to do my duty every single day and to thereby become a hero and a Saint.

46 · MY HEART LAID BARE

A chapter on the indestructible, eternal, universal and ingenious ferocity of mankind.
On the love of bloodshed.
On the inebriation by bloodshed.
On the inebriation of crowds.
On the inebriation of the torture victim (Damiens.)†

47 · MY HEART LAID BARE

The only figures who stand apart from other men are the poet, the priest, and the soldier,
the man who sings, the man who blesses, the man who sacrifices and sacrifices himself.
The rest deserve the whip.

———

Let us be suspicious of the masses, of common sense, of the heart, of inspiration, and of the obvious.

* *Mariette:* Baudelaire's childhood nurse; see *Hygiene*, section 93.
† *Damiens:* Robert-François Damiens, publicly drawn and quartered in 1757 for having threatened Louis XV with a knife. His torture is treated in the opening chapter of Michel Foucault's *Surveiller et punir* (1975). Another entry directly inspired by Maistre's theories of sacrificial violence.

48 · MY HEART LAID BARE

I have always been astonished that women are allowed in churches. What kind of conversation could they possibly hold with God?

———

The Eternal Venus (caprice, hysteria, fantasy) is one of the most seductive shapes of the Devil.

———

The day a young writer corrects his first set of proofs he is as proud as a schoolboy who has just caught his first dose of the clap.

———

Not to forget the major chapter on the arts of divination—by water, by cards, by readings of the palm, etc. . . . .

49 · MY HEART LAID BARE

Woman cannot distinguish her soul from her body. She is simplistic, like all animals. —A satirist might opine that this is because she has nothing but a body.

———

A chapter on
Male Apparel.
The ethics of Apparel.
The joys of Apparel.

50 · MY HEART LAID BARE

On prigs and pedants
professors

judges
priests
ministers

————

Minor celebrities of our day.*
Renan.
Feydeau.
Octave Feuillet.
Scholl.

————

Newspaper editors. François, Buloz, Houssaye, Rouy, Girardin,
Texier, de Calonne, Solar, Turgan, Dalloz.†
—List all the scoundrels. Solar at the head of the list.

51 · MY HEART LAID BARE

To be a great man and a saint *in one's own eyes*, this is all that matters.

52 · MY HEART LAID BARE

Nadar is the most astonishing expression of vitality.‡ Adrien told me
that his brother Félix had a double set of viscera. I was jealous seeing
how well he succeeded in everything that was not abstract.

---

* *Minor celebrities of our day:* Ernest Renan, author of a "historical" *Life of Jesus*
(1863), to which Baudelaire again alludes on folio 82; Ernest Feydeau, author of the
best-selling novel of adultery *Fanny* (1858); Octave Feuillet, an ex-classmate of Baude-
laire's and member of the French Academy; Auriélien Scholl, editor of *Le Nain jaune*,
where Baudelaire had hoped to publish his essay "The Painter of Modern Life."

† *Newspaper editors:* Additions to the previous honor role of journalistic incompe-
tence and ignominy: Edmond Texier (*L'Illustration*), Félix Solar (*La Presse*), and Julien
Turgan and Paul Dalloz (*Le Moniteur universel*).

‡ *Nadar:* The photographer Félix Nadar, author of a posthumously published
Charles Baudelaire intime (1911), was one of Baudelaire's oldest and closest friends—

———

Veuillot is so uncouth and such an enemy of the arts that it would appear that all of the world's *Democracy* had taken refuge in his breast.*

Flesh out the portrait.

Supremacy of the pure idea—among Christians as among the communist disciples of Babeuf.†

The fanaticism of humility. Not even to aspire to understand Religion.

53 · MY HEART LAID BARE

Music.
On slavery.
On society women.
On loose women.
On magistrates.
On the sacraments.
The man of letters is the enemy of the world.
On bureaucrats.

54 · MY HEART LAID BARE

In lovemaking as in almost all human affairs, any *entente cordiale* is the result of a misunderstanding. The misunderstanding is pleasure. The man cries out: "O my angel!" The woman purrs: "Mamma! Mamma!" And these two imbeciles are persuaded that they are of the same mind. —The abyss of incommunicability will not have been bridged.

———

one of the few persons (other than his mother) whom he addresses with a familiar "tu" in his correspondence.

 * *Veuillot:* Louis Veuillot, author and journalist known for his polemical ultramontanist (i.e., pro-papacy) writings.

 † *Babeuf:* François-Noël Babeuf, a hard-left ideologue of the French Revolution, guillotined in 1797.

55 · MY HEART LAID BARE

Why is the spectacle of the sea so infinitely and so eternally satisfying?

Because the sea simultaneously suggests to us the idea of immensity and the idea of movement. Six or seven leagues represent the radius of the infinite for man. A diminutive infinity, true. But what does it matter, if it succeeds in suggesting the idea of infinity in its totality? Twelve or fourteen leagues (measured in diameter), twelve or fourteen leagues of liquid in motion are enough to provide man with the most exalted idea of beauty during his brief residence on earth.

56 · MY HEART LAID BARE

Religions are the only interesting things on earth.

What is the universal Religion? (Chateaubriand, de Maistre, the Alexandrians, Capé).*

There is a Universal Religion fit for the Alchemists of Thought, a Religion that emerges from man, considered as a memento of God.

57 · MY HEART LAID BARE

Saint-Marc Girardin has uttered a phrase that will long endure: *Let's be average.*†

Juxtapose this with Robespierre's dictum: "Those who do not believe in the immortality of their being do themselves justice."

Saint-Marc Girardin's injunction implies an immense hatred of the sublime.

---

* *What is the universal religion?:* Alludes to Chateaubriand's *Genius of Christianity* (1802), Joseph de Maistre's *Treatise on Sacrifices* (1821), Philo of Alexandria's synthesis of Greek and Jewish philosophy, and (perhaps, slightly misspelled) Etienne Cabet's heavily Christianized early nineteenth-century utopian socialism.

† *Saint-Marc Girardin:* A liberal, antiromantic literary critic and establishment member of the Académie française. His exact phrase was "Soyons médiocres."

To have seen Saint-Marc Girardin making his way down the street is to have immediately recognized a fat, conceited goose seized by panic and racing this way and that as the coach bears down upon him.

58 · MY HEART LAID BARE

Theory of true civilization.

It does not entail gas, steam, or table-turning; it entails the diminution of the traces of original sin.

Nomadic peoples, hunters, farmers, and even cannibals can *all* prove superior—by their energy, by their personal dignity—to our Western races.*

Which shall possibly be destroyed.

Theocracy and communism.

59 · MY HEART LAID BARE

I grew up, for the most part, on laziness and leisure.

To my great detriment; for idleness, without a fortune, leads to debts and to the affronts that ensue from debts.

But to my great advantage—when it came to sensibility, meditation, and the capacity for dandyism and dilettantism.

Other men of letters are, for the most, vile and ignorant money-grubbers.

60 · MY HEART LAID BARE

The "young lady" of publishers.†
The "young lady" of editors-in-chief.

---

* *our Western races:* Baudelaire here goes against Maistre's demystification of the Rousseauistic "noble savage" in the second of his *Soirées de Saint-Petersbourg*.

† *The "young lady" of publishers:* The *jeune fille*, that fictive figure of female innocence whom publishers and editors and judges would invoke when rejecting material (such as *Madame Bovary* or *Les Fleurs du mal*) that might be deemed offensive or dangerous to the general public.

The scarecrow figure of the "young lady," a monster, an assassin of art. Who and what this "young lady" is in reality.

A little idiot and a little bitch; extreme silliness coupled with extreme depravity.
"Young ladies" combine the despicability of the juvenile delinquent with that of the boarding-school student.

61 · MY HEART LAID BARE

Advice to noncommunists:
Everything is common, even God.

62 · MY HEART LAID BARE

The Frenchman is a barnyard animal, so well domesticated that he dares not break through a single picket fence. Witness his tastes in art and literature.

He's an animal of the Latin race: he does not object to manure in his home, or in his literature. He loves to eat shit. He's crazy about excrement. Barfly littérateurs call this *Gallic salt*.*
A fine example of crassness of the French, this from the nation that thinks of itself as independent before all others.

The following extract from the fine book of M. de Vaulabelle will suffice to give an idea of the impression that Lavalette's escape from prison made on the least enlightened members of the royalist party:†

---

* *Gallic salt:* The ribald version of the dry wit called "Attic salt."
† *Lavalette's escape from prison:* The Count of Lavalette, a prominent official during the Empire of Napoleon, was condemned to death by the Ultras in 1815 at the outset of the Restoration. On the eve of his scheduled execution, he was visited in jail by his wife and daughter (later to become Delacroix's mistress). He escaped by exchanging clothes and places with his wife, who remained in prison in his stead. Vaulabelle's account of this celebrated prison break, taken from his *History of the Two Revolutions* (1855–56), comes from a newspaper clipping pasted in here by Baudelaire.

"The enthusiasm of the royalists, at this particular juncture of the second Restoration, knew no bounds. The young Joséphine de Lavalette was then attending one of the principal convent schools in Paris (l'Abbaye-au-Bois); the only reason she had left its grounds was to go greet her father. When she returned to school after his escape and when it became known that she had played a small part in it, an immense outcry was raised against this child; the nuns and her friends avoided her, and a good number of parents declared that they would withdraw their children from the school were she permitted to remain there. They said that they didn't want their children to be in contact with a young girl who had acted in such a fashion and who had provided such a bad example. When Mme. de Lavalette regained her freedom six weeks later, she was obliged to remove her daughter from the school."

63 · MY HEART LAID BARE

Princes et generations

It is equally unjust to ascribe to ruling sovereigns either the merits or the vices of the nation they are currently governing.

These merits and vices are almost always, as statistics and logic prove, attributable to the climate of the preceding administration.

Louis XIV inherits the administration of Louis XIII. Glory.

Napoleon I inherits the administration of the Republic. Glory.

Louis-Philippe inherits the administration of Charles X. Glory.

Napoleon III inherits the administration of Louis-Philippe. Dishonor.

It's always the previous administration that is responsible for the morals of the following one, inasmuch as an administration can be responsible for anything whatsoever.

The sudden interruptions caused by circumstances do not allow this law to be absolutely exact when it comes to the timing of regime change. One cannot exactly mark out where a given influence ends— but this influence will be felt among the entire generation that experienced it during its younger days.

64 · MY HEART LAID BARE

How the young hate those who quote. They consider a man given to quotations their enemy.

I would even make misspelling a capital offense (Th. Gautier).

———

A fine picture to be drawn: Literary Crooks.

———

Not to forget the portrait of Forgues—the Pirate or Buccaneer of Letters.*

———

The overpowering appetite for prostitution at the heart of man, hence his horror of solitude. —He wants to be *two*. The man of genius want to be *one*, hence solitary.
Glory involves remaining *one*, and prostituting oneself in a special way.
It is this horror of solitude, this need to forget one's *self* in flesh not one's own, that man nobly refers to as *the need to love*.

———

Two noble Religions—graffiti immortalized on walls, permanent obsessions of the masses: a prick (the phallus of antiquity), flanked by "Long Live Barbès!"† or "Down with Philippe!" or "Long Live the Republic!"

---

* *Forgues:* Émile Daurand Forgues had published a virtual plagiarism of Poe's "Murders of the Rue Morgue" in the magazine *Le Commerce* in 1846. In one of his "Marginalia," Poe had similarly accused Eugène Sue of plagiarizing the same story in the ape episode of his *Mysteries of Paris* (1842–43).

† *Long live Barbès:* Armand Barbès, imprisoned for life in 1839 for his participation in a republican plot to overthrow King Louis Philippe. Released in February 1848, he

65 · MY HEART LAID BARE

Examine in all of its modalities—be it in the works of nature or the works of man—the universal and eternal law of gradation: the *by and by*, the *little by little*, with things progressively growing in force, like compound interest on an investment.

The same thing goes for *artistic and literary achievement,* as well as for the variable funds of *willpower.*

66 · MY HEART LAID BARE

The throng of minor scribblers whom one sees at funerals, shaking hands on all sides and recommending themselves to the notice of the newspaper reporter in attendance.
On the funerals of famous men.

67 · MY HEART LAID BARE

Molière. My opinion of *Tartuffe* is that it is not a comedy but a pamphlet. If he considers this play, a proper atheist will observe that one should never leave certain momentous questions to the rabble.

68 · MY HEART LAID BARE

To glorify the cult of images (my great, my single, my earliest passion).

To glorify vagrancy and what might be called Bohemianism, the cult of multiplied sensation, as expressed by music. Refer to Liszt here.*

---

was again imprisoned that May, accused of organizing a coup d'état to create a new provisional government.

* *Liszt:* The composer Franz Liszt had published an essay on the music of the "Bohemians" (i.e., the Gypsies) of Hungary in 1859. Baudelaire's prose poem "The Thyrsus" is dedicated to Liszt.

———

On the necessity of beating women.*
One can punish what one loves. As with children. But this implies
the sorrow of despising what one loves.

———

On Cuckolds and Cuckoldry.
The Sorrows of the Cuckold.

They arise from pride, from a faulty understanding of honor and
happiness, and from a love that has been foolishly turned away from
God and instead assigned to the creaturely realm.
Again and again: the animal who worships, mistaking his idol.

69 · MY HEART LAID BARE

Analyze the insolence of utter imbecility: Clément de Ris and Paul
Pérignon.†

70 · MY HEART LAID BARE

The more a man cultivates the arts, the fewer hard-ons he gets.
He makes a more marked distinction between mind and beast.

---

* *On the necessity of beating women:* Baudelaire at his most Schopenhauerian. As for
the remark on punishing children that follows, the twentieth of Poe's "Fifty Sugges-
tions" reads: "Children are never too tender to be whipped: —like tough beefsteaks,
the more you beat them the more tender they become" (*Brevities,* 487). This meta-
phor returns in Baudelaire's late prose poem "Let's Beat Up the Poor!"
  † *The insolence of utter imbecility:* The aforementioned critic Clément de Ris had de-
nounced the "lasciviousness" of *The Flowers of Evil.* Paul Pérignon was Baudelaire's
mother's half-brother and a member of the hated family council that oversaw the
poet's finances.

Only brutes get great hard-ons, and fucking is the lyricism of the masses.

———

To fuck is to aspire to enter into another, and the artist never leaves himself.

———

I've forgotten the name of that bitch. . . . Ah, what the hell, I'll remember it on Judgment Day.

———

Music conveys the idea of space.
As do all the arts, more or less. Because they are *number* and number is a translation of space.

———

To desire to be the greatest of men, each and every day!!!

71 · MY HEART LAID BARE

As a child, I by turns wanted to be a pope (but a military pope) or an actor.
The intense pleasures that I derived from these two hallucinations.

72 · MY HEART LAID BARE

Still a child, I felt two contradictory emotions pulling at my heart: the horror of life and the ecstasy of life.
A fair characterization of a lazy nervous type.

73 · MY HEART LAID BARE

Nations only produce great men despite themselves.

———

Apropos of the actor and my childhood fantasies, a chapter devoted to what in the human soul gives rise to the vocation of the actor, the glory of the actor, the condition of the actor, and his position in the world.

Legouvé's theory.* Is Legouvé merely a cold-hearted practical joker, a Swift trying to see whether he could get France to swallow another absurdity?

His choice. A good one, in that Samson is not an actor.

On the true grandeur of pariahs.

———

Virtue might very well damage the talents of pariahs.

74 · MY HEART LAID BARE

Commerce is, by its very essence, *satanic.*

—Commerce is tit for tat, it's lending something to someone with the understanding: *Give me back more than I gave you.*

—The mind of the merchant is completely depraved.

—Commerce is *natural* and *therefore despicable.*

—The least despicable of merchants is the one who says: Let's be virtuous so that we can make far more money than those vice-ridden fools.

—For the merchant, even honesty offers a money-making opportunity.

—Commerce is satanic because it is the basest and vilest form of egoism.

* *Legouvé's theory:* Playwright and French Academician Ernest Legouvé published a pamphlet in 1863 recommending that the Croix d'Honneur be henceforth awarded to actors, notably to Samson, author of comedies and professor at the Conservatoire.

75 · MY HEART LAID BARE

When Jesus Christ says, "Blessed are those who are starving, for their hunger shall be satisfied," he is calculating probabilities.

76 · MY HEART LAID BARE

The world works only through Misunderstanding.

—It's through universal Misunderstanding that everybody comes to agreement.

—If, by some misfortune, everybody understood each other, one could never come to agree.

———

The man of wit—who will never be in agreement with anybody—should make it a point to enjoy the conversation of imbeciles and the reading of worthless books. He will derive bitter pleasures from this, pleasures that will largely compensate him for his efforts.

77 · MY HEART LAID BARE

Bureaucrats, ministers, theater directors, newspaper editors can sometimes be estimable creatures, but they are never divine. They are persons with no personality, creatures without originality, born to exercise their profession, that is, to be the servants of the public.

78 · MY HEART LAID BARE

God and his profundity.

It takes insight to seek in God the accomplice and friend one has always lacked. God is the eternal confidant in this tragedy of which every man is the hero. There perhaps exist usurers and murderers who say to God: "Lord, arrange things so that my next venture might prove successful!" But the prayers of these loathsome creatures do not spoil the honor and the pleasure of mine.

79 · MY HEART LAID BARE

Every idea is, in and of itself, blessed with an immortal life, as is every human being.

Every form that is created, even by man, is immortal. For form is independent of matter; form is not made up of molecules.

———

Anecdotes about Émile Douay and Constantin Guys, destroying or rather thinking they were destroying their works.*

80 · MY HEART LAID BARE

It is impossible to read through any newspaper, whatever the day or month or year, without discovering in every line the signs of the most appalling perversity of man, and at the same time the most astonishing *boasts* of integrity, kindness, and charity, along with the most outrageous affirmations concerning progress and civilization.

Every newspaper, from the first line to the last, is a tissue of horrors. War, crime, theft, shamelessness, torture, crimes of kings, crimes of nations, crimes of individuals, the whole world drunk on atrocities.

And this is the disgusting aperitif that accompanies the morning repast of civilized man every day. Everything in this world positively reeks of crime: newspapers, walls, human faces.

* *Émile Douay and Constantin Guys:* Douay was a composer whom Baudelaire approached for a musical setting of his translation of Henry Wadsworth Longfellow's *Song of Hiawatha* (1861). Baudelaire describes Guys ripping up or burning the drawings of his youth in "The Painter of Modern Life." Cf. the painter Frenhofer in Balzac's short story "The Unknown Masterpiece" (1831).

I cannot understand how a clean hand could touch a newspaper without a shudder of disgust.

81 · MY HEART LAID BARE

The power of amulets proved by philosophy. Piercings of the ground, talismans, everyone's memories.

Treatise on moral Dynamics.*
On the virtue of the Sacraments.

Ever since childhood, a tendency toward mysticism. My conversations with God.

82 · MY HEART LAID BARE

On Obsession, on Possession
On Prayer, on Faith.
The moral Dynamics of Jesus.

(Renan thinks it ridiculous that Jesus might have believed in the omnipotence, or even the material power, of Prayer and Faith.)

The sacraments are how these Dynamics are effectuated.

———

On the infamy of print, a major obstacle to the development of Beauty.

———

* *moral Dynamics:* See the note to folio 8 of *Flares*.

To organize a fine conspiracy for the extermination of the Jewish race.*

The Jews, *Librarians* and witnesses of the *Redemption.*†

83 · MY HEART LAID BARE

All these imbeciles of the Bourgeoisie who prattle on about "morality and immorality in art" and other such nonsense make me think of Louise Villedieu, a two-bit whore who, accompanying me one day to the Louvre, which she had never before visited, started to blush and cover up her face and, pulling me this way and that by the sleeve, asked me, as we stood there gazing upon the immortal paintings and statues, how one dared place indecencies of this sort on public display.

---

* *To organize a fine conspiracy for the extermination of the Jewish race:* In his essay "The Paris of the Second Empire in Baudelaire" (in *The Writer of Modern Life,* 46), Walter Benjamin discusses Baudelaire's "metaphysics of the *provocateur*" and cites this extravagant proposal as a precursor of the *culte de la blague* found in Céline's 1937 pamphlet, *Bagatelles pour un massacre* (*Trifles for a Massacre*). A similar instance of incendiary *blague* may be found in chapter 21 of Baudelaire's *Belgium Disrobed,* where he suggests that the country not be annexed but rather be subjected to an Algeria-style colonialist *razzia,* that is, a punitive *raid* that would pillage all its valuable works of art and bring them back as war plunder to the Louvre in the fashion of Napoleon. That Baudelaire might indeed be speaking tongue in cheek in this much-debated passage of *My Heart Laid Bare* is borne out in part by his satire of Belgian anti-Semitism in chapter 11 of *Belgium Disrobed:* "General lack of integrity. / 'Beware of the Jews!' / 'Especially beware of the German-Russians!' / What a German-Russian is." See Richard Burton, "Baudelaire, Belgians, Jews," *Essays in French Literature* 6 (1998–99): 69–112.

† *The Jews, Librarians:* According to Jean Starobinski ("Notes de Lecture III," *L'Année Baudelaire* 6 [2002]: 148–54), these are standard Christian topoi regarding the Jews, which Baudelaire may well be critiquing as clichés. Saint Augustine famously referred to the Jews as "our librarians" and "guardians of our books." Pascal similarly describes them as "witnesses" to the Messiah and preservers of sacred books they do not comprehend. Does this, however, link them to the "infamy of print" of which Baudelaire speaks two lines earlier (in which some have read an allusion to his Jewish publisher, Michel Lévy, whose "avarice" Baudelaire described as "ignoble" in an 1865 letter to Ancelle)? See Brett Bowles, "Poetic Practice and Historical Paradigm: Charles Baudelaire's Anti-Semitism," *PMLA* 115 (2000): 195–208.

———

The fig leaves of Monsieur Nieuwerkerke.*

84 · MY HEART LAID BARE

For the law of progress to exist, everyone would have to want to implement it; that is, only when every individual had made efforts to progress, then, only then, would mankind experience progress.

This hypothesis may serve to explain the identity of two contradictory ideas—freedom and fate. –Not only will there be, in the case of progress, an identity between freedom and fate, but this identity has always existed. This identity is *history*, the history of nations and of individuals.

85 · MY HEART LAID BARE

Sonnet to be quoted in *My Heart Laid Bare*.
Also quote the piece on *Roland*.

I dreamt last night that I saw Phyllis as proud
And lovely as ere she was in the light of day;
She hoped her ghost with me again might lay,
And that, Ixion-like, I might embrace a cloud.

Into my bed her naked shade did slip,
Saying, "Damon, dear, do you recognize my face?
I have grown yet lovelier in that sad old place
Where since I left you Fate hath made me live.

* *Monsieur Nieuwerkerke:* General director of French museums and superintendent of fine arts (1849–70), responsible for covering up the male genitals of classical statuary.

I have come to kiss the handsomest of faces,
I have come to die again in your fierce embraces."
Then, when this idol had devoured me whole,

She said, "Adieu! I now return among the dead,
You who once boasted of having fucked my flesh,
You can now boast of having fucked my soul."
                                    Parnasse satyrique

I think this sonnet is by Maynard.*
Malassis is convinced it is by Racan.

---

* *Maynard:* This 1620 sonnet (which turns out to be by the poet Théophile de Viau) was first published without attribution in 1861 by Malassis in his Brussels-based magazine, *Parnasse satyrique*. Baudelaire also quotes this sonnet in a letter to Sainte-Beuve of January 2, 1866, which helps date this page. Baudelaire apparently intended to contrast the erotic verve of this sonnet with "the piece on Roland," a twenty-stanza 1833 poem in alexandrines by Napoléon Preyat, written shortly after France's invasion of Algeria and which was addressed to the heroic memory of Roland the Paladin while also celebrating the eventual historic French defeat of the Moors. This wretched, proto-Kiplingesque colonialist ballad ("Malheur aux mécréants! Malheur aux circoncis! / "Malheur," dit Charlemagne, en fronçant ses sourcils") had been included in the fourth volume of Eugène Crépet's *Poètes français: Recueil des chefs-d'oeuvre de la poésie française depuis les origines jusqu'à nos jours,* published by Hachette in 1862. This same volume of modern poets edited by Crépet (for whom Baudelaire had great contempt as an arriviste editor and anthologist) also included a selection from *Les Fleurs du mal*, introduced by Gautier. With the publication of Baudelaire's *Oeuvres posthumes* in 1887, Eugène Crépet came to dominate Baudelaire studies through his acquisitions of manuscripts and editions of the poet's various works and correspondence; in this family venture, he was succeeded in the twentieth century by his son Jacques. Peyrat's poem "Roland" is reproduced in full in André Guyaux's recent revised Folio edition of *Fusées, Mon Coeur mis à nu, et autres fragments posthumes* (Paris: Gallimard, 2016), 200–204.

PART TWO

*Late Prose
Poems and
Projects*

Introduction

Whereas the scraps of *Flares, My Heart Laid Bare,* and *Belgian Disrobed* remained unpublished during Baudelaire's lifetime, most of his poèmes en prose appeared in print over the last six years of his life, their places of publication ranging from little magazines and bohemian journals to mass-circulation dailies. As with his other contributions to the periodical press, Baudelaire counted on his prose poems as a source of literary revenue, however modest. It has been estimated that for each one of these "fragments" (as he inevitably referred to them in his correspondence, just as Rimbaud referred to the prose poems of his *Illuminations* as "fraguements") he received a hundred francs.[1] Hence his temptation to submit the same texts over and over to various editors without disclosing their prior appearance elsewhere: of the forty-two separate prose poems published by Baudelaire, he managed to reprint nearly a quarter of them (some as many as four times) in twelve separate periodicals, amounting to seventy-one publications in all—a dubious tactic that allowed him to squeeze the utmost out of his dwindling literary capital. Eventually, he began to think of gathering these dispersed fragments into an independent volume to be entitled *Le Spleen de Paris*, conceived as a "pendant" to the verse of the *Fleurs du mal*. The precise content and organization of this *livre à venir*, however, continued to elude him, and at his death this major work-in-progress still lay unfinished, like all his other late projects.

Baudelaire's first substantial batch of prose poems appeared in August 1857 in an obscure little magazine, *Le Présent*, that soon went bankrupt. Published the very same month that he learned of the imperial court's decision to mutilate his *Flowers of Evil*, this series of *Poèmes nocturnes* (or *Night Poems*) consisted of six thematically interlinked texts, three of which were transpositions (or "doublets") of poems previously composed in verse. At the very outset, then, Baudelaire's invention of a new genre of *poème en prose* emerged out of his common practice of *rewriting*, whether this involved his tendency to tinker with (or *triturer*, as he called it) his own poetry in revision or, in the case of his translations of Poe or De Quincey, to reword his English-language alter egos into French—to which might be added his habit of often citing previously published passages of his own work in his critical essays, a form of self-plagiarism that allowed him to advantageously pad out his paid articles when short on cash or inspiration. By quoting himself, by "translating" himself, by repeating himself with a difference, by transposing himself out of rhyme and meter onto the unlineated page, Baudelaire's innovation when it came to the prose poem was to conceive it as the revisionary *après coup* or aftermath of the lyric, and not just merely (as he observed in one of his letters) as a preparatory sketch for some perfected verse composition to come.[2]

After this initial 1857 burst of experimentation (which was greeted with mockery by the wags of the Parisian *petits journaux*, for whom Baudelaire in the wake of his trial had become a figure of fun), he seems to have left work on his *Night Poems* in abeyance for four years, when, after the publication of the second, revised edition of his *Flowers of Evil* in 1861, he issued another assemblage of prose poems in Catulle Mendès's *Revue fantaisiste*—nine texts in all, six of which had already been published and three new ones, explicitly urban in inspiration and taking their cue from the "Tableaux parisiens" ("Parisian Views") section recently added to his *Fleurs du mal*. These three, "Les Foules" ("Crowds"), "Les Veuves" ("Widows"), and "Le Vieux Saltimbanque" ("The Old Acrobat"), attracted the attention of the eminent critic Sainte-Beuve, who in one of his articles referred to what he called these "*petits poèmes en prose*" as "jewels." As Antoine Compagnon observes, Saint-Beuve's adjective "petit" (short, small, brief) served not only to distinguish these prose poems from the preexisting genre of epic "poems in prose" (such as Fénelon's *Télémaque*) but also to suggest that their brevity placed them in the category of miniature—if not outright minor—works of art.[3] Indeed, to the very end, Sainte-Beuve would persist in seeing Baudelaire as a *poeta minor*. In his letters to the critic, the poet would out of deference to his master accordingly refer to his prose poems in the diminutive as mere "baubles" or "trifles"—while secretly hoping that Sainte-Beuve would finally recognize them as the true "masterpieces" they were.

Baudelaire's work in progress continued to evolve through 1861. In December of that year, he wrote to Arsène Houssaye, the literary editor of the city's second-largest daily, *La Presse*, proposing the publication of a series of forty to fifty prose poems tentatively to be entitled *Le Promeneur solitaire* (in homage to Rousseau's *Reveries of a Solitary Walker)* or *Le Rôdeur parisien* (in evocation of Rétif de la Bretonne's and Sébastien Mercier's nocturnal prowlings through the capital). Both titles placed the mobile consciousness of the *flâneur* at the center of these compositions—a figure whose peripatetic immersions into the urban crowd he had already portrayed in his unpublished essay on Constantin Guys, "The Painter of Modern Life." Baudelaire's breakthrough was to take the roving, filmic sensibility of the flâneur, ever subject to the shocks (or "soubresauts") of the modern metropolis, and to make it the basis for a new kind of poetic structure entirely made up of colliding, transitory parts. In a rough draft of this same letter to Houssaye (see appendix 1), he described how he imagined the eventual serial newspaper publication of these prose poems might work:

The title.
The dedication.

Without head or tail. Everything head and tail.
Convenient for you. Convenient for me. Convenient for the Reader.
We can all break off wherever we so choose—I my reverie, you the manuscript, the reader his reading. I refuse to hitch anybody's unruly will to the endless thread of some superfluous plot.
I've looked for titles. 66 of them. Even though this work, which is like both a screw and a kaleidoscope, could be pushed toward the cabbalistic 666 or even 6666. . . .
This is worth more than a plot strung out over 6000 pages. So let one at least be grateful for my moderation.

The draft ends with an allusion to "the small stumps" ("petits tronçons") into which the "whole snake" of this work might be cut—a metaphor made more explicit in the published version of his dedicatory letter to Houssaye: "Remove a vertebra, and the two pieces of this tortuous fantasy will easily rejoin. Hack it into numerous fragments, and you will see that each of them can exist apart."[4]

At the time of this writing, Baudelaire had published only nine separate prose poems. That he should claim to have sixty-six titles on hand indicates that his project was indeed still largely a "tortuous fantasy" or a "cabbalistic" reverie on the number 6. (Around this same period, he would also offer Houssaye the bits and pieces of another imaginary work, *Sixty-Six Suggestions* in the manner of Poe.) Six is traditionally the numeral of sin, evil, and imperfection, while 666 is the very name of the Beast—appropriate allegories for this satanic snake that, like a screw (or thyrsus), would spiral around itself in serpentine coils or, like a kaleidoscope, twist everything it refracted into a swirling pattern of imagistic shards. The exponential progression of the number 6 suggests that Baudelaire at this stage conceived his work in progress as an open, infinitely extensible montage of cinematic shots that could be recombined (or respliced) according to the editor's or reader's or poet's directorial whim (in another 1861 letter he noted that his collection of prose poems would be of "indefinite length").[5] Recognizing that the average newspaper subscriber consumed his daily fare in a state of wayward distraction that could only be overcome by addicting him to "a plot strung out over 6000 pages," Baudelaire offered his work as a nonnarrative alternative to the popular suspense fictions published by *La Presse*. Indeed, when they finally appeared in its pages in the late summer of 1862, Baudelaire's "Petits poèmes en prose," prefaced by his dedicatory letter to Houssaye, were featured in the space normally reserved for its *romans feuilleton*—printed in six lateral columns on the rez-de-chausée (or bottom third) of the first and second leaves of the newspaper, the title of each poem preceded by a Roman numeral, in imitation of the separate chapters of a serial novel.[6] Appealing to the attention deficit disorder of his readers, Baudelaire had reduced Poe's recommended length for a short story to even less than a single sitting.

A total of twenty prose poems (fourteen of them brand-new) were published in *La Presse* over three issues in August and September. A fourth installment was set up in galleys but withdrawn from print at the last moment, presumably because Houssaye had discovered that five of the six poems submitted by Baudelaire had previously appeared elsewhere. Baudelaire was devastated. He attempted to justify himself to Houssaye: a number of his more dated pieces had been completely revised (which was true), and if he had blended "the old, the new, and the rejuvenated" in his submissions, it was because "I wanted to give the reader a complete idea of the full extent of the work, conceived ages ago." He requested that "the *totality* of the manuscript" be printed in *La Presse* before he decided to issue the work as a separate volume. To no avail.[7]

While pursuing his dream of their ongoing serial publication, Baudelaire had also been negotiating with Pierre-Jules Hetzel for the publication of his prose poems in book form, possibly as a "romantic book with images"—indeed, it was Hetzel who had applied pressure on Houssaye to publish them in the first place, informing him that "Baudelaire is certainly the most original prose-writer and the most personal poet of our time—there is no newspaper that should delay the publication of this strange classicist of things unclassical."[8] Hetzel, the publisher of George Sand and Balzac, was an ex-forty-eighter who after Louis Napoleon's coup d'état had chosen sanctuary in Brussels, where he brought out the exiled Victor Hugo's jeremiads against the emperor (*Les Châtiments*) in 1853—a distant verse precursor to the prophetic wrath of Baudelaire's *Belgium Disrobed*. After the amnesty of 1859, Hetzel returned to Paris, where he published left-wing works by Proudhon and Zola and, most profitably, illustrated children's books and the science fiction of Jules Verne. He was to be among Baudelaire's warmest supporters during his difficult later years, sharing the occasional *faro* beer with him in Brussels and visiting him in the Dubois clinic in the months before his death.

In early 1863, Hetzel gave Baudelaire an advance of 1,200 francs against the rights to his *Poèmes en prose* (unfinished), *Les Fleurs du mal* (which already belonged to Malassis), and the (barely extant) *Mon Coeur mis à nu*. Hetzel patiently waited two and half years before absolving Baudelaire of his contractual obligations. Meanwhile, the poet kept him abreast of his inability to complete the work he had now come to call *Le Spleen de Paris*. That March he wrote him: "The truth is I am unhappy with the book: I have to revise it, *remold* it"—but promised to deliver the manuscript within a month, assuring Hetzel that it would make a book at once "singular" and "easy to sell."[9] In October, he lied to him that the third, revised and enlarged edition of his *Flowers of Evil* was almost ready to go; as for *Paris Spleen*, "it will contain a hundred pieces—of which thirty are still lacking," but he swore to him that once he managed to escape from the irritations of Paris, he could easily complete the missing thirty texts in Honfleur within a fortnight, for a book publication the following month—a patently delusional pledge.[10] The mention of "a hundred pieces," however, represented a significant departure from his earlier conception of his work in progress as an open-ended (66, 666, 6,666) montage of fragments, for the number "a hundred" hearkened back to the century of titles that had made up the original 1857 edition of *Les Fleurs du mal*—before its careful architecture was destroyed by the courts. Not only would the hundred prose poems of *Paris Spleen* therefore provide the exact numerical (and reparative) "pendant" to his volume of verse as originally published, but they would also, like his *Flowers of Evil*, be grouped along a series of major thematic axes. Baudelaire's notes for the book show that, while in Belgium, he considered dividing it into three major categories: (1) "Choses Parisiennes" ("Things Parisian"); (2) "Onéirocritie" ("Interpretations of Dreams"); and (3) "Symboles et Moralités" ("Symbols and Moral Lessons")—an amalgam of the urban, the oneiric, and the allegorical that echoed the new "Tableaux parisiens" section of his 1861 *Fleurs du mal*.[11]

Baudelaire never resolved the formal contradictions of his *Paris Spleen* project. Through the early 1860s he continued to pursue it as a work in progress, placing successive batches of poems in various magazines and newspapers such as *Revue nationale et étrangère*, *L'Artiste*, and *Le Figaro*. His tone with editors was sometimes taunting: to reimburse a debt still owed to the director of *La Vie parisienne*, he offered to send him "a packet" of some thirty *Poems in Prose* that he had sitting on his table while warning him that they contained "horrors and monstrosities that would cause your pregnant lady readers to abort"—a surefire guarantee of rejection.[12] With other editors, he endlessly quibbled about commas and unauthorized cuts, leading him to withdraw his manuscripts in pique. Meanwhile, he stalled on the actual physical book he still owed Hetzel—to be published in tandem with his *Flowers of Evil* and whose one hundred titles would recall its lost perfection of yore. As late as April 1865, already in Brussels for a year and having received numerous extensions from his indulgent publisher, Baudelaire was still announcing (in a letter only recently rediscovered) the imminent appearance of this virtual book: "The *poems in prose* will appear in the second half of this year with Hetzel under the title *Paris Spleen,* so as to provide a pendant to *The Flowers of Evil.* The fragments that have so far appeared were arranged in no order. In the volume, however, there will be a specific classification."[13] With his mother, however, he was more cautious:

> Yes, I'm continuing with the *Poems in Prose.* And well I should, because they have been under contract for two years. . . . But I am proceeding slowly, very slowly. The atmosphere of this country is most depressing, and what's more, as you might have noticed from the forty or fifty that have already appeared, the crafting of these little trifles demands a great concentration of mind. Nonetheless, I hope to succeed in producing a singular work, more singular or at least more spontaneous than the *Flowers of Evil,* a work in which I'll mingle the frightening with the farcical and even tenderness with hate.[14]

To Sainte-Beuve he similarly blamed his plight on Brussels, largely because the city offered no occasion for real *flânerie:*

> Alas, the *Poems in Prose* are lagging behind. I'm always taking on difficult tasks. Coming up with a *hundred* laborious bagatelles demands that one constantly be in good spirits (necessary even to treat subjects that are sad), in a bizarre state of excitement that feeds on spectacles, on crowds, on music, on gaslights even—this is what I had in mind! I'm only up to *sixty* [that is, forty], and cannot advance any further. What I need is a good *bath of multitude,* to use that disreputable term which so justifiably shocked you [in the prose poem "Crowds"].[15]

Baudelaire was stuck. Fortunately (or unfortunately) for him, three months later Hetzel would release him from his contract in order to avoid litigation with Malassis (who, unbeknown to Hetzel, still owned the rights to *Les Fleurs du mal*). In July 1865, Baudelaire made a panicked visit to Paris to settle the Balzacian legal mess into which he had manipulated his two close publisher friends: in the end, Malassis's creditors (who owned Baudelaire's promissory notes) were temporarily paid off and Hetzel's advance would later be quietly reimbursed by the poet's mother. While in Paris, Baudelaire deposited a "packet" of recent prose poems with his new literary agent Julien Lemer in the hopes of further magazine and eventual book publication. Whether through Lemer's incompetence or dishonesty, both propositions fell through—and, upon the poet's return to Brussels, in failing health, Baudelaire eventually abandoned all hope for his chimerical project. Its remains were published in 1869, two years after his death, under the Sainte-Beuvian title *Petits Poèmes en prose* (and *not* as *Le Spleen de Paris*), in volume 4 of his collected works—whose pages it shared with *Les Paradis artificiels*, a compendium of his writings on drugs and of his translation of De Quincey's *Confessions of an English Opium Eater*, as well as with an early novella, *La Fanfarlo*, and his proto-Benjaminian 1855 essay on children's toys, "Morale du joujou." Edited by Asselineau and Banville, the *Little Poems in Prose* came to a mere fifty texts, prefaced by Baudelaire's dedicatory epistle to Houssaye—a trace of its early origins as a serial newspaper poem.

*   *   *

The eleven prose poems I have translated below all date from Baudelaire's final years in Belgium. I have followed the order in which they appear as numbers XL–L of the 1869 edition, which was based on a late table of contents the poet had compiled in Brussels and on the "packet" of manuscripts deposited in Paris in July 1865 with Gervais Charpentier, editor of the staid *Revue nationale et étrangère*. Charpentier refused to publish any of these pieces during the poet's lifetime, no doubt offended by what Baudelaire in a late letter to Sainte-Beuve referred to as the "disagreeable moral lessons" that his poet-flâneur had extracted from every object or figure accidently encountered in the course of his "rhapsodic" wanderings.[16] With the exception of three pieces, the publications of these prose poems were therefore all posthumous, like all the other fragments I have gathered in this volume.

The sequence opens with two short poems, "The Mirror" and "The Port," both published in the *Revue de Paris* on Christmas Day 1864, and both Belgian in inspiration. "The Mirror" is what critics call a *poème-boutade,* a sarcastic flash of wit, an ill-tempered quip, a come-dian's shtick, ending (as do many of Baudelaire's prose poems) with a punch line:

> A frightful-looking man comes in and looks at himself in the mirror.
> "Why look at yourself in the mirror? You'll only feel disgust at what you see."
> The frightful-looking man answers me: "Monsieur, according to the immortal principles of '89, all men are equal in their rights. Therefore it is my right to look at myself in the mirror. Whether I do so with plea-sure or disgust is of concern only to my conscience." Common sense was no doubt on my side. But from a legal standpoint, he could hardly be faulted.

This poem has been compared to the legends Daumier used to affix to his caricatures—in which an anecdote drawn from everyday bour-geois life is heightened into comic allegory (here, the traditional scene of Vanitas at its mirror).[17] At the antipodes of Baudelaire's aristocratic dandy who "must aspire to be sublime without interruption" and who therefore "must live and sleep before a mirror," this hideous individ-ual, convinced of the equal rights of every man to political or aesthetic representation, no matter how lowly or ugly he may be, is incapable of irony—that is, of self-reflexivity—taking his own democratized image at the letter, mistaking man (instead of God) for the measure of all things. Of this monster Oscar Wilde would later quip in the preface to *The Pic-ture of Dorian Gray*: "The nineteenth-century dislike of romanticism is the rage of Caliban not seeing his own face in a glass. The nineteenth-century dislike of realism is the rage of Caliban seeing his own face in a glass."[18] Seen from the perspective of Baudelaire's Hôtel du Grand Miroir in Brussels, the modern world had become a grotesque fun-house mirror in which every shade of difference and distinction was now being distorted into the egalitarian reproduction of the same.

The lyrical cadences of "The Port," the companion poem in the Christ-mas issue of the *Revue de Paris*, provide a pastoral corrective to the terse satire of "The Mirror," its dockside seascape lensed through the "prism" of the imagination rather than through the literal-minded mimesis of

the looking glass, and its "mysterious and aristocratic pleasure" en-
tirely derived from the nonproductive, nonutilitarian act of aesthetic
contemplation:

> For a soul worn out by the battles of life, a port offers a pleasant re-
> treat. The vast expanse of the sky, the mobile architecture of the clouds,
> the changing colors of the sea, the scintillations of the lighthouses—all
> provide a prism marvelously suited to entertain the eye without ever
> wearying it. The soaring shapes of the ships with their intricate rig-
> gings, harmoniously swaying to and fro in the sea swell, serve to en-
> tertain the soul's appetite for rhythm and beauty. And above all, for
> someone who has lost all curiosity and ambition, there is a kind of mys-
> terious and aristocratic pleasure to be had in contemplating, as he re-
> clines on the belvedere or props his elbows on the jetty, all this activity
> of people leaving or returning, people still possessed of willpower, of
> the desire to travel or to make their fortunes.

This reverie may have been inspired by Baudelaire's visit to the bus-
tling Flemish port of Anvers/Antwerp in the summer of 1864—by far
his favorite city in Belgium (and, as his last line indicates, the country's
most prosperous mercantile link to the colonial riches of the Dutch
East Indies). Behind this "Invitation au voyage," however, lies the nos-
talgic memory of his mother's cottage overlooking the harbor of Hon-
fleur, a fantasy safe haven where he dreamed he might finally complete
all his unfinished projects, all his failed departures.[19]

This disabused desire to multiply (or annihilate) the here and now
by its constant displacement into an ever-receding elsewhere provides
the subject for the late "Anywhere Out of the World," the manuscript of
which was, according to Huysman's 1884 novel *À rebours*, said to hang in
its hero Des Esseintes's library. A Yeatsian dialogue of self and soul, the
poem rehearses a series of imaginary ports of call: Lisbon, Rotterdam,
Batavia (in Dutch Surinam), and then, veering north into the septen-
trion, Tornio (in Lapland), gateway to those polar wastes where "the
sun only glances the earth obliquely and the slow alternations of light
and night eliminate variety and heighten monotony—this moiety the
void." The fluid death wish of the poem is structurally held into place
by two quotations from English-speaking authors: its first line, "Life is

a hospital where each patient is driven by the desire to change beds," is an apothegm translated from Emerson, while its last line (in French) and its title (in English) are taken from Thomas Hood's ballad "The Bridge of Sighs," praised by Poe in "The Poetic Principle," narrating the suicide of a homeless pregnant girl who, as she leaps to her death from London's Waterloo Bridge, hopes she will be "Swift to be hurl'd / —Anywhere, anywhere / Out of the world."[20] In one of his late unpublished compositions, transcribed under his dictation by his Belgian friend Arthur Stevens in April 1865, Baudelaire pursued the translational drive of "Anywhere out of the World" one step further: he rendered all 106 lines of Hood's original poem into (unrhymed, unmetered) verse, in the process imagining *vers libre*, the next great revolution in French poetics after the prose poem, twenty years before Gustave Kahn, Jules Laforgue, and Arthur Rimbaud.[21]

With the exception of "Good Dogs," explicitly situated in Brussels, the locales of the various other prose poems Baudelaire composed in Belgium remain deliberately vague: the scenes they evoke could, as he had explained to Houssaye, take place anywhere in "a modern and more abstract life."[22] "Portraits of Mistresses," the closest Baudelaire comes to writing a full-fledged short story in the style of a Barbey d'Aurevilly or a Maupassant (and which, in a denouement straight out of Poe, culminates in a murder), is set in a smoking lounge adjoining an elegant brothel where four anonymous roués misogynistically weigh the relative merits of their former mistresses in order to kill time. "The Gallant Marksman" in turn involves an excursion to the countryside to visit a nameless shooting gallery where, again to kill time, a husband targets the effigy of a doll and, telling his wife and muse, "I'm figuring it's you," decapitates it with a single shot, before thanking her for having inspired his perfect (because both literal and figurative) homicidal aim.[23] The cartoonish "Soup and Clouds" is staged in a generic dining room, with its first-person narrator absent-mindedly contemplating the "mobile architecture" of the clouds beyond the window while his mistress violently tries to drag him back down to earth, shouting that his soup is about to get cold: "Allez-vous bientôt manger votre soupe, sacré bougre de marchand de nuages?"—this unprintable obscenity ("you blasted bugger") hurled at her "cloudmonger" no doubt being one of the reasons this poem was also rejected by the *Revue nationale et étrangère*. The slapstick catastrophe in which the poet loses his laurels in "Lost Halo," another image out of the annals of nineteenth-century French carica-ture, occurs while he is crossing the traffic of some unidentified ur-ban thoroughfare—although the equine (and egalitarian) "muck of the macadam" into which his poetic halo unceremoniously plops suggests a memory of Haussmann's paved Paris rather than the experience of cobblestoned Brussels.

Baudelaire often made visits to his friend Arthur Stevens in Uccle, a suburb of Brussels. On one of these summer strolls he apparently sighted a road sign advertising a drinking establishment called Tavern on the Tombs, the source of the epigraph for the poem "Cemetery and Shooting Range"—*À la vue du cimitière, Estaminet*. "*Estaminet*," a north-ern regionalism for a lower-class bar, suggests a site in Belgium, but Baudelaire is more interested in underscoring the universal locus of this *memento mori*, turning as does on the traditional trope of "The Skel-eton at the Banquet."[24] After a paragraph devoted to a jokey allegorical interpretation of the tavern's sepulchral name, the poet-flâneur wan-ders down to the cemetery grounds, where the prose suddenly blos-soms into an impressionist plein-air passage straight out of Flaubert: "Indeed, the light and the heat down there were blazing; one would have said that the sun was drunk, pitched headlong across the carpet of magnificent flowers that fed off the ripe loam of decomposition. An im-mense murmur of life filled the air—the life of infinitely small things—punctuated at regular intervals by the crackle of gunfire from a nearby shooting range, champagne corks exploding through the muted hum of a symphony." Just as abruptly, the poem again shifts back into the reg-ister of allegory, ending with a rather baroque prosopopoeia in which the voice of Death, rising from among the tombs, warns the marksmen that they are merely wasting their time disturbing the dead instead of aiming their carbines at what should be their true target: "life in all its unspeakable horror."

Baudelaire's final prose poems are shot through with violence—as are the contemporary notes for *Belgium Disrobed* in which he reports on the savagery of the local customs ("Rape of a child of fourteen years," "Dog eaten alive: Price of admission: 20 francs," "A father gets drunk: he castrates his son") while indicating, only half-ironically, that he too has gotten caught up in this contagion of ferocity: "Packs of women

by whom I was attacked, only managing to fend them off with my ci-
gar." In an 1864 letter to Nadar, he confesses how he had for no reason
assaulted a stranger on the street: "Can you believe that *I* could have
beaten up a Belgian? Unbelievable, no? Entirely absurd that I should
beat anybody up. And what was even more monstrous in this case, I
was completely in the wrong. So, my sense of justice regaining its hold
on me, I ran after the man to offer him my excuses. But he was nowhere
to be found."[25] This Chaplinesque *acte gratuit* apparently provided the
seed for "Let's Beat Up the Poor!" the most enigmatically political of
Baudelaire's late prose poems—in which, playing the role of an agent
provocateur, he tosses a verbal grenade at both the complacent pieties
of bourgeois philanthropy and the utopian projects of socialist revolu-
tion. Narrated in a first-person impersonation of a boulevardier wit,
the poem tells the retrospective story of a dandy-intellectual who, back
in 1848, had holed himself up in his room to devour the political tracts
of the day. Driven into a state of "vertigo or idiocy" by his readings and
desperately in need of a drink, he ventures outdoors. As he is about to
enter a café, he crosses paths with an old beggar and, seized by Poe's
hysterical imp of the perverse (or, more precisely, by Socrates's *daimon*
whispering in his ear), decides to administer a beating to the mendi-
cant—in order to demonstrate the axiom that "to be someone else's
equal, you have to prove it; to be truly worthy of liberty, you have to
conquer it" (a Nietzschean precept that the hideous democrat in "The
Mirror" refused to grasp). Having first made sure that there are no po-
lice around in the deserted *banlieue*, he proceeds to punch the beggar
in the eye and then smashes his head against a wall and thrashes him
with the branch of a tree. But instead of taking his punishment lying
down, the old man reacts—"O what a joy for the philosopher verifying
his theory"—and, filled with hate, returns his attacker's blows, black-
ening both of his eyes and breaking four of his teeth. Signaling that he
now considers the discussion closed, our philosopher gets back up on
his feet to inform the pauper, "Monsieur, *you are now my equal!*" and
asks him to do him the honor of sharing his purse, instructing him that
"should any of your colleagues ask you for a handout, don't forget (if
you are truly a philanthropist) to apply the theory that it has been my
pain to test out on your back." The beggar agrees. Story over. Theory
proved—by the sadomasochistic exchange of pleasure for pain.[26]

The manuscript version of the poem, however, adds the following present-tense kicker to its retrospective narrative: "What do you have to say to this, Citizen Proudhon?"—which was subsequently eliminated in all printed versions of the text. This censored apostrophe to the celebrated anarcho-socialist philosopher Pierre-Joseph Proudhon (most famously associated with the slogan "Property is theft"), here delivered in the familiar, republican *tu* form (as opposed to the formal *vous* in which the beggar is addressed) considerably complicates any easy reading of this poem as a reactionary Maistrian practical joke. Baudelaire had known Proudhon back in 1848, just before the philosopher was clapped into jail for three years for having insulted President Louis-Napoléon Bonaparte. Two letters from that August survive in which the young poet-activist (and *mouchard*) Baudelaire warns his mentor that there is a plot afoot to have him assassinated—this, around the same time that Baudelaire was promulgating the philosopher's theories of "egalitarian exchange" during his brief career as a political journalist. Proudhon's death in January 1865 thus came as a blow: *L'Indépendance belge* ran a disparaging obituary notice that Baudelaire clipped for inclusion in his *Belgium Disrobed*, where he also remembered the philosopher's political exile in Brussels and the publicity surrounding his expulsion from the kingdom in 1863 for having published a letter facetiously inviting the French emperor to annex his neighbor—a deportation that Baudelaire feared might equally befall him were his own satirical book ever to be published in the land of *bêtise*.[27]

"Citizen Proudhon," the object of the poem's address (at least in its manuscript version), is thus a secret sharer of its autobiographical narrator—a comrade in arms back in 1848, a fellow exile in Belgium, and now a shade ambivalently to be mourned. Left-wing readings of "Let's Beat Up the Poor!" discover in the dandy's charitable sharing of his purse with the beggar an homage to Proudhon's theories of "mutualism," in which the working class would secede from the institutions of finance capitalism (and its state-sponsored organs of philanthropic social welfare) in order to establish its own alternative bank, based on a usury-free and egalitarian exchange of goods and services—something approaching the pure anarchic gift economy of Georges Bataille's potlatch. The problem with these readings lies in the poem's central scene of redemptive violence, to which Proudhon was notoriously averse. According to his more hardcore Marxist-Leninist commentators (such as Dolf Oehler), Baudelaire would therefore be offering a caustic critique of Proudhon for having shied away from the necessary bloodshed of revolutionary class warfare (as was the case during the insurrectional days of June 1848, in which Baudelaire had by contrast briefly participated).

The various levels of irony at work in this text render it politically unreadable. What remains at the end of the poem (with its canceled address, at once fraternal and hostile, to Proudhon) is a Dada shortcircuiting of interpretation that opens the way to the uncompromising revolutionary nihilism registered on one of the last pages of *Belgium Disrobed*—in which all the hortatory calls to action are italicized so as to lay bare their rhetorical equivalence as clichés: "Yes! *Long Live the Revolution!* / Forever! What the hell! / But as for myself, I'm not taken in! I was never taken in! I say *Long Live the Revolution!* the way I'd say: *Long Live Destruction! Long Live Expiation! Long Live Punishment! Long Live Death!* / Not only would I be happy to be the victim, but I wouldn't mind being the executioner either—to feel the Revolution from both sides!"[28]

This same desire to play both victim and executioner (or both "the wound and the blade," as Baudelaire described the workings of Irony in his great poem of self-torment, "L'Héautoutimoroumenos") structures the chance encounter with the mysterious "Mademoiselle Bistoury" in the most scandalous of his late unpublished prose poems, also rejected outright by *La Revue nationale et étrangère*. One evening, under the guttering gaslights of the outskirts of Paris, a flâneur (the poem's first-person narrator) is accosted by a streetwalker who comes on to him by addressing him as a doctor. The stroller insists he is nothing of the sort, but so adamant is the hooker about maintaining the mistaken identity of her prey that he eventually agrees to accompany her back to her lodgings, given that her bizarre behavior at least promises (as in Poe's "Man of the Crowd" or André Breton's *Nadja*) that here might be the opportunity for some urban "mystery," some "unhoped-for enigma" to be solved. Once the two have repaired to her squalid lodgings, she lights herself a cigar (the first of her several masculine traits) and proceeds to remind her client of all the (purely fictitious) memories they had shared back during his days as an intern when she used to frequent the operating theaters of his hospital. The narrator again vainly protests that he has never been a doctor, but his heroine refuses to abandon her idée fixe. Proceeding to pull out a stack of lithographs of all the celebrity surgeons she has known in the past, followed by a packet of photographs of younger residents (the only occurrence of photography in Baudelaire's poetry), she asks for a picture of him to add to her trove of medical memorabilia the next time they meet. With her client thus passively reduced to the role of baffled listener or future object in her collection, the prostitute recounts how she habitually has plied her trade among the medical staff of hospitals and how she had at one point picked up a young, impoverished intern to whom she had offered her services for free, in the hopes that he would understand her particular sexual kink and come visit her at home "with his doctor's kit and apron—perhaps with a few bloodstains on it" ("the way a discriminating lover," comments the narrator, "might ask his actress mistress to dress up in the costume of her first starring role"). After this purely matter-of-fact confession of her fetish for surgical instruments and their attendant gore, Mademoiselle Bistoury (or Miss Scalpel) is cut short by the male narrator, who now assumes the role he had previously resisted—that of a (mad-) doctor:

> "Can you remember the first time or occasion when you experienced this particular urge?"
> I had difficulty making myself understood; at long last, I managed to get through. But she seemed quite crestfallen and, if I remember correctly, averted her eyes: "I have no idea. . . . I can't remember."

The memory of the analysand's original scene of trauma—rape, abortion, menstruation?—is never recovered, however. The riddle remains intact, and instead of the denouement that might have been expected, the *moraliste* voice of the flâneur sententiously intrudes: "What *bizarreries* one comes across in a large city, when one knows how to keep one's eyes open as one strolls about. Life teems with innocent monsters!" The poem closes with an impassioned address to God in which the perplexed narrator wonders whether his own perverse appetite for the lurid and monstrous might not be the Lord's indirect way of offering him a homeopathic lesson in charity—"the cure at the tip of a blade."

The words "monster" and "monstrous" reoccur with great regularity in Baudelaire's late vocabulary: he uses them to portray his beating up of a Belgian, to describe *My Heart Laid Bare* and *Belgium Disrobed* (both "monster books"). Indeed, one of the last poems he wrote before his collapse in Namur was a pastiche of baroque verse entitled "Le Monstre, ou le paranymphe d'une nymphe macabre" ("The Monster, or Encomium for a Macabre Nymph"), included in *Les Épaves*—an allegorical self-portrait (in the manner of Félicien Rops) of the ravaged poet as a hideously enticing over-the-hill forty-year-old monstrous whore.[29] "Mademoiselle Bistoury" ranks high among these teratological texts, for under the impress of its double-edged scalpel-pen the various dyads of identity—subject/object, self/other, male/female, doctor/patient, prostitute/client, consumer/commodity, narrator/protagonist, author/reader, poetry/prose—are rendered reciprocal and reversible, which is to say monstrously equal or grotesquely undecidable.[30]

Compared to the pugnacious "Let's Beat Up the Poor!" or the scabrous "Mademoiselle Bistoury," Baudelaire's final prose poem, "Good Dogs," published in the pages of *L'Indépendance belge* in June 1865, seems upon first reading to be, at best, a good-humored farewell to spleen or, at worst, a campy exercise in canine kitsch. When it appeared in the newspaper, the poem was accompanied by the following editorial header (likely suggested by Malassis), which framed it as an amusing Brussels *fait divers*: "We give our readers a curious unpublished piece, composed by M. Charles Baudelaire on the occasion of a vest that had been given to him by M. Joseph Stevens under the condition that he write something about the dogs of the poor. In some of the lines of this poem that deal with the dogs of the acrobat, the reader will recognize the brief description of one of the finest canvases of this painter."[31] Like so many of the pieces in *Paris Spleen*, "Good Dogs" turns on the slippery question of *exchange*. We are told it was composed in gratitude for the gift of a vest belonging to the Belgian painter of *L'Intérieur du saltimbanque* whose canvas depicting two mutts belonging to a traveling acrobat is in turn described (in *mise en abyme* fashion) in the body of the poem. Malassis probably engineered this as a puff piece—a good newspaper plug for two of his friends in which both poet and painter come out as fine fellows indeed. But the painter's gift, it should be noted, is not unconditional: it is a *don contraignant*, a gift with strings attached. As becomes clearer in the poem itself, the poet is not only in debt to him for the vest he has been awarded, but like a trained minstrel (or dog) performing for his patron—he compares himself to Virgil or Theocritus or Aretino—must sing for his supper. And what he has been commanded to sing is a humanitarian ode to "the dogs of the poor" in the manner of Joseph Stevens, the brother of his art-dealer friend Alfred Stevens, a successful *animalier* painter who specialized in coy genre scenes featuring canines of various species. When he first came across *L'Intérieur du saltimbanque* in the collection of a prominent Belgian art collector (see appendix 4), Baudelaire, the author of "Le Vieux Saltimbanque" (the prose poem so admired by Sainte-Beuve), was less than impressed: "*Joseph Stevens:* The run-down living quarters of a traveling showman. A suggestive painting. Dogs in costume. The acrobat has gone out and placed a hussar's busby on one of the dog's heads in order to force him to sit still in front of the cooking pot that is warming on the stove. Too slick [*trop d'esprit*]." This was the kind of piece Baudelaire was expected to write in order to repay the painter for his "gift." Malassis would then turn the poem into a commodity by selling it to *L'Indépendance belge*, which was now generously "giving" it to its readers—market transactions dressed up as gift exchange.[32]

Before being commissioned by the painter Stevens, "Good Dogs" originated as a series of notes for a chapter of *Belgium Disrobed*. Among the first things that apparently struck Baudelaire upon his arrival in Brussels was the prevalence of dogs—not only stray dogs but, above all, working service dogs:

A chapter on dogs, in which the vitality so conspicuously absent elsewhere seems to have taken refuge. Dogs in harnesses.

[The painter] Dubois's quip about dogs ("Don't bring your dog here, he would be humiliated to see his fellow canines dragging carts." "But Monsieur, at least we don't muzzle them here"). A fine chapter to write about these energetic dogs, all zeal and pride. It would seem as if they wanted to show horses a thing or two.

Symbols of (proletarian) vigor, their exuberant barking adding to the cacophony of Brussels streets, these worker dogs are elsewhere viewed by Baudelaire as the battered victims of exploitation:

Sadness of the animals. The dogs are no more petted than are the women. Impossible to get them to play or frisk about. If one tries, they act as surprised as the prostitute whom one addresses as Mademoiselle. But what tireless workers they are!

I have seen a very fat strong man plop himself down in a cart and have himself pulled up a steep slope by his dog.

It's truly the dictatorship of the savage in those uncivilized countries where the male does nothing.

This entire passage is preceded by the laconic observation: "Dogs, the negroes [*nègres*] of Belgium"—and in his prose poem Baudelaire will similarly refer to the packs of strays at the outskirts of cities as *marrons*, that is, as maroons, or organized communities of runaway Black slaves. Belgium, this bastard colony of France, may well be an (African) "uncivilized country" in which lazy male savages rule, but it also possesses its own (colonial) share of *nègres* (that is, slave dogs) to do its work for it—as if Baudelaire were presciently imagining the heart of darkness that was soon to be the Belgian Congo under the reign of Leopold II. Hence the notation in *Belgium Disrobed*: "The man who makes money at a fair by eating dogs alive." A dog-eat-dog world.

"Good Dogs" is very much a poem about who or what gets fed to whom.[33] It opens with an allusion to a comic scene in *Tristram Shandy* in which the author, in a typically Sternean admixture of sentimental empathy and whimsical cruelty, offers his donkey a macaroon, a dainty morsel clearly far beyond the capacity of its palate and certainly not enough to satisfy its hunger. Further on, vagrant dogs are shown dining on leftovers at the rear of fancy restaurants or on the handouts provided by lonely spinsters. In the central scene of the poem—the description of Stevens's painting *L'Intérieur du saltimbanque*—two circus dogs, immobilized by the absurd theatrical outfits they have been forced to wear by their master, salivate in front of a boiling pot of soup, craving this tempting *oeuvre sans nom* like frustrated sorcerers or alchemists (or like a poet hungry for his *oeuvre-à-venir*?). At the poem's close, the shepherds of Virgil or Theocritus are said to have received "a good piece of cheese" or "a nanny goat swollen with milk" in recompense for their pastoral songs, in the same way that the author of the poem we have just read is finally thrown a morsel in reward for his performance—the painter's vest.

In this poem Baudelaire occupies both the place of the dog *and* the master. As a performing dog or *chien de saltimbanque*, he is awarded a tidbit for his labors—a vest that, according to Malassis's eye-witness account of the scene, "most people would have considered no more than a scrap of velvet that had been squashed by so many people sitting on it" but that Baudelaire instead highly admired, finding its worn-out colors and distressed textures particularly "suggestive." As a master, on the other hand, the poet perfectly condescends to his Belgian readers by feeding them dog food. The poem begins with a creaky invocation of the shade of Laurence Sterne, then proceeds to the ritual address to the Muse: "Away with you, O academic muse! I want nothing to do with this stuffy old prude. I invoke familiar muse, the city muse, the lively muse. Let her inspire me to sing of good dogs, of poor dogs, of mud-caked dogs—those dogs whom everyone avoids like the plague, everybody, that is, except the poor, of whom they are the kindred spirits, and except poets, who look upon them with a fraternal eye." The epideictic rhetoric turns from praise to blame in the following two paragraphs—which excoriate the bourgeoisie's pet or purebred dogs (King Charles [sic] spaniels, pugs, greyhounds) before returning to the formal cadences of the ode: "I sing the mud-caked dog, the poor dog, the dog with no home, the flâneur dog, the performing dog . . . ." This is followed by a pastiche of one of those *physiologies* (such as *Les Français peints par eux-mêmes*) that were in great journalistic vogue back in the early 1840s—here providing a humorous pseudosociological overview of the urban comings-and-goings of the canine outcasts.[34] The poem then quickly shifts, by a rhetorical question, to Brussels ("Have you visited lazy old Belgium?"), in order to praise its energetic working dogs, before moving into that hoariest of literary devices, the formal ekphrasis of a painting, as it proceeds to translate Stevens's canvas into words. Baudelaire has agreed to sing; yes, he will toss his tongue to the dogs—but all he chooses to offer his audience is a stale repast of leftover rhetorical scraps, a parodic inventory in prose of all the outworn formal machinery of old-fashioned verse.

The poem ends with a double refrain in gratitude for Stevens's symbolic gift: "A beautiful vest, at once rich and faded in color, a vest that makes one think of autumn suns, of the beauty of women ripe in years and of Indian summers." And again, as a finale: "And every time the poet slips on the vest, he is forced to think of the good dogs, of the philosopher dogs, of Indian summers, and of the beauty of women most ripe in years." Like most of the other previous translators of this poem into English, I have Anglicized Baudelaire's "étés de la Saint-Martin" into "Indian summers"—a term first used in the meteorological sense by Crèvecoeur in his 1788 *Letters from an American Farmer* but that by the early nineteenth century had come to be used metaphorically to refer to any late flowering or warmth following upon a period of chill or decline—as in "the Indian summer of the heart" (John Greenleaf Whittier, 1834), or "an Indian summer crept stealthily over his closing days" (Thomas De Quincey, 1855), or "an Indian summer of serene Widowhood" (Oliver Wendell Holmes, 1867). The older English term, Saint Martin's Summer, is identical to Baudelaire's French. It refers to the late harvest festival celebrated each year on November 11 (or October 31 in the Gregorian calendar) in honor of Saint Martin of Tours, a fourth-century Roman soldier and early Catholic bishop. Legend has it that Martin once tore his cloak in half to share it with a beggar during a fierce winter snowstorm. That night, Martin dreamed of Jesus surrounded by angels and wearing the half-cloak he had bestowed the beggar—a vision that precipitated his conversion from pagan warrior into exemplary Christian. In Baudelaire's (ironic? melancholic?) evocation of the legend, here in the late Indian summer of his career, it is the painter Stevens who incarnates Saint Martin's act of *caritas*, while the poet plays the role of the poor beggar, transfigured into a vision of a half-cloaked Christ.

*   *   *

Also discovered among the papers in Baudelaire's Brussels trunk after his death were the titles and sketches for an additional sixty-five prose poems, as well as an inventory of all the various associated short stories and novels that he had failed to write through his career.[35] The *reliquiae* of these phantom works in progress or works never to be may be found below under the rubric "Projects"—the title of one of Baudelaire's earliest and most frequently recycled prose poems (which he had published for the third and fourth time during his first year in Belgium). In this text, the narrator rehearses a sequence of erotic fantasies in which he attempts to enthrone the sovereign queen of his desires in various settings—a palace, a tropical isle, a rustic Parisian inn—only to decide in the end that he would prefer that her estates remain ideal rather than real, mental rather than physical, and to conclude that, when all is said and done, the entertainment of such dreams is far more pleasurable than their meager fulfillment. "What's the point of bringing projects to completion," the poem concludes, "given that the project in itself provides sufficient pleasure?" ("Et à quoi bon exécuter des projets, puisque le projet est en lui-même une jouissance suffisante?").

The stray autograph sheets of Baudelaire's "Projects"—most of them held by the Bibliothèque littéraire Jacques Doucet and here (to the best of my knowledge) translated in full for the first time[36]—constitute the most *virtual* of Baudelaire's writings, consisting as they do for the most part of a string of titles and thereby observing the central symbolist tenet that poems primarily exist as occasions for *suggestion* (the very term, it will be remembered, that Baudelaire wanted to borrow from Poe for his *Flares*). As Mallarmé put it, the (Lacanian) *jouissance* of a poem therefore does not lie in the explicit naming of an object but rather in the gradual process of divining what this object might imaginatively be—or, better yet, never have been at all. Hence, according to Mallarmé: "le suggérer, voilà le rêve" ("to suggest it, that's the dream"). And what would therefore be more suggestive, more engaging of readerly reverie and *jouissance* than the title of a poem absent any accompanying text?

Like any habitual procrastinator, Baudelaire was a compulsive compiler of lists, given that lists are written down not only in order to *remember* but, perhaps more important, to allow one to *forget*. In the case of the more than one hundred titles for prose poems, short stories, and novels that Baudelaire committed to lists during the final years of his life—the boundaries between these prose genres always having remained remarkably fluid in his mind—these *feuilles volantes* provide a series of indices that point to works at once anticipated and abandoned. A title that stands in for an unrealized work—that is, that serves as an unanchored *paratext* (Genette) or as an autonomous *parergon* (Derrida)—defines a form that is without subsidiary content or that acts as a supplement to (or replacement for) something not yet (or never to be) in existence. An orphaned title (or fragment) of this sort therefore functions as an open frame or unclosed parenthesis—or as a head without a body.[37]

Although Baudelaire's late lists of titles for prose poems *à faire* observe no recognizable order—a first list is numbered 1 through 54, a second list is numbered 48 through 112, and a third list (entitled "Poems easy to do") consists of sixteen items (all crossed out), with many of the same titles circulating among these three lists—he was clearly trying to organize these random projects into some sort of broader tripartite thematic organization of *Le Spleen de Paris* as late as the spring of 1865. The first rubric, which contains thirty-four titles, is entitled "Choses parisiennes" (or "Things Parisian") and seems to be divided into two types of poems. The first of these is focused on representations of urban social types:

The Little Old Atheist
The Alienists
The Seductive Undertaker
The Old Pimp
The Gracious Guest
The Two Drunkards
A Parisian Lazzarone

Among these "Things Parisian," a second type of poem recalls the origins of the modern *poème en prose* (in Aloysius Bertrand's *Gaspard de la nuit*) as an ekphrastic response to genre painting, here exemplified by Baudelaire's "Courtyard of the *Messageries*," a scene copied from an 1803 painting by Louis-Léopold Boilly held by the Louvre (see p. 210 below). Other genre or cityscape paintings are evoked by such titles as:

From the Heights of the Butte Chaumont
The Philosopher at the Carnival
The Hurdy Gurdy
The Distribution of Provisions
Cholera at the Opera
An Ash Wednesday

Baudelaire's second rubric (numbered 35 through 47) is entitled "Onéi-rocritie" (or "Interpretation of Dreams"). Its titles include the evocative (and very Poesque):

Symptoms of Ruin
Return to Boarding School
Unknown Apartments
Sentenced to Death
The Mousetrap
The Palace by the Sea
The Stairs
Prisoner in a Lighthouse

The third and final rubric (made up of ten titles) is entitled "Symbols and Moralities," all of which are patently more allegorical and didactic in intent:

Filial Ingratitude
The Last Words of Jan Hus
Without Remorse or Regret
The Rococo Sphinx
The Pharisee's Prayer
The Rosary
No Offense to the Shades

In the end, Baudelaire never managed to reorganize the fragments of his *Spleen de Paris* into a cohesive volume that would work as a "pendant" to his *Fleurs du mal*—and whose parallel architectonics would be thematically organized around the three major axes he had discovered while writing the poems of "Tableaux parisiens"—the urban scene, the dreamscape, and the allegorical moral tale.

Among the pages of Baudelaire's various late lists of prose poem titles (some of which migrate into his lists for projected "Novels and Short Stories"), a few drafts of these unrealized works have nonetheless survived. The most extended of these sketches is entitled "Elegy for Hats" (intended for inclusion in "Things Parisian"). This is a fragment that Baudelaire probably conceived in the margins of his great 1859–63 essay "The Painter of Modern Life," where he notes at the outset that fashion provides a crucial index of "the moral or aesthetic feeling" of any given era. Worthy of *La Dernière Mode*, the fashion magazine that Mallarmé single-handedly wrote and published a decade later, Baudelaire's sketch for this "Elegy for Hats" is a brilliant (and proto-Benjaminian) study of the temporality of what he was among the first to call *la modernité*, its nomenclature ever new, ever falling out of date:

The *Maintenon*, a small lace headscarf that goes with the hat, knotted above the bonnet strings.

The *Marie Stuart*, designed with flattened point, saracen or ogival style.

The *Lavallière* hat (now out of fashion), with two plumes that converge at the back.

Russian hat. An aigrette.

The *Toquet* features a pompon or tassel.

A (pink) flower worn à la *Marie Louise*.

The *Marinière*, sailor-style bonnet with posy.

The *Longueville*, a Lavallière hat with a single plume drooping behind it, fluttering through space.

The *Highland* bonnet, in checked poplin, with cockade, silver brooch, and eagle or raven feathers.

Trimmings: puffs, ruches, cloth cut on the bias, edgings.

Here the Baudelairean prose poem, at its most modern, takes form as an inventory—a paratactic display of the commodity fetish, a monument to the ephemeral, an elegiac memory of all that is about to die: "The hats make one think of heads, a gallery of heads. Because every hat by its specific features evokes a head in the mind's eye. Severed heads. How sad it is, all this solitary frivolity. The depressing sensation of mindless carefree ruin. A monument of gaiety in the desert. A wanton frivolity."

Another title that wends its way through these late lists of Baudelaire's unwritten prose poems, short stories, and novels is the "End of the World"—the subject of the celebrated final page of *Flares*, so admired by Proust for its prophetic woefulness.[38] Among his sketches for hypothetical novels—which he continued to mention as plausibly publishable projects in late letters to his mother from Brussels—was an end-of-the-world fiction derived from Mary Shelley's 1826 work *The Last Man* (or, more distantly, from Jean-Baptiste Cousin de Grainville's two-volume 1805 prose poem of the same title): "A novel / on the *Last Man* / The same vices as before. Immense distances / On warfare, marriage, politics, etc. . . . among the last men. / Brigands / Sorcery / Imprisonments / Palaces and (subterranean) prisons / Scenes of torture and horror." Or again, on one of the late sheets devoted to his drafts of novels: "The last gasps of the world. / The last men. / Conflicts, rivalries. Hate, the taste for destruction and financial gain. / Their lives, in mankind's waning days. / (Avoid *The Last Man*) / Immense distances."

Yet another title that courses through these late lists of never-to-be-accomplished projects is "Symptoms of Ruin" (a title that Baudelaire intended for inclusion under the *Paris Spleen* rubric of "Interpretation of Dreams" or "Oneirocracy"). Robert Kopp, the most respected editor of Baudelaire's prose poems, suggests that this fragment may well have been among the very last things that Baudelaire wrote in Belgium before his stroke, while also noting how many of its elements are derived from Piranesi's *Prisons* and De Quincey's *Confessions of an English Opium Eater* (and, I would add, Nerval's *Aurelia*).[39] Roberto Calasso cites this text in the coda to his work *The Unnamable Present* (2017), seeing in it a prophetic prefiguration of 9/11:

> Symptoms of ruin. Colossal buildings. Many of them, one on top of another, apartments, rooms, *temples*, galleries, stairways, caecums, belvederes, lanterns, fountains, statues. —*Fissures, cracks. Humidity seeping in from a cistern located near the sky.* —How to warn the people of this, how to warn the nations? Warn the most intelligent, whisper in their ears. High up, a column buckles and its two ends heave. Nothing has yet collapsed. I can no longer find my way out. I climb downwards, then back upwards. *A tower-labyrinth. I have managed to make my way out. I forever inhabit a building about to collapse, a building attacked by some secret disease.* —Just to amuse myself, I mentally envisage to what extent this stupendous mass of stone and marble, with all its statuary and walls about to crash down into each other, will be besplattered by human brains and body parts and shattered bones. —I see such terrible things in my dreams that there are times when I would rather stop sleeping

altogether, were I not convinced that this would only further contribute to my fatigue.

Symptoms of Ruin—a nightmare from which Baudelaire is no longer trying to awake.

NOTES

1. See André Guyaux, *Poétique du fragment* (Neuchâtel: À la Baconnière, 1985), 8.
2. C2: 207.
3. Antoine Compagnon, *Baudelaire l'irréductible* (Paris: Flammarion, 2014), 15–18.
4. OC1: 275.
5. C2: 129.
6. A reproduction of the first page of the August 26, 1862, issue of *La Presse* featuring Baudelaire's *feuilleton* may be found in Compagnon, *Baudelaire l'irréductible*, 193.
7. C2: 264.
8. C2: 1007.
9. C2: 295.
10. C2: 324.
11. OC1: 366.
12. C2: 465.
13. Baudelaire, *Nouvelles lettres*, ed. Claude Pichois (Paris: Fayard, 2000), 96.
14. C2: 473.
15. C2: 493.
16. C2: 583.
17. Compare, for example, the bourgeois contemplating himself in the mirror in Daumier's *10 Heures du matin* (1839). Compagnon, *Baudelaire l'irréductible*, 33–40, provides a bravura reading of the poem.
18. The preface was added in 1891 when *The Picture of Dorian Gray* was first published in book form.
19. "The Port" echoes the contemplation of ships (most likely at Honfleur) evoked in fragments 11 and 22 of *Flares*.
20. See J. A. Hiddelston, *Baudelaire and "Le Spleen de Paris"* (Oxford: Oxford University Press, 1995), for the role of maxims and quotations throughout Baudelaire's prose poems.
21. OC1: 269.
22. OC1: 275.
23. Barbara Johnson, *Défigurations du langage poétique: La Seconde Révolution baudelairienne* (Paris: Flammarion, 1979), 84–92, engages in a classic De Manian deconstruction of the play of the literal and the figurative in this poem.
24. Steve Murphy, *Logiques du dernier Baudelaire* (Paris: Honoré Champion, 2007), 452–76. A doggerel verse version of this poem was also included in the "Bouffoneries" section of *Les Épaves*—another example of Baudelaire's habit of transposing his material into various genres.

25. C2: 401. This scene of violence is prefigured in a passage from section 17 of Baudelaire's *Salon de 1846*, directed at left-wing workers: "Have you ever felt, all you who have been drawn by your flâneur's curiosity to the heart of a riot, the pleasure that I feel when I see a guardian of the public sleep—a policeman or municipal guard—beat up a republican? Like me, you said in your heart: "Beat him up, beat him up a little harder, O policeman of my heart. . . . The man you're beating up is against roses, against perfumes, he's obsessed with household utensils; he's an enemy of Watteau, of Raphael, a passionate enemy of luxury, the fine arts, and literature; a sworn iconoclast, the executioner of Venus and Apollo! A humble and anonymous worker, he no longer wishes to produce roses and public perfumes: he just wants to be free, the ignoramus. . . . Beat the anarchist about the shoulders with religious fervor!" (OC1: 490). Two years later, during the 1848 Revolution, siding with the workers (and such worker poets as Pierre Dupont), Baudelaire would reverse his position. His late 1865 prose poem "Let's Beat Up the Poor!" addressed to the anarchist Proudhon further complicates these political volte-faces.

26. For two influential psychoanalytic readings of the sadomasochism of "Let's Beat Up the Poor!" see Jeffrey Mehlman, "Baudelaire with Freud: Theory and Pain," *Diacritics* (1974): 7–13; and Leo Bersani, *Baudelaire and Freud* (Berkeley: University of California Press, 1977), 139–50. A fuller interpretation is provided by Françoise Meltzer, *Seeing Double: Baudelaire's Modernity* (Chicago: University of Chicago Press, 2011), 11–74.

27. Richard Burton, *Baudelaire and the Second Republic: Writing and Revolution* (Oxford: Oxford University Press, 1991), provides a detailed account of Baudelaire's activities between 1848 and 1851 while also analyzing in a separate chapter the poet's ambivalent treatment of Proudhon in "Let's Beat Up the Poor!"—to which my own reading is indebted. Shortly after Proudhon's death on January 19, 1865, Malassis published a series of notes on "Proudhon en Belgique" in the February 25 number of *La Petite Revue*, to which Baudelaire published a response on March 11. Also in February, Baudelaire wrote Ancelle that his old friend the French art critic Théophile Thoré (a republican and ardent supporter of Manet) had during a visit to Brussels shared with him a packet of Proudhon's late correspondence. In this same letter to Ancelle Baudelaire recounts that Proudhon had been lent a copy of Hugo's *Les Misérables* upon its publication in Brussels in 1862 and that he had critically annotated its first two volumes line by line, taking issue with Hugo's facile humanitarianism. When Proudhon returned the novel to its Belgian owner, the latter, finding the book soiled, carefully erased all the philosopher's marginal notes. "Admirez le belge!" comments Baudelaire, adding, "thus a monument has been lost." All this points to a composition date of February–March 1865 for "Assommons les pauvres!"

28. OC2: 960.

29. OC1: 164.

30. See Anne E. Linton, "Baudelaire's Monsters: 'Mademoiselle Bistoury' and Teratology," *Yale French Studies*, 125–26 (2014): 134–48; and Marie-Hélène Huet, *Monstrous Imagination* (Cambridge, MA: Harvard University Press, 1993). The detailed readings of Cheryl Krueger, "Surgical Imprecision and the Baudelairean *poème en prose*," *French Forum* 27 (2002): 55–72 and of Maria C. Scott, *Baudelaire's "Le Spleen de Paris"* (Burlington, VT: Ashgate, 2005), 55–72, further explore the various metaphors of surgery (and castration) that cut through this poem. The "Mademoiselle Bistoury"

of the title may allude homophonically to Madame Bovary (diagnosed as a male hysteric in Baudelaire's review of the novel) while also recalling the celebrated caricature of 1857 that depicted Flaubert in doctor's garb triumphantly holding aloft his heroine's bleeding heart at the tip of his scalpel while she lies supine on the operating table, her most private recesses dissected by the inhumane surgical precision of the realist novel—just as, that very same year, Baudelaire's *Fleurs du mal*, also accused of excessive "realism," had been subjected to the invasive lancet of the law.

31. Charles Baudelaire, *Le Spleen de Paris/Petits Poèmes en prose*, ed. Robert Kopp (Paris: *Poésie* / Gallimard, 2006), 330.

32. See Jacques Derrida's analysis of the crisis of the gift economy in Baudelaire's prose poem "La Fausse Monnaie" in his *Given Time: I, Counterfeit Money*, trans. Peggy Kamuf (Chicago: University of Chicago Press, 1992).

33. My reading of "Good Dogs" responds to Julien Weber, *"Jeter sa langue aux chiens*: Collective Memory in Baudelaire's 'Les Bon Chiens,'" and to Anne Emmanuelle Berger, "Reigning Cats or Dogs? Baudelaire's Cynicism," both included in the special *Yale French Studies* issue (125–26, 2014) devoted to Baudelaire. I have also profited from Jean-Louis Cornille's essay, "L'Oeuvre sans nom," in his *Fin de Baudelaire* (Paris: Hermann Éditeurs, 2009).

34. See my "Same Difference: The French *Physiologies*, 1840–1842," *Notebooks in Cultural Analysis* 1 (1984): 163–200.

35. These may be found in OC1: 365–74, 588–99.

36. Francis Scarfe, in his translation of Baudelaire's *Paris Blues / Le Spleein de Paris* (London: Anvil, 1989), translates, without gloss or commentary, the "Drafts and Notes" of Baudelaire's prose poems but not the ruins of his short stories and novels. Rainer J. Hanshe's edition of *My Heart Laid Bare and Other Texts* (New York: Contra Mundum, 2007) provides a brief sampling.

37. See Gérard Genette, *Paratexts: Thresholds of Interpretation*, trans. Jane E. Lewis (Cambridge: Cambridge University Press, 1987); and Jacques Derrida, *The Truth in Painting*, trans. Geoff Bennington and Ian McLeod (Chicago: University of Chicago Press, 1987).

38. For a careful assessment of Baudelaire's and Benjamin's respective senses of an ending, see André Hirt, *Baudelaire: Le Monde va finir* (Paris: Éditions Kimé, 2010).

39. See Kopp, *Le Spleen de Paris/Petit Poèmes en prose*, 339.

Late Prose Poems

THE MIRROR

A frightful-looking man comes in and looks at himself in the mirror.

"Why look at yourself in the mirror? You'll only feel disgust at what you see."

The frightful-looking man answers me: "Monsieur, according to the immortal principles of '89, all men are equal in their rights. Therefore it is my right to look at myself in the mirror. Whether I do so with pleasure or disgust is of concern only to my conscience."

Common sense was no doubt on my side. But from a legal standpoint, he could hardly be faulted.

[*Nouvelle Revue de Paris*, December 25, 1864]

THE PORT

For a soul worn out by the battles of life, a port offers a pleasant retreat. The vast expanse of the sky, the mobile architecture of the clouds, the changing colors of the sea, the sparkles of the lighthouses—all provide a prism marvelously suited to entertain the eye without ever wearying it. The soaring shapes of the ships with their intricate riggings, harmoniously swaying to and fro in the sea swell, serve to maintain the soul's appetite for rhythm and beauty. And above all, for someone who has lost all curiosity and ambition, there is a kind of mysterious and aristocratic pleasure to be had in contemplating, as he reclines on the belvedere or props his elbows on the jetty, all these people busy leaving or returning, people still possessed of willpower, of the desire to travel or make their fortunes.

[*Nouvelle Revue de Paris*, December 25, 1864]

PORTRAITS OF MISTRESSSES

In a male sanctum, that is, in a lounge adjoining an elegant brothel, four men sat smoking and drinking. They were neither precisely young or old, handsome or ugly; but whatever their age, they all bore that unmistakable mark of distinction which announces veterans of plea-sure, that indescribable *je ne sais quoi*, that cold and sardonic sullen-ness which clearly declares to the world: "We have lived life to the hilt—and are still on the lookout for something worthy of our love and admiration."

One of them brought up the subject of women. It would have been far more philosophical not to mention the matter at all; but even men of wit, after a few drinks, find themselves drawn into idle talk. One listens to the man holding forth as one might attend to dance music.

"Every man," the gentleman was saying, "starts out life like Cheru-bino:* at that tender age, lacking dryads, you embrace any old tree trunk, without the slightest feeling of disgust. This is the first degree of love. Having reached the second degree, you become more discrimi-nating. The faculty of judgment already implies a degree of decadence. It's at this point that one definitely sets one's sights on beauty. In my case, gentleman, I'm rather proud of having achieved for some time now the climacteric of the third degree: here beauty alone no longer suffices, if not accented by perfume, jewelry, and the like. I'll even ad-mit that I sometimes aspire to the undiscovered joys of a certain fourth degree—which would be marked by absolute calm. But over the course of my entire life, except when I was the tender age of Cherubino, I have been perhaps more susceptible than the next man to the debilitating stupidity and irritating mediocrity of women. What I above all love about animals is their candor. You can therefore judge just how my last mistress made me suffer.

"She was the bastard child of a prince. Gorgeous, of course—why else

* *Cherubino:* Young page in Beaumarchais's *Le Mariage de Figaro* (1784).

would I have taken her on? But she spoiled this great quality of hers by an ambition as twisted as it was unbecoming. This was a woman who always wanted to play the man. 'You're not a man! Oh! If only I were a man! I'm more of a man than either of us!' Over and over, the same relentless refrain coming from a mouth which I had hoped would give flight to song. When I expressed my admiration for a given poem or opera, she would immediately cut me off: 'So you truly think this is powerful? What do you know about power?'—and then proceed to make her case.

"One fine day she decided to take up chemistry—and from then on all I found between her lips and mine was a glass facemask. And quite a prude, into the bargain. If I happened to ruffle her with a gesture that was a bit too amorous, she would recoil from the violation like a sensitive plant."

"How did things finally end?" asked one of the three others. "I had no idea you could display such patience."

"God," he continued, "brings blessings in disguise. One day I found this Minerva, famished as she was for the ideal of power, in a *tête à tête* with my manservant, the situation being such that I had to withdraw discreetly in order not to make the two blush with shame. That evening I let both of them go, having paid them their back wages."

"As for me," continued the man who had interrupted him, "I only have myself to blame. Bliss had descended upon my humble abode, and I did not recognize it for what it was. Fate had lately granted me the favors of a woman who was without a doubt the sweetest, the meekest, the most devoted of creatures—and always ready for it! but without the slightest enthusiasm! 'It's fine by me, seeing as how much you enjoy it.' This was her standard response. You could give this wall or couch a good drubbing and you wouldn't raise more of a reaction from them than I ever managed to extract from the bosom of my mistress, however madly I made love to her. After we had lived together a year, she admitted to me that she had never known real pleasure. I grew disgusted with this lopsided duel, and this exceptional creature went on to get married. Later, on a whim, I decided to get in touch with her again and she said to me, pointing to her six lovely children, 'Well, my dear friend, the wife is still as much a *virgin* as was your mistress.' Nothing about her had changed. There are times when I have my regrets: I should have married the girl."

The others all laughed, and a third fellow chimed in:

"Gentleman, I have known pleasures that you have perhaps over-looked. I'm speaking of the comic element in love—an element that does not exclude admiration. I admired my last mistress more than any of you could have possibly loved or hated yours. And everybody shared in my admiration. Whenever we entered a restaurant, after several minutes everyone would stop eating just to feast their eyes upon her. Even the waiters and the barmaids were so caught up in this contagion of ecstasy that they would forget their duties. In short, for a time there, I was on intimate terms with a living *phenomenon*. She would eat, chew, chomp, gobble down her food—but ever so casually, with the utmost of ease. She was a never-ending source of delight to me. She had such a sweet, dreamy, and romantically English way of saying: 'I'm starving.' And she would repeat these words day and night, displaying the pret-tiest teeth in the world, a set that would both melt and gladden your heart. I could have made a fortune by displaying her at fairs as a *poly-phagous freak*. I fed her quite well; and yet in the end she left me. . . ."

"For a grocer, no doubt?"

"Something of the sort—for somebody in the quartermaster corps who knew the ropes and was able to keep the poor girl supplied with enough rations to feed a platoon of soldiers. Or at least this is what I assumed."

"As for me," said the fourth fellow, "I have endured atrocious suffer-ings, but not on account of the egoism that we so often impute the fe-male of the species. Quite the contrary! I find you are in no position, O far too blessèd mortals, to complain about the imperfections of your mistresses."

This was said in a most serious tone of voice by a man whose manner was calm and collected and whose face was almost that of a clergyman, mismatched by the flash of pale gray eyes, eyes that always seem to be commanding: "Do this! Do that! Never do I show mercy!"

"If you, G. . . . , high-strung as I know you to be, or if the two of you, K. . . . and J. . . . , cowardly philanderers that you are, had ever been the lovers of a certain female of my acquaintance, you would have ei-ther taken flight or died as a result. In my case, as you can well see, I managed to survive. Imagine a person entirely incapable of the slight-est error in her feelings or her calculations; imagine someone so even-natured as to inspire despair; a devotion without drama or exaggeration; a gentleness without fragility; an energy without violence. The story of my love resembles an endless voyage over a surface as pure and polished, and as vertiginously monotonous, as a mirror reflecting all my emotions and all my gestures with the ironic exactitude of my own conscience—with the result that I could not permit myself a single unreasonable gesture or emotion without immediately recognizing the mute reproach uttered by my inseparable specter. I was not her lover, I was her ward. How many foolhardy things my mistress prevented me from doing—to my great regret! How many debts I paid back, despite my better judgment! She robbed me of all the gains I might have gotten out of my private follies. Laying down the rule with unwavering determination, she interdicted my every whim. And to make matters worse, O horrors, she never asked for any gratitude in return once the danger had passed. How many times I had to restrain myself from grabbing her by the throat and screaming at her: 'Can't you stop being perfect, you miserable creature? Let me love you without anger and without dismay!' I admired her for several years, my heart filled with hate. In the event, I was not the one who ended up dead."

"Oh?" the others asked, "so she died?"

"Yes. Things could not go on this way. Love had become an enormous nightmare for me. Win or die, as they say in Politics—such was the alternative that fate had dealt me. One evening, in a forest . . . near a pond . . . after a melancholy stroll together, her eyes reflecting the mildness of the sky, my heart like some twisted thing out of hell . . . ."

"My Lord!"

"Unbelievable!"

"What are you saying?"

"It was inevitable. My sense of fairness is such that I would never beat, insult, or dismiss a servant whose conduct was irreproachable. But I had to weigh this conviction against the horror that this creature inspired in me—to get rid of her without showing her disrespect. What was I supposed to do with her, *given that she was perfect*?"

The three other fellows looked at him, their eyes dazed and somewhat bewildered—as if pretending not to believe him and as if implicitly admitting that they did not feel, as far as they were concerned, capable of an action this rigorous, although entirely justifiable, as had been explained.

They then called for a new round of drinks—to kill Time, whose life is so hard, and to quicken Life, whose flow is so slow.

[Posthumous: *Revue nationale et étrangère*, September 21, 1867]

THE GALLANT MARKSMAN

As the carriage was crossing through the woods, he ordered it to pull up near a shooting range, saying it might be amusing to fire off a few rounds, just to *kill* Time. To kill this monster—is this not everybody's most ordinary and legitimate occupation? He gallantly offered his hand to his dear, delicious, despicable wife—this mysterious woman to whom he owed so much pleasure, so much pain, and, very likely, a good portion of his genius.

Several bullets landed wide of the target; one of them even lodged itself in the ceiling. And as the charming creature doubled over with laughter, mocking the clumsiness of her husband, the latter wheeled around and said to her: "See that doll over there, to the right, her nose so high in the air, so full of disdain? Well, my sweet angel, *I'm figuring it's you.*" And he closed his eyes and pulled the trigger. The doll was cleanly decapitated.

Bowing to his dear, delicious, despicable wife, his inevitable and pitiless Muse, and respectfully kissing her hand, he added: "Ah, my dear angel, how grateful I am to you for the trueness of my aim."*

[Refused by the *Revue nationale et étrangère* in 1865; first published in 1869]

SOUP AND CLOUDS

My crazy little sweetheart† was serving me dinner, and through the open window of the dining room I was musing on the mobile architec-

---

* *The trueness of my aim:* A sketch of this poem appears on folio 17 of *Flares*.

† *My crazy little sweetheart:* Baudelaire drew an ink portrait of a certain "Berthe" and dated it "Brussels, 1864." It bore the following dedication: "While we were having dinner [in Paris] and I was watching the clouds through the open window, she said to me: *Are you going to eat your soup now, you blasted cloudmonger!* To a horrible little

tures that God creates out of sheer vapor—marvelous constructions of impalpability. And amid my contemplation, I said to myself: "All these phantasmagorias are almost as gorgeous as the eyes of my little sweetheart, my crazy little green-eyed monster."

And suddenly I felt a violent punch land on my back, and I heard a voice husky and seductive, a voice full of hysteria, as if coarsened by cheap liquor—the voice of my dear little sweetheart saying to me: "So, are you going to eat your soup now, you goddamn good-for-nothing cloudmonger?"

[Refused by the *Revue nationale et étrangère* in 1865; first published in 1869]

CEMETERY AND SHOOTING RANGE

—*Tavern on the Tombs.** "An unusual sign," thought our passerby, "but well calculated to appeal to one's thirst! I wager the owner of this place is an admirer of Horace and the poets of the school of Epicurus. Perhaps he's even familiar with the profound refinement of the ancient Egyptians, for whom no great banquet went without its skeleton or some other fitting emblem of the brevity of life."

So he made his way in, drank a glass of ale, and slowly smoked a cigar while viewing the graves. Then he decided to treat himself to a walk through the cemetery below, its grass so high and inviting, the sun so richly in season.

Indeed, the light and the heat down there were blazing; one would have said that the sun was drunk, pitched headlong across the carpet of magnificent flowers that fed off the ripe loam of decomposition. An immense murmur of life filled the air—the life of infinitely small things— punctuated at regular intervals by the crackle of gunfire from a nearby

fool, a memory of the even greater fool who was looking for a girl to adopt and who had neither studied the character of Berthe, nor the laws of adoption" (OC1: 1140). A late poem, "Les Yeux de Berthe," also appears in *Les Épaves*.

* *Tavern on the Tombs: À la vue du cimitiere, Estaminet.* Sign observed by Baudelaire on the route from Brussels to Uccle. A shorter verse version of the poem was included in *Les Épaves*.

shooting range, champagne corks exploding through the muted hum of a symphony.

With the heat of the sun beating down on his brains and the fiery scent of Death wafting up all around him, he heard a voice whispering beneath the tombstone on which he was sitting. And this voice was saying: "Cursed be your carbines and your targets, O unquiet mortals, who show such little concern for the dead and their blessèd rest! Cursed be your ambitions, cursed be your calculations, O impatient mortals, who come here to study the art of killing, so near to this sanctuary of Death! If you only knew how easy it is to obtain the prize, to hit the mark, and how nothing amounts to anything, except Death, you would not tire yourselves out with all this senseless activity and you would be less eager to trouble the sleep of those who long ago scored their bull's eye, taking aim at the only true Target—life in all its unspeakable horror."

[Posthumous: *Revue nationale et étrangère*, October 11, 1867]

LOST HALO

"Fancy seeing you here, my dear fellow. You, slumming it? You, the quaffer of quintessences? You, the imbiber of ambrosia? To tell the truth, I'm quite dumbfounded."

"My dear fellow, you know just how terrified I am of horses and carriages. A short while ago, as I was rushing across the boulevard, skipping through the mud, weaving my way through the chaos of traffic where death comes galloping down on you from every direction at once, my halo suddenly got dislodged from my head and fell into the muck of the macadam. I did not have the courage to pick it back up. I decided it would be less annoying to lose my badge of honor than to get my bones broken. What's more, I said to myself, every cloud has its silver lining. I can now walk about incognito, indulge in mean-spirited acts, and wallow in vice, like any ordinary mortal. So here I am—alike you in every way, as you can see!"

"You should at least post a notice about your lost halo, or have the police look into the matter."

"Heaven forbid! I'm doing perfectly well here. You're the only person who has recognized me. Besides, being dignified is such a bore. And just think, perhaps some lousy poet will pick it up and be brazen enough to wear it with pride. I rather enjoy the idea of making some fellow happy—and especially one who'll provide me with a few laughs! Think of X, or of Z! Ha! What a riot!"*

[Refused by the *Revue nationale et étrangère* in 1865; first published in 1869]

MADEMOISELLE BISTOURY

As I was nearing the outskirts of town, beneath the glimmer of the gas lights, I felt an arm slip softly under mine, and heard a voice say into my ear: "Sir, are you a doctor?"

I took a look; she was a tall, well-built thing, wide-eyed, slightly rouged, her hair and bonnet strings fluttering in the wind.

"No; I am not a doctor. Let me pass."

"Of course you're a doctor! It's plain to see. Come to my place. I'll show you a good time. Come along!"

"I'll be sure to drop by, but only *after the doctor does*†—what the hell . . . !"

"Aha!" she said, still clinging to my arm and bursting into laughter, "So you're a doctor who likes to joke around, I've known several of your kind. Come along!"

I'm a passionate devotee of mystery, because I always have such high hopes of unraveling it. So I allowed myself to be led away by this companion, or rather, by this unhoped-for enigma.

I'll skip the description of her hovel; you can find it in any number of well-known French poets of old. Except that (a detail Régnier missed)‡ two or three portraits of famous doctors hung on the walls.

---

* *What a riot!:* A sketch of this poem appears on folio 17 of *Flares*.

† *After the doctor does . . . :* that is, drops in on her for the regular hygienic *visite sanitaire* (or medical checkup) required by the authorities.

‡ *Régnier: Mathurin Régnier,* French satirical poet of the seventeenth century, much admired by Baudelaire. One of Régnier's "Satyres" contains an extended description of a prostitute's chamber, including the various syringes, sponges, and probes used to induce abortions.

How she pampered me! Blazing fire, mulled wine, cigars; and as she was plying me with all these fine things, this ludicrous creature said to me, as she lit herself a cigar: "Make yourself at home, my friend, feel completely at your ease. It'll remind you of your younger years at the hospital. My Lord! Where did you come by all these white hairs? This is not the way you used to look, and it wasn't that long ago either, when you were interning with L. . . . I remember it was you who acted as his assistant on major operations. Now there was a man who really liked to slice and dice and snip away! And you were the fellow who used to hand him his instruments, his sutures, and his sponges. And once the operation was completed, he'd check his watch and proudly announce: 'Five minutes in all, gentlemen!' Oh yes, I do get around. I know all these gentlemen quite well."

A few instants later, now addressing me in a more familiar vein, she again struck up the same old tune: "You're a doctor, ain't you, my pet?"

This unintelligible refrain brought me to my feet: "No I am *not*," I shouted in rage.

"A surgeon, perhaps?"

"No! and no again!—unless I had a mind to cut off your head! Jesus H. Christ!"*

"Wait," she replied, "you'll see."

And she pulled out a stack of sheets from an armoire—which turned out to be a portfolio of portraits of illustrious doctors of the day, a collection of lithographs by Maurin† that had been on public display for a number of years on the quai Voltaire.

"Here! You recognize this one?"

"Yes. That's X. There's his name at the bottom of the picture; I happen to know him personally."

"See, I told you so! Here! That's Z., who used to say of X. during his lectures: 'This monster wears the blackness of his soul on his very face.' All because X. had had a professional disagreement with him. Every-

* *Jesus H. Christ:* Baudelaire's manuscript here reads: "Sacré Saint Ciboire de Sainte Maquerelle"—a blasphemous oath ("Blessed Holy Ciborium of Saint Procuress") perhaps only intelligible today to French Canadians.

† *Maurin:* Nicolas-Eustache Maurin, lithographer of a series of *Célébrités contemporains* (1842).

body got such a kick out of this at Medical School back in those days. You remember? Here! That's K., who turned the insurgents he was treating at his hospital over to the government—that was back during the riots. How could a man that handsome be so heartless? And here's W., a famous British doctor; I scooped him up during his visit to Paris. He looks like a fine young lady, doesn't he?"

I was fingering a string-wrapped packet lying nearby on the pedestal table. "Hold off a minute," she said, "that's the residents; this here packet is the nonresidents."

And she arrayed the bunch of photographic images into a fan; the faces pictured on them were indeed far younger.

"The next time we meet, you'll give me a picture of yourself too, won't you, sweetheart?"

"But," I said, returning to the question that was preying on my mind, "Why do you insist on taking me for a doctor?"

"Because you're such a gentleman, so nice to the ladies."

"What twisted logic," I thought to myself.

"Mind me, I never make a mistake; I've known a great number of them. I have such a liking for these gentlemen that even if there's nothing wrong with me, I sometimes take appointments with them, just to lay my eyes on them. There are those who react quite coldly: 'But there is nothing wrong with you whatsoever.' But there are others who are more understanding, because I flirt around with them."

"And what if they don't catch your drift . . . ?"

"Well, in that case, since I have inconvenienced them *for no good reason*, I just leave them ten francs on the mantelpiece. They're so nice and sweet, these fellows! At the Pitié Hospital, I discovered a young intern— as pretty as an angel, and so polite, so hard-working, the poor boy! His fellow students told me that he was penniless because his parents were too poor to put him through school. This gave me confidence. After all, I'm a fairly good-looking woman, even if I'm getting a little on in years. I said to him: 'Come see me, come as often as you want. With me, no need to feel embarrassed. I don't need the money.' But, mind you, I didn't put it to him that crudely, I just hinted around: I was so afraid of humiliating him, sweet thing that he was. You may find this hard to believe, but I have this little quirk that I couldn't bring myself to admit to him. I wanted him to come see me with his doctor's kit and apron—perhaps with a few bloodstains on it!"

She said this quite straightforwardly, the way a discriminating man might ask the actress he was in love with: "I'd like to see you in that costume you wore in your first starring role."

Ever persistent, I continued on: "Can you remember the first time or occasion you experienced this rather peculiar urge?"

I had difficulty making myself understood; at long last, I managed to get through. But she seemed quite crestfallen and, if I remember correctly, averted her eyes: "I have no idea . . . I can't remember."

What bizarreries* one comes across in a large city, if one knows how to keep one's eyes open as one strolls about. Life teems with innocent monsters.

"O Lord, my God—you the Creator, the Almighty; you who have granted us both Liberty and Law; you, the sovereign who allows men to do as they will; you, the judge who pardons; you who have so many hidden ways, and who have perhaps instilled this taste for horror in my mind to convert my heart—like a cure at the tip of a blade. Lord, have pity on madmen and madwomen! O Creator, can *monsters* truly exist in the eyes of the One who alone knows why they exist, how it was *they came into being,* and how they might *never have come into being at all?*"

[Refused by the *Revue nationale et étrangère* in 1865; first published in 1869]

ANYWHERE OUT OF THE WORLD

Life is a hospital where each patient is driven by the desire to change beds.† This one would prefer to be suffering by the stove, and that one believes he'd recover better by the window.

It seems to me that I'd always do better wherever I'm not, and this

---

* *Bizarreries:* Nineteenth-century usage attested by the *OED*. In his review of the 1855 Exposition Universelle, Baudelaire noted in italics: "*The beautiful is always bizarre.*"

† *Life is a hospital:* From Emerson's *Conduct of Life:* "Like sick men in hospitals, we change from bed to bed, from one folly to another." The title of the poem, "Anywhere out of the World," in English in the original, is drawn from Thomas Hood's "Bridge of Sighs," translated into free verse by Baudelaire in Brussels in 1865. Hood's 1844 poem, praised in Poe's essay "The Poetic Principle," evokes the suicide of a homeless young woman who threw herself off Waterloo Bridge in London, hoping she would be "Swift to be hurl'd / —Anywhere, anywhere / Out of the world."

whole question of changing locations is one I endlessly discuss with my soul.

"Tell me, my soul, my poor shivering soul, what would you think about going to live in Lisbon? It must be warm there, and soon you'd be darting about like a lizard. The city lies on the sea; they say it's built of marble, and that its inhabitants so loathe vegetation that they tear down all the trees. Here's a landscape after your heart—a landscape made of mineral and light, with the liquid to catch their reflections."

My soul offers no reply.

"Seeing as you so love stillness, accompanied by the spectacle of motion, how'd you like to come live in Holland, that fabled land of contentment? Perhaps you'd find amusement in a country whose image you've so often admired in museums. What would you think of Rotterdam—you who adore forests of masts and ships moored at the foot of houses?"

My soul remains silent.

"Would Batavia* perhaps be more to your liking? It would offer us the spirit of Europe, married to the beauty of the tropics."

Not a word. Could it be that my soul has died?

"Have you gone so numb as to take pleasure only in your misery? If this is indeed the case, let's escape toward those lands that provide analogies to Death. I've found a solution, poor soul! We'll pack our bags for Tornio.† Let's push on even further, to the extremities of the Baltic; or even further from life, if possible. Let's settle down at the Pole, where the sun only glances the earth obliquely and the slow alternations of light and night eliminate variety and heighten monotony—this moiety of the void. There we shall be able to take long baths of darkness while the northern lights entertain us with occasional sheaves of pink—reflections of the fireworks of Hell!"

At long last, my soul erupts, shouting out these words to the wise: "Anywhere! Anywhere! As long as it's out of this world!"

[Posthumous: *Revue nationale et étrangère*, September 28, 1867]

---

* *Batavia:* Capital of Dutch Guiana (or Surinam).

† *Tornio:* Town in Lapland on the Finnish-Russian border, springboard for Maupertuis's celebrated arctic expedition of 1737. Mentioned at the outset of Alphonse de Custine's *Russia in 1839*—a favorite book of Baudelaire's.

LET'S BEAT UP THE POOR!

I had confined myself to my room for a fortnight, holed up with the sorts of books that were all the rage back then (sixteen or seventeen years ago)*—books dealing with the art of making the masses healthy, wealthy, and wise in twenty-four hours. I had therefore digested—or should I say, wolfed down—all the pedantic fare of these purveyors of public happiness, some exhorting the poor to become slaves, others persuading them that every pauper is a dethroned king. No surprise, then, if I found myself in a state of mind verging on vertigo—or idiocy.

Yet I somehow seemed to sense, stirring in the depths of my intellect, the inkling of an idea far superior to the entire catalog of old wives' remedies that I had just been perusing. But it was no more than the idea of an idea, something as of yet infinitely vague.

So I ventured outdoors, dying of thirst—for the severe addictions to trashy books create proportional cravings for fresh air and cool drinks.

As I was about to enter a pub, a beggar held out his hat to me, shooting me one of those unforgettable looks that could topple thrones—if mind could move matter or the eye of a mesmerist ripen grapes.

At that very moment, I heard a voice whispering into my ear, one I immediately recognized; it was the voice of that good Angel—or good Demon—who is always by my side. If Socrates had his good Demon, why shouldn't I have my good Angel?

Why shouldn't I be honored as Socrates has been of late—issued a certificate of insanity signed by the artful Dr. Lélut and the knowledgeable Dr. Baillarger?†

The Demon of Socrates differs from mine in that the former would only manifest itself to the philosopher in order to forbid, warn, hinder him, whereas mine favors me with counsel, suggestion, persuasion. Poor old Socrates had a Demon who was merely prohibitive; mine works in the affirmative. Mine's a Demon of action—a fighter Demon.

So this is what its voice was whispering to me: "To truly be someone

---

* *Sixteen or seventeen years ago:* During the revolutionary years of 1848–49, given that this poem was almost certainly composed in 1865.

† *Dr. Lélut and Dr. Baillarger:* Two celebrated alienists; the former had published *Du Démon de Socrate* (1836), in which he argued that Socrates was clinically insane—as were Tasso, Pascal, Rousseau, and Swedenborg.

else's equal, you have to prove it; to truly be worthy of liberty, you have to conquer it."*

I immediately lunged out at my beggar. With a single punch, I blackened his eye, which within the space of a second swelled up like a ball. I broke one of my nails as I relieved him of two of his teeth; and since I didn't feel I had the strength to deliver the knockout blow to the old fellow (being of delicate disposition and having rarely boxed), I grabbed his collar with one hand while I caught his throat with the other, and then proceeded to vigorously bash his head against the wall. I must admit that I had previously inspected the neighborhood with a quick glance, making sure that no policeman would disturb me in this deserted suburb any time soon.

Having finally knocked the weakened sexagenarian to the ground with a kick in the back energetic enough to break his shoulder blades, I grabbed a thick tree branch that was lying nearby and pounded him with the obstinate energy of a cook trying to tenderize a piece of steak.†

Suddenly—O what a miracle! O what a joy for the philosopher verifying the excellence of his theory!—I saw the ancient carcass turn over and rise to its feet with an energy I would have never suspected in a machine so utterly thrown out of whack. With a look of hate that struck me as quite *auspicious*, the decrepit desperado flailed out at me, blackening my two eyes, breaking four of my teeth, and, taking up the same tree branch, beat the living daylights out of me. The energetic medication that I had administered to him had restored his pride and his life.

I finally managed to signal to him that I now considered the discussion closed, and getting back up on my feet and as satisfied as a Sophist of old, I said to him: "Sir, *you are my equal!* Please do me the honor of sharing my purse with you; and should any of your colleagues ask you for a handout, don't forget (if you are truly a philanthropist) to apply the theory that it has been my *pain* to test out on your back."

---

* *To be truly worthy of liberty:* A reworking of Nerval's translation of *Faust*, 2:574–75: "Celui-là seul est digne de la liberté comme de la vie, qui tous les jours se dévoue à les conquérir."

† *Tenderize a piece of steak:* Baudelaire draws the metaphor from Poe's *Fifty Suggestions, 20*: "Children are never too tender to be whipped: —like tough beef-steaks, the more you beat them the more tender they become" (*The Brevities*, ed. Burton R. Pollin [New York: Gordian, 1985], 487).

He heartily swore that he had understood my theory and that he would obey my advice.

"What do you have to say to this, Citizen Proudhon?"*

> [Refused by the *Revue nationale et étrangère*
> in 1865; first published in 1869]

GOOD DOGS

To M. Joseph Stevens†

I have never been ashamed to confess my admiration for Buffon‡— even to the young writers of my century. But today I shall not be invoking the shade of this painter of nature in all her pomp. No.

Instead, I'd prefer to call on Sterne:§ "Descend from heaven, or rise up from the Elysian Fields, to inspire me to sing the praises of good dogs and poor dogs—a song worthy of you, you sentimental wag, you incomparable jester! Return among us, straddling that celebrated ass who forever accompanies you in the memory of posterity; and above all, let that ass not forget to munch on that immortal macaroon which you so delicately pressed between its lips!"

---

* *Citizen Proudhon:* This final line was omitted from all publications of the poem and is still not included in current printings of *Paris Spleen*. When the celebrated anarchosocialist philosopher Jean-Joseph Proudhon died on January 19, 1865, Baudelaire clipped his derogatory obituary notice for inclusion in the *sottisier* of his *Belgium Disrobed*.

† *Joseph Stevens:* Belgian painter (and brother of Arthur Stevens) whose acquaintance Baudelaire made in Brussels.

‡ *Buffon:* French naturalist of the eighteenth century whose chapter title "Homo duplex" (in the "Mammals" section of his "Discourse on the Nature of Animals") Baudelaire was fond of citing and whose description of the (antediluvian) monstrosity of the flora and fauna of North America rhymed with his vision of Poe's America— or of contemporary Belgium.

§ *Sterne:* See Laurence Sterne's *Tristram Shandy*, 7:xxxii, with the commentary: "There was more a pleasantry in the conceit, of seeing *how* an ass would eat a macaroon—than of benevolence in giving him one, which presided in the act." Baudelaire alludes to the same scene in his *Salon de 1859* but interprets it in the opposite sense: "The ass's comic appearance while eating a cake does nothing to diminish the feeling of compassion when we see the miserable serf receiving a few dainties from the philosopher."

Away with you, O academic muse! I want nothing to do with this stuffy old prude. I invoke the household muse, the city muse, alive and well. Let her inspire me to sing of good dogs, of poor dogs, of mud-caked dogs—those dogs whom everyone avoids like the plague, everybody, that is, except the poor, of whom they are the kindred spirits, and except poets, who look upon them with a fraternal eye.

To hell with all those dandified dogs, all those foppish quadrupeds—lesser Danes, King Charles spaniels, pugs, or other tiny rogues—so full of themselves that they thoughtlessly throw themselves between the legs or onto the laps of guests, so sure are they of pleasing them, as unruly as any child, as silly as any strumpet, at times as ill-tempered and insolent as a domestic servant. To hell especially with those four-legged serpents—so high-strung, so jaded—that go by the name of Italian greyhounds and whose muzzles are so pointy that their nostrils cannot track the scent of a friend, and whose heads are so flattened that they lack the brains to play dominos.

Send them back to their kennels, all these tiresome parasites!

Let them return to their silk-lined, well-upholstered kennels! I sing the mud-caked dog, the poor dog, the dog with no home, the *flâneur* dog, the traveling circus dog, the dog whose instincts—like the instincts of the poor, of the gypsies, or of ham actors—have been exquisitely honed by necessity, that most generous of mothers, that true benefactress of intelligence.

I sing of dogs down on their luck—either those who wander, all alone, around the sinuous ravines of great cities, or those who say to the homeless man with a sly gleam in their eye: "Take me along with you; perhaps we could join up together and turn our two hand-to-mouth existences into a decent life!"

"*Where do dogs go?*" Nestor Roqueplan* once asked in an immortal newspaper piece that he has no doubt forgotten—and that I am the only person (perhaps together with Sainte-Beuve) to remember to this day.

Where do dogs go, you ask, O unobservant mankind? They go off to tend to their affairs.

* *Nestor Roqueplan:* Roqueplan's vignette about dogs, a major inspiration behind this poem, had appeared in *La Presse* in 1857. Baudelaire maintained cordial relations with the French critic Charles-Augustin Sainte-Beuve throughout his exile in Brussels, especially given the latter's initial admiration of his prose poems.

Business meetings, lovers' assignations. Making their way through the fog, through the snow, through the mud, under the hammering sun, under the driving rain, they come, they go, they trot, they slip beneath carriages, spurred onward by fleas, by passion, by duty, by need. Like us, they have gotten up early, just trying to get by, or already out looking for a good time.

There are those who spend their nights in a ruin on the outskirts of town and who turn up every day at the same hour to ask for their ritual handout at the kitchen door of a Palais-Royal restaurant;* there are others who travel together in packs over five leagues to take advantage of the meal charitably prepared for them by some sixty-year-old spinster who has given her unoccupied heart over to these animals, given that the shortsighted males of the world no longer take any interest in it.

There are others who, like runaway negro slaves,† creep back into the city on certain days from their rural hideouts, starved for love, and spend an hour frolicking around some pretty little bitch, somewhat shabbily dressed perhaps, but proud and grateful for the attention.

And all these dogs are extremely punctual, doing their rounds without notebook, time schedule, or briefcase.

Have you visited lazy old Belgium, and have you admired as I have all these energetic dogs pulling the carts of the butchers and milkmen and bakers, all barking in jubilation, all expressing the pleasure and pride they feel in competing with workhorses?

Here are two dogs who belong to an even more civilized sphere.‡ Allow me to usher you into the room of a traveling showman, absent for the moment. A bedstead of painted wood, without curtains, bedbug-stained blankets all in disarray, two cane chairs, a cast-iron stove, one or two battered musical instruments. Ah, how dismal these furnish-

---

* *A Palais-Royal restaurant:* Such as Le Grand Véfour, opened in the arcades of the Palais-Royal in 1784?

† *Runaway negro slaves:* Baudelaire's French term is *nègres marrons*. In his notes toward *Belgium Disrobed*, he calls dogs "the negroes of Belgium."

‡ *Here are two dogs:* What follows is an ekphrastic translation of Joseph Stevens's painting *L'Intérieur du saltimbanque*, also mentioned in Baudelaire's inventory of the art collection of Prosper Crabbe (see appendix 4): "*Joseph Stevens.* The run-down living quarters of a traveling showman. A suggestive painting. Dogs dressed up. The showman has gone out and placed a hussar's busby on one of the dog's heads in order to force him to sit still in front of the cooking pot that is warming on the stove. Too slick."

ings! But have a look, I beg you, at these two intelligent characters in the middle of the room, dressed in garments at once sumptuous and frayed, wearing headgear worthy of troubadours or soldiers, and who with their keen sorcerers' eyes sit there watching over *the work without a name** that is bubbling in its pot on the stove, with a long spoon emerging from the brew, planted there like one of those aerial masts indicating that the chimney masonry has now been completed.

Why shouldn't these two hard-working actors stock up on some strong, thick soup before setting out on the road? And wouldn't you forgive them if their mouths were watering at the sight of it, seeing as how these poor devils have to put up with apathetic audiences all day long, not the mention the unfairness of their director, who takes the lion's share and downs more soup than four actors combined?

How often have I cast a tender smile upon all these four-legged philosophers—these slaves whose obedience is a matter of sheer devotion or mere submission—and whom the republican dictionary might well define as *honorary* citizens, were the Republic less concerned with the *happiness* of mankind and more intent on saving the *honor* of dogs.

How often have I imagined that somewhere there was a paradise (who knows, after all?) that would reward all this courage, all this patience, all this hard labor, a special paradise for good dogs, poor dogs, mud-caked, broken-down dogs. After all, Swedenborg claims there is a special paradise for the Turks, and another for the Dutch.

The shepherds of Virgil and Theocritus expected that their pastoral songs would be rewarded with a piece of good cheese, a well-fashioned lute, or a nanny goat swollen with milk. The poet who sang of these poor old dogs was awarded a fine vest whose color, at once rich and faded, is reminiscent of autumn suns, of beautiful women ripe in years, and of Indian summers.†

---

* *The work without a name:* May parodically allude to the "deed without a name" in *Macbeth* 4.1—or to the Great Work of alchemy.

† *Indian summers:* Baudelaire's French runs "aux étés de la Saint-Martin." Saint Martin's Day was a late harvest festival celebrated each year on November 11 (or on October 31, in the Gregorian calendar) in honor of Saint Martin of Tours, a fourth-century Roman soldier and an early Christian bishop. Legend had it that Martin once cut his cloak in half to share it with a beggar during a fierce snowstorm. That very night he dreamed of Jesus surrounded by angels and wearing the half-cloak he

Nobody present at the tavern on the rue Villa-Hermosa* will ever forget how exuberantly the painter peeled off his vest and presented it to the poet, so well had he understood how fine and noble it was to sing of poor dogs.

It was as if some magnificent Italian tyrant of yore had offered the divine Aretino† either a dagger inlaid with jewels or a courtier's cloak in exchange for a precious sonnet or a curious bit of erotic verse.

And each time the poet dons the painter's vest, he inevitably thinks of good dogs, of philosopher dogs, of Indian summers, and of the beauty of women most ripe in years.

[*L'Indépendance belge*, June 21, 1865]

had given away—a vision that precipitated his conversion from pagan warrior into the exemplary Christian remembered on Michaelmas.

* *The tavern on the rue Villa-Hermosa:* A British-style pub in Brussels, Horton's Prince of Wales, a hangout for local painters and poets. Baudelaire describes Horton's (with his usual dyspepsia) in folio 49 of *Belgium Disrobed*: "The story of the gentleman who didn't want to pay for the pickles at Horton's. / Faro, 2 sous 3 centimes. / Obsessed with centimes. / Chairs without cross-bars. / The custom of serving drinks by the shot, as if the barman were assigned to monitor the cravings of the customer." In 1865, the same year as this prose poem was published, Charles Dickens stopped in at Horton's for drinks with his mistress, Ellen Ternan.

† *Aretino:* Sixteenth-century Italian playwright, poet, and satirist, known for his ribald verse.

Projects

---

* *[Lists of Titles]:* These three lists of projects—the pages editorially indicated as [I], [II], [III]—were most likely compiled between the fall of 1863 and the spring of 1865 when Baudelaire was trying to expand his *Paris Spleen* to one hundred poems. The first list indicates Baudelaire's attempt to divide up his collection of prose poems into three thematic zones: "Things Parisian" ("Choses parisiennes"), "Interpretation of Dreams" ("Onéirocritie"), and "Symbols and Moralities" ("Symboles et Moralités").

† *The Courtyard of the Messageries:* See the sketch of this poem on p. 210 below.

‡ *The End of the World:* See the final section of *Flares*.

* *A Parisian Lazzarone: Lazzarone,* a Neapolitan term for a homeless person who lives by begging or doing odd jobs.

† *Cholera at the Opera:* An allegorical engraving by the nineteenth-century German artist Alfred Rethel, whose baroque imagery of Death Baudelaire discusses in his 1859 essay on *L'Art philosophique.*

‡ *Melencolia:* Baudelaire's peculiar spelling of this term indicates he might have been thinking about Albrecht Dürer's 1514 engraving *Melencolia.*

INTERPRETATION OF DREAMS*

SYMBOLS AND MORALITIES

* *Interpretation of Dreams:* In French, Baudelaire's title is "Onéirocritque"—or in *OED* English "oneirocracy," the practice of dream interpretation.

† *Last Words of Jan Hus:* When a peasant added another log to the stake at which the heretic Jan Hus was burned, the martyr exclaimed, "Sancta simplicitas."

‡ *Lucan's Last Cantos:* Baudelaire considered translating Lucan's (unfinished) *Pharsalia* in 1860. He wrote Sainte-Beuve from Brussels in January 1866: "The *Pharsalia*— as scintillating, as melancholic, as stoic as ever—has provided solace to my neural- gias" (C2: 583).

§ *The Pharisee's Prayer:* Luke 18:10: "God, I thank thee, that I am not as other men are, extortioners, unjust, adulterers, or even as this publican." Baudelaire writes his

[II]

PARIS SPLEEN

To do

48 ᵇⁱˢ No Offense to the Shades
48 ᵗᵉʳ The Rosary
48 To Those Philosophers Who Enjoy Masked Balls
49 The Seductive Undertaker
50 The Black Hen
51 The Courtyard of the *Messageries*
52 The Reproachful Portrait (the Portrait of my Father)*
53 The End of the World
54 The Alienists (A Communion gone bad. Universal ministry of justice)
55 The Goldfish
56 The Hall of the Martyrs
57 The Diamond Man
58 Honeymoon Nights (The trials. The new pair of boots. The prayer)
59 The Old Pimp
60 Underripe
61 The Two Drunkards
62 The Hurdy-gurdy
63 The Altar of Moloch
64 The Deaf and Dumb Girl
65 The Theft of the Horsemen (Collectors. Maniacs. Kleptomaniacs. Portraits with eyeglasses)
66 Elegy for Hats
67 An Ash Wednesday ~~at the Saint Jacques Tollgate~~
68 Distribution of Provisions

mother from Brussels, "God, I thank thee for not having granted me the *bêtise* of Victor Hugo."

 * *The Reproachful Portrait:* Baudelaire claimed to have carried a painting of his dead father, Alphonse, from apartment to apartment during his frequent changes of address.

69 Festival in a Deserted City (Paris at Night, during Italian War era)*

70 The Little Old Atheist

71 Church Chants (In exitû Israel . . . ponam inimicos tuos . . .)†

72 Self-Cuckoldry or Incest

73 The Madagascan Pretender (memory rewitnessed in Paris via a wax doll) (short story)

74 The Boa (memory of India) (short story)

75 Orestes and Pylades

76 For Five Pennies

77 A Sudden Change of Wind

78 A Mollified Grudge (The story of Feuchères, *perhaps a short story*)‡

79 The Awaiting Father (Clown costume and toys, *perhaps a short story*)

80 The Lazzarone (in Paris)

81 In Honor of My Boss (The pool hall)

82 Filial Ingratitude (Birds) (experiment)

83 The Monitory Dream (*perhaps a short story*)

84 The Grove Inn (a boyhood memory, brought back by smell, color, and fresh breeze)

85 The Poet and the Historian (Carlyle and Tennyson)

86 Symptoms of Ruin

87 My Beginnings

88 Return to Boarding School (consultation)

89 Unknown Apartments (Places known and unknown, yet recognized. Dusty apartments. Moving days. Rediscovered books)

90 The Palace by the Sea

---

* *Festival in a Deserted City:* Probably alludes to the national celebrations of August 15, 1859, which featured a parade of the French army upon its victorious return from Italy, led by Napoleon III. In other words, a newspaper illustration in the manner of Constantin Guys.

† *In exitû Israel:* "When Israel went out of Egypt . . . I make thine enemies thy footstool."

‡ *Feuchères:* A minor French sculptor praised by Baudelaire in his *Salon de 1845*, then outright dismissed by him as a fraud the following year.

91	Landscapes Without Trees	
92	The Mousetrap	
93	Stairs (Vertigo. Great curves. Suspended men, a sphere, fog above and below.)	
94	Prisoner in a Lighthouse.	
95	Sentenced to Death (for a misdeed forgotten by me but suddenly regained, after the Sentence)	
96	Death	
97	The Sacred Illusion	
98	Melencolia [sic]	
99	A Desire	ORGANIZATION
100	The Dream of Socrates	Things Parisian
101	The Last Words of Jan Hus	Dreams
102	Without Remorse or Regret (?)	Symbols and Moralities
103	Lucan's Final Cantos	Other categories to be devised
104	The Rococo Sphinx	
105	The Gracious Guest	
106	Cholera at the Masked Ball	
107	Statistics and the Theater (Hell on Stage)	
108	Anywhere Out of the World (done)	
109	The Great Prayer	
110	Let's Beat Up the Poor (done)	
111	Good Dogs (done)*	
112	The Pharisee's Prayer	

[III]

Poems easy to do

~~The Courtyard of the *Messageries*~~
~~Elegy for Hats~~
~~From the Heights of the Buttes Chaumont~~
~~End of the World~~
~~The Altar of Moloch~~

* *Good Dogs (done):* This title, together with the previous mentions of the prose poems "Anywhere Out of The World" (#108) and "Let's Beat Up the Poor!" (#110), indicates that this list was made in Brussels in the spring of 1865.

~~Symptoms of Ruin~~
~~The Last Words of Jan Hus~~
~~The Dream of Socrates~~
~~The Black Hen~~
~~The Alienists~~
~~An Ash Wednesday~~
~~Self-cuckoldry or Incest?~~
~~The Little Old Atheist~~
~~For Five Pennies~~
~~Orestes and Pylades~~
~~The Poet and the Historian~~
~~The Sacred Illusion~~

*   *   *

[NOTES AND DRAFTS]

[A]

PROSE POEMS

Jean Hus (analysis of his last words).

The tall melancholy widow* loitering in front of the gardens of Musard's music hall.

The poor people in front of a brand-new café.

My dreams.

Comedy in the provinces.

Boarding school.

Death

The void (Sense of infinite void.)

Sentenced to death for a misdeed I have forgotten (Sensation of

---

* *The tall melancholy widow:* The seed of Baudelaire's prose poem "The Widows" (1861). The urban snapshot that follows would be developed into "The Eyes of the Poor" (1864).

fear. I do not argue with the sentence. Major misdeed not explained by the dream.)

Apartments unfamiliar to me, but noble and poetic.

The Old Acrobat.*

Elegy for Hats. Flowers in the desert. Thomas Gray's lines.†

[B]

PROSE POEMS

(For the Civil War)‡

The cannon thunders . . . limbs flying this way and that . . . the groans of the victims and the howls of those performing the sacrifice. . . . Humanity in its quest for happiness.

[C]

NIGHT POEMS

A Letter from a Fool

High-flown prose, at times sincere, at times ironic.

There are days when I feel so full of strength that . . .

World atlas.

---

* *The Old Acrobat:* Published in 1861 in the *Revue fantaisiste* as "Le Vieux Saltimbanque."

† *Thomas Gray's lines:* "Full many a flower is born to blush unseen / And waste its sweetness on the desert air," from "Elegy Written in a Country Churchyard." These lines also appear in Baudelaire's French adaptation in his 1852 poem "Le Guignon": "Mainte fleur épanche à regret / Son parfum doux comme un secret / Dans les solitudes profondes."

‡ *Civil war:* Among Baudelaire's favorite late readings in Brussels was Lucan's *Pharsalia*, also known as *De bello civili* or *Of Civil War*. He also followed the course of the American Civil War in the newspapers. As for the factional disputes between Catholics and Free Thinkers in Belgium, these too constituted for Baudelaire a civil war—but *en farce*.

[D]

Symptoms of ruin.* Colossal buildings. Many of them, one on top of another, apartments, rooms, *temples*, galleries, stairways, cecums, belvederes, lanterns, fountains, statues. —*Fissures, cracks. Humidity seeping in from a cistern located near the sky.* —How to warn the people of this, how to warn the nations? Warn the most intelligent, whisper in their ears.

High up, a column buckles and its two ends heave. Nothing has yet collapsed. I can no longer find my way out. I climb downward, then back upward. *A tower-labyrinth. I have managed to make my way out. I forever inhabit a building about to collapse, a building attacked by some secret disease.* —Just to amuse myself, I mentally envisage to what extent this stupendous mass of stone and marble, with all its statuary and walls about to crash down into each other, will be besplattered by human brains and body parts and shattered bones. —I see such terrible things in my dreams that there are times when I would rather stop sleeping altogether, were I not convinced that this would only further contribute to my fatigue.

[E]

Notes for the *Elegy for Hats*†

A hat. Smooth surface.
A bonnet. Pleated or ruffed surface.
The brim (extending from the place that no longer rests on the head).

---

* *Symptoms of Ruin:* A lone, undated sheet (now at the Bibliothèque Jacques Doucet), which Robert Kopp believes to be one of the last things Baudelaire wrote. A dream, many of whose architectural elements are taken from Piranesi's *Prisons*, De Quincey's *Confessions of an English Opium Eater*, and Nerval's *Aurelia*.

† *Elegy for Hats:* At the outset of his essay on Constantin Guys, "The Painter of Modern Life," Baudelaire describes leafing through a series of fashion-plates from the time of the Revolution through the Consulate. Fashion, he goes on to note (as will Benjamin and Barthes in his wake), provides a crucial index of "the moral or aesthetic feeling" of any given era. The *mundus muliebris* of this proto-Mallarméan "Elegy for Hats" is a study of the temporality of modernity as *la dernière mode*.

The rear portion of the crown is called *fond* or *calotte,* or *coiffe* when goffered.

Bonnet strings. Straps or thin little strings.

Plumes, marabou trims, aigrettes.

Hatbands made of feathers or flowers.

The *Maintenon,* a small lace headscarf that goes with the hat, knotted above the bonnet strings.

The *Marie Stuart,* designed with flattened point, saracen or ogival style.

The *Lavallière* hat (now out of fashion), with two plumes that converge at the back.

Russian hat. An aigrette.

The *Toquet* features a pompon or tassel.

A (pink) flower worn à la *Marie Louise.*

The *Marinière,* sailor-style bonnet with posy.

The *Longueville,* a Lavallière hat with a single plume drooping behind it, fluttering through space.

The *Highland* bonnet, in checked poplin, with cockade, silver brooch, and eagle or raven feathers.

Trimmings: Puffs, ruches, cloth cut on the bias, edgings.

A milliner's shop furnishings:

Curtains made of muslin or pure white silk. Couches. A cheval glass with polished surface. Oval or tilting mirrors. Large oval table with long-legged mushroom chairs. A fairies' laboratory. A clean line of work.

General appearance: freshness, brightness, whiteness, a flowerbed's vivid colors.

Ribbons, frills and flounces, tulles, gauzes, muslins, feathers, etc.

The hats make one think of heads, a gallery of heads. Because every hat by its specific features evokes a head in the mind's eye. Severed heads.

How sad it is, all this solitary frivolity! The depressing sensation of mindless, carefree ruin. A monument of gaiety in the desert. A wanton frivolity.

The suburban milliner, pale, consumptive, café au lait skin, like an ancient tobacconist in her stall.

[F]

The Courtyard of the Messageries*

In the midst of a group of various people alighting from a coach, a woman surrounded by her children throws her arms around a traveler in a cotton cap. Chilly Parisian day. A small child stands on tiptoes to be kissed.

In the background, another traveler loads his luggage onto a porter's hooks.

In the foreground, to the left, a beggar holds out his cap toward a military man sporting a yellow plume, a soldier of fortune as lean as Bonaparte, and a national guardsman tries to steal a kiss from a luscious shopgirl who's holding a tray and who's half-heartedly resisting.

To the right, a gentleman, hat in hand, speaks to a woman holding a child; near this group, two dogs fighting. Boilly, 1803

[G]

Der Tod as Erwürger.†
Erster Austritt der Cholera auf einem Maskenball in Paris. 1831.
Der tod als Freud.
Death as executioner.
First appearance of cholera at a masked ball in Paris, 1831.
Death as friend.

*   *   *

---

* *Courtyard of the Messageries:* Ekphrastic description of the 1803 genre painting by Louis-Léopold Boilly held by the Louvre.
† *Der Tod als Erwürger:* Title of a lithograph by Alfred Rethel, translated into French by Baudelaire.

[PROJECTS FOR SHORT STORIES AND NOVELS]*

[I]

NOVELS AND SHORT STORIES

The Invisible Marquis?
The Fatal Portrait?
Parricide Love
The Almanac
The End of the World
Icelandic Hemlock?
Heads or Tails
Young Boniface Triumphs
The Unicorn
The Idiot's Mistress
White Slavery
A Black Sheep?
To Loathe Her Is to Adore Her
Holocaust at Will

[II]

NOVELS

The Automaton	*The Prophetic Dream* x
The Blue-Eyed Negress	*A Hungry Man* {conspiracy
The Lessons of a Monster	*Head or Tails* x
To Loathe Her Is to Adore Her	The Madagascan Pretender†

---

* [Projects for Short Stories and Novels]: Pichois's editorial title for the fragments gathered in OC1: 588–99, of his Pléiade edition. He dates them as ranging from the early 1850s through Baudelaire's Brussels years.

† *The Madagascan Pretender:* Based on an 1861 article in *Le Monde illustré* describing the intense and often murderous rivalries between the pretenders to the throne after the death of Madagascar's queen, Ranavalo-Manjaka.

The Virgin Mistress

The Precocious Children
A Black Sheep
High School Crime
White Slavery   x
The Idiot's Mistress—
The Unicorn   x

The Catechism of the Woman
     in Love
The Disgraceful Husband

The Monsters
The World's Happy Few
Lesbians
The Friend of the Red
The Undersea World
A City Within a City
Miners
Glassmakers
The Holocaust
The Altar of the Will   x
The Virgin Mistress
Young Boniface Triumphs

[III]

SHORT STORIES

A Mollified Grudge
(my adventures with Feuchères)
The Ever-Awaiting Father
The Portentous Dream
The Madagascan Pretender
The Boa

*The Reasonable Fool and the Beautiful
Adventuress*   x
Speculations on the Postal Service
The Deserter   x
The Fatal Portrait   x

The Boa   x
Icelandic Hemlock
A Grudge

The Almanac (engage in a
speculation on the calculus of
probabilities involving packages
that never arrive and the resulting
indemnities)

The End of the World

A Change of Wind
The Incorrigible Deserter

[IV]

Man in a Lottery
The Invisible Marquis
The Impossible Portrait
    (due to antipathy)
The Fatal Portrait

[V]

NOVELS

The Invisible Marquis
    Most important

[VI]

NOVELS

A Grudge (Feuchères)
    His daughter
    The Mare
    The Visits to the concierge

[VII]

NOVELS

    Icelandic Hemlock
        (see Goerres on mystic states)*

---

* *See Goerres on mystic states:* Joseph Görres, nineteenth-century German author of various works on mysticism, mentions the Icelanders' use of hemlock for hallucinogenic purposes.

[VIII]

See the question of Sultana Alida.* —*The Circus of Official Honors.*
—*Gazette des Tribunaux* —30 Sept. 1858
M. Ducreux, deputy judge

A series of scenes from the Directoire or Consulate.
The fashions of those times.
The erotic engravings of those times.

Montesquieu's style.

The sensual delights of the Church. Libertine urges felt at
Saint-Paul.

A little old lady whom one follows.

The sculpture or painting gallery for the new Don Juan.

Theory of Faith.

[IX]

No remorse no regrets

What does great suffering matter when one has known great joys?
It's a law, an equilibrium.
Work out the moral algebra of this common saying.
Various refrains.
                    The Keeper of a mistress

The Beautiful Adventuress (more of a novel than a poem)

---

* *Sultina Alida:* The trial of Alida Daldir, a faith-healer who had passed herself off
as a sultana, as reported by the *Gazette des tribunaux.*

[X]

Apply to the notion of joy, of *feeling oneself alive,* the idea of the hyperacuity of the senses, which Poe applied to the notion of pain.*
Create a work through the sheer logic of contraries. The path lies open, against the grain.

[XI]

NOVELS

The Madagascan Pretender
(Locate the issue of the *Monde illustré*
See Messieurs Reynaud, Poethey et Delvau, *9 rue Véron.*)

[XII]

DRAFTS, PROJECTS

Suicide in a Bathtub.

THE FATAL PORTRAIT

Analytical method to verify the miracle. Portrait of the departed.
Discovery of the will. Depiction of a family marked by fatal sorrow.
  —The Deserter, or the military man as comedian
  Armand Baschet.

The old lady's lover.
Prohibited because belief in ghosts.

The *Sortes Biblicae.*†

---

* *Which Poe applied to the notion of pain:* In his description of Roderick Usher.
  † *Sortes Biblicae:* Magical bibliomancy based on chance openings of the pages of the Bible.

The drunkard espying and studying the drunkard.

The perfect man: everything just so, his carriage, his watch.

Of the power of philters and magic in love, like the power of the evil eye.

Divine essence of the vicious circle *(Flares)*.

THE DRUNKARD. —Not to forget that drunkenness is the negation of time, like every violent state of mind, and that, as a result, all the consequences of wasted time must parade before the drunkard's eyes, without however destroying his tendency to put his conversion off to tomorrow—this until all his emotions have been completely perverted and the ultimate catastrophe ensues.

The Conspiracy. I belong to a race which . . . . The taste for death and the taste for life have always had equal sway over me. I have taken a bitter joy in life.

I am several centuries old, for it seems to me my thoughts and actions have occurred in different eras. Who could prove me wrong?

Who will deny the right to suicide? I have nonetheless attempted, such is the modest, critical bent of my mind, to read everything that has been written about suicide. The patent absurdity of Jean-Jacques's maxim.*

—If the conspirators give up their game, my life will lose interest. So it serves my purpose to encourage conspiracy.

(Portrait of the prince. His follies. These follies make him interesting to me. A scoundrel in his youth: *Inde* what vices and what qualities?

(Life is a gamble, the gamblers number some three billion. The odds. *The minute*, to the loser who takes all.)

It was Robespierre, I think, who once observed, "Man never sees his fellow man without pleasure," with that concision that so impressed me in my youth. . . . How many years has it now been that this maxim

---

* *Jean-Jacques's maxim:* Rousseau discusses the pros and cons of suicide in letters 21 and 22 of part 3 of *La Nouvelle Héloïse* (1761). In the years immediately after his death, a legend grew up that Rousseau, like Socrates, had indeed committed suicide, drinking not hemlock but poisoned café au lait.

has ceased to make sense to me? Has nobody else but me felt such a horror at the sight of his fellow man? . . . From the moment I awake to the blessed and often fearsome moment when I go to sleep, there is not a single activity of life that doesn't require the presence and the help of one's fellow man. . . .

Now that I have again discovered the conspiracy, my youth returns. My eyes take a new interest in life. Memories no longer weigh down on me. (A supper with the poor. So there is some virtue in humanity. Humility, willingness to help, generosity.) But once the conspiracy disappears, the taste of nothingness returns.

Jean-Jacques Rousseau's idiotic comment about the way to stop suicide.

[XIII]

NOVELS

Write to Malassis to ask him for books about brigands, highway-men, and sorcerers, especially during the period just after the French Revolution.

Vendée
Schinderhannes*

A novel
   on the *Last Men*
The same vices as before
Immense distances

On warfare, marriage, politics, etc. . . . among the last men.

Brigands
Sorcery

---

* *Schinderhannes:* Johannes Bückler, nicknamed Schinderhannes, eighteenth-century German outlaw who orchestrated one of the most famous crime sprees in German history.

Imprisonments
Palaces and (subterranean) prisons
Scenes of torture and horror

[XIV]

A mere child, the skirts, the silk, the perfumes, the knees of women.
The love of perfection. Everything that disgusts him, he destroys.
He finds an excuse.
Devise the denouement applying the analytic method.

Explore the (vague and general) meaning of colors. Divisions and subdivisions.

[XV]

Jeanne and the automaton.*

An ancient ladies' man.
Every libertine act imaginable.

————

The dance of grammar.
The voice of the adjective penetrated me right down to my bones.

————

A. is a libertine
a. is not yet one
The late A. is one no more.
a. becomes a libertine woman
The frigid wife becomes the torrid lover of a dead man.

————

* *Jeanne and the automaton:* Presumably his mistress, Jeanne Duval.

No doubt there were moments of delirium when I showered him with caresses that were most unrestrained; for he told me on several occasions that he had never imagined that an honest woman could be capable of such diabolical errors when it came to love, especially a woman philosopher.

———

Voice of paradise
The rub? The drama of Revelation.

———

The style all the more decorous as the ideas become less so.

———

What the note of mystery should involve.

———

Scrawniness has something indecent to it which renders it all the more enticing.

[XVI]

NOVELS AND SHORT STORIES

Imagine a poor, starving man wanting to take advantage of a public festival and the distribution of free food just in order to get something to eat.
He is shoved this way and that and beaten up by the crowd.

———

To have discovered a conspiracy.
This is almost a work of art.

This is a novel whose denouement I have already established.

I hold the Empire in my hands.

Alternative, hesitation.

Why save the Empire?

Why destroy it?

Therefore Heads or tails.

Perhaps a comedy

[XVII]

NOVELS

The Reasonable Fool and the Beautiful Adventuress

Thrill of pleasure in the Company of the Profligate.

What horrors and what joys reserved for someone in love with a female spy or thief, etc. . . . !

The moral reason for such joys.

One must always go back to De Sade, that is, to *Natural Man*, to explain evil.

Open with a discussion of love among a group of finicky gentlemen.*

Monstrous feelings of friendship or admiration for a depraved woman.

My *Sisina* sonnet.†

To come up with weird and horrible adventures, in various capitals.

[XVIII]

The man who believes his dog or cat to be the Devil, or some sort of spirit locked up within them.

The man who sees a flaw or an imaginary (physical) defect in his mistress. Obsession.

---

* *A group of finicky gentlemen:* Seed of the late prose poem "Portraits of Mistresses."

† *My Sisina sonnet:* First published in 1859 and evoking the Italian adventuress Elisa Gu(i)erri (or Nieri), the "E. G." mentioned in the second folio of *Flares*.

The man who believes himself ugly—or who sees in himself an imaginary (physical?) defect. Obsession.

A man dreams that he is in such and such a place, surrounded by such and such objects, and that by some inexplicable association of ideas, he is reduced to killing himself—

One day, he actually finds himself in this very place, surrounded by these same objects—and kills himself.

[XIX]

NOVELS

The man of despair need not be as beautiful as his woman.
The man who is not handsome can take no joy in love.

———

Reason for immediate [ ]
A dog or a cat.

[XX]

THE AUTOMATON

What he is, as a lover.
A sorcerer, hoping to fend off any unforeseen accident, he wants to fight against the laws of Nature.
His last will and testament ("If you truly love me . . . ")
And he automatically comes back to life.
His mistress wonders to herself which of these two existences is a dream.
The automaton, prompted by his soul, persuades her that *she had been dreaming* all along and that now he is truly alive.
But his soul, ashamed that it has created this illusion of happiness with a lie, prefers to commit a murder and awakes his beloved through Death, hoping to explain everything to her in Paradise.
What is Paradise?

[XXI]

THE VIRGIN MISTRESS

The woman who does not come is the woman one loves.

The woman who does not make one come is the woman one loves.

A question of aesthetic delicacy, the idol-worship of the man who's seen it all.

Your mistress becomes more endearing to you when you debauch yourself with other women. What she loses in sexual pleasures, she makes up for in adoration.

The realization that he needs to be forgiven makes the man far more loving, more attentive.

On chastity in love.

[XXII]

NOVELS AND SHORT STORIES

Parricide Love.*

Description of the inn.

The wife, the husband, the husband's father.

The lovers, the whole town, including the Imperial Prosecutor and the police.

The reason the wife so hates the father.

The husband's jealousy.

The murder.

The trial.

The execution.

[XXIII]

For the Lover of Beauty,

To Loathe Her is to Adore Her
  or The Disgraceful Husband

* *Parricide Love:* Written in Brussels, on Hôtel du Grand Miroir stationery.

my castle
my wife
The waterfall

———

I am truly debauched. I enjoy orgies, to which I bring the condiment
of irony.

[XXIV]

The defense of the deserter facing court-martial.

———

The reverse of Claude Gueux.* Theory of sacrifice.
Legitimization of the death penalty. The sacrifice only becomes
complete with the *sponte sua*† of the victim.

———

The voluptuary, having long vacillated, is drawn from ferocity into
charity. What kind of misfortune might have caused his conversion?
The illness of his old female accomplice. Battle between egoism, pity,
and Remorse. His mistress (now become his daughter) allows him to
discover fatherly feelings. —Remorse: who knows whether he is not
the author of the misfortune.

[XXV]

A man condemned to death, the job bungled by the executioner,
set free by the people, would return to the executioner. —Yet another
justification for the death penalty.

———

* *Claude Gueux:* An 1834 short story by Victor Hugo, illustrative of the barbarity of
capital punishment.
† *Sponte sua:* Legal term: "of one's own accord; voluntarily."

[XXVI]

NOVELS

The last gasps of the world.
The last men.
Conflicts, rivalries. Hate, the taste for destruction and prosperity.
Their loves, in mankind's waning days.
(Avoid The Last Man)*
Immense distances.
Each sovereign left with but 50 armed men.

---

* *The Last Man:* Jean-Baptiste Cousin de Grainville's prose poem *Le Dernier Homme* (1803), the first story of modern speculative fiction to depict the End of the World. Or possibly Mary Shelley's apocalyptic science fiction novel, *The Last Man* (1826).

PART THREE

Belgium
Disrobed

Introduction BRUSSELS SPLEEN

Among the precious *reliquiae* published for the first time in Eugène Crépet's 1887 edition of Baudelaire's *Oeuvres posthumes* was a brief fifteen-page selection from his "Fragments of an Unfinished Book on Belgium" that contained the author's observations on the country's fine arts and architecture as well as a few jottings relating his travels to the towns of Malines, Antwerp, and Namur. Here too Malassis had prepared the path to publication by delving into the contents of Baudelaire's Brussels trunk and organizing and numbering the 360 loose leaves of the unfinished book—which consisted of sheets in Baudelaire's hand (on hotel stationery or graph paper) as well as other folios featuring newspaper clippings or printed ephemera that he had pasted onto the page and marked in red ink with furious underlinings and sarcastic marginal comments. This "farrago of notes" (as Malassis called it) was divided into thirty-three sheaves, each containing materials relevant to the book's various chapters on Customs, Religion, Politics, the Fine Arts, and so on. A separate "Argument of the Book on Belgium," neatly penned on blue paper in early 1866 and intended by Baudelaire as a prospectus for publishers, accompanied the thirty-three sheaves. Crépet subsequently oversaw the independent publication of this ten-page "Argument" in an 1890 issue of the *Revue d'aujourd'hui*—and this summary remained the only portion of the book available to readers until the appearance in 1953 under the title *Pauvre Belgique* of the first critical edition of the entire manuscript by Crépet's son Jacques and Claude Pichois.[1] This is the version reprinted in Pichois's one-volume Pléiade edition of 1961 and (now having acquired an exclamation mark as *Pau-*

vre Belgique!) in volume 2 of his 1976 Pléiade Oeuvres complètes. In 1986 André Guyaux presented an expanded version of these materials in Gallimard's Folio series under the title La Belgique déshabillée.[2]

Baudelaire never seems to have settled on a definitive name for this great ruin—or construction site—of a book. In his correspondence of 1864 he refers to it as his Lettres belges (or Belgian Letters), a project whose "fragments" he hoped to publish in the pages of the Figaro under the pseudonym he used for his juvenilia, "Charles de Féyis" (his mother's maiden name)—a ruse to protect himself from the fate of his old acquaintance from 1848, the exiled philosopher Pierre-Joseph Proudhon, who had recently been expelled from Belgium for a humorous open letter to Napoleon III sarcastically suggesting that France, in fulfillment of its imperialist ambitions (namely, its recent military forays into Italy and Mexico), simply go ahead and annex its neighbor outright. The possibility of the newspaper publication of these letters having evaporated, Baudelaire subsequently adopted the mock-commiserative title Pauvre Belgique (Poor Belgium), but the publication in Brussels in 1865 of a virulently anti-imperial pamphlet similarly entitled Pauvre France seems to have led him to change his mind later that same year and to choose the tentative title La Belgique déshabillée instead. As Guyaux remarks, this late working title established a rhyme with Mon Coeur mis à nu, the other magnum opus that Baudelaire planned to complete in Brussels. With Goya's Maja desnuda in mind—of which Baudelaire had asked Nadar to make a photographic copy and of whose impact on Manet's recently exhibited Olympia he was no doubt aware—I have therefore chosen to render the title in English as Belgium Disrobed.[3] A bride stripped bare (by her bachelor, even), lying there stark naked, in the raw, her monstrosity on display for all to see.

Unlike Pichois and Guyaux, I have printed the "Argument for the Book on Belgium" at the very outset of my selection from the mass of its preparatory notes.[4] Composed in January 1866, this summary was Baudelaire's last stab at getting his book into some sort of synoptic shape in order to present it to publishers in Paris. In the event, the firms of Lévy, Dentu, and Garnier all turned the project down, fearing that its merciless portrayal of la bêtise belge would hurt their commercial interests in Belgium. This prospectus is probably the most convenient portal into the debris that Baudelaire had amassed for his im-

mense *mise à nu* of Belgium. As it announced, he would devote nearly
ten of his initial chapters to the study of the *moeurs* of Brussels—its
manners, morals, and customs. This would be followed by chapters on
the country's educational system, on the peculiarities of its usage of
French, on its journalists and literati, on the conflicts between its anti-
clerical freethinkers and its Catholic clergy, on the dysfunctional work-
ings of its parliamentary democracy and electoral system, on its mil-
itary forces, and finally (and most topically in December 1865) on its
farcical national mourning of its equally farcical constitutional mon-
arch Leopold I, *Roi des Belges,* lately deceased—all this to be rounded
out by a consideration of the country's fine arts and architecture, sup-
plemented by a series of *promenades artistiques* to its various other cit-
ies and towns, with the whole amounting to thirty-three chapters in all.
The book, as this prospectus suggests, was something of a hybrid mon-
ster—part guidebook, part reportage, part political pamphlet, part self-
portrait, part sheer tomfoolery (or *bouffonerie*)—with careful first-hand
newspaper documentation (for example, on the partisan politics of
electoral gerrymandering and campaign finance reform) interleaved
with coarse satirical squibs and vignettes. Given the virulence—or what
Judith Butler might call the "excitable speech"—of its language (which
rendered it unpublishable), Baudelaire's delirious satire of Belgium has
been compared by critics to Octave Mirbeau's account of his automo-
bile visit to the country, recorded in his 1907 novel bearing the num-
ber of his license plate, *628-E3,* or to Céline's account of his 1936 tour
through Russia, *Mea culpa.*

Following this initial "Argument," I have included a substantial selec-
tion from Baudelaire's notes toward this unfinished book, slightly ed-
ited down in order to avoid their nearly verbatim repetition of identical
observations—a sign of what his friend Malassis termed Baudelaire's
tendency to *radoter* (or to just rattle on and on) when it came to all
things Belgian. I have also for the most part merely summarized the
various newspaper clippings that Baudelaire glued onto the pages of
his manuscript—although I have fully translated all those materials
that he actually copied out by hand or whose specific language singled
them out as particularly salient *objets trouvés* worthy of inclusion in this
immense montage whose citational strategies of mimetic satire and
impersonation anticipate those of Flaubert's *Bouvard and Pecuchet,* of

Karl Kraus's cabaret readings of newspapers aloud, or of Walter Benja-
min's *Arcades Project*. As Bertolt Brecht observed of Kraus, "When the
age laid hands upon itself, he was the hands."[5] And the same might
be said of Baudelaire in Belgium—except that in his case when he laid
his hands upon the age, it resulted in his own self-strangulation, his
tongue tossed to the dogs . . . .

*   *   *

Baudelaire, Sartre reminds us, was forever the accomplished architect
of his own ruin; T. S. Eliot similarly points out his "mulish determi-
nation to make the worst of everything." On his arrival in Brussels in
late April 1864, Baudelaire promptly set into motion the plan he had
long premeditated. In order to convince Albert Lacroix to bring out a
number of his uncollected writings in book form, he would embark on
a series of lectures throughout the land in order to impress the pub-
lisher with his literary celebrity (and marketability). His first lecture,
on Delacroix, in early May at the Cercle artistique et littéraire went rel-
atively well. *L'Indépendance belge* described it as a "most brilliant and
well-deserved success," but in a letter to his mother, Baudelaire con-
fessed: "Between the two of us, everything is going very badly. I ar-
rived too late. There is a great deal of greed here, and an infinite slow-
ness in all things, a vast mass of empty brains. In a word, these people
are dumber than the French."[6] He had learned that it was too late in the
lecture season to schedule the lucrative cross-country speaking tour on
which he had counted; in addition, the winter funds of the Cercle hav-
ing been exhausted, he was forced to accept a fee of 50 francs per lec-
ture instead of the 200 he had been promised. Besides, Lacroix was
away in Paris and couldn't attend—and as a result, Baudelaire offered
to give three more lectures absolutely free of charge to reel in the pub-
lisher when he returned. The following week, his second lecture—this
time a reading of his study of Théophile Gautier (published as a pam-
phlet by Malassis in 1859)—proved to be a disaster. In his opening re-
marks, Baudelaire reminded his audience that "at my first lecture I lost
what might be called the virginity of the word; which, I might add, is
no more of a loss than the other"—which promptly caused a number of
the female audience members to withdraw. A young Belgian writer in

attendance would later remember the poet-officiant standing there "in his white cravat in the circle of light cast by an oil lamp, his pale clean-shaven face darkened by the half-light of the lampshade, his eyes moving about like black suns, his mouth thin and trembling, delicately vibrant under the violin bow of the words." By the time he had completed his hieratic performance, there was not a soul left in the hall. At the end of his three subsequent lectures (entitled "Intoxicants" and drawn from his 1860 study of drugs, *Artificial Paradises*, also published by Malassis), his audience had dwindled to eight—and Lacroix had still not shown his face. One of those present described him during his final lecture as being seized by a terrible case of stage fright (*le trac*), "reading and stammering, trembling, with his teeth chattering, his nose buried in his manuscript."[7] For the entire lecture series, Baudelaire received an honorarium of 100 francs, barely enough to cover his hotel bill.

In the immediate wake of this series of embarrassments and disappointments, Baudelaire sent off a furious note to his friend Manet back in Paris in late May:

> The Belgians are idiots [*bêtes*], liars, and thieves. I have been the victim of the most bare-faced bit of trickery. Here the practice of deceit is the rule, almost a badge of honor. I have not yet addressed the major piece of business that brought me here [his negotiations with Lacroix]; but everything that's happened so far bodes very ill—not to mention that I am here taken to be an associate of the French police. —Don't believe a word they tell you about Belgian good-heartedness. Cunning, wariness, fake affability, vulgarity, underhand dealing—for sure.[8]

For the remainder of his stay in Belgium, Baudelaire would not budge from this initial rancorous assessment of its people's character—formed, it should be noted, by his contacts with the French-speaking bourgeoisie of the Brabant region of Brussels and not by any observation of the Flemish speakers of agricultural Flanders to the north or of the francophone proletarians of industrialized Wallonia to the east and south.

As to the rumors that he had come to Belgium as an agent of the French police, Baudelaire ascribed these to the "Hugo gang." After the coup d'état of December 5, 1851, like thousands of other Republican political refugees, Victor Hugo had slipped over the border into Belgium and installed himself on the Grand-Place in Brussels. Here, over the course of a month he composed his extraordinary eyewitness account of what Marx would call *The 18th Brumaire of Louis Napoleon*, published the following year in London as *Napoléon le Petit* (*Napoleon the Small*). From his subsequent outposts of exile, first on the isle of Jersey and then on Guernsey, Hugo continued to fulminate against the French dictator in his 1853 volume of satirical verse, *Les Châtiments* (*The Punishments*). In the spring of 1861, having refused the recent amnesty granted by the Second Empire to its *proscrits*, he was back in Belgium, finishing up the manuscript of *Les Misérables* at Waterloo. Lacroix brought it out the following year in Brussels, having paid its author an eye-popping 300,000 francs for the rights (and netting his firm 517,000 francs in profit on its international sales). When the novel appeared, Baudelaire reviewed it, damning it with faint praise while in private descrying its sentimental humanism as "vile and inept." Hugo effusively thanked him for the notice—which, as Baudelaire wrote his mother, only confirmed what a numbskull its author was. After its publication, Hugo (or "Olympio," as Baudelaire derisively called him) returned to the prophetic haunts of his Hauteville House on Guernsey, but finding life there too constricting, his sons, Charles and François-Victor, decamped to Brussels in February 1864, where they were joined by their mother, Adèle. In mid-April, barely two weeks before he too would move to Brussels, Baudelaire published his denunciation of the planned celebration of the Shakespeare tricentenary in Paris as a "socialist" plot to honor Hugo's new book, *William Shakespeare* (published by Lacroix), and his son François-Victor's translations of the Bard. Apparently, as a result of Baudelaire's article in the *Figaro*, the French government canceled the festivities, causing a minor diplomatic flap with Great Britain (see appendix 3). Little wonder if Hugo's sons took the recently arrived poet to be a *mouchard*—a police informer or outright spy. In any event, they considered him a suspicious reactionary blackguard (which was true), wholly lacking in the exilic grandeur of their world-famous father (also true).[9]

Baudelaire reveled in the rumors that surrounded him in Brussels. As he had confessed in *Flares*: "When I've inspired universal disgust and horror, I'll have conquered solitude." To one of his correspondents he boasted shortly after his arrival: "They have taken me to be a *police officer* (*good for them!*) (on account of that fine article that I wrote about the Shakespeare banquet), to be a *pederast* (it was I who spread this rumor; and *they believed it!*), then they took me to be a *copy editor*, sent from Paris to correct the proofs of *obscene books* [Malassis's Belgian editions of erotica]. *Exasperated at always being believed,* I spread the rumor that I had *murdered* my father and that *I had eaten him. . . . I swim in opprobrium like a fish in the sea.*"[10] In a section of his *Poor Belgium* devoted to the Belgians' taste for bad-mouthing and slander, he recounts with great verve his delight in playing the *agent provocateur* to the credulity of the local populace:

> When I wanted to put an end to this national passion for slander, at least insofar as my own case was concerned, I resorted to irony, poor simpleton that I am.
>
> To all those who wanted to know why I was staying on so long in Belgium (they don't like foreigners to stay on too long), I explained, quite *confidentially*, that I was a *mouchard*.
>
> And they believed me!
>
> To others I confided that I had been forced to flee France because I had committed a number of crimes too atrocious to describe, but that I was hoping that, thanks to appalling corruption of the French regime, I would soon be amnestied.
>
> And they believed me!
>
> Exasperated, I went on to declare that I was not only a murderer but a pederast. This latter revelation had completely unexpected consequences. The Belgian musicians concluded that Mr. Richard Wagner was a pederast.
>
> For a Belgian cannot get it through his skull that a man might praise another man for entirely disinterested reasons.

All this notwithstanding, Walter Benjamin was certainly right to see in Baudelaire a "secret agent"—"an agent of the secret discontent of his class with its own hegemony."[11]

*   *   *

Meanwhile, after the fiasco of his lecture series, Baudelaire had still not managed to enter into negotiations with Lacroix for the publication of two volumes of his collected criticism and a decent new edition of his *Artificial Paradises*, the rights to which he hoped to sell for 20,000 francs. This sum, he fantasized, would finally release him from chronic debt. Through the good offices of his friend the art dealer Arthur Stevens, a last attempt was made to beard Hugo's elusive publisher. On the evening of June 13, a *soirée* in Baudelaire's honor was arranged at the home of wealthy stockbroker and art collector Prosper Crabbe. Lacroix had been personally invited, as had the editor-in-chief of *L'Indépendance belge*, but only a handful of guests showed up. Baudelaire described the scene to his mother in Daumieresque strokes: "Just imagine *three enormous drawing rooms*, lit with *chandeliers and candelabras*, decorated with superb paintings, an *absurd* profusion of cakes and wine—and all this for ten or twelve *very glum* people. A journalist leaned over and said to me: '*There is something* CHRISTIAN in your works that has not been sufficiently remarked upon.' At the other end of the room, on the sofa of stockbrokers, I heard a murmur: '*He's saying that we are all* CRETINS!'"[12] In this act of suspicious eavesdropping, in the enormity of this tiny phonetic gap between *chrétien* and *crétin*, Baudelaire suddenly seized the comic potential that lay dormant in the gaping abyss of Belgian *bêtise*. In a postscript to the letter, he informed his mother that the book on Belgium he was currently considering might contain "some extremely humorous things, things that nobody has dared to say." Baudelaire made two more attempts to contact Lacroix and his associate Verboeckhoven in the offices of their publishing house, only to be informed that they had no interest at all in his literary or art criticism but that if he managed to come up with a *novel* they might be willing to consider it. The last one hears of Lacroix in Baudelaire's letters is that the publisher was now standing as a candidate for local election and that the poet (*mouchard* that he was) had tracked him down to the hustings—in order to boo him roundly.

His three-volume Lacroix venture having gone up in smoke, Baudelaire nonetheless retained the possibility of turning his trip to Belgium into a more conventional volume—namely, a series of essays on the country's art and architecture, providing the record of an aesthetic sensibility on tour, perhaps in the vein of a Dumas, Nerval, Gautier, or Heine; this was the project for which he had unsuccessfully sought funding from the French Ministries of Education and of the Fine Arts the previous year. With Arthur Stevens acting as his cicerone, he visited several private art collections in Brussels, to his great disappointment.

Baudelaire had recently become more and more interested in the fig-
ure of the *collectionneur* and, in a piece published in the *Le Figaro* just
before he left for Brussels, had praised the French art collector Eugène
Piot as an example of "those who have slowly, passionately amassed
objets d'art completely appropriate to their own natures, transforming
them into family members of their choice."[13] By contrast, in the private
art collection of Belgian stockbroker and recent host Prosper Crabbe,
he saw no trace of elective affinity but merely the ignorant desire to
acquire "specimen" examples of contemporary painters for invest-
ment purposes—painters primarily French, primarily second-rate, or
if Belgian, "all *pasticheurs*, all duplicates of French talent" (see appen-
dix 4 for Baudelaire's catalog of Crabbe's collection). The only painting
in the stockbroker's private gallery that truly challenged Baudelaire's
eye was, predictably, Delacroix's 1854 *Tiger Hunt* (currently held by the
Musée d'Orsay in Paris), a heroic battle between man and beast. Baude-
laire's notes on the painting amount to a telegraphic poem in prose:
"Delacroix, alchemist of Color. Miraculous, profound, mysterious, sen-
sual, terrifying. Colors brilliant and dark, penetrating harmony. The
man's gesture, and the gesture of the beast. The grimace of the beast,
the sniffs of animality. Green, lilac, dark green, soft lilac, vermillion,
dark red, a sinister bouquet."

Although Baudelaire was certainly no stranger to the operations of
the art market in Paris—one of his most persistent creditors remained
the shady art dealer Arondel, from whom he had ruinously purchased
a number of fakes in his youth—the conflation of commerce with aes-
thetics was even more blatant here in Brussels, it being the function of
Belgian *bêtise* to lay all things unashamedly bare:

> A government minister whose gallery I am visiting says to me as I am
> singing the praises of David: "It would seem that the market for Davids
> is going up."
> I retort: "David's stock has never fallen among those possessed of
> any intelligence at all."[14]

On the same page he further noted:

> The manner in which Belgians discuss the value of paintings. It al-
> ways comes down to numbers. This goes on for hours at end. Having

spent three hours quoting the various market prices, they think they have held forth on painting.

Furthermore, the paintings need to be hidden in order to increase their value. The eye wears out paintings.

"L'oeil use les tableaux"—a rather decent *blague belge,* or Belgian joke, as it turns out, its humor turning on the literal-minded confusion between (in Walter Benjamin's terms) the auratic dimension of a work of art and its exhibition value as a commodity.

Surveying the contemporary Belgian art scene, Baudelaire concluded (with a jab at his *bête noire* Courbet): "Composition, a thing unknown. The philosophy of these brutes—a philosophy à la Courbet. Only paint what you see. Therefore *you* are not allowed to paint what *I don't see.* Specialists. One painter for the sun, one for the moon, one for furniture, one for fabrics, one for flowers—with infinite subdivisions of these specialties, as in industry."

The extremely successful painter Alfred Stevens (brother of Baudelaire's cicerone, the art dealer Arthur Stevens) illustrated to perfection the industrialization and commodification of art in Belgium.

> M. Alfred Stevens normally paints a little woman (his particular tulip), always the same one, writing a letter, receiving a letter, hiding a letter, receiving a bouquet, hiding a bouquet, etc. . . . The unfortunate thing about this scrupulous painter is that the letter, the bouquet, the chair, the ring, the guipure, etc., become, in their turn, the crucial object, the object obvious to all eyes. In short, he is a *perfectly* Flemish painter, in that he seeks perfection in little *nothings* or in the *imitation of nature,* which amounts to the same thing.

"Perfection in little *nothings,*" or as Baudelaire's French has it, "la perfection dans le *néant*"—*néant* in nineteenth-century usage meaning "things (or persons) of no value" in addition to the more philosophical "nothingness."[15] This serial and specialized production of *le néant,* this fetishistic attention to objectified (or reified) nugatory detail was, as Baudelaire observed, not only part of the legacy of seventeenth-century Flemish genre painting (he mentions Ostade and Teniers as egregious examples) but also a symptom of the impact of Courbet's doctrine of realism on contemporary Belgian art.

Baudelaire had reason to be allergic to the practice and concept of realism. This after all was the term (with its tincture of subversive socialism) on the basis of which both Flaubert's *Madame Bovary* and his own *Les Fleurs du mal* had been brought to trial by the imperial censors in 1857.[16] But despite his early left-wing associations with Courbet and Champfleury (who popularized the term in the manifestoes of his magazine *Le Réalisme*), Baudelaire was quick to dismiss "realism" as a crude aesthetic doctrine whose claims to "imitate nature" utterly ignored the sovereignty of the "supernaturalist" poetic imagination. As he wrote in 1855: "Poetry is that which is most real, that which is not completely real except *in another world*." As for what was taken to be the actual "real" material world here below, Baudelaire the allegorist considered it to be but a "hieroglyphical dictionary" whose signs always pointed *elsewhere* or *beyond*.[17] In his estimation, the modern painters of Belgium were therefore merely a bunch of hacks, "painters who never looked at an engraving of Raphael, and who do paintings after photographs." The doctrine of realism—which privileged mimesis over poiesis, detail over composition, literalism over irony—was perfectly suited for a nation of counterfeiters, imitators, forgers, plagiarists, and *pasticheurs*.

Belgium's most famous living modern painter, "the darling of the English tourists" and the Salvador Dalí of his day, was Antoine Wiertz. For Walter Benjamin (who mentions the artist at various points in his *Arcades Project*), Wiertz represented the marriage of art with commerce and technology, notably in the development of those illusionistic trompe l'oeil techniques deployed by the painters of the panoramas and dioramas of the Parisian arcades. An ardent advocate of photography and of the arts of mechanical reproduction, Wiertz grandiosely dreamed of decorating railway stations with his monumental allegorical scenes, hoping to break down the space between the museum and the public sphere. He had convinced the Belgian government to construct a vast gallery to house his colossal canvases, decorated with posters featuring pompous humanitarian slogans and proclaiming the supremacy of Belgian art: "BRUSSELS CAPITAL OF THE WORLD. PARIS PROVINCE." In Wiertz's "grandiose mechanical-materialistic divinations" Benjamin discerned nineteenth-century capitalism's delirious phantasmagorias of a utopian future.[18] For Baudelaire, however, Wiertz's kitschy blend of classical academism and lurid romanticism merely confirmed him as the *pompier* painter par excellence: "Wiertz.

Charlatan. Idiot. Thief. . . . A literary painter. Modern hogwash. . . . Plagiarisms. He doesn't know how to draw, and his *bêtise* is as enormous as his colossi." When Wiertz died in June 1865, Baudelaire clipped his obituary from the newspaper ("the greatest painter of our country, and perhaps of our era") and glued it to the official invitation to his funeral at the state-supported Antoine Wiertz Museum—another document to be included in his great *sottisier* of Belgian *bêtise*. Comparing Wiertz's megalomania to Hugo's, he quipped: "les fous sont trop bêtes." Madmen are such morons.

As for Belgium's other great celebrity painter, Peter Paul Rubens, Baudelaire's visit to the Fine Arts Museum of Brussels provoked a similarly dyspeptic reaction: "I knew Rubens perfectly before coming here. Rubens, Decadence. Rubens, antireligious. Rubens, bland. Rubens, fountain of banality." This, from the poet who had signaled out Rubens as one of the great beacons of Western art in the first stanza of his magnificent early poem "Les Phares":

> Rubens, fleuve d'oubli, jardin de la paresse,
> Oreiller de chair fraîche, où l'on ne peut aimer,
> Mais où la vie afflue et s'agite sans cesse,
> Comme l'air dans le ciel et la mer dans la mer.

> (Rubens, river of oblivion, garden of lazy delight,
> Pillow of fresh flesh, off-limits to love,
> Yet infused with the continuous moil of life,
> Like the sea in the sea and the air in the sky.)

All this vibrant pictorial cosmos of Rubens, viewed from Baudelaire's late gnostic perspective, is now drained of its Venetian light and Florentine *disegno* to stand revealed as nothing more than the corpulent expression of the debased Belgian appetition for flesh, for *incarnation*. (Ezra Pound would similarly observe in his *Pisan Cantos*: "all that Sandro knew, and Jacopo / and that Velasquez never suspected / lost in the brown meat of Rembrandt / and the raw meat of Rubens and Jordaens.")[19] Eugène Fromentin, a painter and writer much admired by Baudelaire, would devote over a hundred laudatory pages to the genius of Rubens in the Belgium chapter of his *Les Maîtres d'au-*

trefois (*The Old Masters*), published ten years later in 1875. Baudelaire, by contrast, inspecting the substantial Rubens holdings of the Brussels Museum of Fine Arts, dismisses his old idol with a few random barbs. The painter he had once praised for his "prolific, radiant, almost jovial abundance" now strikes him as merely "fatuous"—"I can't stand people so ostentatiously happy (blandness of all that good cheer, all that pink)." Worse, he discovers in Rubens that same tendency toward grandiloquence that he so detested in Wiertz (or, for that matter, in Hugo, *auteur belge*)—"bombast, which is part and parcel of *bêtise*." In the end, he reduces his cherished Old Master to a dismissive one-liner: "Rubens is a lout [*goujat*] decked out in satins."

Having toured the museums and private collections of Brussels, Baudelaire set off to see the rest of the country, visiting Antwerp and Namur shortly after his arrival in the spring of 1864. Antwerp (or Anvers, as he always called it) he positively loved—and its busy harbor may well have inspired his late prose poem "The Port." In Namur he made the acquaintance of Félicien Rops, whom he described to Manet as "the only true *artist* (in the sense that I perhaps alone understand the term *artist*) that I have come across in Belgium" and about whom he intended to write a "fine chapter" for his book in progress.[20] Baudelaire greatly admired a recent lithograph of his, *A Burial in Wallonia*, in which the brooding realism of Courbet's huge, pathbreaking painting of 1850, *The Burial at Ornans*, had been satirically sharpened and condensed into an incisive anticlerical caricature (which delighted Baudelaire no end, for as much as he detested Belgium's freethinkers, he loathed its Catholic clergy even more for its sheer "ugliness, villainy, nastiness, and *bêtise*"). Trying to find a visual analogue for Baudelaire's neobaroque poem "Danse macabre" (included in the new 1861 "Tableaux parisiens" section of the *Fleurs*), Rops also produced in his honor a charcoal sketch entitled *The Dance of Death*, picturing an emaciated prostitute, seen from behind, her skirt raised, her body ravaged by syphilis, executing a bony can-can of Death. If Rubens was the painter of the flesh in all its inane and postlapsarian carnality, Rops instead offered Baudelaire a modern refashioning of the baroque skeleton. As Benjamin remarked, "Baroque allegory sees the corpse only from the outside; Baudelaire sees it from within."[21]

Baudelaire's various visits to Rops in Namur furthermore confirmed his sense that the finest architecture in Belgium was to be found in the baroque churches built by the Spanish-inspired Jesuits in the seventeenth century, of which Namur's Church of Saint-Loup was the outstanding example. Here again he was going against received opinion, which ever since the publication of Victor Hugo's *Notre-Dame de Paris* in 1831 had proclaimed the supremacy of the Gothic: "V. Hugo's championing of the Gothic has done much to damage our understanding of architecture. We have gotten stuck on it for far too long. —The philosophy of the history of architecture, *according to me*. —Analogies with corals, madreporia, the formation of continents, and finally with the entire life of nature. —No gaps. —A permanent state of transitions. —One can say that Rococo is the final flowering of Gothic." Baudelaire most frequently refers to this late baroque bloom of medieval and renaissance art as "the Jesuit style," which he pronounced "a style with genius," a "complex and ambiguous style," a "monstrous style," describing it in a characteristic oxymoron as *coquet et terrible*—smart, stylish, dainty on the one hand yet terrifying on the other (this is after all a style of the Spanish-sponsored Counter-Reformation). Here is his description of the Jesuit church in Antwerp (dedicated in 1621, but renamed Saint Charles Borromeo in 1803 after the Jesuit order was disbanded by the pope): "Here again, the *Jesuit style* (salmagundi, chessboard, chandeliers, a Boudoir at once mystical and terrifying, mourning in marble, theatrical confessional, Theater and Boudoir, rings of light and transparent glorias, angels and cupids, apotheoses and beatifications)."[22] In the elaborately carved wooden pulpits of these Jesuit churches, executed in what he termed *le style joujou* (the "toy style" or "furniture style" characteristic of Belgium), Baudelaire discovered "a universe of emblems, an ornate chaos of religious symbols," in short, a profusion of signs that defeated easy intelligibility. He was trying to frame a new aesthetic for the sacred, somewhere between the mannerism of sheer camp and the terror of the true sublime:

> Attempt to define the Jesuit style.
> A composite style.
> Stylish barbarity.
> Chessboard.
> Delightful bad taste.
> The boudoir of Religion.

Immense glorias.

Mourning in marble.

(black and white)

Solomonic columns.

(Rococo) statues suspended from the capitals of the columns.

Ex-votos (great ship). . . .

A gigantic polychrome crucifix is commonly suspended from the vault in front of the chancel of the great nave.

(I adore polychrome sculpture)

It's what one of my photographer friends calls Jesus-Christ-on-a-trapeze.

At the heart of this baroque cult lay the devotion to the Mater Dolorosa. In the Church of Notre Dame de la Chapelle in Brussels, he was transfixed by a polychrome statue of *Nuesta Señora de la Soledad*, Our Lady of Solitude, imported from Spain in the sixteenth century, a figure of mourning like the Andromache of his great poem "Le Cygne" ("The Swan") or the bejeweled widow of his sonnet "À une passante" ("To a Passerby"):

The outfit of a *beguine* nun. In full mourning, large veils, black and white, cloak of black muslin.

Life-size.

Diadem of gold encrusted with glass jewels.

Halo of gold with rays.

Heavy rosary, which must come from her convent.

Her face is painted.

The color is terrific, in the terrifying style of the Spaniards.

(De Quincey's "Our Ladies of Sorrow")

A white skeleton peeking out of a black marble tomb suspended on the wall.

This is one of the few glimpses we get of Baudelaire overcome by religious rapture in the debased world of modern Belgium—a petrified erotic encounter with the image of the Mother, represented as a life-size painted puppet dressed in widow's weeds, overseen by a skeleton. A moment of pure disincarnation. "Tout, pour moi, devient allégorie."

Visiting Rops and Malassis in Namur in mid-March 1866, Baudelaire would be similarly overcome. He wanted to inspect the Church of Saint-Loup one more time, this "sinister and stylish marvel" of the Jesuit style. The entire church reminded him of "the interior of a bier embroidered in *black, pink,* and *silver*," with "confessionals in a style that is varied, refined, subtle, baroque, a *new antiquity*." While wandering around this eroticized rococo boudoir of Death, admiring the lavish carvings of its *terrible et délicieux* catafalque (etymologically, "scaffold"), Baudelaire experienced a dizzy spell, tottered, and fell to the ground. He never fully recovered from the stroke.

*   *   *

Meanwhile, soon after his arrival, a completely different kind of "Book on Belgium" was simultaneously taking shape in his mind—a sadistic act of revenge against all the humiliations, real or perceived, to which he had been subject since his arrival in the country in the spring of 1864. Just as the United States had driven his hero Edgar Poe to death, so now Belgium—this little upstart America of Europe—was slowly killing him as well, with all its modern democratic, freethinking filth and meretricious *bêtise*. For the next two years Baudelaire would experience Brussels, not simply as a tourist passing through (à la Gautier),[23] nor as an émigré or political exile (as was the case for Marx, Engels, and Bakunin in the 1840s as well as for Proudhon, Hugo, and Dumas in the wake of 1851), but rather as someone who had chosen the place as a temporary refuge from his Parisian creditors—and who as a result has sometimes been compared by his biographers to the broken-down, debt-ridden British dandy Beau Brummell living out his last syphilitic days in Calais and Caen.

To his conseil judiciaire, Ancelle (who was, oddly enough, now becoming his major confidante), he wrote in the early fall of 1864:

I must admit that over the last two or three months I have allowed my character to run free, and have taken particular pleasure in being hurtful, in displaying my *impertinence*, a talent in which I excel, when I so wish. But here, even this falls short, one has to be *crude in order to be understood.*—

What a bunch of scoundrels! —and I who thought France was an absolutely barbarous country, here I am having to recognize that there is a country even more barbarous than France!

At any rate, whether I be forced to remain here to escape my [Paris] debts or whether I find a safe haven in Honfleur, I shall finish up this little book which, in a word, has forced me to sharpen my claws. I'll make use of them later against France. —It's the first time that I'm being forced to write a book that is absolutely humoristic, at once farcical [*bouffon*] and serious, and in which I'll have to speak of everything. It marks my separation from modern *bêtise*. Perhaps people will understand me, at long last.[24]

In the same letter, however, he confessed that he thereby had placed himself into a perfect vicious circle: he was writing a book so offensive and so repellent that it could never be officially published in Belgium, yet stuck as he was in Brussels with no literary means of income, he was too broke to return to Paris to see it into print. Living off the monthly pittance doled out by Ancelle from his trust fund, extracting whatever small sums he could emotionally blackmail out of his mother in Honfleur, in arrears on his hotel bill, unwilling to leave Belgium, unable to return to France for fear of encountering his various creditors, Baudelaire would spend the remainder of his stay in Brussels in a state of creative paralysis and rapidly declining health, accumulating the "notes" (as he called them) for a book that he knew deep down he would never finish, despite his assurances to all and sundry that the work was nearly complete.[25]

Baudelaire started jotting down the sketches for his satirical study of Belgium in the early summer of 1864. As he ventured forth from the Hôtel du Grand Miroir like a misanthropologist eager to proceed with the fieldwork of his hatred, he was surprised to discover a city whose public spaces were completely vacant. All he could register in a series of negatives is what the place *lacked*:

No life in the Street.
Many balconies. No one on the balconies.
Miniscule gardens to the back of the houses.
Everybody indoors. Doors closed.
No public toilets in the Streets.

No displays in front of the shops.

. . .

—A city without a river.

And all these steep hills interfere with *flânerie*.

. . .

No shops with display cases.

Dawdling in front of shops, this pleasure, this learning process, impossible!—

Everybody at home!

Noting down his "first sensations" of this new environment, he observes its impact on his own sensorium. As the century's supreme poet of olfaction, he is struck, first and foremost, by the *smell* of the place (which he compares to his early visits to the islands of the Indian Ocean and the Cape of Good Hope back in 1841, his only trips outside France before Belgium). The rhythms—or beats—of his sentences are those of a stand-up comedian engaged (à la Seinfeld) in observational jokes about the trivially quotidian, that is to say, about *nothing*:

First impressions. It is said that every city, every country has its smell. Paris, they say, smells or *used to smell* of acrid cabbage. Cape Town smells of sheep. There are tropical isles that smell of roses, musk, or coconut oil. Russia smells of leather. Lyon smells of coal. The Orient generally smells of musk and corpses. Brussels smells of black soap. The hotel rooms smell of black soap. The beds smell of black soap. The napkins smell of black soap. The sidewalks smell of black soap. The continual scrubbing of sidewalks and stoops, even in the pouring rain. A national mania.

After the offense to the nose, the assault upon the ear:

Brussels, a city far noisier than Paris. —Why?

1) Lousy *cobblestones*, which cause carriage wheels to clatter.

2) *Clumsiness, brutality, oafishness* of its populace, creating any number of accidents.

. . .

3) Everybody whistling.

4) All the shouting, braying, yawping. Howls of the Belgian beast.

Paris, infinitely larger and far more bustling, instead produces a vast vague hum, a velvety drone, as it were.

. . .

The Belgians are a breed of whistlers, like brainless birds.
What they whistle are not tunes.
The whistle sharply projected. Splitting my ears.
A habit picked up in childhood, incurable.

. . .

A breed of whistlers who burst into laughter, for no reason. Sign of cretinism.
All Belgians, without exception, have empty skulls.

"All Belgians, without exception"—typical of the categorical judgments into which Baudelaire carelessly (and provocatively) lapses in these notes, despite his half-ironic warning to himself a few pages earlier: "Let us be on our guard against that dangerous Parisian penchant for overgeneralization." But then again, Baudelaire rarely takes his own advice; in fact, generalizing about Belgians—that is, sinking into the sewer of ethnophobic prejudice and racialist stereotype—will more and more become his preferred mode of preventive *bêtise* as he pursues his Swiftian satire of this land of Yahoos.

As for the sense of taste, the first thing Baudelaire discovers upon his arrival is the insistent *fadeur* of a world without savor—insipid, bland:

Blandness.
The bread.
The rancid butter.
Even the vegetables, peas, asparagus, potatoes.
Eggs with blackened butter.
Absence of fruits.
Absence of hors-d'oeuvres.
No spicy stews.

As concerns the sense of touch, he studiously avoids, dandy that he is ("many friends, many gloves"), any tactile contact with the other, unless it be in anger or irritation—as in the perverse attack on the Belgian that seems to have inspired his prose poem "Let's Beat Up the Poor!" The following, with its typical object of derision dehumanized into an automaton, is a textbook example of Henri Bergson's definition of the comic as "du mécanique plaqué sur le vivant"—the fluidity of the organic violently wrenched into the rigidity of the machinic. It also illustrates Baudelaire's (Belgian?) fondness for the cartoon aesthetic of the B.D. (or *bande dessinée*), here inspired by Cruikshank and Hogarth:[26]

> The crazy way Belgians lurch along.
>
> Belgians walk while looking over their shoulders. One would say that some inane curiosity tugs their heads backward while an automatic movement propels them forward. —A Belgian can manage thirty or forty steps with his head craned backward, but inevitably there will come the moment when he bumps into someone or something. I have made many a detour to avoid Belgians walking.
>
> In a crowd, the Belgian pushes forward by poking his two fists into your back. Your only recourse is to wheel around and, as it were accidentally, give him a good jab in the stomach with your elbow.

In his essay on "The Essence of Laughter," Baudelaire cites a similar example of the hilarity induced by the spectacle of some hapless creature stumbling on a sidewalk—slipping and (as it were, theologically) falling on the proverbial banana peel. His analysis of the phenomenon of laughter takes on a Pascalian cast: "Laughter is satanic: it is thus profoundly human. It is the consequence in man of the idea of his own superiority. And since laughter is essentially human, it is, in fact, essentially contradictory; that is to say that it is at once a token of an infinite grandeur and an infinite misery—the latter in relation to the absolute Being of whom man has an inkling, the former in relation to the beast. It is from the perpetual collision of these two infinites that laughter is struck."[27]

Brussels provides the perfect allegorical cityscape in which the infinite grandeur and infinite misery of laughter collide to produce Baudelaire's most intense moments of black humor—most of which take the form of caricatures addressed to the reader's eye. As he jots down his perceptions—Guyaux observes that many of the loose sheets of paper he worked on were folded into four, indicating that he probably carried them around in his pockets (like a mouchard?) in order to take notes on the fly—he works at a fast clip (or as he calls it, *à la diable*), trying to achieve that same rapidity and violence of brushstroke that he so admired in Delacroix and in Guys.[28] Here, quickly traced by his chronic misogyny, are the repulsive outlines of the "typical" Brussels female:

A Punch-and-Judy nose, a ram's brow, onionskin eyelids, colorless vacant eyes, monstrously tiny mouth, or simply an absence of mouth (sans speech or kisses!), the lower jaw retreating, flat feet, elephantine legs (beams on boards), lilac complexion, and with all this, as bird-brained and puffed up as a pigeon.

. . .

Women in the Street.
  Their feet.
  Their calves.
  Their reek.

His sketches of Belgian faces take the physiognomic elements of Lavater, so crucial to nineteenth-century caricature, and twist them into something on the order of the dismantled visages of Francis Bacon:[29]

The Belgian, or rather Brussels face.
Chaos.
Formless, deformed, rough, heavy, hard, unfinished, carved by knife.
Teeth at angles.
Mouths not made for smiles.
Capable of laughter, for sure, but inept, enormous guffaws à propos of nothing.
The face cloudy, bereft of any gaze, like that of a cyclops—not a one-eyed cyclops but a blind one. . . .
The absence of gaze terrifying.
Some of them display monstrously thick tongues, which accounts for their slurred, sibilant speech.

The key word in this passage is "formless"—or *informe*, a term favored by Georges Bataille to describe a "heterogeneous" universe prior to shape or meaning or an abject substance such as spittle or shit.[30] Baudelaire's grotesque close-up shot of the Belgian mouth is a perfect illustration of the (anti-)aesthetic of *l'informe*, worthy of that "absolute comicity" (or "comique absolu") that he associated with *Los Caprichos*

of Goya—a comedy so hyperbolic and so monstrous as to resist all at-
tempts at interpretation, instantly and vertiginously generative of a *fou
rire* akin to hysteria or delirium.[31] Once again he has recourse to the
anaphora of negation:

> Particular look of the mouths in the street and elsewhere.
> >no voluptuous lips.
> >no commanding lips.
> >no ironic lips.
> >no eloquent lips.
> Gaping latrines of imbecility.
>
> Gaping cloaca.
> Formless mouths.
> Unfinished faces.

The word "eye," according to the concordances of *Les Fleurs du mal*,
is the most frequently occurring noun in Baudelaire's poetry. In Brus-
sels, ever on the outlook for eyes, or for the specific quality of a glance,
he instead discovers a population vulnerable to ophthalmia and partial
to fake pince-nez:

> The pince-nez, with its cord, perched on the nose.
> A multitude of vitreous eyes, even among the officers.
> An optician told me that the majority of pince-nez that sells are clear
> glass. Thus this national pince-nez craze is nothing more than a pa-
> thetic effort to appear elegant and yet one more sign of the spirit of im-
> itation and conformity.

As for the gaze of the Belgian, it is at once innocent, malevolent, and
vacant:

> The Belgian eye, wide, enormous, staring steadily, insolent (when it
> comes to foreigners).
> The innocent eye of people who can't manage to take in everything at
> a single glance.
> One of Cyrano's characters says to another: you're so damn fat I
> couldn't beat all of you up in a single day.

Whatever the Belgian eye looks upon is so vast that it takes him ages just to register it.

The Belgian eye has the innocent insolence of a microscope.

Even worse, in the gaze of the Belgian Baudelaire sees a reflection of his own paranoid apprehension of him (or her) as a threatening Other:

Coldness of their gaze, crafty, wary. Expression at once fierce and timid. The eye unfocused and, even when looking right at you, always shifty. A mistrustful race, because it believes itself to be weaker than it is.

. . .

Hostile atmosphere.

The eye and the face of the enemy everywhere, everywhere.

In the planned "Epilogue" to his book, Baudelaire again returns to the "general characteristics" of his mythical Belgian:

Having long wondered why exactly the Belgians existed, I imagined they were perhaps ancient souls who, because of their disgusting vices, had gotten trapped in the hideous bodies that are their image.

A Belgian is a living hell on earth.

. . .

It has occasionally occurred to me that Belgium was perhaps one of those hells that are graduated and disseminated throughout the creation and that the Belgians as [Athanasius] Kircher suspected, were in fact certain animals or certain ancient abject and criminal spirits imprisoned in deformed bodies.

One becomes Belgian for having sinned.

A Belgian is a hell unto himself.

In these lines tacked on at the end of his manuscript, Baudelaire finally experiences a moment of anagnorisis in which he recognizes himself as hellishly *belge*. We have met the enemy and he is us.[32]

* * *

Baudelaire's "physiognomic" caricatures of Brussels street life, which occupy the initial portions of his notes toward *Poor Belgium*, remain among the most provocative fragments of his late style—savage, laconic, paratactic, and (self-)lacerating in their utterly "satanic" sense of superiority over the comic objects of their disdain and disgust. Nobody else in Europe, England, or America is writing this way in 1864, unless it be the Dostoevsky of the hallucinatory *Notes from the Underground*.[33] The remainder of his notes for the first twelve chapters of his book, devoted to the *moeurs* of the inhabitants of Brussels, are more predictable in their (Parisian) disparagement of all things Belgian. Like Balzac in his *Études de moeurs* or Flaubert in his *Moeurs de province* (the subtitle of *Madame Bovary*) Baudelaire uses the term *moeurs* (or mores) to include customs, manners, and morals—in short, the full range of socialized *habitus*. The majority of pages are devoted to the minute (and numbingly repetitive) registering of his reactions to life in the "near abroad" (as the Russians might call it) of Belgium, whose relation to France is at once metonymic (via its contiguity) and metaphoric (via its similarity/dissimilarity).

Baudelaire's stray notes on "The French language in Belgium" (chapter 15) best embody this figural relation. As his correspondence with his various publishers and editors indicates, Baudelaire was notoriously finicky when it came to correct orthography, syntax, and punctuation: in *My Heart Laid Bare*, he quotes with approval his friend Théophile Gautier's suggestion that the act of misspelling be made a capital offense, and in the very last letter to his mother that he managed to compose in his own hand just shortly after his collapse in Namur, he gently corrects her spelling of the adjective *inquiète*, noting that it should be written with one rather than two *t*s. A daily reader (and clipper) of Brussels newspapers and a careful scrutinizer of its shop signs and advertisements, he was similarly attentive to the metonymic distortions (or metatheses) of "correct" French into comic malapropisms: "ophthalmie" becoming "hopitalmie," "cavalcade" turning into "calvacade," the recently coined "photographie" rendered as "potographie." We are here in the domain of what Marcel Duchamp called the *inframince* or *infrathin*—minute differences within the same.[34] For the French of Brussels is of course not a *foreign* language (as was the English of Poe or De Quincey that Baudelaire had translated), and yet, struck by its deviations from the standard idiom of the hexagon, Baudelaire ridicules it for being faulty, for being dissimilar—and hence for being comically inferior. The very *likeness* that obtains between the standard French of Brussels—adopted as the official language of the Belgian government in 1830, even though spoken by only a minority of the nation's population—and that of Paris makes the former's tiny *unlikenesses* on the lexical, syntactical, or grammatical level all the more ludicrous from the imperial (and colonialist) perspective of Baudelaire's (equally despised, though still normative) France.[35]

As he inspects the moeurs of Brussels, Baudelaire is irked (as only a *vates irritabilis* could be) by the enormity of small differences: the paucity of matches, the rarity of lamps at which to relight the bland stubs of Belgian cigars. Here are his comments (perhaps jotted down in situ) on Horton's, the English-style pub that he often frequented, a locale that also features in his final published prose poem, "Good Dogs":

> The story of the gentleman who didn't want to pay for the pickles at Horton's.
> Faro, 2 sous 3 centimes.
> Obsessed with centimes.
> Chairs without crossbars.
> The custom of serving drinks by the shot, as if the barman were assigned to monitor the cravings of the customer.
> Appalling drunkenness of the lower classes. Cheap drinks. Faro and gin.
> The wine cellars of the bourgeoisie extraordinarily well-stocked. Aging their wines [for show—ed.].
> . . .
> Faro is drawn from the great latrine of the [river] Senne; it's a drink extracted from the excrements of the city and then filtered. Thus, for centuries the city has been drinking its own urine.

Here, as elsewhere, while commenting on the mores of the Belgians, Baudelaire the Swiftian satirist frequently veers into gleeful scatology.

> Belgian ladies pissing and shitting.
> The Belgian mother in the latrine (door open) playing with her child and smiling to the neighbors.
> Prodigious love of excrement which one finds in the old paint-

ings. The painters of those days were certainly painting their native land.

Six Belgian ladies pissing in a narrow street, barring one's passage, some standing, some crouching, all dressed to the nines.

. . .

Everywhere else childhood is a pretty thing; here it is hideous, scabby, mangy, grimy, smeared with shit.

One should go to the poor neighborhoods and see the naked children rolling around in shit. Though I don't think they actually eat it.

If the Belgians are nothing but filth for Baudelaire—and dirt, as Mary Douglas reminds us, is basically "matter out of place"—it is but a small step for him to imagine them as *beasts*, that is, to render them into the lowest of the low, into *bêtes* whose sacrality and untouchability, at least according to Derrida, paradoxically mirrors that of the highest of the high—namely, that of the Sovereign (in this case, the alien Baudelaire, a *homo sacer* in all his extralegal state of exceptionality).[36] Baudelaire's notes are filled with comparisons between Belgians and animals: they are most frequently situated as a phylum somewhere between the Mollusk (for their inertia) and the Monkey (for their mimicry), but they are also variously described as rabbits, dogs, sheep, cows, rams, chickens, ducks, shrikes, elephants, and bears. More than their mere animality, Baudelaire underscores their deep and barbarous *bestiality*: as he combs through the newspapers for criminal *faits divers*, he comes across cases involving a rape of a fourteen-month-old child, a father who has castrated his son while drunk, a couple who has strangled their newborn baby and thrown it to the pigs, a man who earns his living by eating live dogs at fairs for 20 francs apiece, a Chaffinch Academy (sponsored by the king) whose members poke out the eyes of their songbirds with hot pins the better to prep them for competition.

Making his Dantescan way his way through the different circles of this Brussels Hell, Baudelaire not only touches on the cardinal sins of its inhabitants (pride, greed, wrath, envy, lust, gluttony, sloth) but is equally attentive—as he is in his poem "Au Lecteur" ("To the Reader")—to all the other venial signs of wickedness that he encounters: slander, servility, mean-spiritedness, boorishness, lack of chivalry, hatred of beauty, vulgarity, absence of hospitality, inefficiency, unscrupulous business practices, interminable slowness in all matters bureaucratic, and (perhaps worst of all, given his own straitened circumstances) the obstinate refusal to extend any credit whatsoever. If Baudelaire devotes so many pages to the minute observation of Belgian *moeurs*, it is because he is ultimately interested (as was Tocqueville in America) in the question of what it means to be free in a modern, democratic society. Compared to that of Second Empire France, Belgium's constitution (drafted in late 1830, just after the kingdom's independence) was the most liberal in Europe in its protection of individual rights, guaranteeing as it did the freedom to assemble, the freedom of religion, the freedom of languages, of education, and of the press. But taking a page out of Burke and Maistre, Baudelaire nonetheless observes: "Constitutions are made of *paper*. Manners and morals are *everything*. —Belgian 'freedom' is a mere word. It's there on paper: but it doesn't exist, *because nobody feels the need for it*." Further on in his notes, while discussing the ludicrousness of a constitutional monarch like Leopold I (not a true sovereign but merely an "automaton in a rooming house"), he returns to this same issue:

> Always the central question of the relation of the Constitution (dead letter) to Customs (living constitution).
> In France, the tyranny of the law is tempered by the ease and freedom of its manners.
> In France, freedom is limited by the fear of its governments.
> —In Belgium, it is suppressed by national *bêtise*.
> —Can one be free, and what purpose does it serve to decree freedom in a country where nobody understands it, wants it, feels a need for it?
> Freedom is a luxury object, like virtue. When the Belgian has eaten his fill of it, what more does he need?

For Baudelaire, only the Imagination (the "queen of all the faculties") can enable the fully sovereign exercise of human freedom. Lacking all imagination, the Belgians are therefore victims of the "spirit of Conformity," vulnerable to what Baudelaire in his essays on Poe's America called "the tyranny of public opinion"—mere sheep following the herd, fleeing the difficult existential challenge of individual solitude for the ease and security of "clubs" and "societies" and "associations":

> Belgians only think in packs
> (Freemasons, freethinkers, societies of all sorts)
> and only amuse themselves in packs
> (societies for entertainment, societies for the raising of chaffinches)
> (little girls walking arm in arm—as do young boys, men, women)
> They only piss in packs.
> Packs of women by whom I was attacked, only managing to fend them off with my cigar.

In their "herd morality" (Nietzsche), *les Belges* complacently place their belief in the doctrine of collective progress—which, for the Maistrian Baudelaire, represents one of the most pernicious philosophical legacies of the Enlightenment. As he had noted in *My Heart Laid Bare*:

> The belief in progress is a lazy man's doctrine, a *Belgian* doctrine. It's the individual counting on his neighbors to do his job for him.
> The only true (that is, moral) progress that can take place is in the individual and by the individual.
> . . .
> Theory of true civilization.
> It does not entail gas, steam, or table-turning; it entails the diminution of the traces of original sin.

If Baudelaire had launched the influential aesthetic concept of *modernity* in his pathbreaking essay "The Painter of Modern Life," in Belgium he was by contrast confronted by something far more economically determined, namely, the historical process of *modernization*—a term that he never specifically uses per se, preferring instead the adjective he introduced into the French language in the final entry of *Flares*: "Machinery will have so *Americanized* us, progress will have so atrophied our spiritual faculties, that none of the bloody, sacrilegious anti-natural reveries of the Utopians could be compared to its actual effects. . . . But it is not specifically in the political institutions that one will observe the effects of universal ruin, or of universal progress—it hardly matters to me what name it goes by. It will be seen in the degradation of the human heart."[37]

As a beacon of "freedom" and "progress," Belgium—like the United

States of America—had by the mid-nineteenth century become the darling of the French liberal press, much to Baudelaire's outrage. But just as his pages on Brussels contain few concrete descriptions of the city's actual topography, demography, or urban infrastructure, so he provides virtually no details about the pace of the country's economic development ever since it was annexed by France between 1795 and 1814 and transformed into one of the major suppliers of war materiel and conscripted soldiers for Napoleon's military industrial complex. After gaining its independence from the United Kingdom of the Netherlands in 1830 and then quickly recomposed into the first artificially created buffer state in Europe—with its French, Dutch, and German swatches stitched together by Lord Palmerston and the Great Powers into what would come to be known as the diplomatic "harlequin of Europe," headed by the puppet Saxe-Cobourg constitutional monarch Leopold I—Belgium became the second industrial power per capita in the world (after England), largely on account of the abundant reserves of pit coal (or *houille*) in Wallonia that fueled the various dark satanic mills around Liège and Charleroi whose iron, zinc, steel, glass, munitions, and locomotives were destined for profitable export to the rest of Europe. The first passenger railway outside of England was constructed on Belgian soil in 1835, and by the 1860s an integrated rail system crisscrossed the country (not once mentioned by Baudelaire, though he certainly traveled on it).[38] Although he occasionally refers to the ever-growing income gap between the poor and the affluent rentier bourgeoisie, Baudelaire—who never ventured farther south into Wallonia than Namur—seems largely indifferent to the fact that Belgium had become the model of a modern plutocratic capitalist state founded on the exploitation of cheap Walloon (or, in the case of the textile factories of Ghent, Flemish) labor, a nation whose wealth was increasingly concentrated in the hands of a few industrial barons who, having consolidated their power against the clergy and large landowners, now controlled the holding companies that were in turn largely financed by the Société Générale de Belgique (the powerful banking interest that contributed to the immense personal wealth of Leopold I and that would later lie behind the untrammeled colonial exploitation of the Congo by his equally rapacious son, Leopold II). In this laissez-faire economy, based on cheap fossil fuel and an impoverished workforce, investment capital in the stock market could yield dividends of up to 40 percent per annum, while the life expectancy in the collieries, metallurgical mills, and textile factories ran to about forty years, factoring in the high mortality rate of child labor.[39]

Friedrich Engels had described this wretched state of affairs in his 1844 *Conditions of the Working Class in England,* and it was not entirely by chance that he would join his collaborator Karl Marx in Brussels to found the first incarnation of the modern Communist Party. Marx, who had been expelled from France in February 1845, after Guizot's government caved in to pressures from Prussia, subsequently found asylum in more "liberal" Brussels, though only on the condition that he publish nothing on the subject of contemporary politics while in residence there. While writing for the *Deutscher Brüsseler Zeitung,* the organ of the radical German émigré faction in Brussels, and organizing the Communist Corresponding Committee, Marx moved between various addresses in Brussels and its suburbs with his wife, Jenny, pursuing his intellectual and political collaboration with his fellow exiles Engels, Bakunin, and the early Zionist Moses Hass. Between 1845 and 1848, he proceeded to write (in German) among the most influential philosophical texts of his career: the posthumously published *Theses on Feuerbach, The German Ideology,* and (in French) *The Poverty of Philosophy,* his reply to Proudhon's recent *The Philosophy of Poverty*—all capped off by his joint authorship with Engels in Brussels of the incendiary *Communist Manifesto* (in German) in February 1848, whose publication in London caused the Belgian authorities to expel him back to (a now more inviting) revolutionary Second Republic France. Marx's favorite conspiratorial haunt on the Grand-Place of Brussels during this period is now marked by a plaque and certified as a UNESCO World Heritage Site. The inn bears the name of *Le Cygne* (or, in Dutch, *Die Swaene*), an uncanny prefiguration of Baudelaire's most celebrated allegory of modern urban mourning and dispossession, "The Swan."

Marx's Brussels writings are perhaps the most important world-historical texts to have emerged from the city in the nineteenth century, together with Hugo's 1862 *Les Misérables* (Lacroix) or—should one be looking for the ancestors of twentieth-century surrealism—the Brussels publications of both Lautréamont's 1869 *Chants de Maldoror* (also by Lacroix) and of Rimbaud's 1873 *Une saison en enfer* (by L'Alliance typographique).[40] In comparison to these works, Baudelaire's (admittedly unpublished) accounts of Belgian politics can seem rather snide and shallow indeed—and too topical, moreover, to be of much interest to to-day's readers (even if uncannily prophetic of contemporary America). Despite his long-standing familiarity with Proudhon's work, he seems to have been ignorant of the whole Marxian legacy in Belgium. The clos-est he comes is in a newspaper clipping that he included in the notes for his chapter 19 on "Politics"—a lengthy description of the international congresses of student radicals held in Liège, Brussels, and Ghent in the fall of 1865, attended by (among others) Marx's future son-in-law Paul Larfargue and loosely affiliated with the First International, founded in London the previous year. As was his habit, Baudelaire exasperat-edly underlined those phrases in this newspaper clipping that he con-sidered to be the most egregious examples of left-wing afflatus: "If we students are the avant-garde of progress, it is because science is on our side." "War on God! This way progress lies!" "Freedom shall soon reign; the slaves shall become masters." "The human brain is divided into two: either one is a complete spiritualist, or one is an experimentalist and positivist." "What is Revolution? The victory of labor over capital, of the worker over the parasite, of man over God!"

To such rhetoric, which Baudelaire also witnessed firsthand at the (drunken) meetings of the Societies for Free Thought that were held at his hotel, he furiously riposted on a stray, late sheet of *Belgium Disrobed*:

Let us add that when one wants to talk to them about *actual* revolu-tion, they are terrified. *Old Maids.* ME, if I agree to be a republican, *I am fully conscious of doing evil.*

Yes! *Long Live the Revolution!*

Forever! What the hell!

But as for myself, I'm not taken in! I was never taken in! I say *Long Live the Revolution!* the way I'd say: *Long Live Destruction! Long Live Ex-piation! Long Live Punishment! Long Live Death!*

Not only would I be happy to be the victim, but I wouldn't mind be-ing the executioner either—to feel the Revolution from both sides!

We all carry the republican spirit in our veins, just as we carry the pox in our marrow. We are Democratized and Syphilized.

Despite his often-quoted claim that Napoleon III's coup d'état had "physically depoliticized" him, Baudelaire nonetheless admitted to his close friend Nadar in 1859 that "even though I have tried to convince myself over and over that I was no longer interested in politics, each time a serious issue arises, I am seized by curiosity and passion." "Politics," he went on to warn him, was "a heartless science" in which "any true politician must inevitably be a Jesuit or a Revolutionary."[41] Ever extravagant in his political *prises de position*, ever seduced by the reversibility of contraries, Baudelaire admitted no middle ground between the apocalyptic Counter-Revolution of Joseph de Maistre or the sacrificial Terror of Robespierre. In the parliamentary politics of Belgium, by contrast, he discovered nothing but a "syphilized" contest between equally mediocre and corrupt opposing parties—the politically correct free-thinking Liberals on the one hand, and the retrograde Catholics on the other (both of whose election campaigns were bankrolled by various powerful financial interests, presumably to encourage ongoing legislative paralysis). The former he ridiculed for their anticlerical propaganda (or what he called their "priestophobia"), for their attempts to desacralize death by the institution of civil burial practices,[42] and, above all, for their programmatic proclamations of atheism—which Baudelaire saw as merely another modern-day (and hence "decrepit") form of religiosity:

> Were religion to disappear from the face of the earth, it would be rediscovered in the heart of an atheist.
>
> . . .
>
> In France, atheism is polite. Here it is violent, idiotic, emphatic. Belgian idiocy is an enormous counterfeit of French idiocy, it is French idiocy cubed.

The Catholics fare no better, Baudelaire issuing his plague upon both houses:

> The priests have no more of an idea of religion here than the prostitutes have of gallantry.
>
> The Belgians make me think of those converted cannibal tribes of South America who dangle Christian symbols on trees, the meaning of which completely escapes them.
>
> The Christian idea of God (invisible, creative, omniscient, all foreseeing) cannot penetrate the brain of a Belgian.
>
> All one has here are atheists or people prone to superstition.

Observing that the Liberal Party had a mere one-vote majority in the Belgian House of Representatives in the spring 1864—which it then lost over the summer, thus throwing the government into disarray—Baudelaire takes a definite schadenfreude in the dysfunctionalities of the Belgian polity, whose schisms in this case were founded not yet on the intense internecine divisions between the Flemish-speaking and French-speaking portions of the country (which in 2011 would lead Belgium to set a world record—after Iraq—for 589 days without an elected government) but rather on the sectarian rivalries between the secularist liberal religion of *laïcité* and the entrenched pieties of the Catholics. Baudelaire's residence in Brussels coincided with the final years of America's War Between the States, which he followed in the newspapers, siding as many Frenchmen did (despite his earlier denunciations in his essays on Poe of America's tolerance of slavery and of the extermination of its "savages") with the traditionalist agrarian South against the progressivist industrialized North. It is typical of his fierce animus against *bien-pensant* bourgeois republicans that he should quip of Lincoln's assassin, "Those who consider Booth a villain are the same ones who adore Charlotte Corday."[43] In his notes on the fractiousness of its corrupt and hyperpartisan parliamentary politics, Baudelaire similarly suggests that as a failed (or utterly sham) democracy imposed on an artificially created state, Belgium was fated to remain forever in some sort of condition of perpetual *différend* or civil war—but a civil war *en farce*. As a nation, in any event, it could never constitute a *whole* for Baudelaire. It would always remain a partial or fragmented object—the projection (or introjection) of his own psychomachia as a *homo duplex*.[44] Late in his notes, he writes that "the Belgian has been hacked into stumps, yet still lives on." The French here reads: "Le Belge a été coupé en tronçons; il vit encore." *Tronçons* is the very word Baudelaire had used to describe his prose poems in his dedication of his *Paris Spleen* to Arsène Houssaye in 1862: "We can cut where we want, I my reveries, you the manuscript, the reader his reading; for I do not hitch the latter's unruly will to the endless thread of some superfluous plot. Remove a vertebra, and the two pieces of this tortuous fantasy will easily rejoin. Hack it into numerous fragments, and you will see that each of them can exist apart. In the hope that some of these stumps [*tronçons*] will be lively enough to please and amuse you, I make bold to dedicate the entire snake to you."[45]

*   *   *

While preparing the "Argument of the Book on Belgium" for distribution to potential Parisian publishers in January 1866, Baudelaire jotted down the following instructions to himself:

> As we proceed to judge the Belgian, let us not stray from certain key ideas: Apery [*Singerie*], Counterfeiting [*Contrefaçon*], Conformity, rancorous Impotence—these various rubrics will enable us to classify our material.
> Their vices are all counterfeits.
> The Belgian fop.
> The Belgian patriot.
> The Belgian bungler.
> The Belgian freethinker . . . . A counterfeit of French impiety. Belgian obscenity, a counterfeit of French smut.

The association of Belgium with the practice of *contrefaçon*—that is, with the production of objects that are counterfeit or counter-fashioned or of things faked or forged—dated back to the 1820s. This was the period when, no longer part of French territory after Napoleon's defeat at Waterloo and now a province of the Kingdom of the Netherlands, the country's authorities decided that only Belgian books would benefit from copyright protection, thus making it legal for its publishers to reprint (primarily French) books for local consumption or for export to the rest of Europe (including back to France, often in cheap and mangled versions). Just as Dickens complained about the many Yankee pirate editions of his works that he encountered during his lecture tour of the United States, so French authors traveling to Brussels (among them Hugo, Gautier, and Dumas) were quick to comment on the various illegal reproductions of their works available in the city's bookstores. By 1840, the situation had reached such a pitch that the French Ministry of Éducation dispatched Gérard de Nerval on a secret mission to Brussels to investigate *la contrefaçon belge*—an uncannily apt project for an author who (like Poe) was obsessed with second selves and *Doppelgänger*.[46] With the onset of the Second Empire in 1852 (which reestablished a firmer French hegemony over Belgium), accords were reached to contain the practice of Belgian book piracy, although (as the careers of Lacroix and of Poulet-Malassis illustrated) banned political or erotic texts (including of course *Les Misérables* and Baudelaire's late *Épaves*) continued to be published across the border for illegal introduction into France.

Visiting Brussels in 1837 with his mistress Juliette Drouet, Victor Hugo was among the first to extend the scope of *la contrefaçon belge* from questions of literary property and copyright infringement (still a very vague zone during the period) to the city at large. As he reported back to his wife, Adèle:

> Brussels is truly the city of counterfeit. There are street urchins as in Paris; the Greek pediment of the Chambre des États resembles the Greek pediment of our Chambre des Députés; the amaranthine ribbon of King Leopold is a counterfeit of our Légion d'Honneur; the two square towers of Sainte-Gudule, quite beautiful by the way, seem to be false replicas of Notre-Dame. Finally, by an unfortunate stroke of bad luck, the river that flows through Brussels is called not exactly the Seine, but rather the *Senne*.[47]

By the mid-nineteenth century, reinforced by the bemused condescension of countless French travelers and journalists, Hugo's comments had been transformed into a far broader national stereotype, as registered in Flaubert's *Dictionary of Received Ideas*, his handbook of obligatory bourgeois *bêtise*: "BELGIAN: One must call Belgians: counterfeit Frenchmen; this is always sure to get a laugh."

Baudelaire ramps up this mild *idée reçue* into a comic (and delirious) catalog of Belgian imposture. Everywhere he looks, he sees the nauseating evidence of its "spirit of imitation of conformity," its idiocy being that of "France cubed." Its so-called Brabant Revolution of 1790 (against the Hapsburgs), not to mention its 1830 uprising (against the Netherlands) that led to its independence, were mere parodies of their French models, thus proving Marx's dictum in his *Eighteenth Brumaire* that all world-historical facts and personages were fated to appear twice—the first time as tragedy, the second time as farce. As for Brussels itself, it was "A Capital of Apes" ("Une Capitale de Singes")—with the word *singe* here acting as the appropriately monkeyed-up anagram of one of

Baudelaire's key conceptual and poetic terms, namely, *le signe* (or, in his most celebrated allegorical pun, *le Cygne*). The examples of its *singerie* were endless: its river Senne, a filthy Styx-like homophone of the Seine; its language, a slurred echo of proper French; its puppet king, Leopold, a minor issue of the house of the Saxe-Coburg; its army of toy soldiers, sent to die for Napoleon III's fiasco of a fake empire in Mexico ruled over by a minor Hapsburg clown, Maximilian I, wedded to Leopold's daughter, Charlotte. Not to mention its hoax of a constitution; its pretense to democracy; its sham socialists and freethinkers; its various societies and associations in the service of groupthink; its fraudulent journalists; its literary plagiarists; its Rembrandt forgers; its adepts of "realism," *pasticheurs* of the imitators of Courbet; its humbug artists painting after photographs; its bogus ladies' men, proud of having caught the clap in emulation of the Parisians; its ersatz Frenchified whores; its wannabe Gallic smutty jokes; its flimflam dandies and swells; its derivative intellectuals and pseudopoets; and, above all, its pitiful excuses for women—tubs of Rubenesque suet, hideous counterfeits of the feminine.

In the infernal hallucination of his great 1859 poem "Les Sept Vieillards" ("The Seven Old Men")—originally entitled "Parisian Phantoms" and the piece in which Baudelaire had proudly boasted that he had finally managed "to exceed the limits assigned to poetry"—the flâneur-narrator by chance encounters an ancient broken-down geezer on a Paris street who suddenly turns into seven identical versions of himself before the narrator's horrified eyes. Stunned by the proliferation of these "baroque specters" and "inexorable twins" who continue to arise Phoenixlike from their own disappearance and reappearance, at once "fathers and sons of themselves," the poet flees this hallucinatory spectacle of the Eternal Return of the Same and, "as exasperated as a drunkard seeing double," retreats back indoors to his rooms to fight off the insanity to which he has now become prey, his mind enfevered by the mystery and absurdity of all this endless *Doppelgängerei*:

> Exaspéré comme un ivrogne qui voit double,
> Je rentrai, je fermai ma porte, épouvanté,
> Malade et morfondu, l'esprit fiévreux et trouble,
> Blessé par le mystère et par l'absurdité!

This, commentators tell us, is one of the first occurrences of the word "absurdity" in the history of French verse, and as Eliot observes in one of the notes to his *Waste Land*, his own "Unreal City" owes much to this breakthrough poem of Baudelaire's (and particularly to its first two lines: "Fourmillante cité, cité pleine de rêves, / Où le spectre en plein jour raccroche le passant"). Of all the poems included in the "Tableaux parisiens" section added to the 1861 edition of *Les Fleurs du mal*, "Les Sept Vieillards" also comes closest to prefiguring Baudelaire's infernal vision of Brussels, the capital of a hoax of a country peopled not just by ghosts, but more precisely by replicants, phantasmagorical doubles of themselves, who move about robotically in a city not merely as "unreal" as Eliot's London but rather as "virtual" as Baudrillard's simulacrum of America. In this (post-)modern waking dream of Hell, the contagion of *contrefaçon* creates a pandemic of simulation in which it is no longer possible to distinguish between model and replica, original and fake, real and counterfeit, self and other, different and same, French and Belgian—in short, in which all meaning-generating oppositions have collapsed into absurdity.[48]

Confronted by this universe of *singerie*, Baudelaire has little choice but to capitulate to its apery. In a move that anticipates the saintly vocation of Flaubert's retired scriveners Bouvard and Pecuchet, he will therefore combat the malady of mimesis homeopathically—that is, by simply counterimitating it, by quoting it verbatim, by copying it down.[49] Among the most astonishing pages of *Belgium Disrobed* are those in which, not content merely to paste (and scornfully underline) some fifty newspaper cuttings onto its 360 loose leaves—his notes indicate that he regularly kept scissors and glue on the writing table of his hotel room for this purpose—Baudelaire also laboriously transcribed by hand a number of documents of modern *bêtise* into his *sottisier* in progress. These include (well before Joyce's *Ulysses*) the raw realia of the flotsam-and-jetsam of printed matter awash in a modern city: theater bills, treacly letters to the editor, snippets of advertisements, newspaper accounts of the legislative machinations of a deadlocked House of Representatives, transcriptions of the proceedings of parliamentary debates concerning gerrymandering and electoral reform, inspirational brochures distributed by the Society for Free Thought, and last but not least, the funeral invitation to the civil burial of a certain abbé

Louis Joseph Dupont, a lapsed *libre penseur* priest (which Baudelaire fiercely attended). In a late underlined note addressed to himself, he writes: "*Comb through all the issues of the newspapers I have on hand and prepare extracts from the articles I have clipped.*" This is one of the last intimate glimpses we get of Baudelaire engaged in his *encylopédie mise en farce* (Flaubert's projected subtitle for *Bouvard and Pecuchet*), as he patiently sifts through the archives of *bêtise*, disappearing into the anonymous murmur of its banalities before finally lapsing into the silence of aphasia, reduced to repeating the syllables *Crénom* over and over, itself a French *contrefaçon* (as he notes in one of his letters) of the Belgian "national swear word"—*Gottverdomme*.[50]

NOTES

1. *Pauvre Belgique*, texte publié par Jacques Crépet et Claude Pichois (Paris: Conard, 1953), based on the manuscript held by the Bibliothèque Spoelberch de Lovenjoul at Chantilly.

2. *Fusées, Mon Coeur mis à nu, La Belgique déshabillée, suivi de Amonetates Belgicae*, ed. André Guyaux (Paris: Gallimard, 1986). My notes to *La Belgique déshabillée* are much indebted to Guyaux's superb edition.

3. See Baudelaire's letter to Félix Nadar of May 14, 1859, and Pichois's notes on Goya (C1: 574, and 1025).

4. In all his editions of *Pauvre Belgique*, Pichois threads the summaries of the chapters given in the "Argument" throughout the body of the text, thus creating an enormous amount of repetition. Guyaux in turn chronologically prints the "Argument" at the very end of Baudelaire's mass of notes. Only Marcel Ruff prints the "Argument" at the very outset of *Pauvre Belgique* in his "l'Intégrale" edition of Baudelaire (Paris: Seuil, 1968). This "Argument du livre sur la Belgique" had previously appeared in volume 2 of Y.-G. Dantec's 1931 Pléiade edition of Baudelaire's *Oeuvres*, which was the edition that Walter Benjamin worked from. It was therefore all he knew of the text of *Pauvre Belgique*.

5. "Karl Kraus" in Walter Benjamin, *Selected Writings*, vol. 2, trans. Edmund Jephcott (Cambridge, MA: Harvard University Press, 1999), 433–57.

6. C2: 362.

7. Claude Pichois, *Baudelaire*, trans. Graham Robb (London: Hamish Hamilton, 1989), 320.

8. C2: 370.

9. Despite their initial suspicions, the Hugo family started inviting Baudelaire for dinner at their home in May 1865—and Adèle even seemed to take a liking to her fellow expatriate (who acted as a go-between with her old flame Sainte-Beuve). Later that year, when Hugo arrived for rest and female recreation in Brussels, he and Baudelaire dined together on several occasions. Hugo had just sold Lacroix and

Verboecken *Les Chansons des rues et des bois* and *Les Travailleurs de la mer* for 120,000 francs—more than Baudelaire had received on his coming of age. Little wonder if the poet was outraged by the profitability of Hugo's *bêtise* in a letter to his mother of November 1865. See Pichois, *Baudelaire*, 330–31; and Léon Cellier, *Baudelaire et Hugo* (Paris: José Corti, 1970).

10. C2: 437.

11. Walter Benjamin, *The Writer of Modern Life: Essays on Charles Baudelaire* (Cambridge, MA: Harvard University Press, 2006), 261.

12. C2: 384.

13. OC2: 771. For Walter Benjamin's (Baudelaire-inspired) observations on the figure of the Collector, see "Convolute H" of his *Arcades Project*, trans. Howard Eiland and Kevin McLaughlin (Cambridge, MA: Harvard University Press, 1999), 203–11; as well as his essay on "Eduard Fuchs, Collector and Historian," in *Selected Writings*, vol. 3, trans. Howard Eiland and Michael Jennings (Cambridge, MA: Harvard University Press, 2002), 260–302.

14. As an example of how Baudelaire transformed many of the prose jottings of his *Poor Belgium* into the satirical verse of his "Amoenitates Beligicae" (or "Belgian Amenities")—which at one point he also wanted to include in his magnum opus— here is his translation into flawless alexandrine couplets of the above encounter with Jules van Praet, one of the king's privy counselors. Entitled "L'Amateur des Beaux-Arts en Belgique," its sardonic bite (and neoclassical firmness of outline) is worthy of Pope or Byron: "Un ministre, qu'on dit le Mecenas flamand, / Me promenait un jour dans son appartement, / Interrogeant mes yeux devant chaque peinture, / Parlant un peu de *l'art*, beaucoup de la *nature*, / Vantant le *paysage*, expliquant le *sujet*, / Et surtout me marquant *le prix* de chaque objet. / —Mais voilà qu'arrivé devant un portrait d'Ingres, / (Pédant dont j'aime peu les facultés malingres) / Je fus pris tout à coup d'une sainte fureur / De célébrer David, le grand peintre empereur! / —Lui, se tourne vers son fournisseur ordinaire, / Qui se tenait debout comme un factionnaire, / Ou comme un chambellan qui savoure avec foi / Les sottises tombant des lèvres de son roi, / Et lui dit, avec l'oeil d'un marchand de la Beauce: / "Je crois, mon cher, je crois que David est en hausse!" For a far more granular analysis of Baudelaire's late Belgian epigrams, see Patrick Thériault, "Baudelaire épigrammatiste: À propos des *Amoenitates Belgicae*," *Poétique* 188 (2020/2): 189–210.

15. The term *néant* reoccurs periodically in Baudelaire's notes toward *Belgium Disrobed*. On folio 97 he speaks of "The Belgian Nullity" (that is, of "Le Néant Belge") when it comes to making conversation. Folio 331, entitled "The Belgian Brain," is followed by the simple lapidary notatation: "Le Néant Belge." Folio 117 observes that "the Belgian is as hard to communicate with as a woman, because he has nothing to communicate, and you are incommunicable to him because of his impenetrability. —Nothing is as mysterious, as deep, as pithy as Nothingness." ("Rien de mystérieux, de profond et de bref comme le Néant.") Unlike the metaphysical angst of his celebrated 1859 poem "Le Goût du Néant," here "Le Néant Belge" comes closer to that radical vacuity (or vacuousness) that Baudelaire names *bêtise*. In the second paragraph of his "Argument" for the book, however, Baudelaire speaks of "the benefit of doing a book on Belgium. To be amusing while speaking of boredom, instructive while speaking of [the] *nothing*." ("Il s'agit d'être amusant en parlant de l'ennui, instructif en parlant du *rien*.") Sensing that Baudelaire's unfinished book on Belgium

was (as Flaubert had described his *Madame Bovary* in a famous 1852 letter to Louise Colet), a "book about nothing," the late Belgian poet and conceptual artist Marcel Broodthaers in 1974 published a facsimile of pages 1315 to 1457 of Claude Pichois's 1961 Pléiade edition of Baudelaire's *Oeuvres complètes*, leaving only the running titles at the top of the page intact ("SUR LA BELGIQUE" . . . "PAUVRE BELGIQUE"), but with all of Baudelaire's text erased, thus creating a virtual book composed of mere blank pages. See the description (with illustrations) of Broodthaers's project in Yves Gevaert, Emile van Blaberghe and John Sheply, "*Pauvre Belgique*: 'An Asterisk in History,'" *October* 42 (1987): 182–95.

16. For the role of "realism" in these 1857 legal proceedings, see Dominque La Capra, *Modern Bovary on Trial* (Ithaca, NY: Cornell University Press, 1982); and my article "Poetry and Obscenity: Baudelaire and Swinburne," *Comparative Literature* 36 (1984): 343–53.

17. See his unpublished essay "Puisque Réalisme il y a" (Since Realism Exists), OC2: 57–59. Written in 1855, this text was contemporary with Courbet's *Painter's Atelier*, which features Baudelaire sitting at a table in the right corner, next to the pentimento of a painted-out Jeanne Duval.

18. See Benjamin, *Arcades Project*, "Convolute S" and "Convolute Y." Benjamin most likely discovered Wiertz through Baudelaire's mention of him in the "Argument for the Book on Belgium." In his "Little History of Photography" of 1931, Benjamin contrasts Wiertz's celebration of the daguerreotype with Baudelaire's denigration of it in his *Salon of 1857*. *Selected Writings*, vol. 2, trans. Edmund Jephcott (Cambridge, MA: Harvard University Press, 1999), 526–27.

19. Canto 80 from *The Pisan Cantos*, ed. Richard Sieburth (New York: New Directions, 2003), 89. My understanding of Baudelaire's late encounter with Rubens and with baroque architecture in Belgium has been shaped by Yves Bonnefoy's essay "Baudelaire contre Rubens" in his *Sous le signe de Baudelaire* (Paris: Gallimard, 2011), 21–85.

20. Baudelaire to Manet, May 11, 1865. In the "Stroll through Namur" included in the "Argument" for his Belgian book, Baudelaire speaks of his plan to do "portraits of Félicien Rops and his father-in-law, a tough local judge and yet quite jovial, a great hunter with a talent for quotation. He has written a book on hunting and quoted me lines from Horace, from my *Fleurs du mal* and sentences by d'Aurevilly . . . the only Belgian with a knowledge of Latin and capable of carrying on in French." Baudelaire here distinguishes between the art of knowledgeable *quotation* and mere Belgian apery. In *My Heart Laid Bare* he had observed: "How the young hate those who quote. They consider a man given to quotations their enemy."

21. Benjamin, *Writer of Modern Life*, 163. Baudelaire's poem "Danse macabre" contains the crucial line "Ô charme d'un néant follement attifé"—which might be loosely translated as "What charm in a nil dressed to kill." See also the discussion of the allegorical skeleton that Rops executed for the frontispiece of Baudelaire's *Épaves* in my introduction.

22. Among the other churches Baudelaire preferred were the Béguinage in Brussels, Saint-Pierre in Malines, and Saint-Loup in Namur. In early 1865, he became particularly interested in the work of the seventeenth-century Flemish architect and painter Wenceslas Cobergher.

23. See Georges van den Abbeele, "La Déception touriste," in *Art et création chez Théophile Gautier* (Paris: Éditions le Manuscrit, 2013).

24. C2: 409.

25. The only portion of the project that he finished was the carefully transcribed "Argument for the Book on Belgium" prepared in January 1866 as a prospectus for publishers in Paris. That same month he admitted to Ancelle that most of the book was still "in the same jumbled state in which Proudhon left what are called his post-humous works" (C2: 571). Proudhon's *Oeuvres posthumes* had just been published in Brussels by (of all people) Lacroix, and Baudelaire no doubt anticipated that his own "Book on Belgium" would similarly see the light of print only after his death. Many of his favorite modern works were in fact published posthumously: Joseph de Maistre's *Les Soirées de Saint Petersbourg* (1821), Alphonse Rabbe's *Album d'un pessimiste* (1835), Joseph Joubert's *Pensées* (1838), Aloysius Bertrand's *Gaspard de la nuit* (1842), and of course Chateaubriand's *Mémoires d'outre-tombe* (1849) and Nerval's *Aurélia, ou le rêve et la vie* (1855).

26. See his 1857 essays "Quelques caricaturistes français" and "Quelques carica-turistes étrangers," themselves a prolongation of his essay on "De l'essence du rire," published two years earlier. All three are available in *The Painter of Modern Life and Other Essays*, trans. and ed. Jonathan Mayne (London: Phaidon, 1964). Michele Han-noosh's *Baudelaire and Caricature: From the Comic to an Art of Modernity* (University Park: Pennsylvania State University Press, 1992) remains the definitive study.

27. OC2: 532. I quote Mayne's translation in *Painter of Modern Life*, 154.

28. In his great obituary essay on Delacroix, Baudelaire quoted the artist as say-ing that if one didn't have the skill to sketch a man throwing himself out of a window during the time it took him to fall from the fifth story to the ground, one would never be able to produce major paintings. Baudelaire comments: "I rediscover in this enor-mous hyperbole the preoccupation of his entire life . . . that one execute with enough rapidity and certainty to allow nothing to evaporate from the intensity of the action or idea" (OC2: 763). He makes similar comments on the feverish celerity of Guy's "ac-tion" sketches in "The Painter of Modern Life."

29. Deleuze's account of Bacon's "dismantling of the face" is discussed in Ger-ald L. Bruns, "Becoming-Animal (Some Simple Ways)," *New Literary History* 38 (2007): 711–13.

30. See Yves-Alain Bois and Rosalind E. Krauss, *Formless: A User's Guide* (Cam-bridge, MA: MIT Press, 1997).

31. He writes in "On the Essence of Laughter": "From now onwards I shall call the grotesque 'the absolute comic,' in antithesis to the ordinary comic, which I shall call 'the significative comic.' The latter is a clearer language, and one easier for the man in the street to understand, and above all easier to analyze, its element being visibly *double*—art and the moral idea. But the absolute comic, which comes much closer to nature, emerges as a *unity* which calls for the intuition to grasp it. There is but one criterion of the grotesque, and that is laughter—immediate laughter. Whereas with the significative comic it is quite permissible to laugh a moment late" (Mayne, *Painter of Modern Life*, 157; OC2: 535). Of Goya he writes: "Goya's great merit in his having created a credible form of the monstrous. His monsters are born viable, har-monious. No one has ventured further than he in the direction of the *possible* absurd.

All those distortions, those bestial faces, those diabolic grimaces of his are impregnated with *humanity*" (Mayne, 192; OC2: 570). Around the same time (in 1853), the German art historian Karl Rosenkranz had coined the term *Aesthetik des Hässlichen*— the aesthetic of the ugly.

32. This recognition of the self in the enemy other is brilliantly explored in Jérôme Thélot, *Baudelaire: Violence et poésie* (Paris: Gallimard, 1993), 187–216. Thélot's theoretical framework for the violence engendered by the rivalry with Same is broadly based on the work of René Girard. Julia Kristeva's *Powers of Horror*, trans. Leon Roubiez (New York: Columbia University Press, 1982), suggests a further psychoanalytical approach to Baudelaire's relation to Belgium—one based on projection, introjection, abjection, rejection, and subjection.

33. Although the impact of Hugo's poetics of the grotesque on Baudelaire is undeniable. Here is the famous description of Quasimodo in part 1, chapter 5 of Hugo's 1831 novel *Notre Dame de Paris*: "We shall not try to give the reader an idea of that tetrahedal nose, of that horseshoe mouth, of that tiny left eye overbristled by a reddish, bushy eyebrow, while the right eye disappeared entirely below an enormous wart, of those teeth in disarray, chipped here and there like the embattled parapets of a fortress, of that callous lip upon which one of these teeth encroached like the tusk of an elephant, of that forked chin and above all, of the overall physiognomy of the face, a mixture of malice, amazement, and sadness." Quasimodo would have fit right into Baudelaire's Brussels, "the land of Hunchbacks and the domain of Rickets." See, more generally, Virginia E. Swain, *Grotesque Figures: Baudelaire, Rousseau, and the Aesthetics of Modernity* (Baltimore: Johns Hopkins University Press, 2005).

34. The *inframince*, according to Duchamp, is that point at which one can just barely begin to perceive a threshold between two states. He gives as examples: the moment between the report of a gun and the appearance of the bullet hole; the temperature change in a seat that has just been vacated; the odor of the smoker's mouth that still lingers in exhaled smoke; the dimensional difference between two massproduced objects made from the same mold, and so on. I follow Craig Dworkin's explanation of this Duchampian concept in his *No Medium* (Cambridge, MA: MIT Press, 2013), 17–18.

35. See the notes to Guyaux's edition of *Fusées, Mon Coeur mis à nu, La Belgique déshabillée* (Paris: Gallimard, 1986), 653–56.

36. Mary Douglas, *Purity and Danger* (London: Routledge and Kegan Paul, 1966); Jacques Derrida, *The Beast and the Sovereign*, vol. 1, trans. Geoffrey Bennington (Chicago: University of Chicago Press, 2009).

37. An extended commentary on this final section of *Flares* is provided by Philippe Roger, *The American Enemy: The History of French Anti-Americanism*, trans. Sharon Bowman (Chicago: University of Chicago Press, 2005), 59–63.

38. Unlike Victor Hugo, who in 1837 described his four-hour roundtrip journey between Antwerp and Brussels (thirty-three miles in all, reaching speeds of ten miles an hour) as follows: "The speed is terrific. The flowers on the edge of the track are no longer flowers, but red or white splotches or rather streaks; no more dots, everything turned into streaks; the wheat fields are large yellow shocks of hair; the alfalfa is long green braids; the towns, the steeples, and the trees dance and blend into each other on the horizon; from time to time, a shadow, a form, a phantom rears up and

then disappears in a flash; it is a highway patrolman who, following custom, salutes the convoy with his weapons. People comment in the compartment: it's still three leagues away, we'll be there in ten minutes." Pierre Arty, *La Belgique selon Victor Hugo* (Liège: Desoer, 1968), 66.

39. Much of this background information is taken from Else Witter, ed., *Political History of Belgium: From 1830 Onwards* (Brussels: Academic and Scientific Publishers, 2009).

40. To this list, in a more minor key, might be added Charlotte Brontë's 1853 *Villete*, a protofeminist novel about the frustrations of female freedom, based on Brontë's experiences in one of Brussels's *pensionnats* in 1842–43. See H. A. T. Ruijssenaars, *Charlotte Brontë's Promised Land* (Haworth, UK: Brontë Society, 2000).

41. C1: 579.

42. Some of Baudelaire's most comic pages involve the freethinkers' campaign for civil burials. In Belgium, an official cemetery had the legal status of a sacred place and thus fell under the authority of the church. Nonbelievers were therefore denied the right of burial on the grounds that they would desecrate the site. Baudelaire takes great pleasure in reporting the freethinkers' complaints that priests would surreptitiously dig up their corpses and throw them over the graveyard walls at night. This battle over corpses between the atheists and the Catholics reminded him of Wiertz's colossally awful painting *The Death of Patrocles*. The corpse of course lies at the core of Baudelaire's neobaroque poetics. As for the Belgian nation as a whole, he refers to it as "a corpse of a people, a garrulous corpse, created by diplomats."

43. For the French attitudes toward the American Civil War, see Roger, *American Enemy*, 65–95.

44. The question remains: if for Baudelaire Belgium symbolized the triumph of mechanized (or "Americanized") fragmentation over organic totality—or in Tönnies's classic formulation, the transformation of traditional *Gemeinschaft* (community) into modern *Gesellschaft* (society)—what does France in turn represent for him? Despite his personal loathing for Napoleon III, Baudelaire nonetheless clearly preferred the "Caesarism" of the Second Empire (as an expression of traditional national power and sovereignty) to the compromise formation of Louis Philippe's bourgeois monarchy. Like Joseph de Maistre, however, he located his true paradise lost in *ancien régime* France, or in some aristocratic feudal never-never land in which, as he notes in fragment 22 of *My Heart Laid Bare*: "There are only three beings worthy of respect. The priest, the warrior, the poet. To know, to kill, to create. All other men are mere stableboys doing their master's bidding, that is, exercising what are known as *professions*."

45. OC1: 275.

46. See my *Selected Writings of Gérard de Nerval* (London: Penguin Books, 1999), xvii. For a fuller account of French reactions to *la contrefaçon belge*, see Claude Pichois, *L'Image de la Belgique dans les lettres françaises de 1830 à 1870* (Paris: Nizet, 1957), 32–37.

47. Arty, *La Belgique selon Victor Hugo*, 111.

48. Jean Baudrillard, *America*, trans. Chris Turner (London: Verso, 1988). See also Jean-Philippe Mathy's discussion of Baudrillard in his *Extrême-Occident: French Intellectuals and America* (Chicago: University of Chicago Press, 1993), 224–50.

49. According to Catherine Gothot-Mersch's introduction and notes to her Folio

edition of *Bouvard et Pécuchet* (Paris: Gallimard, 1979), in the projected second volume of his posthumous novel, Flaubert's scriveners were to devote themselves entirely to *la copie* of examples of modern *bêtise*.

50. See the letter to Mme. Paul Meurice in appendix 7. A full 130-page reproduction of the hundreds of press clippings (or *coupures*) that Baudelaire had collected as documentary evidence (or *pièces à conviction*) for the *sottisier* of his book on Belgium may be found in Guyaux's 1986 Folio edition, 321–454. The recent edition of *Belgium Stripped Bare*, translated and introduced by Rainer J. Hanshe (New York: Contra Mundum, 2019), usefully includes extended summaries of the fifty or so press clippings that Baudelaire actually folded or pasted into the body of his manuscript. Whether Baudelaire intended to include the rest of his vast collection of newspaper clippings within his eventual book or whether they just constituted preliminary research data or items to be later excerpted remains open to question. In any event, the mimetic act of citation remains central to his entire project, paradoxically conceived as a *critique* of mimesis. The parallels with Walter Benjamin's *Arcades Project* are notable. For a broader discussion of Benjamin's poetics and politics of quotation and copying, see my "Benjamin the Scrivener," in *Benjamin: Philosophy, Aesthetics, History*, ed. Gary Smith (Chicago: University of Chicago Press, 1989), 1337.

Argument of the Book on Belgium

Possible titles:

The true Belgium. Belgium stark naked.
  Belgium disrobed. A Ludicrous Capital.
  A Capital of Apes.
                    ?

1 · PRELIMINARIES

That one should always "carry along one's fatherland on the sole of one's shoes"—whatever Danton* might say.

France seems quite barbaric, seen up close. But go to Belgium, and you will become less critical of your own country.

Just as Joubert† gave thanks to God for having made him a man and not a woman, so you too will thank him for having created you French and not Belgian.

The great benefit of doing a book on Belgium. To be amusing while speaking of boredom, instructive while speaking of *nothing*.

A sketch of Belgium offers this further advantage: it allows one by the same token to caricature the idiocies of France.

---

* *Danton:* Refusing to flee France after his arrest in 1794, Danton claimed that it would be impossible "d'emporter sa patrie à la semelle de ses souliers."

† *Joubert:* Joseph Joubert, French moralist and essayist, much admired by Baudelaire. Chateaubriand first published Joubert's posthumous *Pensées* in 1838.

Europe has entered into a conspiracy to flatter Belgium. Craving compliments, Belgium inevitably takes them seriously.

How, some twenty years ago, we used to chant the praises of the United States of America in all their liberty, glory, and good fortune!* Belgium inspires similar idiocies.

Why the French who have resided in Belgium won't tell the truth about this country. Because, given how French they are, they don't want to admit that they were *had*.

Voltaire's verses on Belgium.†

2 · BRUSSELS. Physiognomy of the Street.

First impressions. It is said that every city, every country has its smell. Paris, they say, smells or *used to smell* of acrid cabbage. Cape Town smells of sheep.‡ There are tropical isles that smell of roses, musk, or coconut oil. Russia smells of leather. Lyon smells of coal. The Orient generally smells of musk and corpses. Brussels smells of black soap. The hotel rooms smell of black soap. The beds smell of black soap. The napkins smell of black soap. The sidewalks smell of black soap. The continual scrubbing of sidewalks and stoops, even in the pouring rain. A national mania.

---

* *We used to chant the praises of the United States of America:* This is how Baudelaire descried the United States in his 1859 "Notes nouvelles sur Edgar Poe": "To burn negroes in shackles, guilty only of having felt their black cheeks flush with the red of honor, to wave revolvers around in the orchestra pits of concert halls, to establish polygamy in the paradises of the West which even the Savages (a term which does them no justice whatsoever) had not yet befouled with these shameful utopias, to place posters on walls, no doubt in order to enshrine the principle of unfettered liberty, advertising *cures for nine-month illnesses*—these are some of the striking features, some of the moral illustrations of the noble country of Franklin, the inventor of shopkeeper morality, the hero of a century given over to matter. It is worth calling attention to these marvels of brutality, at a time when Americanomania has almost become a respectable passion."

† *Voltaire's verses on Belgium:* Quoted in full later on in Baudelaire's notes, on folio 20.

‡ *Cape Town smells of sheep:* On his return trip from Mauritius and Réunion, Baudelaire had stopped over in Cape Town in December 1841—his first contact with Dutch/ Flemish culture.

The general *blandness* of life. Cigars, vegetables, flowers, fruits, cuisine, eyes, hair, everything *bland*, everything sad, flavorless, asleep. The human face itself, blurred, clouded, asleep. A Frenchman goes in fear of this *Soporific Contagion*.

Only the dogs are alive; they are the negroes [*nègres*] of Belgium.

Brussels much noisier than Paris; reasons for this. The cobblestones, uneven; the houses, rickety and creaky; the streets, narrow; the local loudmouthed accent, atrocious; the clumsiness, widespread; the *whistling* (describe), a national trait; the dogs forever barking. . . .

Few sidewalks, or sidewalks blocked (the result of individual liberty pushed to the extreme). Lousy paving. No life in the street. —Many balconies, nobody on the balconies. The *spy-mirrors*,* signs of boredom, curiosity, inhospitality.

Gloominess of a city without a river.

Nothing on display in the shops. *Flânerie*, so dear to nations endowed with imagination, impossible in Brussels. Nothing to see, and strolling out of the question.

Innumerable pince-nez. The reason for this. The remark of a local optician. An amazing quantity of Hunchbacks.

The Belgian, or rather the Brussels, face—vague, shapeless, pasty, or splotchy, bizarre build of the jaws, menacing stupidity.

The ludicrous way the Belgians lurch along. They proceed forward by looking over their shoulders, endlessly bumping into things.

3 · BRUSSELS. Customs. Tobacco, cuisine, wines.

The question of tobacco. The drawbacks of liberty.
The question of cuisine. No roast meats. Everything braised. Every-

---

* *Spy-mirrors:* Mirrors placed laterally to house windows, allowing one to check, unobserved, who is at the door.

thing prepared with rancid butter (to save money or as a matter of taste). Execrable vegetables, either because of their poor quality or on account of the butter. No spicy stews. (Belgian cooks believe that highly seasoned fare means highly salted fare.)

The elimination of the dessert course is also quite symptomatic. No fruits (those from Tournai—are they even decent?—are exported to England). One therefore has to import them from France or Algeria.

And to top it off, the bread is execrable, damp, soft, charred.

Alongside the *common myth* of *Belgian liberty* and of *Belgian cleanliness*, let's place the *myth* of *how cheap it is to live* in Belgium.

Everything is *four times* more expensive than in Paris, where the only expensive thing is rent.

Here, everything is expensive, except rent.

You can, if you have the stomach for it, live *à la Belge*. Description of the Belgian diet and hygiene.

—The question of wine. —Wine, an object of curiosity, a collector's item. Magnificent wine cellars, richly furnished, *all identical*. Expensive, heady wines. The Belgians *display* their wines. They drink wine, not because they have any taste for it, but out of vanity, to validate their *Conformity*, their resemblance to the French.

—Belgium, a paradise for traveling wine salesmen. What the common folk drink. Faro and gin.

4 · CUSTOMS. Women and Love.

No *women*, no *love*.

Why.

No gallantry among the men, no sense of modesty among the women.

Modesty, something forbidden, no need felt for it. Broad portrait of the Flemish woman, or at least of the Brabant woman* (setting the Walloon woman aside for the moment).

---

* *Brabant woman:* Brabant was from 1830 to 1995 the central province of Belgium, with Brussels as its chief city. The French-speaking Walloons lived primarily in the south and east of the country.

Typical physiognomy comparable to that of the sheep or ram.
—Smiles impossible because of the recalcitrance of the muscles and
the set of the teeth and jaws.

The complexion generally pasty, sometimes splotchy. The hair yel-
low. The legs, breasts, huge—tubs of lard. The feet, horrors!!!

Monstrous bosoms typically developing quite precociously, swelling
like swamps owing to the humidity of the climate and the gluttony of
the women.

The stench of the women. Anecdotes.

Obscenity of Belgian females. Anecdotes about latrines and street
corners.

As concerns love, refer to the indecency of the old Flemish paint-
ers. Sixty-year-olds having sex. This people has not changed, and the
Flemish painters remain true to life.

—Belgian prostitution, high- and low-end. Counterfeit French tarts.
French prostitution in Brussels.

—Excerpts from the rules and regulations governing prostitution.

5 · CUSTOMS (continued)

Belgian coarseness (even among officers).
Back-biting comments about colleagues in the press.
The tone of Belgian critics and newspapermen.
Belgian vanity ruffled.
Belgian vanity in Mexico.*
Mean-spiritedness and servility.
Belgian morality. The monstrosity of Belgian crime.
Orphans and old men put up for auction.
(The Flemish party. Victor Joly.† His well-founded criticism of the
Belgians' tendency to ape everything—which perhaps needs to be
inserted elsewhere.)

* *Mexico:* Belgium sent troops in support of the French intervention in Mexico
(1861–67).
† *Victor Joly:* Publisher of the satirical newspaper *Sancho* and the only Belgian jour-
nalist to find favor in Baudelaire's eyes.

6 · CUSTOMS (continued).

The Belgian Brain.
Belgian Conversation.

It is as difficult to define the Belgian character as it is to classify the Belgian on the scale of living creatures.

He is an *ape*, but he is also a *mollusk*.

Extraordinarily scattered-brained, amazingly thick-headed. It is easy to oppress him, as is borne out by history; it is almost impossible to crush him.

As we proceed to judge the Belgian, let us not stray from certain key ideas: Apery, Counterfeiting, Conformity, rancorous Impotence—these various rubrics will enable us to classify our material.

Their vices are all counterfeits.

The Belgian fop.

The Belgian patriot.

The Belgian bungler.

The Belgian freethinker, whose most salient feature is to *believe* that *you do not believe what you are saying*, since *he* cannot grasp it. A counterfeit of French impiety. Belgian obscenity, a counterfeit of French smut.

Presumption and fatuousness. —Familiarity. —Portrait of a Walloon *loser*.

Widespread and absolute distrust of wit. The misadventures of M. de Valbezen, the French consul in Antwerp.

Distrust of laughter. —Bursts of laughter for no apparent reason. —One tells a heartwarming story; the Belgian bursts into laughter just to prove he has gotten it. —Belgians are ruminants who digest nothing.

And yet—who would believe it?—Belgium has its own *Carpentras*, its own Boeotian, the butt of Brussels jokes. By the name of Poperinghe.*

So there may well be people even dumber than all those I have so far seen.

* * *

* *Poperinghe:* Town in West Flanders, an object of ridicule, as were the Boeotians of antiquity, whose dullness and ignorance were proverbial.

7 · BRUSSELS CUSTOMS

Small-town mentality. Jealousies. Calumnies. Defamations.
Noses in other people's business. Pleasure in the misfortune of others.
Products of laziness and incompetence.

8 · BRUSSELS CUSTOMS

Spirit of obedience and CONFORMITY.
Spirit of associability.
Numberless Societies (the remains of earlier Guilds).
On the individual level, laziness of thought.
By coming together into associations, individuals relieve themselves
of the burden of having to think on their own.
The Pranksters Club.
A Belgian would not believe himself happy unless he saw others who
had achieved happiness in the same manner. Therefore, he cannot be
happy *on his own*.

9 · BRUSSELS CUSTOMS

The *Spy-mirrors*.
Belgian cordiality.
Impoliteness.
And again, how gross they are. *The "Gallic salt" of the Belgians*.
The *pisser* and the *vomiter*,* national statues I find symbolic. —Scato-
logical jokes.

10 · BRUSSELS CUSTOMS

Slow-wittedness and laziness of the Belgians; true of its leaders,
employees, and workers.
Its bureaucracies, torpid and convoluted.

---

* *The pisser and the vomiter:* Famous fountains in Brussels: the *Manneken-pis* and
the *Cracheur*.

The Postal Service, the Telegraph Service, the CUSTOMS Warehouse. Anecdotes about its government agencies.

11 · BRUSSELS CUSTOMS

Belgian Morality. The Merchants. Nothing but success matters. Money. —The story of a painter who would have gladly handed over Jefferson Davis just to earn the reward.

Everybody mistrusting everybody else, the sign of general immorality. A Belgian will suspect the motivation behind every act, no matter how noble it be.

Unscrupulous business practices (anecdotes).

The Belgian is always quick to rejoice in the misfortunes of others. Which provides food for conversation, bored as he is.

Everybody eager to engage in Slander. Of which I have been the victim on a number of occasions.

Widespread avarice. Immense fortunes. No charity. One would say that there is a conspiracy to keep the common folk in a state of dire poverty and stupefaction.

Everybody in sales, even the rich. Everybody has something they want to unload secondhand.

Hatred of beauty, to complement the *hatred of wit*.

Not to Conform, the ultimate crime.

12 · BRUSSELS CUSTOMS

The myth of *Belgian cleanliness*. Its basis. —Clean things and dirty things in Belgium. Profitable businesses: ceiling whitewashers. Losing businesses: Bathing Establishments.

Poor neighborhoods. Working-class mores. Nakedness. Drunkenness. Beggary.

13 · BELGIAN ENTERTAINMENT

The atmosphere stiff and awkward.
Lugubrious silence.

The *Conformist* mentality, always. They only amuse themselves in packs.

The Vaux Hall.

The Casino.

The Théâtre Lyrique.

The Théâtre de la Monnaie.

The French Vaudeville.

Mozart at the Théâtre du Cirque.

Julius Langenbach's troupe (which flopped because of its talent).

How I managed to incite an entire hall into applauding an over-the-hill second-rate dancer.

French vaudevilles.

Neighborhood dances.

Ball games.

Archery contests.

The Brussels Carnival. Drinks are never offered to one's dance partner. Everyone jumping up and down in place, in utter silence.

The barbarity of children's entertainment.

14 · EDUCATION

State or City Universities. Free Universities. Athenaeums.

No Latin, no Greek. Professional studies. Hatred of poetry. Education to train engineers or bankers.

No metaphysics.

Positivism in Belgium. M. Hannon and M. Altmeyer,* whom Proudhon dubbed: *this old harpy!* His portrait. His style.

General loathing of literature.

15 · THE FRENCH LANGUAGE IN BELGIUM

—The style of the books (few and far between) they write here.

—Some specimens of the Belgian idiom.

---

* *M. Hannon:* Joseph Hannon succeeded Jacques Altmayer as rector of the Free University of Brussels in 1864.

They don't know French, *nobody* knows it, but everybody *affects* not to know Flemish. It shows good taste. The proof that they know how to speak it quite well—they *curse out* their servants in Flemish.

16 · JOURNALISTS AND LITERATI

In general, the literati (?) here hold other jobs as well. Most often as office employees.

Moreover, no literature. At least no French literature. One or two *chansonniers*, disgusting apes of Béranger's off-color songs.* One Novelist, an imitator of the copiers of the Apes of Champfleury.† Savants, annalists, or chroniclers—that is, people who collect and others who buy up stacks of paper at a low price (the financial accounts of buildings and other documents, the entries of princes, the transcripts of the sessions of municipal councils, copies of archives) and then resell all this material in a single block as a history book.

In fact, everybody here is an *annalist* (in Anvers, everybody is an art dealer; in Brussels, there are rich art collectors who also deal in secondhand curios).

The Tone of the Newspapers. Numerous Examples. Ridiculous letter columns in the *Office de publicité*. —*L'Indépendance belge*. —*L'Écho du parlement*. —*L'Étoile belge*. —*Le Journal de Bruxelles*. —*Le Bien public*. —*Le Sancho*. —*Le Grelot*. —*L'Espiègle*. —Etc., etc.

Literary patriotism. A poster announcing a play.

17 · BELGIAN IMPIETY. *Quite a chapter, this! As is the following one.*

Insults directed at the Pope. —Antireligious propaganda. —Account of the death of the archbishop of Paris (1848). —Staging of Pixéré-

---

* *Béranger: Pierre-Jean de Béranger*, the most popular *chansonnier* of the early nineteenth century, imprisoned in 1821 and 1828 for his antiestablishment songs.

† *Champfleury:* Pseudonym of Jules Fleury-Husson, early supporter of the work of Courbet and editor of the periodical *Le Réalisme* (1856–57). His novel, *Les Bourgeois de Molinchart* (1855), is considered among the earliest works of literary realism.

court's play, *Le Jésuite,* at the *Théâtre Lyrique.* —The Jesuit-bogeyman.
—A procession. —Royal subscription for burials. —Campaign against a
Catholic schoolteacher. —The law regulating Cemeteries. —Civil buri-
als. —Corpses under contention or stolen. —The burial of a *Solidarist.*
—Civil burial of a woman. —Analysis of the regulations of the societies
of *freethinkers.* —Rules for making out one's will. —A wager made by
the Body of Our Lord Eating Society!

18 · IMPIETY AND PRIESTOPHOBIA*

More on the *freethinkers!* More on the *Solidarists* and the *Emanci-
pated!* Another last will and testament formulated in order to filch
yet another corpse from the Church. An article by M. Sauvestre in
L'Opinion nationale on *free thought.* Again, more corpses stolen. —The
funeral services for a clergyman who died a *freethinker.* —Jesuitopho-
bia. —Who exactly is *our brave De Buck,* a former criminal, persecuted
by the Jesuits. —An assembly of *freethinkers* at my hotel, the *Grand
Miroir.* —Belgians philosophizing. —Another burial of a *Solidarist* to
the tune of: *"Oh damn it all! Nadar's caught a dose!"*

The clerical party and the liberal party. Equally dumb. —The cele-
brated Boniface, or Defré† (a Belgian Paul-Louis Courier) is afraid of
ghosts, digs up the corpses of children who died without final sacra-
ment in order to rebury them in sanctified ground, and thinks he will
meet a tragic death like Courier and has escorts to accompany him at
night for fear he be assassinated by the Jesuits. —My first interview
with this imbecile. He was drunk. —Returning from the garden where
he had gone to vomit, he interrupted the piano playing in order to
launch into a speech in favor of *Progress* and against Rubens as a Cath-
olic painter.

—Those who want to abolish capital punishment do so out of sheer
self-interest, in Belgium as in France.

---

* *Priestophobia:* Or *prêtrophobie,* a nonce word coined by Joseph de Maistre.
† *Defré:* Louis-Joseph Defré, vociferous member of the anti-Catholic party and fre-
quent object of Baudelaire's ridicule. Paul-Louis Courrier, French political pamphle-
teer of the turn of the nineteenth century.

—Belgian anticlericalism is a counterfeit of French anticlericalism, but raised to the cubic power.

—The area in cemeteries reserved for dogs or reprobates.

—Belgian bigotry.

—Ugliness, villainy, nastiness, and *bêtise* of the Flemish clergy. –See Rops's lithography of the *Burial*.*

—Pious Belgians make one think of the cannibal Christians of South America.

—The only religious program that would work for the *freethinkers* of Belgium is the program of M. de Caston, a French magician.

—Curious opinion of a friend of Dumouriez on the political parties in Belgium: "There are only two parties, the drunkards and the Catholics." —This country has not changed.

19 · POLITICS

Electoral practices. Venality. The cost of an election in any given locality is an open secret. Voting scandals.

Parliamentary favors. (Many illustrations of this.)

Belgian eloquence.

A grotesque discussion about campaign financing.

The republican caucus. A duplicate of the Jacobins.

In the sands of time, Belgium always so far behind.

20 · POLITICS

There is, strictly speaking, no such thing as a Belgian people. There are the Flemish and Walloon races, and there are rival towns. Take Anvers. Belgium, a harlequin patched together by diplomats.

The baroque story of the 1789 Brabant Revolution, undertaken

* *Rops's lithography of the* Burial: Félicien Rops's anticlerical lithograph *A Burial in Wallonia* (1863) was often compared to Gustave Courbet's painting *A Burial at Ornans* (1850).

against a Philosopher-King,* and finding itself facing the French Rev-
olution, a philosophic revolution.

A constitutional monarch is an automaton in a rooming house.
—Belgium is the victim of the property qualification that determines
the right to vote. Why nobody here wants universal suffrage. The
constitution is nothing but a rag. Constitutions are made of *paper*.
Manners and morals are *everything*. —Belgian "freedom" is a mere
word. It's there on paper, but it doesn't exist, *because nobody feels the
need for it.*

At a certain moment, this comic situation in the House. The two
parties equal, minus *one* vote. —The *magnificent spectacle* of the elec-
tions, as the French newspapers put it.

Description of an electoral assembly. —Political powwows. Political
oratory. Bombast. Disproportion between speech and object.

21 · ANNEXATION

Annexation is a prime topic of Belgian conversation. It was the first
word I heard when I arrived here two years ago. They have talked of
it so much that they have convinced the parrots of French journalism
to repeat the word after them. —A good portion of Belgium is pro-
annexation. But this is not reason enough. First of all, France would
have to agree to do so. Belgium is a sniveling little ragamuffin who
throws himself around the neck of a fine gentleman and says to him:
"Adopt me, be my father!" —but the gentleman first has to be willing
to do so.

I am against annexation. There are already enough morons in
France, not to mention all those we have annexed in the past, the
people of Bordeaux, of Alsace, and others.

But I would not object to an invasion, to a Razzia,† a raid in the

---

* *Philosopher-King:* Joseph II, Holy Roman Emperor and ruler of the Hapsburg
lands (which included Belgium) from 1780 to 1790.

† *Razzia:* A term derived from the Arabic, originally signifying an invasion into
foreign or enemy territory to seize livestock and harvest. Also used to describe the
French military raiding tactics during the conquest of Algeria.

ancient fashion, in the fashion of Attila. Everything beautiful could be carted off to the *Louvre*. All this belongs to us far more legitimately than it does to the Belgians, given that they no longer have a clue about it. —And the fairer Belgian sex would make the acquaintance of the Turcos,* who are not very hard to please.

Belgian is the *shitty end of the stick*; this is above all what makes it so inviolable. *Hands off Belgium!*

On the tyranny of the weak. Women and animals. This is what accounts for the tyranny of Belgium over European opinion.

Belgian is safeguarded by the balance of rivalries. Yes; but what if these rivals reached an agreement among themselves! What would happen in that case?

(Place the rest in the Epilogue, among conjectures as to the future and advice to the French.)

22 · THE ARMY

Is, on a comparative basis, far larger than the armies of the rest of Europe: but never engages in war. Odd allocation of governmental funds!

This army, were it to undertake a campaign, would have problems with its infantry troops because of the particular configuration of the Belgian foot. But there are many men who could be quickly made battle-ready.

All these young beardless recruits (military service is quite short in duration) have the faces of children.

In this army, an officer's only hope for advancement depends on the natural death or suicide of a superior.

Many of the younger officers are quite disheartened—they are for the most well educated and would make excellent soldiers should the occasion arise.

Classes in Rhetoric at the military academy, studies of imaginary battles—paltry consolations for the inactivity of minds educated for the art of war.

* *Turcos:* French sharpshooters in the Algerian war.

Better manners in the army than in the rest of the nation. Which is not very surprising. The sword has always proved an ennobling and civilizing force.

23 · KING LEOPOLD I. HIS PORTRAIT. ANECDOTES. HIS DEATH. NATIONAL MOURNING.

Leopold, this pathetic minor German princeling, managed (as one says) to make his brave little way. He didn't flee into exile in a coach. Having arrived on the throne in his wooden clogs, he died with a fortune estimated at a *hundred million,* amid European apotheosis. In recent days, he has been declared *immortal.* Ludicrous panegyrics. Leopold and Vapereau.*

A perfect mediocrity, but with a peasant's canniness and perseverance, this young sprout of the Saxe-Coburg family managed to hoodwink everybody, laid away a nice little *nest egg,* and in the end filched the fulsome praise usually reserved for heroes.

Napoleon I's opinion of him.

His avarice, his rapaciousness. —A German princeling's moronic ideas about court protocol. His relations with his family. —His allowances. The "pension" he received from Napoleon III.

Anecdote about the gardener.

His ideas about parks and gardens, which caused him to be taken for a lover of the *great outdoors,* but which were simply the products of his tightfistedness.

Newspapers are censored so that the King will read nothing alarming about his poor state of health.

What the Minister of the Interior said within my hearing one morning. The King's ridiculous aversion to dying. —His incredulous reaction to his demise. —He sends away his doctors. —He steals from his mistress.

* *Leopold and Vapereau:* Louis Gustave Vapereau's standard *Dictionnaire universel des contemporains* (1858) contained a very flattering portrait of Léopold de Saxe-Coburg, who became king of the Belgians in 1831. Baudelaire felt that the coverage of the current events surrounding Leopold's death on December 10, 1865, would grant his proposed book on Belgium "une brutale actualité."

Invasion of the duchess of Brabant and her children. She slaps a crucifix on his mouth and asks him whether there is anything for which he wants to repent.

Parallels between the death of the King and all other Belgian deaths. —His three chaplains quarrel over his corpse. —M. Becker wins out in the end, *given his superior command of French!*

—The great comedy of Mourning begins. —Black bunting, panegyrics, apotheoses. —Public drinking, public pissing, public vomiting everywhere. —All the Belgians in the street, soused, crowded together in silence as if at some masked ball. —They find this entertaining. —Brussels had *in reality* never seen such a *party.* —After all, here was its *first king* ever to have died. —The new King makes his entry to the tune of an Offenbach air (*factual*). —Nobody laughs. —There are some Belgians singing: *Let's Soldier On,* a fine reply to those miserable *Frenchies* who would annex them.

24 · FINE ARTS

In Belgium, no Art; Art has withdrawn from the country.

No artists, except Rops.*

Composition, a thing unknown. The philosophy of these brutes—a philosophy à la Courbet. Only paint what you see. Therefore *you* are not allowed to paint what *I* do not see. Specialists. —One painter for the sun, one for the moon, one for furniture, one for fabrics, one for flowers—with infinite subdivisions of these specialties, as in industry. —Collaboration becomes essential.

The national taste for vile and revolting things. The old painters are therefore the truthful historians of the Flemish mentality. —Here, bombast is part and parcel of *bêtise*—which explains good old Rubens, a lout decked out in satins.

On several modern painters, all *pasticheurs,* all duplicates of French

---

* *No artists, except Rops:* Baudelaire first met Félicien Rops in Namur in late May 1864. He would subsequently design the baroque frontispiece for the 1866 Malassis edition of Baudelaire's *Épaves.*

talents. —The tastes of those who follow art. —M. Prosper Crabbe.*
—The vulgarity of the celebrated M. Van Praet, minister of the palace.
—My single interview with him. —How one puts together a collec-
tion. —Belgians measure the value of artists by the market price of
their paintings. —Several pages on this despicable *self-promoter* called
Wiertz,† the darling of English tourists. —Analysis of the Museum of
Brussels. —Contrary to received opinion, its Rubens are far inferior to
those in Paris.

Sculpture, nil [*néant*].

25 · ARCHITECTURE. CHURCHES. WORSHIP

Modern urban architecture. Junk. Ricketiness of the houses. No har-
mony. Clashing architectures. —Good materials. —Blue stone. —Pas-
tiches of the past. —The monuments are Counterfeits of France. —As
for the Churches, Counterfeits of the past.

The past. The gothic. —The 17th century.

— Description of the Grand-Place of Brussels (very well tended).

— In Belgium, they are always out of date; the styles lag behind and
last far longer.

—In praise of the 17th-century style, an unrecognized style, of which
there are magnificent specimens in Belgium.

—The *Renaissance* in Belgium. —Transition. —The Jesuit styles.
—Styles of the 17th century. The Rubens style.

The Church of *Béguinage* in Brussels, *Saint-Pierre* in Malines, the
Church of the Jesuits in Anvers, *Saint-Loup* in Namur, etc., etc. . . . .

—V. Hugo's championing of the Gothic has done much to damage
our understanding of architecture. We have gotten stuck on it too
long. —The philosophy of the history of architecture, *according to me.*
—Analogies with corals, madrepora, the formation of continents, and

---

* *M. Prosper Crabbe:* Wealthy Belgian stockbroker who sponsored a lecture by
Baudelaire in his home. Baudelaire also wrote a brief (critical) catalog of Crabbe's
art collection (see appendix 4).

† *Wiertz, the darling of the English tourists:* For further on the Belgian painter An-
toine Wiertz, see p. 364n below.

finally with the entire life of nature. —No gaps. —A permanent state of transition. —One can say that Rococo is the final flowering of Gothic.

—Cobergher, Faid'herbe and Franquart.*

—Victor Joly's opinion of Cobergher, as usual deriving from Victor Hugo.

—The immense riches of the Churches. —A bit of the curiosity shop, a bit of the junk store.

Description of this type of wealth.

Some churches, either Gothic, either 17th century.

Polychrome statues. The confessionals highly decorated; —the confessionals at the Béguinage, at Malines, at Anvers, at Namur, etc.....

The Pulpits of Truth. —Extremely varied. —The true Flemish sculpture is made of wood and is at its most stunning in the churches. —A sculpture that is not sculptural, not monumental; toy sculpture. A sculpture of patience. —Yet this art has died out as have all the others, even at Malines, where it flowered so successfully.

—Description of a few processions. Traces of the past still subsisting in religious practices. —The sumptuousness of it all. —Astonishing naivete in the dramatization of religious ideas.

Passing observations about the sheer number of Belgian festivals. Every day a feast day. A telling indication of the laziness of its people.

—Belgian piety, dim-witted. —Superstition. The Christian God is beyond the capacity of the Belgian Brain.

—The Clergy, ponderous, crude, cynical, lubricious, rapacious. In a word, Belgian. The Clergy was behind the Revolution of 1831 and therefore believes it owns the country.

—To return to the Jesuits and to the Jesuit style. A style with genius. The complex and ambiguous character of this style. —(Stylish yet terrifying.) —Large openings, large bays, large light—a mélange of figures, styles, ornaments, symbols. —A few examples. I have seen tiger paws functioning as volutes. —In general, the exteriors of these churches are plain, except for the facade.

---

* *Cobergher, Faid'herbe, Franquart:* Wenceslas Cobergher, Louis Faidherbe, and Jacob Franquart, three major architects associated with the development of the baroque style in 17th-century Belgium.

26 · THE COUNTRYSIDE AROUND BRUSSELS

Fat, buxom, moist, like the Flemish female—murky, like the Flemish male. —The vegetation is quite black. —The climate is humid, cold, hot, humid, four seasons in a single day. —Not much animal life. No insects, no birds. Even the beasts flee these accursèd climes.

27 · A STROLL THROUGH MALINES

Malines is a nice little Beguine nun snug in her hood. —Mechanical music wafts through the air. —The *Marseillaise* on the carillon. —Every day is a Sunday. —Crowds in Churches. Grass growing in the streets. The ancient smell of Spain. The Beguine nunnery. Several Churches. —Saint-Rombaut. Notre Dame. Saint-Pierre. —Paintings of two Jesuit brothers on the Mission. *Continuous* confessionals. The marvelous symbol of the Pulpit, promising world domination to the Jesuits—the sole sculptural piece of sculpture that I have seen. —The smell of wax and incense. —Rubens and Van Dyck. —The Botanical Garden. The stream clear, fast-flowing. —A fine Moselle wine at the *Greyhound* Inn. —Explain what a *Private Society* is.

28 · A STROLL THROUGH ANVERS

Encounter with the archbishop of Malines. —Flat country, the vegetation black. —Fortifications new (!) and ancient, with English gardens. Here finally is a town that could pass for a Capital! —The Meir square. The Rubens House. The House of the King. The Flemish *Renaissance*. The Town Hall. —The Church of the Jesuits, a masterpiece. —Here again, the *Jesuit style* (salmagundi, chessboard, chandeliers, a Boudoir at once mystical and terrifying, mourning in marble, theatrical confessionals, Theater and Boudoir, rings of light and transparent glorias, angels and cupids, apotheoses and beatifications). —What I think of the celebrated Rubens, of churches that are closed, of sacristans. —Calvaries and Madonnas. —Certain houses done in modern (pompous) style. —The majesty of Anvers. The beauty of a major river.

From which Anvers should be viewed. —Napoleon I's docks. —M. Leys. —The Plantin house. —The Rydeck dancehall, balls and prostitution. The Rydeck is a *joke*. It's the kind of sprawling brothel one finds on the outskirts of Paris.

Anvers mores, atrociously coarse. The funereal air of the waiters in restaurants. –Anvers politics (*will already have been treated in* the chapter *on political mores*).

29 · A STROLL THROUGH NAMUR

People rarely visit Namur. A town overlooked by travelers, not surprisingly because the *Donkey-Guides* never mention it. —The town of Vauban, of Boileau, of Van der Meulen, of Bossuet, of Fénélon, of Jouvenet, of Rigaud, of Restout, etc. . . . Memories of Boileau's *Le Lutrin*.* —*Saint-Loup*, the absolute masterpiece of the Jesuits. General impression. A few details. Jesuits as architects, as painters, as sculptors, as decorators. —*Les Récollets*. Saint-Aubin, a St. Peter's of Rome in miniature, an exterior of brick and blue stone, its interior white, with a convex portal. —Nicolaï, a fake Rubens. —The Street of Blind Chaffinches. (The duke of Brabant, currently Leopold II, president of a Chaffinch Academy.)

—The peculiarities of prostitution in Namur.

—Walloon population. —Better manners.

—Portraits of Félicien Rops and his father-in-law, a tough local judge and yet quite jovial, a great hunter with a talent for quotation. He has written a book on hunting and quoted me lines from Horace, from my *Fleurs du mal*, and sentences by D'Aurevilly. —Struck me as charming. —The only Belgian with a knowledge of Latin and capable of carrying on in French.

— I'm heading for Luxembourg, without knowing it.

— The countryside, black. The river *Meuse*, steep-sloped and misty.

— Namur wine.

* *Boileau's* Le Lutrin: In addition to this mock-heroic epic in six cantos, the French poet Nicolas Boileau-Despréaux had also published a neoclassical ode celebrating the French occupation of Namur in 1692.

30 · A STROLL THROUGH LIEGE

The palace of the Bishop-Princes. —Cellars. —Drunkenness. —Major pretensions to Frenchness.

31 · A STROLL THROUGH GAND

Saint-Bavon, a few nice things. Mausoleums. —Uncouth locals. —An ancient town made up of yokels in revolt, thinks of itself as special, and puts on the airs of a Capital. Depressing town.

32 · A STROLL THROUGH BRUGES

A ghost town, a mummy of a town, more or less preserved. It smells of death, the Middle Ages, Venice in black, humdrum specters and tombs. —The great Beguine nunnery; carillons. A few monuments. A work attributed to Michelangelo. Yet Bruges, too, is on its way out.

33 · EPILOGUE. *The future. Advice to the French.*

Belgium is what France might well have become had it remained in the hands of the Bourgeoisie. Belgium is without life, but not without corruption. —Hacked into pieces, divided up, invaded, defeated, soundly thrashed, pillaged, the Belgian continues to vegetate, a pure marvel of mollusk existence. —*Noli me tangere*, a fit motto for it. —But who would want to grasp hold of this *shitty end of the stick*? — Belgium is a monster. Who would want to adopt it? And yet it contains within itself *several* elements that could contribute to its dissolution. This diplomatic harlequin could be torn apart from one moment to the next. —A portion of it could go to Prussia, the Flemish portion to Holland, the Walloon portion to France. —A great misfortune for us. —Portrait of the Walloon. —Races that are ungovernable not because of their excess of vitality but because of their total absence of ideas and feelings. Nothing there. [*C'est le néant.*] (The quotes by Maturin and Demouriez's friend). —Commercial interests in play, with which I don't want to bother myself. —Anvers aspires to become a *free city*. —Once again, the question of annexation. — Small cities (Brussels, Geneva), nasty cities. Small nations, nasty nations.

Tips to the French who are condemned to live in Belgium: how to avoid getting robbed, insulted, poisoned.

FINIS

Selections from
Belgium Disrobed

1 · OPENING

4 · OPENING

Danton. Carp and rabbit.* *America and Belgium.* I'd love to possess the faculties of . . . so many of the writers I have always envied. A certain style, not the style of Hugo, that *Belgian* author. This is my pipe dream.
A slapdash, devil-may-care book.
To toss off an amusing book on a boring topic. —(Third-rate actors.)
The slack rope and the asphalt lake.

A little poem on Amina Boschetti.†

---

* *Carp and Rabbit:* A French expression designating two things that don't go together or that are mismatched or incompatible, like cold-blooded fish and warm-blooded mammals. Over the course of the nineteenth century "a marriage of carp and rabbit" came to signify a morganatic (or left-handed) marriage between an aristocrat and a commoner or between two persons of unequal social status. Two pages later Baudelaire describes Belgium as the "offspring of Carp and Rabbit"—that is, as a kind of mongrel or half-caste nation. On the other hand, Baudelaire's comparison of Belgium to America as two monstrous examples of liberal, progressive, rapidly industrializing versions of modernity would suggest the alternative translation of "Chalk and Cheese"—that is, two things different but difficult to tell apart.

† *Amina Boschetti:* Baudelaire's light verse about the debut performance of this (somewhat fleshy) Italian ballerina at Théâtre de la Monnaie in September 1865 was later published in his *Épaves.*

A poor man dazzled by luxury objects, a sorrowful man inhaling his childhood in the fragrance of a Church, such was I as I beheld Amina.

The arms and legs of Amina. The preconception that sylphids are always thin.

Tour de force of gaiety. That sweet old gossip—Guerri.* Gin.

Talent in the Desert.

They say Amina is disconsolate.

She smiles amid a people that knows not how to smile. She flutters about amid a people where any given woman could, with one of her elephantine feet, crush thousands of eggs.

5 · OPENING

France is, no doubt, an extremely barbaric country.

Belgium as well.

Perhaps Civilization has gone into hiding among some small, as of yet undiscovered tribe.

Let us be on our guard against that dangerous Parisian penchant for over-generalization.

We have perhaps been too disparaging of France.

One should always carry along one's fatherland on the sole of one's shoes. It acts as a disinfectant.

One fears one will become *bête* here. Everything asleep. Everything slow. (The signalman who lopes ahead of the trains as they enter the city a symbol of all this.)

The offspring of Carp and Rabbit.

The French prefer to deceive rather than to admit they have been deceived. French vanity.

---

* *Guerri:* Perhaps the "adventuress" Elisa Guerri, whom Baudelaire had met via Mme. Sabatier.

6 · BRUSSELS
OPENING

The purpose of a satirical piece of writing is to kill two birds with
one stone. The additional advantage of doing a sketch of Belgium is
that it provides a caricature of France.

8 · OPENING

Shall we say that the world has become uninhabitable for me?

10 · OPENING

To produce an amusing work on a thankless subject.
Belgium and the United States. The newspapers' spoiled brats.

12

My Heart Laid Bare,
Notes on *Belgium*
(not in order) Paris Spleen.
Stanzas for Defré.*
Guidebook.

10 · BELGIUM

Incapable of conversation. —"I dislike the Belgians." —"Pray why,
sir?" —"Because they know no French." —"But sir," says the Belgian,
"what about the Hottentots?" —"Sir, the Hottentots live very far away
and you live quite nearby, besides, I have been told by reliable sources
that the Hottentots have long since been . . . consigned to Hell."
—"Why so? For not knowing French?" "Indeed, sir."

* *Defré:* See p. 281n above.

14 · PHYSIOGNOMY OF THE BELGIANS

The gaze cautious, heavy, stupid, staring. Apparent rudeness simply the result of the slowness of their vision.

Belgians walking while turning around to look over their shoulders and finally ending up flat on their faces.

Build of their jaws.
Thickness of their tongues.
Whistling.
Pronunciation slow, slurred.

15 · BRUSSELS
OVERALL IMPRESSIONS
HUMAN PHYSIOGNOMY

The Belgian eye, wide, enormous, staring steadily, insolent (when it comes to foreigners).
The innocent eye of people who can't manage to take in everything at a single glance.
One of Cyrano's characters says to another: you're so damn fat I couldn't beat all of you up in a single day.
Whatever the Belgian eye looks upon is so vast that it takes him ages just to register it.
The Belgian eye has the innocent insolence of a microscope.

16 · THE *BON MOT* IN BELGIUM

Here the *bon mot* (for example: *why here's another Frenchman come to discover Belgium*), a witticism usually borrowed from some French vaudeville comedian, does not fare very well. A hundred thousand people can deliver a single such *mot* ten times a day without exhausting it. Like the grain of musk that retains its scent without losing any of its weight. Like the brandied cherry suspended from the ceiling by a string and which, licked by numberless children, still remains intact. With this difference, however: sometimes a cleverer child will swallow the cherry, whereas the thousands of Belgians never quite manage to seize the *bon mot* in its entirety, or rather they swallow it without digesting it, vomit it back up, pass it further along, swallow it all over again without disgust, and then revomit it as if nothing were. O happy nation, so thrifty and so moderate in its pleasures! O happy nation whose organic constitution is such that it will never allow itself to splurge on wit!

17

Paris Spleen.*
  A Most Peculiar Conversation.
  No Offense to the Shades.
  The Rosary.

Belgian civilization.
The Belgian is most civilized.
He is outfitted with trousers, overcoat, umbrella, like any other man. He gets drunk and fucks just as they do in the lands beyond Quiévrain.† He pretends he's come down with the clap, in order to take after the French. He knows how use a fork. He's an outrageous liar, he's devious, he's highly civilized.

20 · BELGIUM
  OPENING

I find this sad little city
A cradle of ignorance,
Of boredom and stolidity,
Of stupidity and indifference,
An ancient land of obedience,
Poor in wit, rich in piety.

---

* *Paris Spleen:* The following three items are the titles for prose poems to come. See Baudelaire's list of projected prose poems, pp. 202–3.
  † *Quiévrain:* Ancient town marking the border between France and Belgium.

Voltaire, from Brussels, 1722

The last three words are over the mark.

2 · BRUSSELS

23 · GENERAL CHARACTERISTICS. BRUSSELS

The smells of cities. Paris, it is said, smells of acrid cabbage. Cape Town smells of sheep. The Orient smells of musk and corpses. Frankfurt . . . ? Brussels smells of black soap.

The bed linens. Insomnia brought on by black soap.

Few perfumes.

Few spicy stews.

General blandness of the cigars, vegetables, flowers (spring late and rainy, summer hot and humid), eyes, hair, gazes.

The animals seem sad and sleepy.

The human face is heavy, pasty.

Large yellow rabbit heads, yellow eyelashes.

Sheep lost in a dream.

Pronunciation slow, slurred. Syllables throttled in the throat.

Peppers become cucumbers here.

A chapter on dogs, in whom the vitality so absent elsewhere seems to have taken refuge.

Dogs harnessed to carts. (Dubois's joke.)

24 · BRUSSELS.

Physiognomy of the Street.

Scrubbing of the sidewalks, even during the pouring rain. A national mania. I have seen little girls scrubbing a small stretch of sidewalk with small rags for hours on end.

An indication of what good imitators they are and a particular sign of a Race that is not at all choosy when it comes to its amusements.

25 · BRUSSELS
   GENERAL CHARACTERISTICS
   CUSTOMS

                              Dogs, the negroes of Belgium.
   Sadness of the animals. The dogs are no more petted than are the
women. Impossible to get them to play or frisk about. If one tries, they
act as surprised as the prostitute whom one addresses as Mademoiselle.
   But what tireless workers they are!
   I have seen a very fat strong man plop himself down in a cart to
have himself pulled up a steep slope by his dog.
   It's truly the dictatorship of the savage in those uncivilized countries
where the male does nothing.

26 · BRUSSELS

   First Sensations.

   Brussels, a city far noisier than Paris. —Why?
      1) Lousy *cobblestones*, which cause carriage wheels to clatter.
      2) *Clumsiness, brutality, oafishness* of its populace, creating any
   number of accidents.
      (à propos of the clumsiness of its denizens, not to forget the way
   the Belgians walk—looking the other way. —The elaborate detours a
   civilized man has to make in order to avoid bumping into a Belgian.
   —A Belgian does not walk, he just lurches along.)
      3) Everybody whistling.
      4) All the shouting, braying, yawping. Howls of the Belgian beast.

   Paris, infinitely larger and far more bustling, instead produces a
vast, vague hum, a velvety drone, as it were.

27 · BRUSSELS

   Boarding Schools

   Whether engaged in amusement or in thought, the Belgians always
act like boarding school students—men, women, boys, girls.

Even the women only piss in groups. As Béroalde remarks, they are team pissers.*

My battle with a group of Brussels women out on the town.

29 · CUSTOMS. BRUSSELS

The habit of laughing for no reason whatsoever, especially among the women.

Smiles almost impossible. Their face muscles not supple enough to execute this gentle feat.

GENERAL CHARACTERISTICS

No life in the Street.
Many balconies. No one on the balconies.
Miniscule gardens to the back of the houses.
Everybody indoors. Doors closed.
No public toilets in the Streets.
No displays in front of the shops.

What you miss is the river, which the canals hardly replace.
—A city without a river.
And all these steep hills interfere with *flânerie*.

30 · BRUSSELS
GENERAL EXTERIOR CHARACTERISTICS
CUSTOMS

Many balconies. Nobody on the balconies. Nothing to see on the street.

Everybody at home! (tiny closed-in gardens).
The complaints of an Italian.

No shops with display cases.

---

* *Team pissers:* Baudelaire takes the remark from François Béroalde de Verville's satirical work *Le Moyen de parvenir* (1796).

Dawdling in front of the shops, this pleasure, this learning process, impossible!—

Everybody at home!

32 · BRUSSELS

Characteristics of the Street and the population at large.
The pince-nez, with its cord, perched on the nose.
A multitude of vitreous eyes, even among the officers.
An optician told me that the majority of the pince-nez that he sells are clear glass. Thus this national pince-nez craze is nothing more than a pathetic effort to appear elegant and yet one more sign of the spirit of imitation and conformity.

33 · BRUSSELS
GENERAL EXTERIOR CHARACTERISTICS

Things in general look quite comfortable.
Cleanliness of the curtains and blinds.
Flowers in profusion.
Rooms that look fairly prosperous.
To the back, a tiny garden choked with flowers.
Astonishing similarity of all the apartments.
Seen up close, the luxury is not only monotonous, but cheap-looking.

34 · BRUSSELS
GENERAL FEATURES

The Belgians are a breed of whistlers, like brainless birds.
What they whistle are not tunes.
The whistle sharply projected. Splitting my ears.
A habit picked up in childhood, incurable.

The hideous ugliness of the kids, filthy, snot-nosed little vermin, repulsive.

Ugliness and filth. Even if scrubbed clean, they would still be hideous.

A breed of whistlers who burst into laughter, for no reason. Sign of cretinism.

All Belgians, without exception, have empty skulls.

35 · BRUSSELS
GENERAL CHARACTERISTICS

The Belgian, or rather Brussels face.
Chaos.
Formless, deformed, rough, heavy, hard, unfinished, carved by knife.
Teeth at angles.
Mouths not made for smiles.
Capable of laughter, for sure, but inept, enormous guffaws à propos of nothing.
The face cloudy, bereft of any gaze, like that of a cyclops—not a one-eyed cyclops but a blind one.
Cite the lines of Petrus Borel.* The absence of gaze, terrifying.
Some of them display monstrously thick tongues, which accounts for their slurred, sibilant speech.

36 · BELGIUM
BRUSSELS
GENERAL PHYSIOGNOMY

Particular look of the mouths in the street and elsewhere.
  no voluptuous lips.
  no commanding lips.

---

* *The lines of Petrus Borel:* From Borel's 1839 *Madame Putiphar*, describing the Stone Commander in *Don Juan:* "A hyperborean, a gnome without eyelid or pupil or forehead, and who rings empty, as when a sword strikes a gutted tomb." Also quoted below on p. 380.

no ironic lips.
no eloquent lips.
Gaping latrines of imbecility.

Gaping cloaca.
Formless mouths.
Unfinished faces.

37 · BRUSSELS
GENERAL PHYSIOGNOMIC CHARACTERISTICS

All Belgian faces have something murky, wary, defensive about them—some have the faces of sacristans, some the faces of savages.

Menacing stupidity.
Maturin's remark.*

Their manner of walking, at once hurried, impulsive, and hesitant, naturally taking up a great deal of place.

Abundance of Hunchbacks.

38 · BRUSSELS

Physical physiognomy.

Brussels is the land of Hunchbacks, the domain of Rickets.
Why?
Is it the water, is it the beer, is it the unsanitariness of the city and its housing?
In short, it's still the same race as always. Just as the pisser and vomiter and the Kermesses of Ostade and Teniers still provide an exact

---

* *Maturin's remark:* From chapter 20 of Charles Maturin's *Melmoth the Wanderer* (1820), which Baudelaire was considering translating for Poulet-Malassis. "It is certain that the gloomiest prospect presents nothing so chilling as the aspect of human faces, in which we try in vain to trace one corresponding expression to what we feel."

expression of Flemish joy and jest, so we discover in the life around us the same rickety cripples found in the primitive painters of the North.

39 · BRUSSELS
GENERAL FEATURES

Ugliness cannot fathom beauty.

Let's relate the general ugliness of this nation to this further fact: its general hatred of Beauty. Examples: bursts of laughter in the street or when gathered before true beauty—Belgian artists' radical inability to understand Raphael.

A young writer* has recently come up with an ingenious idea, but one which is not absolutely correct. The world is about to end. Humanity has reached a state of decrepitude. To amaze the degenerate men of his day, some Barnum of the future puts on display a beautiful woman from the distant past who has been artificially preserved. "Goodness gracious," they exclaim, "could humanity have been as beautiful as all that?" I say this does not ring true. These degenerates would be filled with such self-admiration that they would deem ugly that which is beautiful. Just witness the wretched Belgians.

40 · BRUSSELS
GENERAL CHARACTERISTICS
CUSTOMS

The Belgians have no idea how to walk. They fill up the entire street with their arms and feet. Lacking any nimbleness whatsoever, they do not know how to stand aside, to give way, they just crash right into the obstacle.

Coldness of their gaze, crafty, wary. Expression at once fierce and

---

* *A young writer:* Baudelaire goes on to paraphrase Stéphane Mallarmé's prose poem "Le Phénomène futur"—which he must have read in manuscript in Belgium in 1865, given that Mallarmé's poem was first published only ten years later.

timid. The eye unfocused and, even when looking right at you, always
shifty. A mistrustful race, because it believes itself to be weaker
than it is.

WOMEN

Woman does not exist. The filthy white of vaginal discharges. And
since she is not accustomed to caresses, she does not know how to
please. Nor does she ever make an effort to.

There are females and males. There is no chivalry. —No care given
to dress.

41 · POOR BELGIUM
  BRUSSELS

The crazy way Belgians lurch along.

Belgians walk while looking over their shoulders. One would say
that some inane curiosity tugs their heads backward while an au-
tomatic movement propels them forward. —A Belgian can manage
thirty or forty steps with his head craned backward, but inevitably
there will come the moment when he bumps into someone or some-
thing. I have made many a detour to avoid Belgians walking.

In a crowd, the Belgian pushes forward by poking his two fists
into your back. Your only recourse is to wheel around and, as
it were accidentally, give him a good jab in the stomach with your
elbow.

3 · BRUSSELS. CUSTOMS. TOBACCO, CUISINE, WINE.

45 · POOR BELGIUM

A major article on the *question of Belgian cuisine.*
  Blandness.
  The bread.
  The rancid butter.

Even the vegetables, peas, asparagus, potatoes.
Eggs with blackened butter.

Absence of fruits.
Absence of hors d'oeuvres.

No spicy stews.
The Belgian is no more of a gourmet than a Papuan.
His cuisine is disgusting and elementary.
But the grocery store owner . . . ?

The question of wine!

47 · BRUSSELS

The question of wines.
Do the Belgians like wine? Yes, as a collectable item.
If they could show it off without offering it up or drinking it them-
selves, they would be most satisfied.
They drink it out of vanity to make one believe they enjoy it.
Always old wines.

The Norman peasant and his cider.

49 · BRUSSELS
GENERAL CHARACTERISTICS
CUSTOMS

The story of the gentleman who didn't want to pay for the pickles at
Horton's.
Faro, 2 sous, 3 centimes.
Obsessed with centimes.
Chairs without crossbars.
The custom of serving drinks by the shot, as if the barman were
assigned to monitor the cravings of the customer.
Appalling drunkenness of the lower classes. Cheap drinks. Faro
and gin.

The wine cellars of the bourgeoisie extraordinarily well stocked. Aging their wines.

50 · Cuisine section

What Brusselites drink

Faro is drawn from the great latrine of the Senne; it's a drink extracted from the excrements of the city and then filtered. Thus, for centuries the city has been drinking its own urine.

4 · CUSTOMS. WOMEN AND LOVE

52 · BRUSSELS

The typical woman.

A Punch-and-Judy nose, a ram's brow, onionskin eyelids, colorless, vacant eyes, monstrously tiny mouth, or simply an absence of mouth (sans speech or kisses!), the lower jaw retreating, flat feet, elephantine legs (beams on boards), lilac complexion, and with all this, as bird-brained and puffed up as a pigeon.

53 · BRUSSELS

Women in the Street.

Their feet.
Their calves.
Their reek.
If you yield the sidewalk to them, seeing as they are accustomed to yield it to men, they step off the sidewalk at the same time as you do, bumping into you—and thank you for your good intentions by calling you an oaf.
Description of several Belgian women. —The nose, the eyes, the bosom. Rubenesque suet.

54 · BRUSSELS
   GENERAL CHARACTERISTICS
   CUSTOMS
   WOMEN

The women walk pigeon-toed. Large flat feet.
Fat arms, fat bosoms, and fat calves.
As overpowering as swamps.

55 · CUSTOMS
   BRUSSELS
   WOMEN

A remedy for love, an expression from the Louis XIII period.
Here, a man deserves little credit for remaining chaste.
Priapus himself would fall into a funk.
The two sexes stick to themselves.
No gallantry among the men.
No coquetry among the women.
No resistance, no modesty.
Among the men, no glory, no conquest, no credit due.
The women all blond, bland, their shallow sheep's eyes blue or gray.
A Kaffir woman would stand out like an Angel here.
Precocious buxomness of the young girls. Adipose precocity.
Vegetables raised in swampy soil.
The women have no idea how to walk. —Go out in public ungroomed.
Frenchwomen here and there—well put together, but quite sad.
—Pick out some of the odder features of the rules and regulations
governing prostitution.

57 · BRUSSELS
   WOMEN
   LOVE

Love is noticeable for its absence. What is called love is here re-
duced to animalistic gymnastics which I need not describe to you.

Vomiting lovers.

The young girl who worked in the stationery shop filled the entire place with her stench. (The ancient Englishwoman suffering from *Delirium tremens*.)

The young girl bursts into laughter when the man asks her for directions, or replies: *Gott for dum!* . . .

58 · BRUSSELS
   GENERAL FEATURES

No gallantry, no modesty. The Belgian female.

Belgian ladies pissing and shitting.

The Belgian mother in the latrine (door open) playing with her child and smiling to the neighbors.

Prodigious love of excrement which one finds in the old paintings. The painters of those days were certainly painting their native land.

Six Belgian ladies pissing in a narrow street, barring one's passage, some standing, some crouching, all dressed to the nines.

Cleanliness of Belgian women. Even in the street, difficult not to smell their stench, as well as that of their daughters (Montagne-de-la-Cour).

59 · CUSTOMS

I have never been able to make a Belgian understand that chivalry is among the signal lessons that a French mother teaches her son.

—Belgians think gallantry means bestiality!

5 · CUSTOMS (continued)

62 · BELGIAN PATRIOTISM

[Clipping from *L'Espiègle*, May 1865. A review of *The Captive*, one-act comic opera by M. Cormon, music by M. Eduard Lassen.* Baudelaire quotes and underlines as follows: "The first performance of

---

* *Lassen:* Eduard Lassen, Danish-born Belgian composer and conductor who led the first performance of Wagner's *Tristan and Isolde* in Weimar. *Cormon:* Eugène Cormon, French librettist who wrote for Bizet, Offenbach, and others.

this new opera at Le Théâtre de la Monnaie on Monday was mobbed. A smashing success, and a well deserved one at that, we are happy to observe—*all the more so because M. Édouard Lassen is a Belgian. Believe me, M. Cormon [a Frenchman] cannot be said to have contributed to this success, for given a libretto this paltry,* it's a miracle that M. Lassen managed to devise such a charming score. *M. Cormon develops an episode from the adventurous life of Miguel Cervantes in makeshift French and limping lines of verse."*]

63

General coarseness, among all the classes.
Five officers' heroic deed.

[Clipping from the *Gazette belge,* November 3, 1865: Five officers from the Seventh Line Regiment force their way into a newspaper office and attack the chief editor for having published an article they considered libelous.]

65

Mexican Expedition. Belgian Vanity.

[Clipping from the *Gazette belge,* November 5, 1865: Latest news from Mexico. The resignation of the commanding colonel and other officers of the Belgian regiment, decimated by combat, sickness, and desertions. Emperor Maximilian reported to have fled the capital.]

The officers resign, therefore it is *obvious* that there is nothing else for Maximilian to do but take flight. An example of Belgian logic.

67

Family affections.
No soul.

[Clipping from the *Gazette belge,* September 23, 1865: "Several weeks ago, an individual living on the rue Haigne in Tournai sold two of his children, age four and eight, to a member of a traveling circus [*sal-timbanque*] for the sum of 325 francs, for which he received 25 francs in cash and the rest in goods. / At the moment that they were being handed over, these unhappy little creatures, having become aware of their fate, started to cry and scream and clasped the knees of their hard-hearted father, begging him not to abandon them, promising to obey his slightest wishes in the future, as long as they could stay on with him at Tournai. The father, cruel to the very end, remained un-moved and the children were taken away. The neighbors could barely suppress their indignation. / The individual in question has been living high on the hog ever since. He was still in possession of another young daughter. We have learned that he offered her to the traveling acrobats now performing at our festivities for the price of 528 francs. / We are unaware whether our laws permit or prohibit this traffic in white slaves; but if courts manage to indict this guilty individual for his malfeasances, we will commend them in the name of morality and of the rights of nature, revolted by such scandalous commerce. This individual should be pursued to the full extent of the law, for he clearly exists beyond the bounds of humanity."]

68

Family affections.
Morality (Ardennes).

[Clipping from the *Écho de Bruxelles*, August 5, 1864: "The Assize Court of the Ardennes has just dealt with a case of incest and infan-ticide whose guilty parties displayed an incredible degree of cruelty. Jean-Baptiste Périn and his sister Léonie were accused of murdering their newborn. After having strangled the baby, they allegedly boiled it, then fed its flesh to a pig, before throwing its bones into the fire. This case caused quite a stir in the department of the Ardennes; the courtroom was therefore packed. After the presiding judge read the indictment, the jury went into deliberation around half past noon. Three quarters of an hour later, it returned a verdict of not guilty for Léonie and a verdict of guilty for Périn, with attenuating circumstances. The Court sentenced Périn to a lifetime of hard labor."]

69 · BRUSSELS
MORALS

Criminality and immorality of Belgium.

Here criminal acts are far more ferocious, more mindless than elsewhere.

Rape of a fourteen-month-old child.

Phenomenal immorality of the parish priests, recruited from the hideous race of peasants.

Dog eaten alive. Price of admission: 20 francs.

70 · BRUSSELS
CUSTOMS
CRIMES
DRUNKENNESS

The peculiarly savage and bestial character of Belgian inebriation.

A father gets drunk. He castrates his son.

Observe in this crime not only its ferocity, but its modus.

A Belgium can only make sexual organs the objects of his jokes or attacks. A true obsession.

71 · *Coarseness.*

Belgian bestiality.

The man who earns a handsome living at fairs by eating live dogs. Audience made up of women and children.

6 · CUSTOMS (continued)

75 · BRUSSELS

Moral characteristics.

It is difficult to assign the Belgian a place on the scale of living creatures. Yet one might maintain that he should be classified somewhere between the Mollusk and the Ape. There is plenty of place available.

76 · BRUSSELS
GENERAL FEATURES

The Belgian manages to eat his soup all on his own, with a spoon. He even knows how to deploy forks and knives, though he is so inept he would prefer to rip his prey apart with his teeth and filthy claws.

77 · IGNORANCE
VANITY
BELGIUM SCUM

I have witnessed extraordinary things in Brussels.

Architects ignorant of the history of architecture.

Painters who have never looked at an engraving of Raphael and who do paintings after photographs.

Women who insult you for having offered them a bouquet.

Ladies who leave the latrine doors open while attending to their *business*.

Pseudo-swells [*gandins contrefaits*] who have raped all the women in sight.

Freethinkers who are frightened to death of ghosts.

Patriots who want to massacre all the French (and who carry their right arms in slings to make it appear they are veterans of duels).

And finally (this is the majority of the nation) a slew of people who, when you mention God to them, tell you: You don't believe a word you're saying. —By which they mean: Because I do not have the faintest understanding.

And officers who gather into a gang of five to go beat up a journalist in his office.

78 · BRUSSELS
GENERAL CHARACTERISTICS
CONVERSATION

The amazing presumptuousness of the Belgians, in all spheres of society. —Someone has done something—a book, a painting, a remarkable deed; —"I could do the same thing just as well" (obviously!), "therefore I am his equal."

79 · BRUSSELS
GENERAL CHARACTERISTICS
CUSTOMS

When a Belgian addresses himself to ten persons, he always directs his remarks to a single one of the listeners and, if need be, turns his back on the rest of the company.

A Belgian never yields the right of way to a woman on a sidewalk.

Only once have I seen a person trying to attract the attention of a theater public by his attitude and manner of dress.
Although his clothing and his overcoat were of a light color and although he was wearing rings on his amethyst gloves, no one paid him the slightest notice.*
Furthermore, Belgians always seem to be poorly dressed, even though they put a great deal of effort into their clothing. But nothing suits them.
The most sparkling of temperaments would be extinguished here amid the universal indifference. Impossibility of living a life of vanity here.
Here, when it comes to art one cannot say, as one does of small towns: *Bis repetita placent.*†

80 · BRUSSELS
GENERAL FEATURES

Belgians' contempt for famous men.
The familiarities they take with a famous man. Right off, they tap him on the stomach and address him with the familiar "tu," as if they

---

* *No one paid him the slightest notice:* Sometimes read as an ironic self-portrait of Baudelaire the Dandy in exile.
† *Bis repetita placent:* "The more they are repeated, the more they please" (Horace).

had known each other since childhood, back in the dusty, filthy streets of the Marolles.*

Everybody is convinced he could have been just as successful, *man that he is. Homo sum, nihil humani a me alienum puto.*† New translation.

81 · BRUSSELS
CUSTOMS

Boasting about everything—about women, about money, about duels, etc.

Every man forced to boast about himself in a country where nobody knows how to do justice to anybody else.

Besides, no one thereby fools anybody else because everyone knows his neighbor is just as huge a liar as he is. At the very most, he believes the half of what he hears!

Here, woe to Modesty—which always goes unrewarded. If some fine upstanding man says: "I have done very little," one automatically concludes that he has done nothing!

82 · BRUSSELS
CUSTOMS
GENERAL FEATURES

With all their ponderousness, nothing solid. Enormous weight, yet surprising inconsistency.

Velocity proportional to weight. Forever the flock of sheep, heading right, left, north, south, rushing this way and that in a single mass.

I have never seen a Belgian who dared stand up not to a thousand people but merely to ten, just to say: "You are making a mistake," or "You are being unjust." These people only think in herds.

Furthermore, there is nothing that it is more widely practiced here, nothing that is more widely admired and honored, than kicking someone when he is down. The *Vae victis* has never found such

---

* *Marolles:* The working-class district of Brussels.

† *Homo sum:* "I am human and consider nothing human alien to me" (Terence).

enthusiasts. Given the number of times this people has been con-
quered, I therefore have the perfect right to enjoy telling it: "Woe to
the vanquished."

83 · *Walloon.*

A brief portrait of the Walloon *loser.*
Unruly,
Indiscrete,
insolent,
conquering the world,
and imitating Napoleon's campaign strategies.
Agitated,
telling you: "You do not believe what you say."
It's above all the Walloon who is the caricature of the Frenchman,
not the Fleming.
Often bandy-legged, clubfooted, or hunchbacked.
Wallonia, a breeding ground for lawyers.

85 · BRUSSELS
GENERAL FEATURES

The Belgians distrust justified laughter; they never laugh when ap-
propriate. But they *burst into laughter* for no reason whatsoever.

"Quite a nice day, isn't it?"
And they burst into laughter.

7 · BRUSSELS CUSTOMS (continued)

89 · BRUSSELS
GENERAL CHARACTERISTICS
CUSTOMS

Small-town mentality.
Belgian mistrust. Belgian gossip. Belgian slander.

They accused me of being a *mouchard*—a spy, an informer.*
Mouchard means someone who does not think like us.
Its 18th-century synonym: pederast.

90 · BRUSSELS
   CUSTOMS

Small-town curiosity.

If the taste for allegories were ever to return to literature, a poet
would find no better place to situate the *Temple of Slander* than in
Brussels.
   A Belgian whispers into your ear: "Avoid so-and-so. He's vile." And
then another in his turn: "Avoid so-and-so. He's a scoundrel." —And so
it goes, everyone behind each other's back.
   Yet they have no fear of keeping the wrong company, for they see
each other, tolerate each other, associate with each other, even though
the entire nation be made up of scoundrels—if one is to take them at
their word.
   When I wanted to put an end to this national passion for slander, at
least insofar as my own case was concerned, I resorted to irony, poor
simpleton that I am.
   To all those who wanted to know why I was staying on so long in Bel-
gium (they don't like foreigners to stay on too long), I explained, quite
confidentially, that I was a *mouchard*.
   And they believed me!
   To others I confided that I had been forced to flee France because I
had committed a number of crimes too atrocious to describe but that I
was hoping that, thanks to appalling corruption of the French regime,
I would soon be amnestied.
   And they believed me!
   Exasperated, I went on to declare that I was not only a murderer but
a pederast. This latter revelation had completely unexpected conse-

---

* *Mouchard:* Baudelaire claimed he had been accused by the sons of Victor Hugo
of being a French police informer planted within the Brussels community of French
political refugees.

quences. The Belgian musicians concluded that Mr. Richard Wagner was a pederast.

For a Belgian cannot get it through his skull that a man might praise another man for entirely disinterested reasons.

92 · BRUSSELS
GENERAL FEATURES

The Belgians are very mistrustful. Nobody on the balconies. You ring, they crack open the door, they look at you as if you were some government agent come to collect the overdue balance on a state loan.

I was taken to be a *Mouchard*.

I added that I was a Jesuit and a pederast. And they believed me, the dimwits!

94 · BRUSSELS
GENERAL CHARACTERISTICS
CUSTOMS

Small-town mentality.

Conversation. Distrust of Wit.
Laughter for no reason.
Gossip.
Endless defamation.
Forever announcing the disgrace or ruin of a neighbor.

When a neighbor is ruined, even if he be the most honest man in the world, everybody shuns him, afraid they might be asked to render him the slightest service.

Poverty, a major disgrace.

Small town
small minds
small hearts.

95 · BRUSSELS
    GENERAL CHARACTERISTICS
    CUSTOMS
    CONVERSATION

Belgian curiosity.
Small-town mentality.

If you stay on here for a while, everybody eventually asks: "Monsieur is no doubt an expatriate?"

So difficult it is for them to fathom that one might remain here *for the pleasure of it* and that one might have decided of one's own free will to live among them.

I'm always tempted to reply: "Yes, Monsieur, because I murdered my father and ate him raw, without even bothering to boil him."

But they would probably believe me.

The Belgian is like the Russian. He's afraid to be studied. He wants to hide his wounds.

8 · **BRUSSELS. CUSTOMS** (continued)

97 · BRUSSELS

> link this to
> Belgian Nothingness
> in conversation, imbecile
> laughter, etc.

SPIRIT OF OBEDIENCE AND CONFORMITY

"If you believed you had discovered happiness, wouldn't you feel the need to share its recipe?"

"No."

"I certainly would—I could not believe myself happy unless I saw everybody else living the same way I did. *This would be the proof of my happiness.*"

—Such were the remarks of a Belgian who, without the slightest encouragement on my part, had buttonholed me for four hours, telling me how rich he was, how many knickknacks he owned, how married he was, how much he had traveled, how often he had gotten seasick, how he had to flee Paris because of the cholera, how he owned a factory in Paris all of whose foremen were decorated—and all this because, hoping to get rid of him, I had told him that as far as I was concerned there was no happiness to be had save in solitude.

98 · BELGIUM
STREET CUSTOMS

Belgians only think in packs
(Freemasons, freethinkers, societies of all sorts)
and only amuse themselves in packs
(societies for entertainment, societies for the raising of chaffinches)
(little girls walking arm in arm—as do young boys, men, women)
They only piss in packs.
Packs of women by whom I was attacked, only managing to fend them off with my cigar.

99 · BRUSSELS
GENERAL CHARACTERISTICS

The Belgians are crazy about societies, demi-societies, quarter-societies. . . . Infinite division.
The disciplinary manner in which they amuse themselves, weep, rejoice, pray. —Everything done Prussian style. Which in fact indicates their inability to weep, pray, amuse themselves as solitary individuals.
The ancient debris of feudal idiocies: solemn oaths, lineages, guilds, juries, nations, trades. Van der Noot still reigns.*
(Curious misunderstanding between the two revolutions, the Brabant Revolution and the French Revolution.)

---

* *Van der Noot still reigns:* Henri van der Noot, highly authoritarian president of Belgium's executive branch after the 1789–90 Brabant uprising against the Hapsburgs.

100 · BRUSSELS
     CUSTOMS

There is no people better suited for conformity than the Belgian people. Here one thinks in packs, entertains oneself in packs, laughs in packs. Belgians establish societies to arrive at an opinion. Hence their absolute astonishment or contempt when faced with anybody whose opinion they don't share. It is therefore impossible for a Belgian to conceive that somebody might believe something that he doesn't. Anyone who disagrees with him is considered suspicious.

I have little knowledge of the Belgian Catholics. I believe they all are as *bêtes*, as wicked, as lazy as the Belgian atheists.

— Proof of Belgian obedience and laziness:
"What are you going to Church for? You ain't even carrying a missal."

101 · BRUSSELS
     GENERAL CHARACTERISTICS
     CUSTOMS

Fondness for societies.
Fondness for guilds (remains of the Middle Ages).
Freemasons.
One thinks in common. Which is to say, one does not think.
Ergo, infatuation with ranks, presidencies, decorations, militarism (civil guard).
However minor your achievement, you are at once rewarded with ranks and honors of every order.
But one minor failure, and you are no longer anything. You are stripped of everything; you fall off every ladder.

333 · BRUSSELS
     CUSTOMS

The spirit of conformity, even in their amusements.

40 men create an association to come up with April Fools' pranks.

Raising chaffinches.
A society dedicated to the blinding of chaffinches.*

The Duke of Brabant, president of a Chaffinch Academy.

Barbarity of the children's games.
Birds attached to a stick by their feet.

9 · BRUSSELS. MORES (continued)

103 · CUSTOMS
      BRUSSELS

Belgian Cordiality is expressed by the *Spy-mirror*, which speaks clearly of how bored its denizens are, how reluctant they are to open to anybody who might knock at their doors.

It is expressed by the absence of lamps for the lighting of cigars. One can only light one's cigar in the place one has purchased it.

—By the rudeness of the people from whom one asks street directions. (Goddammit! Why the hell don't you stop bothering me?)

There are those who will perhaps agree to help you with the directions; but they get things so bungled up that you understand nothing.

"Monsieur, just go down there and then take the avenue and then turn at . . ." often using place names which require prior knowledge to understand them.

"To the right . . . to the left," unknown terms.

104 · BRUSSELS
      GENERAL CHARACTERISTICS
      CUSTOMS

Everybody at home. Nobody on the balconies. The spy-mirror. The tiny patch of a garden.

---

* *The blinding of chaffinches:* It being believed that sightless birds sang best, their eyes were poked out with hot pins.

Substantial fortunes. Substantial savings.

Notes by Malassis. —The king brushes his hat, lest the rain stain the dust on it. Several million men brush their hats and flick the dust off their shoulders.

Their worship of hats. Belgians love their hats the way the peasants Pierre Dupont sang about loved their cattle.*

Matches are equally precious. You have to use them sparingly.

Chairs without crossbars.

Dubois's comment on dogs ("Don't bring your dog here, he would be humiliated to see his fellow canines dragging carts." "But Monsieur, at least we don't muzzle them here.") A fine chapter to write about these energetic dogs, all zeal and pride. It would seem as if they wanted to show horses a thing or two.

105 · CUSTOMS
BRUSSELS

"Scratch a civilized Russian," said Bonaparte, "and you will find a Tartar."

This holds true for even the most charming of my Russian acquaintances.

Scratch a Belgian prince, and you will find a hick.

106 · CUSTOMS
BRUSSELS

Coarseness of the street manners.

—One does not yield to a woman on the sidewalk.

—French workers are aristocrats compared to the princes of this country.

—Grossness of the jokes.

—The *Gallic salt* of the Belgians. My loathing for the fabled *Gallic salt* of the French.

---

* *Pierre Dupont:* A populist balladeer of the rural and urban poor, praised by Baudelaire in an 1851 essay.

—French shit and Belgian shit, two forms of the same kind of humor.

—*The pisser. The vomiter.*

This crassness is reproduced in love. Even in paternal love. The bare bottoms of Jordaens. Part of Flemish life.

It is reproduced in their politics. Cite examples from the newspapers.

It is reproduced in the clergy. A bunch of offensive dolts.

10 · BRUSSELS. CUSTOMS (continued)

108 · BRUSSELS
GENERAL FEATURES

Belgian sluggishness.
  Their laziness.
  They get up late.
  Even the shopkeepers have no notion of work.

The money changer takes me for a beggar.

109 · BRUSSELS

Ponderousness

ADMINISTRATIVE DELAYS

Interminable Deliberations
In all matters.

Belgian sluggishness

A well collapses onto one of the workers who is digging it.
Proclamations. Search parties. Calls for help.
Several days pass. Sunday is observed as a day of rest, despite the parables of Jesus Christ.
Finally they discover the corpse. At which point they try to prove

that the buried man must have died of asphyxiation from the very outset.

325

Belgian bureaucracy.

My adventures with THE POST OFFICE, when dealing with my proofs.* No law for objects that are not correspondence (i.e., manuscripts).
M. Hoschtein.
The administration. Van Gend (re manuscripts).
THE TELEGRAPH OFFICE does not take telegrams. My adventures with the Telegraph Office.

CUSTOMS OFFICE. The vulgarity and stupidity of the employees.
13 offices, 20 signatures on my part, 20 signatures by the administration. The CUSTOMS Inspector. His portrait. The CUSTOMS Director. The Minister of the Interior. The Minister of Finances. "The real reason why I had my watch sent to me in Belgium?" —None of my former tribulations equal to this.

11 · BRUSSELS. CUSTOMS

113 · POOR BELGIUM
GENERAL FEATURES

Belgian morality.

Here, no professional thieves. But their absence is largely compensated for by the universal lack of integrity.

---

* *My proofs:* Shortly after his arrival in Brussels, Baudelaire was frantically trying to finish up the proofs to his translation of Poe's *Histoires grotesques et sérieuses*— which he needed to mail back to the printer in Paris. A few lines later, Baudelaire describes the difficulties he had retrieving a watch from Belgian Customs: he had pawned this pocket watch before leaving Paris and, having no time-keeping piece in his Brussels hotel room, had asked his conseil judiciaire, Ancelle, to get it out of hock and send it across the border.

Similarly, in those states where prostitution remains illegal, all women can be bought.

[Stray page]

POOR BELGIUM
GENERAL FEATURES
BELGIAN MORALITY

The painter Verwée is eager to earn 500,000 francs by turning Jefferson Davis in.* Babou is scandalized. "My Lord! He's a scoundrel, isn't he?" Babou shoots back: "If today you turn in a scoundrel for whatever reward, tomorrow you will turn in an honest man."

J. Leys, ashamed of his compatriot, tries to smooth things over.

"You will turn him out of patriotism; and then you'll have yourself a painting commissioned by the Washington Museum."

(Provided there be a museum in that den of Yankees.)

"Not at all," says Verwée, who naively persists in his infamy, "first I'll take the 500,000 francs, and only then would I consider doing a picture for their Museum."

Belgian morality.

115 · BRUSSELS
CUSTOMS

Apply to the Belgians the passage where Emerson speaks of the Yankees' opinion of *Cobden* and *Kossuth*.† (*The Conduct of Life*)

Similarly, as concerns Liszt . . .‡

---

* *Jefferson Davis:* Davis fled Richmond, Va., on April 3, 1865, and remained at large for a month.

† *Cobden and Kossuth:* Emerson observes in *Representative Men* ("Worship"): "How prompt the suggestion of a low motive! Certain patriots in England devoted themselves for years to creating a public opinion that should break down the corn-laws and establish free trade. 'Well,' says the man in the street, 'Cobden got a stipend out of it.' Kossuth fled hither across the ocean to try if he could rouse the New World to a sympathy for European liberty. 'Aye,' says New York, 'he made a handsome thing of it, enough to make him comfortable for life.'"

‡ *Liszt:* Alludes to the aspersions cast upon Liszt's residence in a monastery of

Never would a Belgian imagine honorable intentions.

He will always try to dig out some base motive, given that this is the only kind of motive he could himself possess.

116 · BRUSSELS
CUSTOMS

General lack of integrity.

"Beware of the Jews!"

"Especially beware of the German Russians!"

What a German Russian is.

A few fine examples of the Belgian lack of integrity.

In fact these people do quite well when it comes to stealing each other blind; great respect is accorded to whoever comes out on top.

117 · BRUSSELS

Moral Characteristics.

The Belgian is as hard to communicate with as woman, because he has nothing to communicate to you, and you are incommunicable to him because of his impenetrability. —Nothing as mysterious, as deep, as pithy as Nothingness [*le Néant*].

His hatred of the foreigner. How he hates and despises the Frenchman! A being essentially lazy and envious, he needs to feed on slander.

Have no fear of hurting his feelings by telling the truth about him. Even when he knows how to read, he does not do so.

No creature is more inclined to take pleasure in the misfortunes of others.

The barbarity and grossness are *universal*, without exception, despite the strenuous affectation of civilized manners. *Manners!!!*

Rome, where he received the tonsure at the hands of Cardinal Hohenlohe on April 25, 1865.

118 · BRUSSELS
CUSTOMS

Hostile atmosphere.

The eye and the face of the enemy everywhere, everywhere.

Slander, theft, etc. . . . . Nonetheless, during the first days, an animal-like curiosity, like ducks paddling toward the slightest sound on the shore.

The myth of Belgian hospitality.

Advice to those Frenchmen who would wish to suffer as little as possible.

337 · BRUSSELS

Belgian hospitality.

So much has been made of this that even the Belgians believe it.

Belgian hospitality consists of rounding up those French who are poor and starving them and immediately putting them on a boat to England.

Or of *muzzling* journalists, of subjecting them to nasty insults, and then dumping them at some border; whereupon they ask for a monetary reward from the French Emperor, who never requested them to do any such thing in the first place.

But if they hear that a Frenchman has money, they treat him like a precious guest, *in order to eat him for supper*. Then, once he is ruined they proceed to toss him into Debtor's Prison, where he is subjected to further extortions (for his cot, table, chairs, etc. . . .)

Thus Belgian hospitality (whatever the nationality of the visitor) is a political economy—or cannibalism.

12 · CUSTOMS (continued)

122 · BRUSSELS
GENERAL CHARACTERISTICS

Among the filthy things:

The Senne, whose waters are so murky they could not reflect even the fiercest ray of sun.

Cleaning up the Senne.

The only way would be to change its course, to keep it from flowing through Brussels, where it serves as a sewer for all the Latrines.

123 · BRUSSELS
    CUSTOMS

BELGIAN CLEANLINESS. An enormous impression of whiteness. Initially agreeable. And then disagreeable. Strange colors: bright pinks and greens.

Clean things: parquet floors, curtains, stoves, facades, lavatories.

Dirty things: the human body and the human soul. (As for perfumes, the eternal black soap.)

The ceiling plasterers and whitewashers. —Thriving businesses. Perhaps the painting of the buildings in bright colors is necessary in this climate.

They water the plants when it rains.

BELGIAN CUISINE. Absent in Restaurants—or rather, no Restaurants to speak of. Lousy bread, for those who appreciate good food. —As a consolation: read a cookbook. —No mistress: read a romance.

Actually, I'm wrong. There is a Flemish cuisine; but you have to visit people's homes to make its acquaintance.

No roasted meats.

124 · BRUSSELS
    GENERAL FEATURES

Ugliness and poverty
On Prostitution

Poverty which in every country so easily softens the heart of the philosopher can here only inspire overwhelming disgust, given how the faces of the poor are so fundamentally marked by incurable vice and vileness.

Everywhere else childhood is a pretty thing; here it is hideous, scabby, mangy, grimy, smeared with shit.

One should go to the poor neighborhoods and see the naked children rolling around in shit. Though I don't think they actually eat it.

Even old women, those sexless creatures whose great virtue it is (at least everywhere else) to melt one's heart without arousing one's senses, here retain upon their faces all the marks of ugliness and stupidity that they inherited in their mothers' wombs. They therefore inspire no politeness, respect, or tenderness.

13 · BELGIAN ENTERTAINMENT

126 · BRUSSELS
GENERAL FEATURES

Multitude of festivals.
Everything an excuse for a festival.
Street *kermesses*.
Triumphal arches for all the victors.

127 · BRUSSELS
CUSTOMS. ENTERTAINMENT

When at a concert, the Belgian accompanies the melody with his foot or cane, to make it clear that he is following it.

128 · BRUSSELS
GENERAL CHARACTERISTICS
CUSTOMS

One listens to serious music with great attentiveness, to broad humor with some trepidation.

To let it be known that one has gotten the beat, one taps the floor with one's cane.

Each concert has its French section; one is afraid, it is true, to be French, but one is also afraid not to appear so.

129 · ENTERTAINMENT SPOTS
      BRUSSELS

There are none.

A ball at *La Louve*.
A majestic dance, but danced by bears. A kind of *pavane*, which a de-
cent choreographer could turn into a charming thing. Then some sort
of dance of ancient origin. (Belgians do not offer any refreshments to
their dance partners.)
Vaux Hall and the Zoological Garden.
The musical medleys quite middling.

The audience cold as ice.
It does not applaud, perhaps for fear of being mistaken.

Théâtre de la Monnaie. Empty hall, the artists, the orchestra, the
audience all half-hearted.
Théâtre Lyrique. (They would do well to place a warning on the
door, as they do on churches: *No dogs allowed!*)
Queen Crinoline, a novelty for me, Epimenides that I am.*

130 · BRUSSELS
      POPULAR ENTERTAINMENT
      MASKED BALLS

> *The space tight enough*
> *for the obedient herd.*

> *Attending one's own funeral would be more fun.*

Deathly silence.
Even the music is *silent*.

---

* *Queen Caroline: La Reine Caroline, ou le Royaume des femmes: Pièce fantastique en cinq
actes et six tableaux*, as witnessed by Baudelaire-Epimenides, the mythical seventh- or
sixth-century BCE Greek seer and philosopher-poet whose name later became asso-
ciated with the famous paradox, "All Cretans are liars."

The dances are lugubrious.

A masked ball is much like a funeral service for a freethinker.

The women cannot dance because their thighbones are so tightly screwed into their hip sockets. The women's legs are dowels stuck into planks.

The men! Oh! Caricature of France!

The costumes. —Dominos in percale. —Bundles of calico. Scum scummier than any known scum. Hideous animality. —Ah! How hideous they are, these barbarian Apes!

How to endure two thousand specimens of absolute Ugliness!

131 · CONCERTS
    ORCHESTRAS

The bitter sound of German brass.

132 · CUSTOMS
    BRUSSELS

The barbarity of children's entertainment.

A string knotted around the leg of a bird and attached to a stick.

A friend of mine cuts the string and spoils all the fun.

The Street of the Chaffinches at Namur, all their eyes poked out.

14 · EDUCATION

134 · BRUSSELS
    BELGIAN MENTALITY

No Latin. No Greek. Professional studies. Create bankers. Hatred of poetry. A Latinist would make a poor businessman.

Monsieur Duruy would like to make of France a Belgium.

Latin studies. To the extent possible, no poets, or a few poets at most. —No metaphysics. No courses in philosophy.

Positivism in Belgium.

Altmeyer and Hannon.

Belgian hatred of all literature, and especially of La Bruyère.*

15 · THE FRENCH LANGUAGE IN BELGIUM

137 · BRUSSELS
GENERAL CHARACTERISTICS
CUSTOMS

Looking at Kaulbach's illustrations of *Werther,* two Belgians. One says to the other: "That's just a bunch of mythology."

Everything they don't understand they call mythology.

Of which there is a great deal.

138 · COMIC BITS

Belgian style.

"M. Reyer nears having finished."

139 · COMIC BITS

Two British tourists mistake me for Monsieur Wiertz.†

140 · BRUSSELS
COMIC BITS

In the street called *Night and Day,* on the occasion of a neighborhood *kermesse,* a lantern:

---

* *La Bruyère:* Baudelaire quotes La Bruyère in his prose poem "Solitude"—"Truly misfortunate are those who are unable to be alone."

† *Wiertz:* See p. 364n below.

"Madame," says Athos, "if *yous* makes a move, I *blows yous* brains out."

To a *Monsieur* asking directions, *"yous* jus' *goes* straight . . . ."

141 · COMIC BITS

The hilarious letter columns in the *Office de publicité*. Consult Arthur.*

Specimens of Belgian style, to be found in the catalog of the perfumeries.
Pro refrigerio animae suae.†
Translation by Monsieur Wauters.

The bizarre Latin of the inscriptions.

Garden of Zoology, Horticulture and *Amusement*.

The grave of the painter David (where?)
If they came all the way here to repatriate the remains of an obscure Cavaignac, they could have just as well done the same for David,‡ who was also a celebrity and an exile.

142 · BRUSSELS
HEALTH. DISEASES

Ophthalmia, which the Belgians generally call *hopithalmia*.

---

* *Consult Arthur:* The art dealer Arthur Stevens, Baudelaire's native informant and cicerone in Brussels.
† *"Pro refrigerio animae suae":* "For the refreshment of your soul."
‡ *David:* Jacques-Louis David, the great painter of the French Revolution and Empire, went into political exile in Brussels after the Restoration of the Bourbons and was buried there in 1825, France having refused to repatriate his remains because he was a "regicide." Jean-Baptiste Cavaignac was an obscure member of the Constitutional Assembly in the French Revolution, a distant relative of the general by that name who put down the June Days Uprising in 1848.

143 · BRUSSELS. BELGIAN STYLE

Le Grelot says in speaking of Napoleon III: "He is said to be quite ill. No matter. He will die of what he must die."

And if one happens to mention that the Emperor is in fact in good health, one is suspected of being a *mouchard*. It is customary, among *persons* of *quality*, to pretend that he is quite ill.

Belgian conformity.
Belgian obedience.
Belgian docility.

Proudhon's friends,* when a riot broke out under his windows, a figure of rhetoric.

145–46 · BRUSSELS

Belgian expressions.

Confidential diseases.

I have truly tried to fathom this Belgian term.

Confidential strikes me as absurd; for even if it is true that these diseases are only communicated in secret and in private, it is quite certain that, at least among the French, one does not announce in advance, even when one is aware of it, the *confidential* nature of the disease in question to the person to whom one *desires* to communicate it.

O joy, O triumph! *Eureka!* This expression probably derives from the excessively prudish, priggish, delicate sensibility of this subtle Belgian people! —Thus I imagine that in the better circles of Brussels, a young girl would not say: "*This young man gave me the bloody pox.*" Or that a

---

* *Proudhon's friends:* The political philosopher Proudhon took up exile in Brussels in 1858. Amid local demonstrations (organized by the freethinker deputy Defré), he was expelled from the kingdom in December 1862, after having published a tongue-in-cheek appeal to Napoleon III to annex Belgium.

young man speaking of a well-raised young girl would not say: "*She dealt me a nasty dose!*"

The former would prefer to say: "*This young man took me into his confidence most cruelly!*" or else: "*This young man was so horribly confidential with me that my hair started falling out!*" And the latter: "*Hers was a confidentiality I shall long remember!*" Or rather: "*I placed my confidence in her! It will be remembered by her posterity for another three generations!*"

O ye fine Belgian pharmacists! I passionately adore your dictionary, and the Euphemism that dominates your advertisements.

147 · BRUSSELS
CUSTOMS

Belgian expressions.

Locate that small book designed for Belgians, which contains the do's and don'ts of French.*

It don't taste me ["Ça ne me goûte pas"]
Does that taste you? ["Gôutez-vous ça?"]
You know?, at the end of sentences ["Savez-vous"]
If'n y'please (curter than vaudeville comics)
For once ["Pour une fois"]
Posit ["poser"] an act (story of the gravedigger)
Confidential diseases
The divagation of dogs
Hydrophobia (rabies)
Hopithalmia
Know how to ["savoir"] for be able to ["pouvoir"]

"When are you leaving?" —"I don't know how to leave." —"Why?" —"I have no money."

---

* *The do's and don'ts of French:* Perhaps *Les Omnibus du langage: Fautes contre la langues signalées par L'Académie et les grammairiens* (Brussels, 1861). It might be noted that the definitive 1936 guide to *Le Bon Usage du français*, obligatory in all French schools, was written by a Belgian, Maurice Grévisse.

"I didn't know how to sleep."

"I don't know how to eat any more."

148 · BRUSSELS

Belgian Expressions.

The ministry has just *posited* an act which . . .

Ever since its inception, this ministry has yet to *posit* a single act.

A gravedigger dug up a coffin, *smashed up* the casket, *raped* the corpse (inasmuch as one can rape something inert), and *stole* the jewelry that had been buried with the deceased. —The gravedigger's lawyer: "I shall prove that my client has not *posited* any of the acts of which he stands accused."

Ah! Victor Joly is quite right to advise them to drop French and to pick up Flemish again. But unfortunately V. Joly is obliged to write this in French.

16 · JOURNALISTS AND LITERATI

152 · BRUSSELS
GENERAL CHACTERISTICS
CUSTOMS

No journalism.

Journalists are not believed.

What journalism!

Here you can call God a swindler in print, but if you said in print that Belgium wasn't perfect, they would stone you.

The prudishness of *L'Espiègle* when it comes to young ladies.

Here one can cheat in business. But offer your arm to your mistress, and you are a disgrace.

153 · BRUSSELS
POLITICS
RELIGION

All of Belgium slavishly follows *Le Siècle*,* a newspaper which is merely ludicrous in France but which, among barbarian nations such as this, proves absolutely nefarious.

155

[Clipping from the *L'Indépendance belge* of January 20, 1865, under-lined by Baudelaire]: "NEWS FROM FRANCE / Paris, January 19. / Although long anticipated, the event that most preoccupied the public today was the death of M. Proudhon. The reputation of this writer is far too well known for us to venture into great detail: he was for many years the bogeyman of both the bourgeoisie and the conservatives, and it was on account of *this celebrity that, in the wake of 1848, he was portrayed in an Aristophanic vaudeville play entitled Property Is Theft. The actor Delannoy provided the spitting image of the fearsome socialist's features*, but the piece concluded with a very courteous couplet that served to mitigate all the gall that had been heaped upon him. *One is aware that M. Proudhon had undergone a complete change of mind in his latter years and that, more than once, he made common cause with legitimist or clerical newspapers, notably against the reunification of Italy.* But however bizarre M. Proudhon's sudden about-turns might have seemed, we no longer have the right to doubt the sincerity of his polit-ical evolutions or his talents as a writer. M. Proudhon died as he lived, in poverty: and he, *who seemed to have so aspired to dissolve the whole of society, appears to have insisted until his dying day on conserving the consolations of family ties.* His funeral services will be held tomorrow." [At the bottom of the clipping Baudelaire writes:] "Remarkable tact on the part of the French foreign correspondent for *L'Indépendance belge* as concerns the death of Proudhon. Perhaps this article was written by an author of vaudeville plays who is here putting in a plug for him-

* *Le Siècle:* Influential Parisian newspaper, too progressivist for Baudelaire's taste.

self? What, this monster truly loved his wife? Just as Catalina did, to the immense surprise of M. Mérimée."

157 · POOR BELGIUM
JOURNALISM

"The Grand Duke, heir to the Russian throne, died in Nice. It is said that the Emperor loved his son a great deal, though one may be permitted to doubt the paternal love of certain Sires." *L'Espiègle,* "The Week in Politics."

I imagine that the witticism pivots on the word: *Sire.*

A fine example of the democratic mentality of the Belgians.

(Comb through all the issues of the newspapers I have on hand and pre-pare extracts from the articles I have clipped.)

158 · CONCLUSION FOR BRUSSELS

. . . . In short, Brussels is what one calls a *Hole,* but hardly an innocuous hole.

A Hole, full of wicked tongues. Use as a new gambit?

159 · BELGIUM
CUSTOMS

Letter columns of *L'Office de publicité*

[copied out by hand]
Nursery of Saint-Josse-Ten-Noode.

"A fond wish that has brought joy to two hearts has at long last been granted: with the fulfillment of this vow so passionately awaited, a promise has been made to Heaven to donate FIVE FRANCS to the *wee little angels* of the nursery.

Please accept, Monsieur Bertram, this *simple donation,* and please ask your *blond cherubs* to pray for the happiness of two souls who have sworn before *God* (the God of the Belgians) to love each other in fidelity come what may.

    S.M."

The idyll among Brutes.
Gessner among Brutes.*
Idealism among Brutes.
(Search for further bits of correspondence in *L'Office*)

160–61 · BRUSSELS
       CUSTOMS
       BELGIAN JOURNALISM

L'Espiègle

[copied out by hand]
THE VOICE OF THE MINISTRY

A representative of the left, well known for his *bon mots*, already foresees the day when his will be the single voice to decide the majority vote of the ministry. This is, in effect, to be predicted, given how weakened and scr. . .d up the left is at the moment. So this joker in question will proudly proclaim: "I am the voice of the majority; salute me!" And in order not to lose his voice, he will hie himself off to Arlon; he will take to bed, like an expectant mother; a carriage will be kept ready at his door, for crucial votes. They will make sure he is well entertained, just to keep him in fine fettle. Little H will tickle his fundament, master Defré will sing vespers for him with an appropriately contrite air, and the happy champion of the ministry will exclaim: "I'm having so much fun, I'd almost give up my fundament."

163 · FINE ARTS AND SAMPLES OF THE
DELICACY OF BELGIAN ART CRITICISM

[Press clipping from *Sancho*, September 15, 1864: "As for Messieurs Corot, Delacroix, and Diaz, we believe that these paintings were

---

* *Gessner:* Salomon Gessner, eighteenth-century Swiss author of sentimental *Idylls*.

meant for some exhibit in New South Wales or Timbuctoo, and that it was by some mistake that they arrived in Brussels. It was perhaps on the moon or somewhere else that these gentlemen caught sight of landscapes that have nothing in common with the nature we see every day: their trees, skies, animals are not of our world. We will therefore abstain from judging these works which, after all, may merely be a trap laid for our naive Flemish gullibility.

Is the committee who organized this exhibit certain that the painting by Courbet* representing two *Gougnottes* [dykes]—initiates will understand this term invented for the needs of the matter at hand in some flophouse of the lowest order—was meant to be displayed to the general public? It belongs in a House of Ill Repute."]

164 · BRUSSELS
    THEATERS
    ENTERTAINMENT
    CUSTOMS

[Hand-copied theater poster, with the following comment in the margin:]
Great care always taken to inform the public that the author in question is a Belgian, *rara avis*

REOPENING OF THE NATIONAL CIRCUS THEATER
By a French troupe (SUMMER SEASON)
Rue du Cirque

———

SATURDAY JUNE 10. PREMIERE OF
THE MAN
IN THE
BLACK MASK

* *The painting by Courbet:* Originally entitled *Femmes damnées* (after the lesbian poem excised from the original edition of *Les Fleurs du mal* and reprinted in *Les Épaves*), the painting was rebaptized *Venus Pursuing Psyche with Her Jealousy* when exhibited in Brussels in the fall of 1864.

A sprawling historical drama, NEVER BEFORE PERFORMED,
In 5 acts and 10 spectacular tableaux, with choruses of 40.
By M. Alexandre Dandoé (YOUNG BELGIAN AUTHOR)
The orchestra and choruses will be directed by M. J. B. Braun
(a future poster will supply all the details of the play)

————

NOTE. The producers are certain that ALL BRUSSELS will come to see
and listen to the work of this young metal caster. Let everybody offer
the tribute of his encouragement to this brave BRUSSELS AUTHOR who
will overcome all public censure with the very first lines of this moving
drama, whose energetic scenes and heartfelt text will cause his COMPA-
TRIOTS to experience DEEP SATISFACTION and JUSTIFIABLE PRIDE.

17 · BELGIAN IMPIETY

[A sheaf entirely composed of some twenty press clippings and
pamphlets selectively underlined by Baudelaire, presumably for the
purposes of future quotation of their *bêtises*. As indicated in section
17 of the "Argument" (see p. 280 above), they document the tenor of
anticlericalism in Belgium: insults directed again Pope Pius and the
archbishop of Paris; the caricature of the Jesuit as a bogeyman or *great
black devil*; criticism of Catholic girls' schools as havens of lesbian-
ism, etc. Other clippings address the contemporary debates over civil
burials, the allocation of grave plots in cemeteries, and the new rites
practiced by various "societies" of freethinkers or "Solidarists," to
mark the separation of church from state.]

18 · PRIESTOPHOBIA. IRRELIGIOUSNESS

188 · BRUSSELS
GENERAL CHARACTERISTICS

Belgium is more filled than any other country with people who
believe that J.C. was *a great man,* that all that *nature* teaches us is good,

that *universal morality* precedes the dogmas of all religions, that *man can do anything,* even create a language, and that steam, railroads, and gas lighting prove the *eternal* progress of mankind.

All these stale litanies of a philosophy merely fit for exportation are swallowed here like sublime delicacies. In short, what Belgium, forever simian, most successfully and *naturally* imitates is French foolishness.

(the Memphite Stone
of progress)*

191 · BRUSSELS
  PRIESTOPHOBIA

Belgian style in all its delicacy.

[copied by hand]
The Wild Jackal and the Catholic Priest.

"Within the zoological realm there exist two specimens for whom corpses exercise a particular attraction. These are the jackal and the Catholic priest. As soon as death has spread, or is about to spread, its veil over a human creature, you observe them both obeying their instinct as they sniff the wind, set off on their track, and unerringly scurry toward the dead, saying to themselves: Here's something that needs doing."
Le Grelot, February 16, 1865

Further along, *Le Grelot* accuses priests of stealing corpses. But take good note, the freethinker is also obsessed with stealing corpses. The priest and the freethinker both go after corpses, the better to tear them apart.

Le Grelot is the rag that always refers to the pope familiarly as *pio nonno. Pio nonno* is changing quarters; which means: the pope is losing his mind.

* *Memphite Stone:* Also known as Shabaka Stone, incised with a mysterious Egyptian text, the Memphite Theology.

192

[copied by hand]*
Brussels, Nov. 15, 1864

FREE THOUGHT
ASSOCIATION
FOR
THE EMANCIPATION OF CONSCIENCES
THROUGH EDUCATION
AND
THE ORGANIZATION OF
CIVIL BURIALS
N° 37
M.

The executive committee invites you to participate in the funeral
services of Monsieur
L'abbé Louis Joseph Dupont,
Former member of the diocese of Tournai,
who died last night as a free thinker after an extended illness.
The services will take place Thursday the 17th of this week at 3PM
at the municipal cemetery, near the porte de Hal.
We will gather at 2:30 at the funeral parlor, 44 rue Blaes

Paul Ithier   Henri Bergé
Secretary   President

194 · POLITICS
PRIESTOPHOBIA

A meeting of the Society for *Freethinkers* at my hotel.
Various speeches.

A fanatic complains that the *freethinkers* are still in such a weak posi-
tion that their households are threatened by contagion.

Thus is it not enough to be a *freethinker* on your own. Your wife
should also be forbidden from attending Mass or taking confession.

---

* [Copied by hand]: Baudelaire sent the original of this document to Ancelle, not-
ing, "I attended the burial of this miserable creature."

Telemachus, Calypso, Jesus Christ, etc., etc., etc., etc. . . . and other mythologies. All boiled down to a question of morals or emotion.

"It's so hot out I have to take off my clothes, now *thaat's* God!" "It's so cold out I have to put them back on, now *thaat's* God!"

They have given a burial ground to Ursuline nuns. They will poison your children.

The civil funeral of Armellini.*

"Followed by the multitude of free thinkers."

O happy nation, blessed with such a multitude!

We French are lucky to have one multitude per century.

195 · MORES
PRIESTOPHOBIA

"They stole one of our corpses, you know?"
To have it for supper?

The pleasure of seeing a politician who's a complete moron. Had he been French, it would have given me the same pleasure.

· M. Defré, a radical. *Useful art.* Rubens should have put his paintbrush in the service of Protestantism.

In short, the picture of French socialism, but even more hideous. The Elephant imitating the fandango or egg dance.

Fourierism.

Alas! He was drunk—*and* a Representative!

Defré, the persecutor of M. J. Proudhon in a land of freedom.†

196 · POLITICS
PRIESTOPHOBIA

The clerical party and the revolutionary party.

Forever accusing each other.

With such violence!

Describe the Revolutionaries. Example: Defré.

* * *

* *Armellini:* Carlo Armellini, Italian republican, forced into political exile in Brussels.
† *Persecutor of M. J. Proudhon:* See p. 281n.

They believe all the tomfoolery exported by French liberals.

(Abolition of the death penalty. Victor Hugo as influential as Courbet.* They tell me that in Paris 30,000 people have petitioned for the abolition of the death penalty. 30,000 people who well deserve it. If you are frightened of capital punishment, you are therefore already deserving of it. At least, you are hardly impartial insofar as it is concerned. The excessive love of life is a descent into animality.) In France, atheism is polite. Here it is violent, idiotic, emphatic. Belgian idiocy is an enormous counterfeit version of French idiocy, it is French idiocy cubed.

Three Societies, whose goal it is to persuade, and even to compel citizens to die like dogs. Explain what the "corner for dogs" is in the cemeteries. The most amusing thing is that these *"future dogs"* want to be buried alongside the Christians.

Free thought, for the upper classes, that is, for wealthy brutes, has its own organ: *The Free Examiner, a Rationalist Journal.* Here are some quotations drawn from it . . . . you can see what it means to be a rationalist.

The two other Societies (for commoners) are the *Affranchis* [The Emancipated] and the *Solidaires* [The Solidarists]. Burials with music. Brass bands. Trombones.

A civil funeral procession passing through the place de la Monnaie.

Corpses at the doors of taverns.

Pilfered corpses. ("One of our corpses got *stole!*"). Do they intend to eat it for supper?

Danger of associating with any group whatsoever. Abdication of the individual.

197 · POLITICS
PRIESTOPHOBIA

And they stumble back drunk, blaring into their trombones: "*Ah zut! alors si ta soeur est malade!*" ["Damn it all, your sister's caught a dose"],

* *Victor Hugo . . . Courbet:* Baudelaire's two hobby horses. Victor Hugo had delivered a series of well-publicized lectures against capital punishment in 1865. As Baudelaire saw it, Hugo was as influential an exponent of abolitionism in Belgium as Courbet was of realism.

deliberately passing in front of a church, circling around it just to torment its priest, oh so proud that they have dumped a *Solidarist* into the void. *"Those who do not believe in the immortality of their existence do themselves justice"*—as Robespierre used to say.*

Quote the Regulation governing the formulation of the last will and testaments of free thinkers.

Quote some of the perorations delivered at the graves of the *Solidarists* and *Free Thinkers*.

[On folio 185, Baudelaire had already pasted in one of these funeral orations, clipped from the pages of the free-thinking *Journal de Bruxelles* of June 5, 1864, and here reproduced with his sarcastic underlinings]:

"Brothers,

Each time that we carry out the sad duty of rendering a final homage to the *heroic death* of one of our own and that we relegate to the earth, *our common mother*, the mortal remains of a republican, of a freethinker, of a true man—each time that this grave opens to receive so many memories of so much greatness and so much suffering, *a cry rings out, a cry of supreme insurrection, a cry of victory and of intellectual rebellion AGAINST GOD, AGAINST HEAVEN AND EARTH, AGAINST iniquity, injustice, and the rule of force*. The Church shudders at the very thought and souls become distraught. The Revolution shall not allow itself to be buried. Immortal, it shall rise from the tomb into which its opponents wish to swallow it along with the deceased, and *the idea of martyrdom* shall henceforth take flesh within us, revivifying us, until its final breath enflame us with the sacred fire of truth.

Here he lies, this warrior, this victor! His task is now accomplished. As we cry out to him with our hearts, he shall now but answer us with the memory of all his travails and all his fortitude, *for Van Peene was a man of great character, of immutable principles, a passionate propagandist who defiantly held his ground against all religious ideas*.

We have seen him maintain this valor in the face of *the slyest of sacerdotal ministrations*. This valor shielded him from the most satiny of seductions and the most elaborately laid traps.

As he looked around himself, he saw how death's scythe fell where it may.

* *As Robespierre used to say:* the same dictum is quoted in *My Heart Laid Bare*.

He saw many who were sick, many who among his closest friends, go to their graves as perfect Catholics. *But he,* as understanding as he was of their sufferings, brought his own moral rigor to bear against this desolating spectacle of weakness and corruption. He knew how *to repudiate the priests, how to die as a free man, and how to prove at long last that* THE PEACE OF THE SOUL LIES IN THE NEGATION OF GOD!

Salve, Van Peene, salve!"

199 · POLITICS
  PRIESTOPHOBIA

The question of cemeteries and funeral services.

The brutality of the clergy. The corner for the dogs, that is, the reprobate. The corpse tossed over the wall.

At any rate, Rops's *The Burial* (the story about the priest scolding Cadart* for having displayed it) demonstrates the grossness of the Belgian clergy. This clergy is gross because it is Belgian, not because it is Roman.

Even I am shocked by the following:

It is forbidden to visit churches at all hours; it is forbidden to stroll about in them; it is forbidden to pray in them at any other hour than the scheduled services.

After all, why wouldn't the clergy be any less gross than the rest of the nation? The priests have no more of an idea of religion here than the prostitutes have of gallantry.

200 · BRUSSELS
  GENERAL CHARACTERISTICS

The Belgians make me think of those converted cannibal tribes of South America who dangle Christian symbols on trees, the meaning of which completely escapes them.

On what rung of the ladder of the human or simian species should the Belgian be placed?

---

* *Cadart:* French publisher of lithographs who had put Rops's 1863 artwork *A Burial in Wallonia* on display in his Brussels shopwindow.

The Christian idea of God (invisible, creative, omniscient, conscious, all-foreseeing) cannot penetrate the brain of a Belgian.

All one has here are atheists or people prone to superstition.

19 · POLITICS

204 · BRUSSELS
POLITICAL CUSTOMS

(Nothing more ridiculous than searching for truth in numbers.)

Universal suffrage and table turning. Man seeking for *truth* within man (!!!).

The vote is therefore merely a way of creating *a police*, a mechanical operation, a last resource, a *desideratum*.*

205 · BRUSSELS
POLITICAL CUSTOMS

The Elections.

The herds of voters.

The hustings (Lacroix.† Various picturesque scenes).

The fine *speechifiers*.

The caricatures.

The price of an election!——

Memories of all the ditties and caricatures directed against the Jesuits.

206 · BRUSSELS
POLITICAL CUSTOMS

Representative Vleminckx, go take a bath!‡ Five centimes.

Voters, have pity on the poor blind.

(Copy the poster)

---

* *Desideratum:* Baudelaire borrows the term from Poe's essay "Maelzel's Chess Player."

† *Lacroix:* Hugo's Belgian publisher and a particular *bête noire* of Baudelaire—who turned up to boo him during one of his electoral speeches.

‡ *Vleminckx, go take a bath!:* Jean-François Vleminckx, the liberal representative of the district of Brussels, made his career as a defender of hygiene measures for the working class. He authored an *Essai sur l'ophthalmie des Pays-Bas*, hence the "Voters, have pity on the blind" of the next line.

I stand by my word! To a man.
Caricatures of the liberals.
Caricatures of the clericals.
Cheek by jowl.

It has been agreed, after receiving a written request from Charleroi, not to insult the Catholic deputy M. Deschamps.

O magnanimous people!

A corpse of a people. A garrulous corpse, created by diplomats.

Haven't the French done enough to praise America and Belgium? I wager that at this very moment, as concerns the elections . . . . . .

207 · BRUSSELS
    POLITICS

Proof of the alarming corruption of the Belgians when it comes to elections.

"Here, according to the documents issued by Parliament, is the text of the legislation intended to eliminate electoral fraud."
The proposed law follows:
37 articles ! ! ! !
to prevent ALL POTENTIAL INSTANCES OF MALFEASANCE
Three full columns in *L'Indépendance belge*.

Besides, in Belgium it is an open secret that a given election in a given district will cost such and such. The price for each district is public knowledge (legal battles over campaign financing).

211

Promise myself to check whether that little old lady is still there on the bank of the canal.

As concerns the low cost of living here, the only cheap item is a seat in the House of Representatives. An election won't run you very much here. There are representatives who have paid not much more than 30,000 francs. Which is cheap compared to England and the United States. This proves that a Belgian conscience can be bought fairly inexpensively, and the Belgian palate is not overly fussy.

213 · BELGIUM
   POLITICAL CUSTOMS

See the discussion of electoral reforms in the *Journal de Liège* (back-room deals).

[Copied by hand]

Friday, July 28, 1865
Écho du Parlement.

M. Tesch (minister):

"The voter has no need to explain himself to anybody. . . . . The voter exercises a sovereign right. . . . . . This is a right he exercises and not a function he fulfills."

M. Coomans (opposition)

"I see, so it's the old feudal system of electors."

M. Tesch:

"Just another one of your usual *mots*."

M. de Borchgrave (ministerially):

"I didn't catch what he said, but had I heard it, I would have rejoindered, Carry on!" (Hilarity.)

(Re campaign finances, electoral indemnities, sundry matters, transportation . . . . . etc.)

214–23

[A series of press clippings chronicling the "grotesque" parliamentary debates between the clerical and liberal parties on such subjects as corruption, electoral reform, and secularization. Further clippings include reports on the late 1865 meeting between the "revolutionary" social democrats of Brussels and French student radicals returning from the Congress of Liège.]

20 · POLITICS

225 · BRUSSELS
POLITICS

There is no such thing as a Belgian people. Ergo, when I say the *Belgian people*, this is a mere abbreviation. What it means: the different races that comprise the population of Belgium.

226 · BRUSSELS
GENERAL FEATURES

Homuncularity of Belgium.
This *homunculus*, the result of an alchemical operation pulled off by diplomats, actually believes himself to be a man.
The fatuousness of the infinitely small.

The tyranny of the weak.
Women.
Children.
Dogs.
Belgium.

227 · BRUSSELS
POLITICAL CUSTOMS

Antwerp wants to be a free city. Ghent wants to be a free city. Everybody wants to be free. And every mayor wants to be King.
As many parties as there are cities.
As many *Kermesses* as there are Streets. Every Street wants its own Fair.

229 · BRUSSELS
POLITICS

The Brabant Revolution and the French Revolution in Belgium.
The Brabant Revolution as an enemy of the French Revolution.
Misunderstanding.

Joseph II was closer to us.* At least he was a Utopian!

Still a question. The Brabant Revolution, a revolution managed by the clergy.

Political meetings here—the French Revolution, but so out of date.

Belgians are ingrates when it comes to the French Revolution or the Empire.

230 · BRUSSELS
  POLITICS

A constitutional monarch is an automaton in a rooming house.

231 · BRUSSELS
  POLITICS

Belgium is the stage where the poll tax is acted out.

What would France have become had it lowered the poll tax? (constitutional retardation).

The poll tax stands at 30 francs.

Universal suffrage would place it at the mercy of the priests. Which is why the liberals want nothing to do with it.

Always the central question of the relation of the Constitution (dead letter) to Custom (living constitution).

In France the tyranny of law is tempered by the ease and freedom of manners.

232 · BRUSSELS
  POLITICAL CUSTOMS

In France, freedom is limited by the fear of its governments.

—In Belgium, it is suppressed by national *bêtise*.

—Can one be free, and what purpose does it serve to decree freedom in a country where nobody understands it, wants it, feels a need for it?

Freedom is a luxury object, like virtue. When the Belgian has eaten

* *Joseph II:* Ruler of the Hapsburg lands, 1780–90. Brabant revolted against the Austrians in 1789, and from 1792 to 1814 it was part of French territory.

his fill of it, what more does he need? *In Mexico, boys, you'll be feasting on leg of lamb.**

234 · POLITICS

The current comical situation in the House.
Two parties, virtually equal.
The majority has a one-vote advantage.
They round up all those who are sick.
One of these sick men dies.
Major speech at the grave of the deceased. (Protestant funeral bombast.)
The party that has just lost its tie-breaking vote is left with one last recourse: to *cast a spell* on one of the members of the opposition party.

No gunshots ever.
Well, if the price of beer were to be raised, things would perhaps take quite a different turn.
But this people doesn't fight for ideas. It loathes ideas.

235 · BRUSSELS
GENERAL CHARACTERISTICS
POLITICS

Bombast. Military metaphors. Disproportion between speech and object.

21 · ANNEXATION

315 · POLITICS

Invasion.

A country that has been so often conquered, and that has known how (despite the frequent intrusions of foreigners) to hold obstinately

---

* *In Mexico, boys:* Slogan used to recruit soldiers for the Mexico Expedition of 1861–67, unpopular in Belgium even though the French puppet emperor Maximilian had married Charlotte, daughter of Leopold I.

on to its own customs, should not pretend to be this afraid of invasion. This is a small people, but stronger than it seems.

316 · BRUSSELS
POLITICS

Invasion
Annexation
Belgium does not want to be invaded, but wants one to want to invade her.
She's this flabby thing who wants to arouse desires.
To tell the truth, would the Walloon region even care?

318 · POOR BELGIUM
HISTORY

*Razzia**

The Flemings put up with everything that the Duke of Alba† imposed on them—and he only had ten thousand Spaniards. They only rose up in revolt when taxes reached twenty percent.

Advice to all European armies. *Never annex.* But *Razzia*, always.

This is where one has to begin. A *Razzia* of its monuments, its paintings, of all its various art objects.

One can transport everything that is beautiful abroad. Every nation has the full right to say: *This belongs to me, since the Belgians take no pleasure in it.*

242 · AGAINST ANNEXATION

Annexation, never!
There are already enough morons in France.

---

* *Razzia:* See p. 283n.

† *Duke of Alba:* Don Fernando Álvarez de Toledo, 3rd Duke of Alba (also known as the Iron Duke), governor of the Spanish Netherlands, 1567–73.

321 r–v · BRUSSELS
POLITICS

Annexation
Razzia

Annexation! And again annexation! All they talk about here.

For the person in charge here is the Emperor. He is the ruling power, as the *Kladderadatsch* episode demonstrates (find the passage).*

(Three powers: the House, *L'Indépendance belge*, and the Emperor of the French). Constitutional government, a triad of powers.

Verwée's opinion. Belgium has forgotten that *annexation* is already a *fait acccompli*, and then that France would have to agree to it. —Just stop the first passerby in the street and tell him: *Be my adoptive father*, especially if you are a filthy, sniveling child. The eel that wants to be skinned but that cries out before being skinned. The churchwarden's nose.

This is how I understand annexation: *occupy their territory, take over their buildings and their treasures,* and *deport all the inhabitants.* Impossible to employ them as slaves. They are too dumb.

Nastiness of small countries (Belgium, Switzerland), *nastiness of the weak,* of runts and hunchbacks.

After all, circumstances could arise that might cut this diplomatic harlequin in twain—half going to Holland, half to France.

My opinion of the Walloons.

There is only *one person* in the world who *fantasizes* about *annexation*, and that's the Belgian. True, the *celebrated* Wiertz thought otherwise.†

Let the Hyperboreans return to the north!

317 · POLITICS

Misleading patriotism.

Belgian patriotism.
A single patriot, Victor Joly, in a country where there is no *patrie*.
His portrait.

* *Kladderadatsch episode:* Belgian satirical journal fined for publishing caricatures of Napoleon III.
† *Wiertz:* See p. 364n.

They are putting Belgium up for auction. Is there any buyer at this price?

Holland remains mum. France as well. Belgium is unsellable. It's the shitty end of the stick.

Invasion and annexation are the fantasies of an old wanton prude. She thinks that one has eyes only for her. For Belgium to be annexed, France would have to agree to do so.

243 · ANNEXATION

Belgium is safeguarded by the equilibrium of its rival factions. But what if these factions should reach an agreement among themselves?

22 · THE ARMY

245 · POLITICS
THE ARMY

Would very much like to be an army.

An enormous budget allocated to an army that does not fight.

All its soldiers look like kids. Observing them, I think of Castelfidardo and of the Franco-Belgian battalion in the recent Italian War.*

246 · BELGIUM
ARMY

In the Belgian army, the only way of advancing one's career is by stepping into a suicide's shoes.

Training in military Rhetoric. Debriefings on imaginary battles.

---

* *Castelfidardo:* The Franco-Belgian volunteers defending the Papal States suffered a humiliating defeat by the Sardinians at Castelfidardo in September 1860.

23 · KING LEOPOLD I. HIS PORTRAIT.
ANECDOTES. HIS DEATH. HIS MOURNING.

248 · THE KING OF THE BELGIANS

Example of mediocrity, with perseverance. He made his brave little way. This youngest sprout of the Saxe-Coburg line arrived "in his clogs" and died in his palace with a fortune of 100 million. —A true example of meretriciousness cut out for success.

The great Judge of European Peace has at last *kicked the bucket.*

"*An officer of no distinction*" was Napoleon's comment on Leopold's request to become his aide-de-camp.

249 · BRUSSELS

The King.

The money he put away.

His avarice.

His rapaciousness. His "pension" from Napoleon III.

Why he passes for a student of Courbet's.*

The mentality of a German princeling. German nonsense from another age.

His relations with his sons.

The Gardener.

The feeling of the *people* toward their King.

251 · BRUSSELS
POLITICS

King Leopold and his sons receive an indemnity from Emperor Napoleon III for their portion of the fortune seized from the princes of the house of Orléans. (Double-check the truth of this.)

These Orléans are vile worshippers of Moloch.†

* *A student of Courbet's:* Presumably because of his cult of Nature, as expressed by his horticultural enthusiasm for parks and gardens.

† *These Orléans:* Baudelaire had a visceral contempt for the French royal house of Orléans—of which his stepfather, General Aupick, had been the faithful and handsomely rewarded servant during the reign of Louis-Philippe.

254 · BRUSSELS
    THE KING

The King's aversion to dying.
How he treats his doctors.

This resistance to Death and this love of life are major signs of
imbecility.
For when would he schedule his death, if he were so permitted?

Always a brute, he kicks out the doctor who dared inform him of the
gravity of his condition.

255 · RE THE DEATH OF THE KING

Because the King pretended he was not sick, they had special issues
of the newspapers printed up for him in which, far from mentioning
his terminal illness, they spoke only of his recovery. This way, he
alone remained in the dark about his imminent death.

National mourning. Stores closed, theaters closed, black arm-
bands. The mourning provides a pretext for festivities. Every-
body drinking, the streets flooded with piss. A solid stream of
grief.
What would the populace of Paris do if it were given eight
days off?

256 · THE DEATH OF THE KING

On the rue de Louvain, three days before his death, I overhear the
Minister of the Interior behind me:
"These prayers are homages rendered to *Roy-awl-tee*, but His
Highness once dead, only the Protestant will remain—a major
bother."
Explanation: The three chaplains (Lutheran, Calvinist, Anglican),
each vying for the corpse of the King.
The death of the King thereby quite *conforming* to the deaths of all
Belgians.

It's the corpse of Patroclus* all over again, M. Wiertz all over again.

Further question: Will he be buried at Laeken or in England?†
The latter would not be a very patriotic gesture on his part.

257 · RE THE KING

The three chaplains.

The Belgians transform everything into an excuse to celebrate, even the death of the King.

The bars are full.

The populace spends eight days doing nothing.

What would happen in Paris if the populace were given eight days off? It would be up to no good, with gusto.

And what fun they all have shooting cannons off for eight straight days! The Belgians thereby become convinced that they are true artillery experts.

258 · RE THE DEATH OF THE KING

The fashion in which the Belgians grieve. —Drinking, pissing, vomiting.

A crowd strolling about aimlessly. —Everybody soused.

The new King is coronated to a tune of Offenbach's. Nobody surprised.

The photographer Neyt's joke‡ about the death of Leopold: *What a banner day for the bars!*

---

* *Patroclus:* Allusion to *The Greeks and Trojans Fighting for the Body of Patroclus*, the title of Antoine Wiertz's most famous painting, finally exhibited at the Paris Salon of 1839 after previous refusals. See p. 364n.

† *Laeken or England:* Leopold I died at his castle at Laeken, outside Brussels, on December 10, 1865. He had been awarded British citizenship in 1815 before marrying Princess Charlotte of Wales, second in line to the throne.

‡ *Neyt's joke:* Belgian photographer Adolphe Neyt's portrait of Baudelaire in Brussels provided the frontispiece for Eugène Crépet's 1887 edition of the *Oeuvres posthumes*.

24 · THE FINE ARTS

260 · POOR BELGIUM

On Flemish painting

Flemish painting only stands out for qualities that are distinct from its intellectual qualities. No intelligence, but sometimes rich coloring and almost always an astonishing level of craftsmanship. No composition. Or laughable composition. Ignoble subjects, pissers, shitters, vomiters. The humor disgusting and monotonous, typical of this race. Horrifying ugliness of the figures. These poor people expended a great deal of talent on copying their own deformity.

In this race of painters, Rubens represents *grandiloquence*, which does not exclude *bêtise*. Rubens is a lout decked out in satins.

[stray leaf]

The strongest of the Belgian painters, the one that these faro drinkers and these potato eaters are quick to compare to Michelangelo, M. Alfred Stevens,* normally paints a little woman (his particular tulip), always the same one, writing a letter, receiving a letter, hiding a letter, receiving a bouquet, hiding a bouquet, in short, all this prettified kind of twaddle that Devéria† used to sell for 200 sols without any great pretensions. —The unfortunate thing about this scrupulous painter is that the letter, the bouquet, the chair, the ring, the guipure, etc. . . . . become, in their turn, the crucial object, the object obvious to all eyes. —In short, he is a *perfectly* Flemish painter, in that he seeks perfection in little *nothings* or in the *imitation of nature*, which amounts to the same thing.

---

* *Alfred Stevens:* Baudelaire dedicated his late prose poem "Good Dogs" to his older brother, the painter Joseph Stevens. Another brother, Arthur, was an art dealer and critic whom Baudelaire also frequented in Brussels.

† *Devéria:* Baudelaire's *Salon of 1845* included a short section on the genre lithographs of Achille Devéria.

261 · BRUSSELS
       MODERN PAINTING

Love of specialization.

There is one painter who only paints peonies.

An artist is criticized for wanting to paint everything.

They say: "How can he know anything if he doesn't *weigh in* on something?"

Because here you have to be *weighty* in order to be considered serious.

262 · MODERN BELGIAN PAINTING

Art has withdrawn from this country.

Coarseness of its art.

Minute depictions of everything that lacks life.

Paintings of livestock.

Philosophy of the Belgian painters. Philosophy of our friend Courbet, a self-serving exporter of this poison. ("Only paint what you see! Therefore *you* are only allowed to paint what *I* see.")

Verboeckhoven* (Calligraphy. His remarkable comment about *numbers*) (Carle and Horace Vernet).

Portaels (decently educated; no natural talent). I think he knows it.

Van de Hecht.

Dubois (innate sensibility. Knows nothing about drawing).

Rops (re Namur. Worth extensive study.)

Marie Collart (extremely curious).

Joseph Stevens.

Alfred Stevens (the heady *scent* of painting. Timid. —Paints for *art-lovers*).

Willems.

Wiertz.   Composition is therefore

Leys.   a thing unknown.

* *Verboeckhoven:* For a fuller identification of these various Belgian painters, see Pichois's notes at OC2: 1503–4.

Keyser (!)	The pleasure I took in
Gallait (!)	again seeing the engravings
	of Carrache.

263 · PAINTING

There are painters who are literary, too literary. But there are also the smutty painters (viz., all that Flemish filth which, however well painted it might be, offends one's taste).

In France, they find me too painterly.
Here, they find me too literary.

Everything that escapes the intellectual grasp of these painters they call literary.

264 · FINE ARTS

The manner in which Belgians discuss the value of paintings. It always comes down to numbers. This goes on for hours on end. Having spent three hours quoting the various market prices, they think they have held forth on painting.

Furthermore, the paintings need to be hidden in order to increase their market value. The eye wears out paintings.

Everybody here is an art dealer.

In Anvers, if you are a failure at everything else, you become an art dealer.

Always minor paintings. Contempt for great art.

329 · FINE ARTS
BRUSSELS

A government minister whose gallery I am visiting says to me as I am singing the praises of David: "It would seem that the market for Davids is going up."

I retort: "David's stock has never fallen among those possessed of any intelligence at all."

265 · BRUSSELS
FINE ARTS

Our Belgian confreres are unaware of the great art of decorative painting. Instead of this great art (which in the past existed in the Jesuit churches), all one finds here is *municipal* painting (always the municipality, the township), which amounts to large-scale anecdotal painting.

267–68

[Newspaper clipping containing an encomiastic obituary of Antoine Wiertz* on the occasion of his death on June 18, 1865, pasted to an invitation to his funeral that Baudelaire had received.]

269 · BRUSSELS
PAINTING

Wiertz's stupidity on a par with that of Doré and Victor Hugo.
Bignon: Madmen are such morons [*les fous sont trop bêtes*].

270 r–v · BRUSSELS
MODERN PAINTING

"Independent" Painting.
Wiertz. Charlatan. Idiot, thief. Believes he has a destiny to fulfill.

* *Wiertz:* The Belgian painter Antoine Wiertz had an enormous studio in Brussels, one hall of which had been built by the Belgian government to house his colossal paintings. Its walls were covered with pseudo-philosophical adages and slogans— such as "Bruxelles Capital, Paris Province," which was also the title of a violent pamphlet he had directed at French art critics for having ignored his submissions to the Paris Salons of the 1830s (which included his gigantic historical painting *Greeks and Romans Fighting over the Body of Patroclus,* referred to above). Upon his death in June 1865, Wiertz willed all his work to the state, and the (national) Musée Antoine Wiertz still exists to this day on the rue Vautier. Walter Benjamin comments on Wiertz at several points in his *Arcades Project* as an advanced symptom of the "phantasmagoria" of nineteenth-century capitalism.

Wiertz, a literary painter. Modern hogwash. The Christ of the humanitarians. Philosophical painting. As dumb as Victor Hugo toward the end of his *Contemplations*. Abolition of the death penalty. Infinite powers of man.

Copper crowds.

His wall inscriptions. Insults directed at France and French art critics. Wiertz's slogans all over the place. M. Gagne.* Utopias. Brussels Capital of the World. Paris Province. Bignon's remark about how moronic madmen can be.

Wiertz's books. Plagiarisms. He doesn't know how to draw, and his *bêtise* is as enormous as his colossi.

In short, this charlatan had an excellent business sense. But what will Brussels do with all of this stuff after his death?

His trompe-l'oeils.

A Belgian Woman Slapped.

Napoleon in Hell.

The Lion of Waterloo.

Wiertz and V. Hugo out to save humanity.

272–73 · MUSEUMS

The Museum of Brussels†

Vanthulden's grossness. Septuagenarians hiking up their skirts. Flemish filth (always the *pisser* and the *vomiter*). Thus what I used to take to be the sheer products of several artists' imagination turns out to be an accurate translation of local MORES. (Lovers kissing while vomiting.)

Van den Plas and *Pierre Meert.*

Paintings as poorly labeled as in France.

Monks and nuns by *Philippe de Champagne.*

---

* *M. Gagne:* Paulin Gagne, author of the *Monopanglotte,* which proposed a utopian universal language, and of the twenty-five-thousand-line poem *Femme-Messie,* sarcastically cited in Lautréamont's *Poésies* as a major masterpiece.

† *Museum of Brussels:* See Pichois's notes at OC2: 507–9, for further details.

A canal by *Canaletto*.

Tintoretto (Mary Magdalene anointing the feet of Jesus).

Paul Veronese. A small sketch of the Louvre's *Last Supper*.

Veronese. The Presentation in the Temple.

Veronese. Juno Showering Gifts on Venice (recalling his ceiling in the Grand Salon).

Guardi, mislabeled *Canaletto*.

A beautiful portrait by *Titian*.

An agreeable *Albani*, the first I have seen.

Preti, rape, battle, blinded eye.

Tintoretto. Shipwreck beyond a palace (see the Catalog).

Metzu. Cuyp. Mass. Teniers. Palamedes.

Fine *Van der Neer. Ryckaert* (reminds one of Le Nain).

Superb *Meert. Janseens*. Superb *Jordaens*.

Rembrandt (cold). *Ruysdael* (sad).

Curious sketch by *Rubens*, very white.

Superb *Rubens*.* The buttocks of Venus, surprised yet flattered by the audacity of the satyr who is kissing them.

Peter Neefs. Gothic church, decorated with Jesuit statues and altars.

David Teniers.

David Teniers (both quite beautiful).

Backhuysen (banal).

Portrait of a woman, a genteel woman à la Maintenon, by Bol.

Jean Ateen, 2 paintings, one of which quite fine.

Flemish filth and foolishness.

274–75 · MUSEUM OF BRUSSELS

Van Dyck, ladies' hairdresser.

Silenus, a superb painting, labeled *Van Dyck*, should be attributed to *Jordaens*.

Jordaens. The Satyr and the Peasant.

(Jordaens far more personal and straightforward than Rubens. Re

---

* *Superb Rubens*: Probably *Venus and Cupid at the Forge of Vulcan*.

Rubens's fatuousness. I can't stand people so ostentatiously happy (blandness of all that good cheer, all that pink).

Isabel Clara Eug. Hisp. Belg et burg. Prin.

Albertus archid. Austriae belg. Et burg. Prin.

Decorative portraits a bit larger than life. Some superb Rubens, *curious* Rubens.

Emmaneul Biset.

Ehrenberg-Emelraet (see the Catalog)

Hubert Goltzius.

Smeyers (a composer. A rare thing here).

Siberechts (reminds one of Le Nain).

Jordaens an exorcism.

Jordaens a triumph.

Re the large Rubens paintings to the rear.*

I knew Rubens perfectly before coming here.

Rubens, Decadence. Rubens, antireligious.

Rubens, bland. Rubens, fountain of banality.

The Museum's incredibly rich holdings in *Primitives*.

Sturbant (?)

Roger de Bruges.† Charles le Téméraire.

Holbein (The Little Dog).

The famous panels of *Van Eyck*. (Superb, but crapulously Flemish).

Breughel of Velours.

Breughel the Elder? (consult Arthur Stevens)

Breughel the Droll.

(Massacre of the Innocents. A town in winter. The entry of the soldiers. White ground. Persian silhouettes.)

Mabuse. The perfumes of Magdalene.

Van Orley. –Van Eyck.

Fortunately for me, the moderns were nowhere to be seen.

---

* *Large Rubens paintings to the rear:* Most likely *The Assumption of the Virgin, The Adoration of the Magi*, and *The Martyrdom of Saint Livinius*, in which the saint's tongue has been ripped out of his mouth by tongs and is being fed to a dog—"je jette ma langue aux chiens." See Jérôme Thélot, *Baudelaire: Violence et poésie* (Paris: Gallimard, 1993), 226–27.

† *Roger de Bruges:* Roger de la Pasture (also Rogier van der Weyden).

25 · ARCHITECTURE, CHURCHES, WORSHIP

277 · BRUSSELS
ARCHITECTURE

A pot and a horseman on the roof are the most visible reminders of their extravagant taste in architecture. A horse on a roof! A flowerpot on a pediment!
This relates to what I call *le style joujou*—the toy style.

Muscovite bell towers. On a Byzantine bell tower, a bell or rather a service bell fit for a dining room—which makes me want to detach it in order to ring for my (giant) servants.

The lovely houses on the *Grand'Place* remind one of those curious pieces of furniture called *Cabinets*. The toy style.

As a matter of fact, fine pieces of furniture are always small monuments.*

278 · BRUSSELS
ARCHITECTURE. SCULPTURE

Pots on roofs.
 (purpose of pots?)
An equestrian statue on a roof. Here's a fellow galloping over roofs.
 In general, no understanding whatsoever of sculpture—except the toy sculpture or ornamental sculpture at which they excel.

279 · ARCHITECTURE

In general, even in the modern buildings, the architecture is ingenious and eye-catching. Absence of classic proportionality.
 Bluestone.

---

* *Small monuments:* See Poe's essay "The Philosophy of Furniture" (1840).

La Grande Place

Before the bombardment by Villeroy,* and even today, amazing décor. Stylish yet solemn. —The equestrian statue. The emblems, the busts, the varied styles, the golds, the pediments, the house attributed to Rubens, the caryatids, the stern of a ship, the Hôtel de Ville, the house of the King, a world of architectural paradoxes. Victor Hugo (see Dubois and Wauters).†

The boat wharf.

282 · BRUSSELS. ARCHITECTURE
AND LITERATI BEHIND THE TIMES

Cobergher and Victor Joly.‡

"If I could get my hands on this Cobergher," says Joly, —"a wretch who has corrupted the religious style."

The existence of Cobergher, the architect of the Church of the Béguines, of the Augustines, and of the Brigittines, was revealed to me by a recent issue of the *Magasin pittoresque*. I had in vain asked a number of Belgians for the name of this architect.

V. Joly has remained stuck on Hugo's *Notre-Dame de Paris*. "I cannot pray," says he, "in a Jesuit-style church." —He needs gothic architecture.

---

* *The bombardment by Villeroy:* The historic city center of Brussels was nearly destroyed by the bombardment of the town in 1695 by the Duke of Villeroy, commander of the French Army of Flanders.

† *Dubois and Wauters:* The painter Louis Dubois was one of Baudelaire's native informants in Brussels and would have known about political refugee Victor Hugo's residence on the Grand-Place in the wake of Napoleon III's coup d'état of December 2, 1851. Alphonse Wauters was the co-author of a three-volume *History of Brussels* that Baudelaire consulted.

‡ *Cobergher . . . Joly:* Wenceslas Cobergher, seventeenth-century Flemish architect, painter and engraver, pioneer of the Flemish Baroque style of architecture, was featured in *Le Magasin pittoresque* of January 1865 (which helps date this page). Though Baudelaire was an admirer of the Belgian journalist Victor Joly in many other matters, he nonetheless condemned his taste for gothic architecture, as celebrated in Hugo's 1831 novel, *Notre-Dame de Paris*.

There are people so lazy that they take the colors of the curtains in their room as an excuse for never getting down to work.

283 · BRUSSELS AND BELGIUM
ARCHITECTURE

The overall aspect of the Churches.
Sometimes their riches are real, sometimes bric-a-brac.
Just as the houses on the Grand-Place appear to be curious pieces of furniture, so the churches often look like curiosity shops.
But this is not displeasing. Childish honors rendered unto the Lord.

186 · CHURCHES. BRUSSELS

Churches closed.
What happens to the money that they charge tourists?

The Catholic religion in Belgium at once resembles Neapolitan Superstition and Protestant Priggishness.

A religious procession. At long last! Banners on a rope, stretched over the street. Delacroix's crack about flags. Religious processions have been outlawed in France out of respect for a handful of assassins and heretics. Do you remember the incense, the rose petals raining down, etc. . . . ?
Byzantine banners, some so heavy that they were carried horizontally.
Bourgeois religious bigots. Types as thickheaded as revolutionaries.

284 · BRUSSLES
GENERAL CHARACTERISTICS
WORSHIP

A 2nd procession, in celebration of the miracle of the Stabbed Hosts.

Large polychrome statues.
Polychrome crucifixes.

Beauty of polychrome sculpture.

The Eternal Crucified above the crowd. —Sprays of artificial roses.

My heart warming.

Thank God I could not see the faces of those who were carrying these magnificent images.

285 · CHURCHES. BRUSSELS

Sainte-Gudule. Magnificent stained-glass windows. The colors beautiful, intense—colors of the sort that a deep soul might infuse into the objects of life.

Sainte-Catherine. Exotic scent. Ex-votos. Painted virgins, rouged, all decked out in finery. The specific scent of wax and incense.

All the pulpits enormous and theatrical. Scenes staged in wood. Excellent craftsmanship, which makes me want to order some furniture from Malines or Louvain.

The churches invariably closed once the services are over. So one is reduced to praying *on time*, in Prussian fashion.

A tax on tourists.

When you enter after the services are over, they point you to a placard where the price of admission is indicated.

286 · BRUSSELS
WORSHIP

Belgian religions.

Atheism.

Allan Kardec.*

A religion to satisfy both heart and mind.

People never find their own religion beautiful enough.

---

* *Allan Kardec:* Nom de plume of Hippolyte Léon Denizard Rivail, a popular nineteenth-century French medium, spirit-tapper, and author of the *Gospel According to Spiritism.* Another stab at Victor Hugo's table-turning séances.

287 · ARCHITECTURE. THE JESUIT STYLE

A brave bookseller who prints books against priests and nuns and who probably educates himself by reading the books he prints, tries to convince me that there is no such thing as the Jesuit style—this, in a country littered with Jesuit monuments.

288–89 · CHURCHES. BRUSSELS

Attempt to define the Jesuit style.
A composite style.
Stylish barbarity.
Chessboard.
Delightful bad taste.
Versailles chapel.
Collège de Lyon.*
The boudoir of Religion.
Immense glorias.
Mourning in marble
(black and white)
Solomonic columns.
(Rococo) statues suspended from the capitals of the columns, even from Gothic columns.
Ex-votos (great ship)

A church made up of various styles is a historical dictionary. It is the natural waste heaped up by history.
Polychrome madonnas, all decked out in finery.
Tombstones. Funerary sculptures suspended from columns. (Jean-Baptiste Rousseau)†
Extraordinary pulpits, rococo, dramatic confessionals. In general,

---

* *Collège de Lyon:* Between the ages of eleven and fifteen, Baudelaire attended boarding school in Lyon, where he was apparently impressed by its rococo architecture.
† *Jean-Baptiste Rousseau:* Eighteenth-century French poet—no relation to Jean-Jacques—banished to Brussels in 1712 for a poem he never wrote, and buried there in 1741.

a style of sculpture fit for domestic interiors—and for the pulpits, the *style joujou.*

The pulpits are a universe of emblems, an ornate chaos of religious symbols, sculpted by skilled chisels from Malines or Louvain.

Palm trees, oxen, eagles, griffons; Sin, Death, pudgy angels, the instruments of the Passion, Adam and Eve, the Crucifix, foliage, rocks, curtains, etc. . . . , etc. . . . .

A gigantic polychrome crucifix is commonly suspended from the vault in front of the chancel of the great nave (?).

(I adore polychrome sculpture.)

It's what a photographer friend of mine calls Jesus-Christ-on-a-trapeze.

290 · CHURCHES. BRUSSELS

Jesuit churches. The *flamboyant* Jesuit style. Rococo of Religion, ancient memories of books of engravings. The miracles of Deacon Pâris.* (But let's be on guard against Jansenism.)

The Beguinage Church. Delicious impression of whiteness. The Jesuit churches, very airy, very well lit.

This church is as snowy in its beauty as a young girl at her first communion.

Fire pots, skylights, busts in niches, wingèd heads, statues perched on capitals.

Charming confessionals.

Religious coquetry.

The worship of Mary, so beautiful in all the churches.

291 · CHURCHES. BRUSSELS

The church of *La Chapelle*

A polychrome crucifix and above it, *Nuestra Señora de la Soledad* (Our Lady of Solitude).

---

* *Deacon Pâris:* François de Pâris, early eighteenth-century miracle-working Jansenist saint.

The outfit of a *beguine* nun. In full mourning, large veils, black and white, cloak of black muslin.

Life-size.

Diadem of gold encrusted with glass jewels.

Halo of gold with rays.

Heavy rosary, which must come from her convent.

Her face is painted.

Terrific [*terrible*] color, terrific style of the Spaniards.

(De Quincey's "Our Ladies of Sorrow").*

A white skeleton peeking out of a black marble tomb suspended on the wall.

(More amazing than the one at Saint-Nicolas du Chardonnet.)

26 · THE COUNTRYSIDE

293 · BRUSSELS
GENERAL CHARACTERISTICS
OF THE SURROUNDING COUNTRYSIDE

The earth is fat and rich and dark around Brussels. The vegetation late but deep. Mist. Humidity. Nature resembling its inhabitants.

The agriculture is amazing. Everything cultivated. Plowmen at work. Slopes cultivated by spade and mattock.

Yet in this rich countryside, there are disgustingly dirty and yellowed children who come up and surround you in packs, obstinate little beggars with exasperating sing-song voices. These are not children of the poor. —Their parents, often rich farmers, sometimes intervene: *O, these greedy little kids, they just want some cake.*†

And this people pretends it is free!

You have to pay a fee at every tollgate, that is, every . . . . The debris of feudalism. The tollgates are rented out as concessions.

---

* *De Quincey's "Our Ladies of Sorrow"*: Chapter 8 of De Quincey's *Confessions of an English Opium-Eater* (translated by Baudelaire) is entitled "Our Ladies of Sorrow."

† *Cake:* See Baudelaire's prose poem "Le Gâteau" ("The Cake").

326 · BRUSSELS

The landscape.

Nature of the Terrain around Brussels—muddy or sandy, making walking impossible.
All the parks neglected, in a state of abandon.
The woods largely uninhabited.
Very few songbirds.

294 · BRUSSELS
GENERAL CHARACTERISTICS

The beauty of the Quai des Barques and of the Allée verte.

The lentils and the duckweed. A most peculiar invasion, quite rapid.
—A carpet of green, which invites you to walk upon it but which robs the waters of their iridescent shimmer.

27 · A STROLL THROUGH MALINES

296–97 · MALINES

Botanical garden.
Overall impression: rest, festivity, devotion.
Mechanical music in the air, representing a race of automata whose diversion depends on discipline. The carillons dispense the individual from searching for his own expression of joy.
—At Malines, every day is Sunday.
The ancient smell of Spain.
Rombaud (Raimbault, Rombauld), Gothic.
The Church of Saint-Pierre.
The story of saint François Xavier painted by two brothers (painters and Jesuits), reverberating symbolically on the facade.
One of two prepares his paintings in red.

Theatrical style in the manner of Restout.

Character of the Jesuit Churches. Brightness and whiteness.

These churches seem to be perpetually taking communion.

The entirety of Saint-Pierre is surrounded by ceremonious confessionals, running alongside each other without interruption, creating a large circle of richly sculpted symbols that are most ingenious, most bizarre.

The Jesuit church finds its recapitulation in the Pulpit. The globe of the earth. The four quarters of the earth. Louis de Gonzague, Stanislas Kostka, François Xavier, saint François Régis.

The old crones and the beguines. Mechanical acts of devotion. Perhaps true happiness. Pronounced scent of wax and incense, long gone in Paris, an emanation one only rediscovers in villages. Halles des Drapiers. Flemish Louis XVI.

298 · MALINES

Malines is traversed by a stream, fast-running, green. But Malines the Sleeper is no nymph but rather a beguine whose bashful gaze barely dares venture out from the darkness of its hood.

It's a small town, not afflicted, not tragic, but just mysterious enough to catch the eye of a foreigner unfamiliar with the minute solemnities of the life of devotion.

Religious paintings—*pious but not confirmed believers* —according to Michelangelo.

Secular tunes adapted for the carillons. Among the melodies that waft about and mingle together, I caught a snatch of what seemed to be the *Marseillaise*. The hymn of the Rabble, soaring forth from the bell towers, lost some of its bitter savor. Chopped into bits by the carillon hammers, it ceased to be that massive howl one traditionally hears and seemed to take on a childish grace. It was as if the Revolution were learning how to stutter forth the language of Heaven. The sky, clear and blue, was not annoyed to receive this homage of the earth mingled with the other melodies.

[Stray leaf]

Having visited so many altarpieces, so many chapels and confessionals, O sybaritic traveler, go to the Hotel of the Levrette, but not to dine there, heaven forbid! (for it is impossible to dine in Belgium, unless you have the stomach to deal with this endless procession of boiled *beef* and *mutton* (or, supposedly, *veal*), all this *beefsteak* and *tête de veau*, with cutlets or *ham* salads for dessert)—but to try a certain Moselle wine, firm, fine, dry, fresh, and sparkling, which left me with a vague memory of honey and musk. Only the incense was missing.

28 · A STROLL THROUGH ANVERS

299–301 · FIRST VISIT TO ANVERS

Leaving Brussels behind. What a joy! M. Neyt. The archbishop of Malines. Flat country. Black greenery. (An employee howling.) New and ancient fortifications of Anvers. English gardens on the fortifications. Place de Meir. The house of Rubens. —The house of the King.

Ancient styles. Flemish Renaissance. The Rubens style. The Jesuit style.

Flemish Renaissance: the Hôtel de Ville of Anvers. (Coquetry, sumptuousness, pink marble, golds).

Jesuit Style: The Jesuit Church of Anvers. The Beguinage Church in Brussels.

An extremely composite style. A salmagundi of styles. Chessboards. —Chandeliers in gold. —Mourning in marble—black and white. Theatrical confessionals. There's a bit of the Theater and bit of the Boudoir in Jesuit décor. The craftsmanship of the wood sculpture from Malines or Louvain.

Catholic luxury in the extreme sacristy or boudoir sense.

The coquetries of Religion.

Calvaries and Madonnas.

Eye-catching modern style in the architecture of the houses. Blue granite. A moderate blend of Renaissance and Rococo.

The style of Capetown.

The Town Hall (pink marble and gold).

In Anvers, finally able to breathe!

The majesty and the breadth of the Escaut river. The large basins. Canals and basins for inshore navigation.

Fairground music near the ships. A stroke of luck.

Church of Saint-Paul. Gothic exterior. Jesuit interior. Ceremonious, theatrical confessionals. Lateral chapels in multicolored marble. Chapel of the Collège de Lyon. (Ridiculous Calvary. Here the dramatic sculpture verges on out-and-out comedy, on unwitting comedy.)

(The Church of Beguinage in Brussels. Finery of a girl taking communion.)

Notre-Dame of Anvers. The pomp of Quinten Metsys, James Tissot.* The rapacity of the sacristans. Paintings by Rubens restored and kept in the sacristy to make the most money off them. Entrance fee: 1 franc (per person). If a French priest ever dared . . .

The cuisine of Anvers.

The herring canal, or the famous Rydeck.

Prostitution.

The place looks like a real capital. Manners coarser than those of Brussels, more Flemish.

29 · A STROLL THROUGH NAMUR

302–3 · TRIP TO NAMUR

FROM BRUSSELS TO NAMUR —Always this *black greenery*. Fertile soil.

Namur. —City of Boileau and Van der Meulen.† During my entire stay I couldn't get *Boileau and Van der Meulen* out of my mind. And then, after having visited the sites, I couldn't get *Le Lutrin* out of my

---

* *Quinten Metsys:* Sixteenth-century Flemish artist, first important painter of the Anvers school. *James Tissot:* Nineteenth-century French society painter, influenced by contemporary Belgian realist painter Henri Leys of Anvers.

† *Van der Meulen:* Adam Frans van der Meulen, seventeenth-century Flemish painter known for his scenes of military campaigns and conquests. For Boileau and *Le Lutrin,* see p. 290n.

mind. At Namur all the monuments date from the Louis XIV or, at the latest, the Louis XV period.

Again the Jesuit style (not Rubens this time or Flemish Renaissance). Three major churches—*Les Récollets, Saint-Aubin, Saint-Loup*. Finally try to nail down the beauty of this style (end of the Gothic). A particular art, a composite art. Seek out its origins (De Brosses).*

Saint-Aubin. Pantheon, St. Peter's in Rome. *Bricks*.

Note the convexity of the portal and pediment.

Magnificent grates. The particular solemnity of the 18th century.

Was it at *Saint-Aubin* or in the *Récollets* that I admired the *Nicolais*.†
Which Nicolai? Paintings by Nicolai, engraved with Rubens's signature. *Nicolai the Jesuit*. Still working.

Saint-Loup. A sinister and stylish marvel. *Saint-Loup* differs from all the Jesuit stuff I've seen. The interior of a catafalque embroidered in *black, pink,* and *silver*. Confessionals in a style that is varied, refined, subtle, baroque, a *new antiquity*. The *Beguinage* church in Brussels is a girl taking communion. *Saint-Loup* is a terrifying [*terrible*] and delicious catafalque.

The sustained majesty of all these Jesuit churches, flooded with light, with large windows, boudoirs of Religion rejected by *Victor Joly*, who claims he can only pray under Gothic arches—*a man who prays but rarely*.

Detailed technical description (inasmuch as possible) of Saint-Loup.

The chaffinches. Blinded. Chaffinch societies. Barbarity.

Prostitution.

The name of the successful female star of the moment.

Sometimes printed on a lantern; in the poorest districts, scrawled in chalk.

—A fine chapter on Rops.‡

—The Walloon population. —What is the Walloon? I take the wrong train. —Gaiety, drollery, teasing, kindness.

---

* *De Brosses:* Charles de Brosses, *Les Lettres familières écrites de l'Italie à quelques amis en 1739–1740*, contains passages devoted to baroque architecture.

† *The Nicolaïs:* Jacques Nicolaï, seventeenth-century disciple of Rubens whose late baroque paintings hung in the Cathedral of Saint-Aubin at Namur.

‡ *Rops:* See p. 286n.

[See "Argument," p. 291 above]

33 · EPILOGUE

309 · BELGIUM
GENERAL FEATURES

The Belgian has been hacked into stumps, yet still lives on. He's a worm one has forgotten to squash.

He's totally *bête*, but as resistant as a mollusk.

A hyperborean, a gnome without eyelid or pupil or forehead, and who rings empty, as when a sword strikes a gutted tomb.*

310 · POOR BELGIUM

Belgium is a case that proves the theory of the tyranny of the weak.
Nobody would dare lay a hand on Belgium.
Noli me tangere, an appropriate motto for her.
She is sacred.

311 · BELGIUM
GENERAL CHARACTERISTICS

Having long wondered why exactly the Belgians existed, I imagined that they were perhaps ancient souls who, because of their disgusting vices, had gotten trapped in the hideous bodies that are their image.

A Belgian is a living hell on earth.

---

* *A hyperborean:* Quoted from Petrus Borel. See p. 302n.

312 · POOR BELGIUM

It has occasionally occurred to me that Belgium was perhaps one of those hells that are graduated and disseminated throughout the creation and that the Belgians, as Kircher* suspected, were in fact certain animals or certain ancient abject and criminal spirits imprisoned in deformed bodies.

One becomes Belgian for having sinned.

A Belgian is a hell unto himself.

313 · BRUSSELS

The fate of Belgium
Perhaps for the *Epilogue*
Annexation?
Dismemberment?
Nothing would be easier. Belgium is ready for it. She would fully cooperate.

Nothing would be easier than to conquer Belgium. Nothing would be more difficult than to tame her.

And then, what to do with her? What purpose would it serve to reduce to slavery a people that doesn't even know how to cook an egg?

314 · POLITICS

Epilogue.
Invasion.

Belgium is what France would have become had the reign of Louis-Philippe lasted—a fine example of constitutional inanity.

The sulking pride of Boeotians.
Frog nations puffing themselves up into oxen.

---

* *Kircher:* Athanasius Kircher, seventeenth-century German Jesuit scholar and polymath. Baudelaire mentions his theories of metempsychosis in a note to his translation of Poe's "Metzengerstein."

There are cities (Brussels, Geneva) that resemble prudes convinced they excite lust.

This issue of invasion comes up endlessly in conversations.

But no one has any designs on you, damn it all!

339 · POOR BELGIUM

Hors d'oeuvre
Nadar.*
Janin's comeuppance.†
Preface to J. Caesar.‡
The Lincoln Affair.§

Those people who consider Booth a villain are the same ones who adore Charlotte Corday.

Did Lincoln get his just deserts? God's government is most complex. The villain is not necessarily divine; but once he exists, God makes use of him to punish the villain.

---

* *Nadar:* Baudelaire's old friend the photographer, caricaturist, and balloonist Nadar visited Brussels for the Independence Day festivities of September 1864, attracting great crowds (the crowd-control fences installed for the occasion are still sometimes called "Nadar barriers" in Belgium). Baudelaire was invited to participate in the ascension of Nadar's balloon, "Le Géant," but declined.

† *Janin:* See the "Letter to Jules Janin" translated in appendix 6. Janin's Académie Française candidacy was rejected in April 1865.

‡ *Preface to J. Caesar:* Napoleon III published a *History of Julius Caesar* in three volumes in 1865. Baudelaire planned to write an essay refuting the great man theory of history and providential view of progress that informed its preface, which concluded as follows: "The aim I have in view in writing this history is to prove that, when Providence raises up such men as Caesar, Charlemagne, and Napoleon, it is to trace out to peoples the path they ought to follow; to stamp with the seal of their genius a new era; and to accomplish in a few years the labor of many centuries. Happy the peoples who comprehend and follow them! woe to those who misunderstand and combat them! They do as the Jews did, they crucify their Messiah; they are blind and culpable: blind, for they do not see the impotence of their efforts to suspend the definitive triumph of good; culpable, for they only retard progress, by impeding its prompt and fruitful application" (*History of Julius Caesar* [New York: Harper and Brothers, 1865], xiv). Baudelaire apparently intended to include his critique of Napoleon III's opportunistic theory of providential progress in the pages of *Poor Belgium*.

§ *The Lincoln Affair:* The arrest and death of Lincoln's assassin, John Wilkes Booth, on April 26, 1865. The *Indépendance belge* of May 17 contained the letter Booth had written to his mother just before his death.

Always following the herd. The journalists who adore America and Belgium. Booth's testament.

Booth a brave man. I'm glad he died a brave man's death. —The surgeon.*

[stray leaf]

BRUSSELS

passim.

Their philosophy is that of boarding school teachers or exam crammers.

I never understood this perfectly until I saw the absolute idiocy of their convictions.

Let us add that when one wants to talk to them about *actual* revolution, they are terrified. *Old Maids.* ME, if I agree to be a republican, *I am fully conscious of doing evil.* Yes! *Long Live the Revolution!*†

Forever! What the hell!

But as for myself, I'm not taken in! I was never taken in! I say *Long Live the Revolution!* the way I would say: *Long Live Destruction! Long Live Expiation! Long Live Punishment! Long Live Death!*

---

* *The surgeon:* Dr. Samuel Mudd, who had treated Booth's injured leg in Maryland during Booth's escape.

† *Long Live the Revolution!:* Baudelaire is probably here reacting to one of the clippings he made for eventual use in chapter 19, "Politics." It consists of several pages (dated November 5, 1865) taken from the radical journal *La Rive gauche*, published by French political exiles in Brussels and one of whose major contributors was Auguste Rogeard, the recent author of a violent pamphlet against the Second Empire of Louis Napoleon entitled *Pauvre France*—a title that probably caused Baudelaire to change the name of his book from *Pauvre Belgique* to (provisionally) *La Belgique déshabillée*. The newspaper report in question transcribed the proceedings and the speeches of the Congress of Liège held in late October 1865 and of another follow-up meeting in Brussels on November 3—an international gathering of "progressive" students (including Karl Marx's future son-in-law Paul Lafargue) loosely affiliated with the First International, founded in London the previous year, and with the Brussels newspaper *Le Peuple*, the organ of the freethinking *Solidariens* and the *Société des Affranchis*. The entire dossier is included in Guyaux, ed., *Fusées, Mon Coeur mis à nu, La Belgique déshabillée* (Paris: Gallimard, 1986), 394–407.

Not only would I be happy to be the victim, but I wouldn't mind being the executioner either—to feel the Revolution from both sides!

We all carry the republican spirit in our veins, just as we carry the pox in our marrow. We are Democratized and Syphilized.

[stray leaf]

POOR BELGIUM
EPILOGUE

Today, Monday the 28th of August 1865, over the course of a hot and humid evening, I followed the meanderings of a street fair (*Kermesse*), and in the streets named *Devil's Corner, Monks' Rampart, Our Lady of Sleep, Six Tokens,* as well as in several others, I discovered, to my great delight and surprise, frequent symptoms of cholera suspended in the air. Have I sufficiently invoked cholera, this monster I adore? Have I studied the advance signs of his arrival attentively enough? How long shall I have to wait for him, this horrific favorite of mine, this impartial Attila, this divine plague who strikes down his victims at random? Haven't I sufficiently pleaded with My Lord God to speed his passage over the stinking banks of the *Senne*? And how much pleasure would I finally derive as I contemplated the grimacing agony of this hideous people caught in the coils of its fake Styx, its *Briareus-river,** whose waters carry off more excrements than the sky above provides sustenance to flies! I shall take great delight, oh certainly, in the terrors and tortures inflicted on this race whose traits are yellow hair, nankeen trousers, and lilac complexions!

A detail worth mentioning: after all the numerous shields dedicated to national *Unity,* to *Friendship,* to *Fidelity,* to the *Constitution,* to the *Virgin Mary,* I discover one dedicated: *To the Police.*

---

* *Briareus-river:* In Greek mythology, Briareus was one of the three-hundred-armed and fifty-headed Hecatoncheires who represented the gigantic forces of nature manifested in earthquakes or the motion of sea waves. The insalubrious river Senne was covered up between 1867 and 1871 to make way for the construction of new public buildings and boulevards in its place.

Excerpts from the *Notebook*

Baudelaire's so-called *Carnet* (or *Notebook*) was, unlike the loose leaves of *Fusées* or *Mon Coeur mis à nu*, a small bound duodecimo agenda consisting of 112 pages (with an additional 46 pages at the end torn out). Jacques Crépet dated its entries as ranging from July 1861 to November 1863. In addition to its lists of names and addresses (including those of prostitutes), it contains, in the manner of an account book, ledgers of debits and credits, daily appointments, and references to the projects Baudelaire was working on, notably his studies of Delacroix and Guys, his translation of Poe's *Eureka*, his unfinished essays on *Literary Dandyism*, and his collection of prose poems (here explained in a late 1861 draft of a letter to the magazine editor Arsène Houssaye). This Carnet, which provides an extraordinary glimpse into the minutiae of Baudelaire's everyday life, was first published in its entirety in 1938 and then in the edition of Baudelaire's *Écrits intimes* prefaced by Sartre in 1946. Its first critical edition was included in the 1949 *Journaux intimes*, edited by Crépet and George Blin and published by Corti. A more recent transcription (with detailed notes) may be found in OC1: 713–80. Rather than reproduce all the topical trivia of this private agenda, I have selected those fragments that complement the thrust of his contemporary *Flares, Hygiene,* and *My Heart Laid Bare.*

*To Houssaye**

The title.
The dedication.

----

* *Houssaye:* Arsène Houssaye, the editor (in 1861–82) of both the newspaper *La Presse* and the magazine *L'Artiste*—and to whom Baudelaire is here describing his submission of prose poems for publication. This is a sketch of both the letter he sent to Houssaye around Christmas 1861 and of the eventual dedication of his "Petits poèmes en prose" when they finally appeared in the August 26, 1862, issue of *La Presse*.

Without head or tail. Everything head and tail.*

Convenient for you. Convenient for me. Convenient for the Reader. We can all break off wherever we so choose—I, my reverie, you, the manuscript, the reader his reading. And I won't be suspending the latter's recalcitrant will on the endless thread of some superfluous plot.

I've looked for titles. 66 of them. Even though this work, which is both like a screw and a kaleidoscope, could be pushed toward the cabbalistic 666 or even 6666. . . .

This is worth more than a plot strung out over 6,000 pages. So let one at least be grateful for my moderation.

Who among us has not dreamed of a special and poetic prose to translate the lyric movements of the spirit, the undulations of reverie, and the sudden jolts of consciousness?

My departure point was Aloysius Bertrand.† What he did for the picturesque days of old, I wanted to do for abstract modern life. And then, from the very outset I realized that I was doing something DIFFERENT from the model I wanted to imitate. Which anybody else would take pride in, but which humiliates me, given that I believe that a poet must always do exactly what he wants to do.

Note on the famous saying.
Finally, small stumps
the whole snake.‡

*   *   *

* *Everything head and tail:* The 1862 version of this dedication letter explains: "My dear friend, I am sending you a small work which cannot be unjustly accused of having neither head nor tail, given that everything in it, on the contrary, is *at once* head and tail, alternatively and reciprocally."

† *Aloysius Bertrand:* Author of the posthumously published *Gaspard de la nuit* (1842), generally considered to be the first major French volume of modern prose poems.

‡ *The whole snake:* Baudelaire makes the metaphor more explicit in the published dedication of 1862: "Remove a vertebra, and the two pieces of this serpentine fantasy [of a book] will effortless join themselves together again. Hack it up into numerous fragments, and you will see that each of them can exist apart. In the hope that a few of these stumps [*tronçons*] will be alive enough to please and amuse you, I make bold to dedicate the entire snake to you."

Salvation lies in the right moment. Salvation lies in money, in success, in security, in the removal of my Trustee, in Jeanne's survival.

*   *   *

chemise slipping off
breasts low and heavy
moral messages

General sadness
Messalina shoulders
sinister, macabre dolls

*   *   *

To be the greatest of men, tell oneself that at every minute.
To have material is to have money.

*   *   *

Prayer. Sobriety. Spirituality
Work, money, chastity.
MY MOTHER

*   *   *

Agathe
   Child's hairdo, ringlets running down her back.
   Makeup. The eyebrows, the lids, the mouth. Rouge, white, beauty spots.
   Earrings, necklaces, bracelets, rings.
   Plunging neckline, arms naked, no crinoline.
   Black open-worked silk stockings if the dress is black or brown, pink if the dress is light-colored. Very revealing shoes. Fancy garters. A bath: feet and hands well tended to, perfumed all over.

Because of her coiffure, leaving the ball with her hood on, should we decide to make our exit.
White sheets.

*   *   *

9 A.M.
prayer straightaway
before ablutions
and work straightaway
after ablutions

Aphorisms and Album Inscriptions

Editorially entitled "Pensées d'Album" and "Aphorismes" in OC1: 709–10, these squibs and witticisms were collected by Baudelaire's friends across the years. His friend and future biographer Charles Asselineau in particular wanted to record the dandy at his most quotable.

[In the album of Philoxène Boyer]*
Among the rights that have been under discussion of late, there is one that has been largely forgotten, and in whose demonstration *absolutely everybody* has a vested interest—the right to contradict oneself.

[In the album of Félix Nadar]
Vitam impendere vero [signed "Louis Blanc"]†
There are three, to my knowledge, who have adopted this austere motto: Jean-Jacques, Louis Blanc, and George Sand. Joseph de Maistre somewhere writes (in his *Considerations on France*, I believe): "If a writer adopts as his motto: *Vitam impendere vero*, the bets are on that he's a liar."

---

* *Philoxène Boyer:* Brilliant polymath who met Baudelaire during his early student days in Paris and remained a lifelong friend.

† *Vitam impendere vero:* "To devote one's life to the truth" (Juvenal), the epigraph of Rousseau's *Confessions. Louis Blanc:* French politician and historian who, as a member of the provisional government of the Second Republic, was an advocate for workers' cooperatives for the urban poor.

[In the album of Édouard Gardet]*

Is it not a fact, my dear Gardet, that rouge is a most agreeable thing, not only because it transforms and exaggerates nature, but because it obliges us to kiss the ladies elsewhere than on their cheeks? —I'm sure I'm not offending you, my dear friend, who like me, are convinced that one should never lose one's dignity, except with the female on whom one's heart is set.

Ch. Baudelaire.

[Copied by Nadar onto a caricature of Baudelaire]

The corollary of every revolution is the massacre of innocents.

["Aphorisms of Ch. Baudelaire," as recorded by Charles Asselineau in his private notebooks]

If a shopkeeper's not a thief, he's a brute.

Pederasty is the only thing that links the law courts to humanity.

Stoicism is a religion that had but a single sacrament—*suicide.*

Sobriety is the mother of gluttony—for whom it provides *moral* support.

A cat is a sweet-talking vampire.

Absurdity descends like grace upon the weary.

Were Jesus Christ to descend to earth a second time, M. Frank-Carré† would exclaim: We've got another backslider here.

Were one to lay a fart on the nose of About,‡ he would mistake it for an idea.

---

* *Édouard Gardet:* Longtime friend of Baudelaire's and literary executor of Charles Asselineau. Baudelaire's comments here echo his "In Praise of Cosmetics" in his 1863 essay "The Painter of Modern Life."

† *M. Frank-Carré:* French magistrate.

‡ *About:* Edmond About, art critic and author of *The Notary's Nose* (1862).

Were religion to disappear from the face of the earth, it would be rediscovered in the heart of an atheist.

Nothing makes one better understand the sheer inanity of virtue better than the novels of La Madeleine.*

To learn is to contradict oneself—there is a degree of implication here that falsehood never attains (Custine)—a quip admired by Bodler.†

---

* *La Madelaine:* Jules de la Madeleine, minor author of the novel *Marquis des Saffras* and model Catholic convert.

† *Bodler:* Asselineau's jokey spelling of Baudelaire. Astolphe-Louis-Léonor, Marquis de Custine, French aristocrat and wit, best known for his travelogue, *Russia in 1839.*

Shakespeare Anniversary

Baudelaire's article was published anonymously in the *Figaro*, April 14, 1864, shortly before his departure for Belgium. Founded as a satirical weekly in 1825, this *petit journal* was published somewhat irregularly until 1851, when it was taken over by Hippolyte de Villemessant. Upon becoming a daily in 1866, it attained the largest circulation (56,000) of any newspaper in France. Baudelaire's relations with the *Figaro* were long and fraught. In its issue of July 5, 1857, the paper had run a front-page article by Villemessant's son-in-law (by the Flaubertian name of Gustave Bourdin) that drew the attention of the French courts to the "monstrosities" contained in Baudelaire's recently published *Flowers of Evil*. An official investigation by the public prosecutor soon followed, leading to Baudelaire's trial and conviction in August. The following year, the *Figaro* again attacked Baudelaire, noting that he had been overheard badmouthing Victor Hugo and in general denigrating the generation of great French romantics to whom he so obviously owed everything. "Luckily," the article maliciously concluded, "the long arm of the law is there to punish him if necessary." In a furious (printed) reply, Baudelaire accused the paper of deliberately misinterpreting his relation to Hugo and indirectly threatened legal action should its attacks on his reputation continue. By late 1863, however, Baudelaire had mended his bridges with Villemessant: after its manuscript had been floating around in search of a publisher for three years, it was in the pages of the *Figaro* that Baudelaire's greatest essay, *The Painter of Modern Life*, finally appeared in three installments. Two months later, in early 1864, the *Figaro* published six of his "Little Poems in Prose" for two weeks running (handsomely introduced by the same Gustave Bourdin), but then immediately dropped the series—because, as Baudelaire wrote his mother, Villemessant had informed him that "everybody found them boring." Later, after having gone into exile in Brussels, Baudelaire was briefly convinced in 1865 that Villemessant would publish his notes on Belgium in the *Figaro* under the title *Lettres belges* (and signed, for the sake of his safety abroad, "Charles de Féyis," his mother's maiden name)—but the potentially lucrative project never went anywhere.

In the spring of 1864, a celebration of the tricentenary of Shakespeare's birth was to be held in the Grand Hôtel of Paris, its blue-ribbon committee of organizers including Berlioz, Dumas, Gautier, and Janin. But as Baudelaire (correctly) surmised, the festivities were designed less to celebrate the memory of the Bard than to honor his new incarnation in the person of Victor Hugo (who was to be represented at the celebration by an empty chair draped in black). The event was timed to coincide with the publication (by Lacroix in Brussels) of Hugo's three-hundred-page essay, *William Shakespeare* (which certain wags suggested should have simply been entitled *Ego*), intended to accompany the eighteen-volume translation of Shakespeare's works by his son François-Victor. Hugo's Shakespeare is, as Baudelaire points out, a palpably "socialist" figure—that is, a *pro populo poeta,* champion of the poor and huddled masses and benefactor of Mankind. Observing that none of France's major Shakespeare scholars or translators from the English (including himself) had been invited to participate in the event, Baudelaire acidly denounces the triumph of liberal-progressive political correctness over aesthetics. Given the wide circulation of the *Figaro,* it is quite likely that Baudelaire's article, a calculated provocation of the "Hugo clan," contributed to the cancellation of the Shakespeare festivities by the government as potentially subversive—hence the rumors among the political refugee community in Brussels when Baudelaire arrived that he was in fact a secret agent (or *mouchard*) of the imperial police.

To Monsieur the Editor in Chief of the *Figaro*

Monsieur,

It has more than once been my lot to read the *Figaro* and to find myself scandalized by the brashness and callowness that passes for talent among your contributors. To put it plainly, the kind of partisan writing associated with what one calls *le petit journal* does not in the least amuse me and almost always offends my sense of justice and decency. Nonetheless, each time I find myself confronted with this level of sheer *bêtise* and monstrous hypocrisy, typical of the kind of thing our century produces in such unrelenting abundance, I suddenly realize that *le petit journal* in fact does serve some purpose. As you see, I am therefore practically putting myself in the wrong, but ever so gracefully.

This is why I thought it was only fitting for me to call to your attention another such typical outrage, another such typical prank, before it actually explodes in everyone's face.

April 23 is the date on which they say that Finland—Finland!—will celebrate the three hundredth anniversary of Shakespeare's birth. I have no idea whether there is some mysterious reason behind Finland's desire to celebrate a poet not born in her land or whether she intends to raise some sort of mischievous toast to the English poet-actor. I can fully understand that the literati of Europe might want to cooperate in a common gesture of admiration for a poet whose greatness (like that of a number of other great poets) renders him universal; let us however note in passing that reasonable though it might be to celebrate the poets of every land, it would be far more just if each country first celebrated its own. Each religion has its own saints, and it pains me to observe that nobody here has thought it appropriate to celebrate the births of Chateaubriand or Balzac. I suppose one might well object that they are not yet ripe enough for glory. What about Rabelais then?

Well, so be it. Let us assume that, moved by a spontaneous sense of gratitude, the collective literati of Europe might wish to honor the memory of Shakespeare with no ulterior motives whatsoever.

But are the literati of Paris moved by a spirit of generosity as disinterested as this? Or rather, are they not unwittingly obeying the marching orders of a tiny coterie whose motives are far more personal and partisan, and thus quite unrelated to the glory of Shakespeare?

I have been, as concerns this matter, privy to several amusing anecdotes and several complaints which I would like to share with you.

A meeting was held somewhere—little matter exactly where. M. Guizot* was to have been named to the committee, no doubt to honor him for having authored a wretched translation of Shakespeare. M. Villemain's† name also came up, given that years ago he had written more or less well on the subject of English theater. This seemed a good enough reason, even though this mandrake without a soul would have cut a rather paltry figure in front of the statue of the world's most passionate poet.

---

* *Guizot:* François Guizot had in the 1820s "refreshed" the classic French translation of Shakespeare by Letourneur (1776–83). Guizot subsequently went on to become the foreign and then the prime minister of the July Monarchy (1840–48).

† *Villemain:* A particular *bête noire* of Baudelaire, Abel-François Villemain was the "perpetual secretary" of the French Academy, and hence largely responsible for the fiasco of the poet's candidacy in early 1862. Baudelaire subsequently wrote a virulent attack on him, which remained unpublished until 1907, entitled *L'Esprit et le style de M. Villemain.*

I wonder whether the name of Philarète Charles,* who has done so much to popularize English literature in our country, was ever brought up. I doubt it, and for good reason. Here at Versailles, at a stone's throw from me, there lives an ancient poet who made his mark, not without honor, upon the romantic literary movement—I am speaking of M. Émile Deschamps,† the translator of *Romeo and Juliet.* Well, Monsieur, would you believe that his name raised a number of objections? If I were to ask you to guess why, you would never come up with the answer. M. Émile Deschamps was for many years a senior employee of the Ministry of Finance. It is now many years since he retired. But when it comes to meting out justice, the factotums of democratic literature don't look into the details: this clique of young whippersnappers is so intent on pursuing its own agenda that it is often surprised to discover that some old geezer (to whom it owes so much) has not yet kicked the bucket. You will be surprised to learn that Théophile Gautier‡ was almost excluded from the committee, on the grounds that he was a *mouchard.* (*Mouchard*—"stooge"—is the term applied to an author who writes drama or art criticism for government newspapers.) I am not all surprised—nor will you be—that the name of M. Philoxène Boyer§ provoked much recrimination. M. Boyer is clever-minded, very clever-minded, in the best sense of the word. Possessed of an enormously supple imagination, he is an extremely erudite writer who (back in the day) improvised brilliant commentaries on the works of Shakespeare. All this is true, without a shadow of a doubt, but alas, the poor fellow sometimes permitted himself flights of lyricism in praise of the monarchy that were deemed too exaggerated. He was no doubt sincere in

---

* *Philarète Charles:* Charles had published a series of *Études sur W. Shakespeare* in 1852.

† *Émile Deschamps:* An early admirer of Baudelaire, and author of translations of *Macbeth* and *Romeo and Juliet* (1844). In 1841, he was briefly interned in the same mental institution as Gérard de Nerval.

‡ *Gautier:* Théophile Gautier, who had once been part of the "Petit Cénacle" that participated in the theater riots surrounding the first performance of Hugo's *Hernani* in early 1830, was now an influential critic of the arts who wrote for the semiofficial governmental newspaper *Le Moniteur universel.* For the term *mouchard,* see p. 395.

§ *Philoxène Boyer:* An eccentric polymath friend of both Baudelaire and Nerval; his ambitious study of Shakespeare lay unfinished at his death in 1867.

his beliefs, but no matter! In the eyes of these young gentlemen, those unfortunate odes negated all his accomplishments as a Shakespearean. As concerns Auguste Barbier,* the translator of *Julius Caesar,* and Berlioz, the author of a *Romeo and Juliet,* I have no information. M. Charles Baudelaire, whose taste for Saxon literature is well known, had been overlooked. Eugène Delacroix† is better off dead. Without doubt, they would have slammed the doors of the festivities in his face—Delacroix, who in his own fashion translated *Hamlet* but who was also the corrupt member of the municipal council, Delacroix, that aristocratic genius who pushed his cowardice so far as to be on polite terms even with his enemies. On the other hand, we shall witness the democrat Biéville offering up a toast—*with some restrictions*—to the immortal author of *Macbeth,* together with the delectable Legouvé and Saint-Marc Girardin,‡ this hideous flatterer of young dullards, not to mention the other Girardin,§ the inventor of telepathic communication between snails and the contriver of a national subscription at a penny a head for the abolition of war!

But the height of grotesquery, the *nec plus ultra* of sheer ridiculousness, the irrefutable symptom of the complete hypocrisy of these proceedings, was the nomination of M. Jules Favre to the committee.¶ Jules Favre and Shakespeare? Can you grasp the enormity of this? M. Jules Favre is no doubt cultivated enough to grasp the beauties of Shakespeare and, in this respect, could easily be invited. But if he has two ounces of common sense, if he doesn't want to compromise the ancient poet, he should refuse the absurd honor that has been bestowed upon

---

* *Auguste Barbier:* Barbier's translation of *Julius Caesar* appeared in 1848; Berlioz's choral symphony *Roméo et Juliette* was first performed in 1839 (with a libretto by Émile Deschamps).

† *Eugène Delacroix:* Delacroix died in the late summer of 1863, with Baudelaire immediately publishing a long obituary in his honor. Delacroix had produced a series of thirteen lithographs based on *Hamlet* in 1843. Like Berlioz, he had attended the 1827 production of the play in Paris with Charles Kemble as Hamlet and Harriet Smithson as Ophelia (whom Berlioz would later marry).

‡ *Legouvé* and *Saint-Marc Girardin:* See *My Heart Laid Bare,* folios 73, 57.

§ *The other Girardin:* Editor of *La Presse.* See *My Heart Laid Bare,* folio 4.

¶ *Jules Favre* and *Dufaure:* Both Jules Favre and Jules Dufaure were political figures associated with the moderate republican opposition to Napoleon III. Dufaure was elected to the French Academy in 1863, Favre in 1867.

him. Jules Favre on a Shakespeare committee! This is more grotesque than Dufaure's election to the Académie française.

But, truth be told, the organizers of these *little* festivities have other things on their minds than glorifying poetry. Two poets who attended the aforementioned initial meeting piped up to observe that one was forgetting this or that person or that one might do this or that—the points they were making were purely literary in intent. But to every suggestion they offered, one of the little humanitarians would object: "You do not understand *what this is all about.*"

This solemn occasion shall not be lacking in absurdity, for Shakespeare will of course also have to be feted on stage. When one wants to honor Racine with a play, one stages *Les Plaideurs* and *Britannicus,* after the customary ode; if it's Corneille one's celebrating, one puts on *Le Menteur* and *Le Cid*; if it's Molière, *Pourceaugnac* and *Le Misanthrope* will do. Well, the director of a major theater, a moderate and sweet-tempered fellow who does not care too much whether he is dealing with apples or oranges, recently said to the poet who was entrusted with coming up with something in honor of the English tragedian: "Try to slip in a word or two in praise of the French classics and then, to honor Shakespeare all the better, let's put on a performance of *Il ne faut jurer de rien.*" Which is a minor closet drama by Alfred de Musset.*

Let's briefly talk about the real purpose of this great jubilee. You are well aware, Monsieur, that in 1848 that literary school of 1830 entered into an adulterous alliance with democracy, an alliance at once monstrous and bizarre. Olympio† renounced his famous doctrine of *art for art's sake,* and ever since then, he and his family and his disciples have not ceased to preach the cause of the people, to speak for the people, to display themselves, whenever the occasion arises, as the friends and ardent benefactors of the people. "A tender and profound love for the people!" Ever since then, the only thing they manage to love in literature has taken on the colors of revolution and philanthropy. Shakespeare is a socialist. He was never aware of the fact, but no matter. There are critics who, playing on paradox, have already tried to twist

---

* *Musset:* Alfred de Musset's dramatic "proverb" was first performed in 1848.

† *Olympio:* A sarcastic reference to Victor Hugo, author of the autobiographical poem "La Tristesse d'Olympio" (1840).

Balzac—a monarchist who swore by the throne and the altar—into an advocate of subversion and demolition. We are all too familiar with this sort of sleight of hand. Well, Monsieur, you know that we are living in divisive times and that there is a class of people whose throats are choked with toasts and fine speeches and hosannas, all of which are struggling to find their object. I have known individuals who follow the obituaries quite closely, especially those of celebrities, and who rush off to cemeteries to sing the praises of people they never knew. Let me mention M. Victor Cousin* as a prince of this particular specialty.

Every banquet, every festivity offers a fine occasion for French verbiage to shine. The requisite speechifiers are always on hand, and the little coterie of hangers-on who cluster around this poet (in whom God, always mysterious in his ways, has amalgamated stupidity with genius) has decided that the time is right to put this unchecked mania of the French in service of the following agenda, for which Shakespeare's birthday will merely serve as the pretext:

1) To engineer and fuel the success of V. Hugo's book on Shakespeare,† a book that (like all his books) is filled with beauties and *bêtises*, and that will cause even further consternation among his most sincere admirers;

2) To propose a toast to Denmark. The fate of Schleswig-Holstein‡ is a burning issue these days, thanks to Hamlet, Denmark's most illustrious prince. This will be far more appropriate than the toast to Poland§ that was offered (so I heard) during a banquet in honor of M. Daumier.

Then, as things develop, and in tune with that particular crescendo of *bêtise* characteristic of crowds gathered under a single roof, there will be toasts to Jean Valjean,¶ to the abolition of capital punishment, to the abolition of poverty, to *Universal Brotherhood*, to the spread of En-

---

* *Victor Cousin:* Prominent French philosopher, best known as a proponent of Eclecticism.

† *V. Hugo's book on Shakespeare:* Victor Hugo's book-length essay on *William Shakespeare*, published by Lacroix in Brussels in April 1864, was intended to accompany the eighteen-volume translation of Shakespeare undertaken by his son François-Victor (1859–66).

‡ *The fate of Schleswig-Holstein:* The Second Schleswig War, in which Denmark fought Prussia and Austria, had broken out in February 1864.

§ *The toast to Poland:* The liberation of Poland from Russian domination was a popular cause among the French radicals of the 1830s.

¶ *Jean Valjean:* Hero of Hugo's *Les Misérables*.

lightenment, to the *true* Jesus Christ, *legislator of the Christians*, as one used to say to M. Renan, M. Havin,* and to all the idiots of this nineteenth century in which it is our tiresome privilege to live, and in which everybody (so it would seem) is robbed of his natural right to *choose his brothers.*

Monsieur, I forgot to mention that women would be excluded from these festivities. Beautiful shoulders, beautiful arms, beautiful faces, and fancy gowns would have threatened the democratic austerity of this solemn event. Nonetheless, I think one might well invite a few actresses, if only to encourage them to perform a bit of Shakespeare so as to compete with the Smithsons and the Faucits.†

Publish this under my own signature, if you think it's appropriate; suppress it if you consider it of too little value.

Please accept, Monsieur, the assurance of my most distinguished respect.

[unsigned]

* *M. Renan, M. Havin:* Ernest Renan had published his "historical" *Vie de Jésus* in 1863. Felix Havin (whose complacency was captured in a magnificent photo by Nadar) was the chief editor of the liberal newspaper *Le Siécle*, the frequent object of Baudelaire's late opprobrium.

† *The Smithsons and the Faucits:* Harriet Smithson and Helena Saville Faucit, the most celebrated English Shakespearean actresses of their day.

Catalog of the Collection of M. Crabbe

Prosper Crabbe was a wealthy stockbroker and art collector whom Baudelaire's friend Arthur Stevens advised on his acquisitions—mostly "specimens" of the artists in question, as Baudelaire observes, rather than major works in their own right. The pièce de résistance of the collection was Eugène Delacroix's Rubens-inspired *Tiger Hunt* (currently in the Musée d'Orsay, Paris), which Baudelaire recognized as a masterpiece. Probably composed in mid-1864 and showing Baudelaire still in command of his acute art critical eye. For a full identification of the works, the reader is referred to the notes in Pichois's Pléiade edition (OC2: 1523–24).

Diaz. Across the enormous shade of trees, flickers of harried light.

Dupré. Magical mirages of evening.

Leys. Archaic manner. First manner, more naive.

Rosa Bonheur. The best I've seen; good cheer standing in for true achievement.

Decamps. One of the best. Huge, hillocked sky, depth of space.

— An enormous landscape in small dimension. Balaam's ass. Preceded the Dorés.

— Three soldiers involved in the Passion. Terrifying bandits à la Salvator Rosa. The crown of thorns and scepter of reeds explain the professions of these highwaymen.

Madou. A Flemish Charlet.

Cabat. Very beautiful, very fine, very shadowy, very leafy, *prodigiously finished*, a bit hard, gives an excellent idea of Cabat, somewhat forgotten these days.

Ricard. A fake Rembrandt. Well executed.

Paul Delaroche. Gives a better idea of him than usual. A simple and sentimental study.

Meissonier. A small, meditative figure of a smoker. A true Meissonier without any great pretensions. A fine specimen.

Troyon. 1860. Fine specimens. A dog standing on a knoll, tense and supple, eyes on the horizon.

— Cows. Large horizon. A river. A bridge.

— An ox on a path.

Robert-Fleury. Two historical scenes. Always selected as the finest specimens. An excellent understanding of Theater.

Jules Breton. Two.

Alfred Stevens. A young girl examining the folds of her dress in front of a swing mirror.

— A young girl, most virginal and high-minded, removes her gloves to sit down at the piano. A bit dry, a bit glassy. Very witty, more precious than the rest of Stevens.

— A young girl gazing at a bouquet on a console. The distinguished and bizarre harmony of Stevens's hues has not been sufficiently praised.

Joseph Stevens.* The run-down living quarters of a traveling showman. A suggestive painting.

Dogs dressed up. The showman has gone out and placed a hussar's busby on one of the dog's heads in order to force him to sit still in front of the cooking pot that is warming on the stove. Too witty.

Jacque. More finished than all the Jacques. A courtyard to be examined with a magnifying glass.

Knyff. Gauzy effect of the sun. Bedazzlement, whiteness. A bit casual. À la Daubigny.

Verboeckhoven. Astonishing, glassy, so disheartening as to provoke the envy of Meissonier, Landsee, H. Vernet. Colors à la Demarne.

Koekkoek. Tinplate, zinc, the work of a so-called amateur. Again, chosen as a specimen.

Verwée. Solid.

Corot. Two. In one, transparency, delicate demi-mourning, crepuscule of the soul.

Th. Rousseau. Marvelous, sheer agate. Too much love of detail, not enough love of the architectonics of nature.

---

* *Joseph Stevens:* Describes Stevens's *L'Intérieur du saltimbanque,* which inspired the second half of Baudelaire's prose poem "Good Dogs." See my commentary on the poem, pp. 169–71 above.

Millet. La Bruyère's beast of burden, his head bowed to the ground.

Bonnington. Interior of a chapel. A marvelous Diorama, no larger than a hand.

Willems. Two. Flemish preciosity. The letter, the washing of hands.

Gustave de Jongh. A young girl dressed up for a ball, reading music.

Eugène Delacroix. Tiger hunt. Delacroix, alchemist of Color. Miraculous, profound, mysterious, sensual, terrifying. Colors brilliant and dark, penetrating harmony. The man's gesture, and the gesture of the beast. The grimace of the beast, the sniffs of animality. Green, lilac, dark green, soft lilac, vermillion, dark red, a sinister bouquet.

Translator's Notes

Baudelaire's "Note du Traducteur" appeared at the end of his translation of Poe's *Eureka*, published by the firm of Michel Lévy in late November 1863, while Baudelaire was still in Paris. The unpublished "Avis du Traducteur" was sent to Lévy from Brussels in November 1864 as a "fragment" that Baudelaire wanted appended to his forthcoming French edition of Poe's *Histoires grotesques et sérieuses,* the fifth volume of his Poe translations to be published by the firm. That June Baudelaire had written a public letter to the art critic Théophile Thoré defending Manet against charges of having pastiched Velázquez, Goya, and El Greco (whose works Baudelaire claimed Manet had never even laid eyes on). He cited himself as a perfect example of such unconscious—and Borgesian—influence. "Well, so they accuse me of imitating Edgar Poe! Do you know why I so patiently translated Poe? Because he resembled me. The first time I opened a book of his, I saw, with terror and delight, not only subjects I had dreamed of, but SENTENCES I had thought up, written by him twenty years earlier."

[POE'S "PREFACE" TO *EUREKA: A PROSE POEM (1848)*]

To the few who love me and whom I love—to those who feel rather than to those who think—to the dreamers and those who put faith in dreams as in the only realities—I offer this Book of Truths, not in its character of Truth-Teller, but for the Beauty that abounds in its Truth; constituting it true. To these I present the composition as an Art-Product alone: —let us say as a Romance; or, if I be not urging too lofty a claim, as a Poem.

What I here propound is true: —therefore it cannot die: —or if by any means it be now trodden down so that it die, it will "rise again to the Life Everlasting."

Nevertheless it is as a Poem only that I wish this work to be judged after I am dead.

E. A. P.

["TRANSLATOR'S NOTE" TO *EUREKA* (1863)]

The last pages of the book indicate to the reader the meaning that should be attributed to the term *Life Everlasting*—which also occurs at the end of the preface.

The word is used in a pantheistic sense, not in the religious sense that is commonly intended. *Life Everlasting* therefore in this case means: *the indeterminate series of God's existences, be it in the state of concentration, or in the state of dissemination.*

[UNPUBLISHED "TRANSLATOR'S AFTERWORD" TO *HISTOIRES GROTESQUES ET SÉRIEUSES* (1864)]

To the sincere appreciators of the talents of Edgar Poe let me say that I consider my task as finished, even though I might have taken pleasure in pleasing them with further installments. The two series of *Histoires extraordinaires* and *Nouvelles Histoires extraordinaires*, as well as the *Aventures d'Arthur Gordon Pym*, will suffice to present Edgar Poe in his various guises as a visionary storyteller, at times terrifying, at times amiable, alternately sarcastic and tenderhearted, always the philosopher and the analyst, a great lover of the magic of absolute verisimilitude and of the most disinterested jest. *Eureka* will have introduced them to the ambitious and subtle dialectician. If my task could have been fruitfully continued in a country such as France, it would remain to me to present Edgar Poe the poet and Edgar Poe the literary critic. Any true lover of poetry will recognize that the former of these duties is almost impossible to carry out and that my very humble and very devoted talents as a translator do not permit me to compensate for the absent sensual delights of rhythm and rhyme. To those readers possessed of insight, the fragments of poetry inserted into his short stories—such as "The Conqueror Worm" in "Ligeia," or "The Haunted Palace" in "The Fall of the House of Usher," or that most mysteriously eloquent poem "The Raven"—will have to suffice to grant them a glimpse of all the wonders of this pure poet.

As for his second field of talent—that of criticism—it is easy to understand why what I might call Edgar Poe's *Causeries du lundi** would stand little chance of pleasing these flighty Parisians, who could not give a fig about those literary quarrels which divide a nation that is still very young and which turn the North against the South both in matters literary and political.

To conclude, let me say to my unknown French friends of Edgar Poe that I am proud and delighted to have introduced a new genre of beauty into their memory; and furthermore—why not admit this outright?—let me say that I found the willpower to do this because of the pleasure it gave me to present them with a man who in many respects resembled me, that is, who was part of myself.

The time will soon come—or so I am led to believe—when the esteemed publishers of the French mass-market editions of the works of Edgar Poe will see the glorious necessity of issuing them in a material form that would be more durable and more attractive to book collectors, and in an edition where the fragments of which they are currently composed would be arranged in a more definitive and analogical fashion.

* *Causeries du lundi:* Sainte-Beuve's popular *Monday Chats* on literary topics. Baudelaire is referring to volume 3 of *The Works of the Late Edgar Allan Poe,* edited by R. W. Griswold and published in 1850: *The Literati: Some Honest Opinions About Authorial Merits and Demerits, with Occasional Words of Personality, Together with Marginalia, Suggestions, and Essays.*

Letter to Jules Janin

Jules Janin (1804–1874), sometimes known as the "prince of critics" (or, among his detractors, as "first among the second-raters"), was a prolific author of theater reviews for the *Journal des débats*, as well as a frequent contributor of feuilletons to the mainstream press. He is perhaps best remembered today for the tasteless pseudo-obituary of Gérard de Nerval that he published in 1841 shortly after Nerval had been briefly committed to a mental institution, ascribing the "death" of the poet's reason to the dangers of the poetic imagination, especially when addled by the reading of too much German literature (Nerval had translated Goethe's *Faust* and would later translate Heine). In his "Heinrich Heine and Poets in Their Youth," which appeared in the February 11, 1865, issue of *L'Indépendance belge*, Janin continues in this jeeringly ethnophobic vein. While generally laudatory of Heine's early work, Janin finds that his poetry is at once too melancholy and too ironic—flaws that he imputes to the poet's worship of Byron and Goethe. To Heine's sickly and self-reflexive irony, so admired by modern "neocritics," Janin opposes "the good old French poets" of the sixteenth and seventeenth centuries (Jean-Antoine de Baïf, Mathurin Régnier, Théophile de Viau, Philippe Desportes), underscoring the naive and robust joy with which they celebrated their muses in simple and affecting songs of love. Among the nineteenth-century French poets whom Janin singles out as being vastly superior to fashionable foreigners, he lists such now-forgotten figures as Mme. de Girardin, Jean-Pons-Guillaume Viennet, Auguste Barbier, Hégésippe Moreau, and Victor de Laprade—pointedly ignoring the work of Baudelaire and Gautier. In his unfinished reply to Janin's article, Baudelaire proposes his own cosmopolitan countercanon of modern poetry: Lord Byron, Alfred, Lord Tennyson, Poe, Mikhail Lermontov, Giacomo Leopardi, José de Espronceda. Janin cruelly concludes his piece with an evocation of Heine's final agony during the long illness that led to his death in his *Matrazingruft* in 1856: "Heine was in fact the first victim of his inexorable irony; since he had assigned himself the task of always laughing—today, tomorrow, forever—he never knew during his own lifetime the sweet delight of tears, nor did he therefore encourage any to be shed over his coffin." Reading the piece, Baudelaire, who was slowly dying à la Heine in Brussels, hit the ceiling and delivered himself of these fragmentary fulminations, which he signed (according to Pichois) with a sketch of a *badelaire*—that is (in ancient usage), of a scimitar. His one consolation: Janin's candidacy to the Académie française was rejected in 1865. "The prince of critics" would have to wait another five years to become an Immortal.

Monsieur, I feast upon your feuilletons—in *L'Indépendance* no less, which, in its moments of ingratitude, sometimes shows less than full respect toward your person. Treating you in the fashion of Buloz. Or like Auguste Barbier by the *Revue de Paris*.* The Official Disclaimer. *L'Indépendance* is possessed of convictions that do not allow it to bemoan the misfortunes of a queen. This is why I read you; for I vaguely count myself among your friends, that is, if you believe as do I that admiration inspires a kind of friendship.

But your article of yesterday caused me to fly into a rage. Let me explain why.

So it turns out Henri Heine was human! Bizarre. It turns out Catalina† was human. A monster nevertheless, since he conspired in favor of the poor. Henri Heine could be nasty—yes, like so many sensitive men, irritated at having to live among scum. By *Scum* I mean those people who have no familiarity with poetry (the *Genus irritable vatum*).‡

Let's therefore examine the heart of Henri Heine in his youth.

The fragments of his that you quote are charming, but I see perfectly well that what shocks you is their sorrowfulness, their irony. If J. J. were emperor he would decree that it was forbidden to weep or to hang oneself under his reign—or even to laugh up one's sleeve. *When Augustus took a drink*, etc.§ *You are a happy man*. I pity you for being so easily happy. A man must fall very low indeed to believe himself happy! Or

---

* *Buloz and Barbier:* François Buloz, editor of the *Revue des deux mondes*, had inserted an "official disclaimer" when publishing eighteen of Baudelaire's poems in 1855. The *Revue de Paris* resorted to the same strategy when it printed Barbier's prorevolutionary poem "La Curée" in 1830, as did *L'Indépendance belge* in a note appended to Janin's recent article on Marie-Antoinette.

† *Catalina:* Lucius Sergius Catilina, first-century BCE Roman senator associated with the second Catilinarian conspiracy to overthrow the Republic.

‡ *Genus irritable vatum:* "The irritable race of poets" (Horace).

§ *When Augustus took a drink:* "When Augustus took a drink, Poland got drunk" (Voltaire).

408 | CHARLES BAUDELAIRE

perhaps this is just a sardonic outburst on your part; perhaps you are merely smiling to hide the fox that is gnawing at your entrails. If this were indeed the case, everything would be forgiven. If my tongue were able to utter words such as yours, it would be seized by paralysis as a result.

———

You do not like discrepancy* or dissonance. Away with those indiscreet individuals who might unsettle the somnolence of your self-content. Long live the *ariettes* of Florian.† Away with the powerful laments of the knight Tannhäuser, *aspiring to pain*. You like the kind of music one can listen to without hearing it, or the kinds of tragedies one can pick up in the middle.

Away with all these poets whose pockets are filled with daggers, with gall, with vials of laudanum. This man is sad, therefore he scandalizes me. —He lacks a Margot, and has never had one. Long live Horace drinking his eggnog or, rather, his falernian wine, and pinching his little Lisette like the jolly good fellow he is, a fine old poetaster without any deviltry or fury—without *aestus*!‡

———

Among the various fine funerals that you cite, I believe you mention Béranger's.§ There was nothing fine about it, believe me. A prefect of police said that he had skipped the affair: the only fine sight was Mme. Louise Colet mixing it up with the police officers. And Pierre Leroux came up with the appropriate quip: "I had always warned Béranger that he would miss his own funeral."

* *Discrepancy:* Baudelaire here gallicizes the English word "discrepancy."

† *Florian* and *Tannhaüser:* Florian Leopold Gassmann, an eighteenth-century composer of light comic operas and fables. Baudelaire had published an important review of Richard Wagner's *Tannhäuser* in 1861.

‡ *Aestus!:* Boiling, agitated, seething.

§ *Béranger:* The popular *chansonnier* was given a state funeral in July 1857—just a month before the trial of *Les Fleurs du mal*—despite his republican sympathies. *Louise Colet:* The poet was at that point still the mistress of Flaubert. *Pierre Leroux*, a prominent disciple of Saint-Simon, introduced the term "socialism" into French discourse.

———

Béranger? People have uttered a number of verities about this ribald poet. Much more could be said about him. Let's move on.

———

De Musset. Poetic facility; but not very cheerful. Which would contradict your thesis. A lousy poet, by the way. You find his work these days lying around girls' rooms among the spun-glass dogs, the Caveau songbook, and porcelain items won at the lottery of Asnières. —A languid undertaker.

———

Sainte-Beuve. O not him, stop right there! Can you explain this particular kind of beauty? An undergrad Werther.* Which again contradicts your thesis.

———

Banville and Viennet.† Major catastrophe. Viennet, the perfect gentleman, heroically setting out to destroy poetry; but what about Rhyme!!! or even Reason!!! —I know that you always have some ulterior purpose in mind. . . . So, who urged you to bring him up?

———

Delphine Gay! —Leconte de Lisle.‡ Do you find the latter all that amusing, suitable to your liking, cross your heart?

---

* *An undergrad Werther:* An allusion to the *Weltschmerz* of Sainte-Beuve's first volume of poems, *Vie, poesies et pensées de Joseph Delorme* (1829), much admired by Baudelaire.

† *Banville* and *Viennet:* Théodore de Banville, author of *Odes funabulesques* (1857). Jean-Pons-Guillaume Viennet, neoclassical poet, playwright, and politician, elected to the French Academy in 1830.

‡ *Delphine Gay* and *Leconte de Lisle:* Delphine Gay, wife of the French newspaper publisher Émile de Girardin, was the author of best-selling romances and popular

—And Gautier? And Valmore?* And me? —My bag of tricks.

I'm providing a paraphrase of the *genus irritabile vatum* in defense not only of Henri Heine but of all poets. These poor devils (the crowning achievements of humanity) are insulted by everybody. When they are thirsty and ask for a glass of water, there are Trimalcions quick to accuse them of being drunkards. Trimalcion† wipes his fingers on the hair of his slaves; but if a poet so much as dared to want to have a few bourgeois in his stable, many would find this outrageous.

———

You say: "Here is something fine and dandy that I shall never understand. . . . The neocritics . . . ."

Stop putting on such old-fashioned airs; they will be of no help to you, not even with Master Villemain.

———

Jules Janin does not want any images that cause him distress.

What about the death of Charlot?‡

And that last kiss in the lunette of the guillotine?

And the Bosphorus, so enchanting when seen, head impaled, from the tip of a stake?

And the Mire?

And the Capuchins? And the cankers smoking under the red-hot sword?

---

verse. *Leconte de Lisle*, whose poetry Baudelaire had damned with faint praise in an 1861 review, was associated with the Parnassian school.

* *Gautier* and *Valmore:* Baudelaire dedicated the 1857 edition of *Les Fleurs du mal* to Théophile Gautier ("Au poète impeccable, au parfait magicien ès lettres française, à mon très-cher et très-vénéré maître et ami"). *Marceline Desbordes-Valmore*, warmly praised by Baudelaire in an 1861 review, would later exercise an important influence on the prosody of Verlaine and Rimbaud through her practice of the *vers impair*.

† *Trimalcion:* Host of the banquet in Petronius's *Satyricon*, which Baudelaire was rereading in Brussels.

‡ *The death of Charlot:* Alludes, together with the following lines, to various episodes in Janin's early gothic novel *L'Ane mort et la femme guillotine* (1827)—his faddish contribution to the craze for *la littérature frénétique* (as Charles Nodier had dubbed it).

When the devil grows old, he turns into a . . . shepherd. Go take your white sheep out to pasture.

Down with suicides. Down with these nasty troublemakers. Under your reign, *Janino Imperatore*, one could never say out loud: Gérard de Nerval* hanged himself. You would even have police inspectors place under house arrest anybody caught without the grimace of happiness on their lips.

Catalina, a man of wit without doubt, because he had friends in the opposition party, which only a Belgian would find unintelligible.

Always Horace and Margoton! You are careful not to choose Juvenal, Lucan, or Petronius. The last with his terrifying filth, his depressing drollery. (You would of course be on Trimalcion's side, *because he is happy*, admit it.) Lucan with his regrets for Brutus and Pompey, his dead come back to life, his witches from Thessaly making the moon dance on deserted plains. And Juvenal with his bursts of laughter so full of rage. For you have not failed to observe that Juvenal's anger is always provoked by the poor or oppressed. O the filthy wretched fellow! Long live Horace and all those to whom Babet so freely dispenses her favors.

Trimalcion is stupid, *but he is happy*. He is so vain that he sends his servants into stiches, but *he is happy*. He is vile and despicable, but

---

* *Gérard de Nerval:* Janin had published a tasteless mock-obituary of Nerval when the poet was committed to a mental institution in 1841. After Nerval's suicide in late January 1855, a number of his literary friends (including Gautier) tried to cover up the nature of his death.

happy. He is ostentatious about his wealth and pretends to be a *bon vi-vant*; he is ridiculous, but *he is happy.* Ah, let us pardon those who are *happy.* Happiness is such a fine and universal *excuse,* isn't it?

———

Ah, you are happy, Monsieur. What! —If you were to say: I am virtuous, I would understand what that implied: I suffer less than the next man. But no: you are *happy.* That is, easy to satisfy? I pity you, and consider my foul humor far more distinguished than your beatitude. —I would even go so far as to ask you whether this earthly spectacle suffices you. What! You have never felt the urge *to make your exit,* if only for a change of scene? I have very serious reasons for pitying the man who is not in love with Death.

Byron, Tennyson, Poe, and Co.
Melancholy firmament of modern poetry. Stars of the first order.
Why have things changed? A serious question, one which I do not have the time to explain to you here. But you haven't even dreamed of asking yourself this question. Things have changed because they had to change. Your old friend Master Villemain whispers into your ear the word: Decadence. It's a word that ignorant schoolmasters find quite useful, a vague word behind which we can hide our laziness and your obliviousness to law.

But why this repeated insistence on happiness? For your own entertainment? Why would sorrow not possess its particular beauty? And horror as well? And anything? Or everything?

———

I can already hear your objections. I know which side you are on. You would probably dare to maintain that one has no right to place dead men's skulls into soup dishes or claim that the tiny corpse of a newborn babe would make a fine headscarf. (A joke that in fact was carried out; but alas, back in the good old days!) —There would nevertheless be a great deal to say about this. —You wound me in my dearest convictions. In these matters, everything depends on the sauce, that is, on genius.

———

Why would the poet not be a grinder of poisons as well as a confectioner of sweets, a man who raises serpents for miracles and fairground displays, an Indian snake-charmer in love with his reptiles, delighting in the icy caresses of their coils at the same time that he delights in the terrors of the crowd?

———

In your article, two parts that are equally ridiculous. Ignorance of Heine and of poetry in general. An absurd thesis concerning poets in their youth. A poet is not old or young, he just is. He is what he wants. A virgin, he sings of debauchery; sober, he sings of drunkenness.

(Your disgusting love for happiness makes me think of M. Véron* calling for a more *affectionate* literature. Your taste for honest decency is, moreover, merely a form of sybaritism. M. Véron said this in pure innocence. Sue's *Wandering Jew* had no doubt depressed him. He too wanted nothing better than sweet, untroubling emotions.)

———

As for poets in their Youth:
  Books *lived*, poems *lived*.
Ask M. Villemain about this. Despite his incorrigible love for solecisms, I doubt he would swallow this one.

Byron, loquacity, redundancy. Some of your qualities, Monsieur. But, in return, those sublime flaws that make for a great poet: melancholy, always inseparable from the sensation of beauty, and a fiery, diabolical personality. A salamander mind.

* *M. Véron:* Publisher of *Le Constitutionnel*, in whose pages Eugène Sue's serial pot-boiler *Le Juif errant* had appeared in 1844.

———

Byron. Tennyson. E. Poe. Lermontov. Leopardi. Espronceda.* —But none of them sang of Margot! —Wait a minute! I didn't name a single Frenchman. France is poor in poets.

French poetry. Its stream ran dry under Louis XIV. Reappears with Chénier† (Marie-Joseph). The other Chénier is merely a Marie-Antoinette furniture maker.

Finally, renewal and explosion under Charles X.

———

Your French band music. Spinet and orchestra. Poetry that's skin-deep. Thomas Hood's Cupid.‡

Your pack of poets running neck to neck like bassets and greyhounds, like weasels and giraffes.

Let's analyze them one by one.

And Théophile Gautier? And me?

———

Lecomte Delille (as you spell it). Your various blunders. *Jean Pharond* for Pharamond. *Jean Beaudlair*.§ Don't spell it *Gauthier* if you want to make up for your absent-mindedness, and don't imitate his publishers who know him so poorly that they always mangle his name. The versification of a prose piece. And you were there. Villefranche's tic.

A congenital tic.

---

* *Lermontov, Leopardi, Espronceda:* This generation of romantics died relatively young: the Italian Leopardi in 1837, at age thirty-nine; the Russian Lermontov in 1841, at age thirty-seven; and the Spaniard Espronceda in 1842, at thirty-four.

† *Chénier:* Baudelaire provocatively prefers the declamatory verse of Marie-Joseph Chénier to that of his older brother, André Chénier, a martyr of the French Revolution and commonly considered the greatest of France's eighteenth-century poets.

‡ *Thomas Hood's Cupid:* The obese, porcine figure of fun of Hood's *Whims and Oddities* (1823).

§ *Jean Beaudlair:* Baudelaire, like Gautier, is nowhere mentioned in Janin's survey of contemporary poetry, but he nonetheless takes delight in mocking the critic's frequent misspellings of names (e.g. "Flobert" for "Flaubert," "Gauthier" for "Gautier").

Natural function.
  Villefranche
   and Argenteuil.
Gascony.
Franche-Comté.
Normandy.
Belgium.

———

You are a happy man. This is enough to console you for all your errors. You understand nothing about the architecture of words, about the plasticity of language; nothing about painting, about music, about poetry. But take consolation in the fact that neither Balzac nor Chateaubriand ever managed to write a decent line of verse. But they at least knew how to recognize good poetry when they saw it.

———

Begin the piece with my flying into a rage. Stone thrown into my garden or rather into our garden.

(In the *Janin* article.)
Janin praises Cicero, a journalist having his little joke. Perhaps it's a kiss blown in Master Villemain's direction.
Cicero the *philippiste*. A dirty little upstart.
He is our own Caesar. (De Sacy.)
Janin probably had his reasons for including Viennet among the poets. Similarly, he probably had his reasons for praising Cicero. Cicero is not of the French Academy, yet one could claim that he is in it, via Villemain and the flunkies of the House of Orléans.

Letter to Mme. Paul Meurice

Madame Paul Meurice, née Eléonore-Palmyre Granger (1819–1874), was the wife of the playwright Paul Meurice, a close associate of Victor Hugo who looked after the latter's financial and literary interests during his twenty years of exile. Her father was the painter Jean-Pierre Granger, a student of David and a friend of Ingres (who did a pencil portrait of her in 1843), which explains her links to the artistic milieu of Manet and Fantin-Latour. Baudelaire had sent her a copy of his *Richard Wagner* in 1861 and, while in Belgium, struck up a warm and slightly flirtatious correspondence with her—the only woman, with the exception of his mother, with whom he maintained any sort of epistolary relation, even though she was clearly a member of the enemy Hugo camp. In August 1866, when Baudelaire was hospitalized in Paris in the Dufour clinic on the rue du Dôme, she visited the aphasic poet and, at Champfleury's suggestion, played excerpts from *Tannhäuser* for him on the piano—apparently to beneficial effect.

[Brussels] Friday, February 3, 1865

When one is in receipt of a letter so charming, and especially so unexpected and so undeserved, one's first duty is to answer it immediately; I thus find myself quite guilty of having put off for nearly a month the pleasure of replying to you and of offering you my thanks. I could tell you—which is true enough—that I am often ill, but this would be a paltry excuse: colds, neuralgias, and fevers never last thirty days. I prefer to tell you the truth—that I am too inclined to take advantage of the indulgence of my friends, and that there is something in the atmosphere of this loathsome climate that not only dulls [*abêtit*] the spirit but also hardens the heart, thereby causing us to become derelict in all our duties.

You will imagine, dear Madame, how much pleasure you have given me when I admit how chagrined I was to have sent you a letter filled with such foolishness—as casually as I might have written a close friend—and that, seeing this letter now set in stone, I was hardly expecting any reply, already casting about for means of asking your forgiveness. Thus, in reading your entirely unexpected reply, I experienced a twofold pleasure—first, the pleasure of simply *hearing you speak,* and second, the pleasure of sheer astonishment. I must admit that you are decidedly possessed of the finest qualities in this world.

Let me immediately address some of your remarks that touched me most deeply. No, let me assure you, there is nothing *specific* that is getting me down. I am, as always, in a foul mood (my particular malady) because of the *bêtise* that surrounds me and because I am discontented with myself. But in France, where there is less *bêtise,* where *bêtise* takes on a politer form, I would suffer just as much: and even if I had strictly nothing to reproach myself for, I would be equally discontented—because I would dream of doing better. Therefore, whether I be living in Paris or Brussels or some other unknown city, I am bound to find myself ill, and incurably so. There is a kind misanthropy that stems, not from poor character, but rather from an exacerbated sensibility and a tendency to fly into outrage too freely. —Why am I staying on in Brussels—a place I in fact loathe? — *First and foremost, because this is where I happen to be,* and in my current state I would be miserable anywhere. Second, because I have decided to do penance and shall continue to do so until I have healed myself of my vices (a slow process) and until a certain person to whom I have entrusted my literary affairs in Paris has resolved certain issues.

Because you forgive me everything and allow me to speak absolutely freely with you, I shall tell you that this Belgium that I loathe so deeply has already rendered me a great service. *It has taught me to do without everything.* Which is considerable. *I have become well behaved, given the impossibility of satisfying myself.* I have always loved pleasure, which has perhaps done me the greatest harm. In a small port town, there is the pleasure of studying the activity of the harbor, the comings and goings of the boats, the pleasure of having drinks in a bar with people whose station may be low but whose sensibilities I find of interest. Here there is nothing. The poor people here don't even inspire any charity on my part. At Paris, there are dinners with friends, museums, music, women. Here there is nothing. Eating well is out of the question. As you know, there is no Belgian cuisine: these people here don't even know how to cook eggs or grill meats. Wine is considered something precious and rare, to be consumed only on special occasions. In fact, I am fairly convinced these animals drink it only out of vanity, to prove that they are connoisseurs. As for cheap, fresh wine, the kind you quaff down by the glassful when you're thirsty, impossible to find any here. —As for chivalry, it is even in shorter supply. The sight of a Belgian woman vaguely makes me want to pass out. Should the god Eros himself want to immediately extinguish all his flames, all he would have to do is look a Belgian female in the face.

In addition, the coarse manners of the women (which equal those of the men) detract from their charm, if these poor creatures indeed were capable of displaying it. A few months ago, I found myself lost one night in an area of town that was unfamiliar to me; I asked two young women for directions and they replied: *Gott for damn!* (or *domn!*) (I'm transcribing this poorly: no Belgian has ever been able to explain the spelling of this national curse word, but it is the equivalent of *Sacré nom de Dieu!*). So these two young ladies answered me: *God dammit all! Stop pestering us!* —As for the men, they never miss a chance to exercise their special vocation for grossness. One day when the streets were iced over, I saw a little actress from the *Théatre du Parc* slip and fall. She had hurt herself quite badly, and as I was struggling to help her back onto her feet, a Belgian who was passing by kicked away the muff she had dropped on the street, saying: "See? Sure you're not forgetting anything?" —The man was perhaps a member of Parliament, a minister, a prince, perhaps the King himself. A Parisian worker would have picked up the muff like a gentleman and returned it to the lady.

As I was saying to you, I would invite all voluptuaries to come live in Belgium. They would quickly be cured of their ways and in a few months their disgust *would allow them to regain their virginity*.

Another service that this country of scoundrels has rendered me. —You have teased me on more than one occasion about my tendencies toward mysticism! —Let me assure you that even you would become a practicing Christian here—if only out of self-respect or nonconformism. The sight of all these atheistical quadrupeds has served to strengthen my ideas about religion. I do not even have nice things to say about their *Catholics.* The liberals here are atheists, the Catholics are superstitious and just as gross as the former, and both parties are dominated by the same hypocrisy.

Two more little anecdotes, as Belgian as can be—just for your amusement.

One day a waiter in a café said to me: "You go to church, Monsieur? You were seen at such and such a church at Christmastime." I replied: "Mum's the word." But I said to myself: "They're surely going to take this up at a cabinet meeting." —Two days later I run into a Belgian who says to me: "Oh, so you're going to mass, are you? *Gott for domn!"* (the same old curse I cannot manage to transcribe). "What are you going to do at mass, SINCE YOU ARE NOT EVEN CARRYING A MISSAL?" This is a perfect example of Belgian logic: One does not pray without a book. One does not think without rules and regulations. But he's getting something quite wrong here too: a missal would be of no use to a Belgian—he wouldn't be able to understand prayers in written form.

One day I am taken, with great ceremony, to visit the home of a minister who owns an extremely valuable collection of paintings. Toward the end of the visit I am escorted to a Bartolini painted by Ingres. This was the moment when I was supposed to go into ecstasy—but I had not been properly forewarned. I said: "This is most likely an Ingres. The hands and the face are too exaggerated; it lacks *style;* it's smudgy red in color. There was a great man who preceded Ingres and who was by far the greater genius. Namely, David." At which point the minister turns toward my keeper (because I think that I too was on *show*) and delicately inquires: "If I am not mistaken, the market for Davids has RISEN of late, has it not?" I could not control myself: I reassured him that among people of intelligence the market for Davids had never *fallen.*

Another service that Belgium has rendered me! Inform Bracquemond* of this. It has disillusioned me insofar as Rubens is concerned. Upon leaving Paris, I had far too high an opinion of this oaf. Rubens is the only type of gentleman that Belgium could produce, that is, a lout

---

* *Braquemond:* Félix Braquemond had designed a frontispiece (featuring a baroque skeleton, but never published) for the 1861 edition of *Les Fleurs du mal,* and later painted a portrait of the aging Mme. Meurice in 1866.

decked out in silks. To the finest Rubens I would now prefer a small Ro-
man bronze, or an Egyptian spoon—in wood.

Please convey my sincere regards to your husband. And greetings to
Fantin and Manet.* —M. Charles Hugo† has asked me to remind you
of his fond memories of you. —It would seem that his father is about
to move here. Zounds! I was about to forget the extremely serious and
interesting question of what fashions you propose to wear. You were
right to bring this up to me, you know how much this interests me. As
far as fashion is concerned I am almost as erudite as is Malassis when
it comes to ancient books or botany. For the poor fellow has gone in for
botany (and not for entomology, for there are no insects in the woods
of this country, just as there are no birds: animals flee the Belgians). I
have understood all your fashion choices; they remind me of times that
still are fresh in my mind.

As for your hairstyle, I have to admit to my shame that I understand
it less. I have only one remark to make to you: when a lovely woman is
possessed of white hair, whatever her hairstyle, she should absolutely
be sure to *show it off*. It adds to her beauty.

I gallantly kiss your two hands and clasp them in mine most fervidly.

C. B.

---

* *Fantin and Manet:* The two were friends: Fantin-Latour would paint a portrait of
Manet in 1867. Baudelaire remained in regular contact with Manet during his Brus-
sels years.

† *Charles Hugo:* Hugo's eldest son, who had moved to Brussels in 1864 with his
brother François-Victor and his mother, Adèle.

Chronology of Baudelaire's Life

1821
Birth of Charles-Pierre Baudelaire in Paris on April 9. His father, Joseph-François Baudelaire, a former priest, retired civil servant, and amateur painter, is sixty-two, and his mother, Caroline Dufaÿs, twenty-seven.

1827
His father dies.

1828
His mother marries Jacques Aupick, a career military officer and veteran of the Napoleonic Wars.

1830–31
Aupick named lieutenant colonel for his part in the conquest of Algiers.

1832–35
Attends boarding school in Lyon, site of worker unrest, which his stepfather is assigned to quell.

1836–39
Attends the Lycée Louis-le-Grand in Paris. Expelled during his final year, he nonetheless passes his *baccalauréat* exam.

1840
Enrolls in law school. First poems. Debts. Prostitutes. Syphilis.

1841

To encourage him to mend his spendthrift ways, the Aupick family council sends him on a long sea voyage. On a steamboat bound for Calcutta, he stops off at Mauritius, then at Réunion, before deciding to return, via Cape Town, to Bordeaux.

1842–44

Comes into a comfortable inheritance, which he proceeds to squander. Rents an apartment in an old *hôtel particulier* on the quai d'Anjou; takes a mistress, Jeanne Duval, a Haitian-born actress and dancer of mixed French and African ancestry; and lives the bohemian life of a dandy. Alarmed by his profligacy, the family council names Narcisse Ancelle, a notary in Neuilly (and later its mayor), as the trustee of his estate, or *conseil judiciaire*. In concert with his mother, Mme. Aupick, Ancelle will control his ward's purse strings for the remainder of his days.

1845

First published poem ("À une dame créole") and first piece of art criticism, *Salon de 1845*, signed Baudelaire Dufaÿis. First known suicide attempt. Working title of the future *Fleurs du mal* is *Les Lesbiennes*.

1846

Salon de 1846. A collection of aphorisms, *Choix de maximes consolantes sur l'amour*, and other fiction projects.

1847

A short novella, *La Fanfarlo*. Portrait of Baudelaire by Courbet. Begins reading Poe. General Aupick named commander of the École Polytechnique, the army's military academy, in Paris.

1848

Participates, alongside Courbet, in the street fighting of the February Revolution. Founds the socialist newspaper *Salut public* with Champfleury. Takes workers' side in June uprising. Contacts with Proudhon and Blanqui. First translation of Poe, "The Magnetic Revelation." Aupick named minister plenipotentiary to Turkey.

1849

A volume of poetry with the socialist title *Les Limbes* is announced for publication on the first anniversary of the February Revolution but never appears. Spends end of year in Dijon, suffering from symptoms of syphilis.

1850

Moves in with Jeanne Duval in Neuilly. Meets his future publisher, the anarchist Poulet-Malassis, recently released from prison for participating in the June 1848 insurrection.

1851

Du vin et du haschisch comparés comme moyens de multiplication de l'individualité and eleven new poems. Aupick named ambassador to Madrid. Discovers the work of Joseph de Maistre. His "fury" at Napoleon's coup d'état of December 2 "physically depoliticizes" him.

1852

Breaks with Jeanne. Publishes a long biographical essay on Poe, who had died three years earlier. Sends his first poem to Mme. Sabatier.

1853

Morale du joujou. Further translations of Poe. Theater projects.

1854

Brief liaison with the actress Marie Daubrun. Further theater projects (*L'Ivrogne*).

1855

Eighteen poems with the title *Les Fleurs du mal* appear in the prestigious *Revue des deux mondes*. Writes an essay on laughter as well as studies of Delacroix and Ingres. Reviews the Paris 1855 Exposition Universelle. Distances himself from Courbet's brand of "realism." First notes for *Fusées*. First two published prose poems. Aupick, now a senator, buys a house at Honfleur on the Normandy coast.

1856

Michel Lévy brings out Baudelaire's translation of Poe's *Histoires extraordinaires*, which will go through five editions. Breaks with Jeanne. Signs a contract with Poulet-Malassis for *Les Fleurs du mal* and a volume of art criticism.

1857

Publishes Poe's *Nouvelles Histoires extraordinaires* with Lévy. Death of Aupick. *Les Fleurs du mal* appears in June and is immediately denounced for its "monstrosities" by *Le Figaro*. Baudelaire and his publisher, Poulet-Malassis, placed on trial for the book in August, are required to remove six of the offending poems and to pay steep fines. Six prose poems appear under the title "Poëmes nocturnes." Essays on French and foreign caricaturists, as well as on Flaubert's *Madame Bovary*, which had been prosecuted the same year.

1858

Takes ether and opium to treat his various physical afflictions. Translates Poe's *Aventures d'Arthur Gordon Pym*. Moves back in with Jeanne in Neuilly.

1859

Jeanne in municipal clinic. Spends a productive six months with his mother in Honfleur on the Normandy coast. Annus mirabilis: First notes toward *Mon Coeur mis à nu*. *Le Salon de 1859*. Essay on Théophile Gautier. Composition of "Le Cygne." Publication of "Les Sept Vieillards," "Les Petites Vieilles," and "Le Voyage." Moves to the Hôtel de Dieppe, rue d'Amsterdam, where he will reside on a more or less permanent basis until his departure for Belgium in 1864.

1860

Experiences "a sort of stroke" and complains of "cerebral congestion," nausea, and dizzy spells. With Poulet-Malassis publishes *Les Paradis artificiels*, which includes his essays on opium and hashish and his adaptation of De Quincey's *Confessions of an English Opium Eater*. Considers suicide. Briefly moves to Neuilly to take care of the ailing Jeanne.

1861

Second Poulet-Malassis edition of *Les Fleurs du mal*, enlarged by the addition of the *Tableaux parisiens* section. Publishes *Richard Wagner et Tannhäuser à Paris*. Major depression: complains of the reappearance of his symptoms of syphilis. Sells the rights to all his past and future literary works to Poulet-Malassis. Publishes a series of studies on contemporary French writers. Presents himself as a candidate for a vacant seat at the French Academy. Breaks with Jeanne.

1862

In January, experiences "the wind of the wing of imbecility" passing over his head. Withdraws his candidacy to the French Academy in February, having failed to garner any votes. Twenty *Poèmes en prose* appear in *La Presse*, with a dedicatory epistle to Arsène Houssaye. Poulet-Malassis, bankrupt, lands in debtor's prison.

1863

Ever deeper in debt, Baudelaire (again) sells the rights to his literary works, this time to the leftwing publisher Hetzel. Publishes a long obituary homage to Delacroix, in addition to nine new prose poems. Sells Lévy his royalties to his complete translations of Poe (five volumes in all, his sole steady source of literary income). *Le Peintre de la vie moderne*, in preparation for several years, finally appears in *Le Figaro*. Poulet-Malassis, released from prison, moves his semiclandestine publishing operations to Brussels.

1864

Le Figaro publishes his anonymous attack on the celebrations of the three-hundredth anniversary of Shakespeare's birth, which he denounces as a publicity stunt for Hugo's new book, *William Shakespeare*. Leaves for Brussels in late April, where he takes up residence at the Hôtel du Grand Miroir and delivers five (poorly paid, poorly attended) lectures—one on Delacroix, one on Gautier, and three on drugs and literature, drawn from his *Paradis artificiels*. Attempts to find a publisher for his works in Brussels also fail. Visits several towns of Belgium during the summer, with a view toward writing a larger book about (or, rather, against) the country, to be entitled *Lettres belges* and signed Charles de Féyis, after his mother's maiden name. Publishes further prose poems from his projected volume *Le Spleen de Paris*.

1865

Health worsens: neuralgias, rheumatisms, digestive problems. Publishes his final volume of Poe translations, *Histoires grotesques et sérieuses*. Attempts without success to place his new book, now called *Pauvre Belgique!*, with Paris publishers. Contractual and legal problems with both Hetzel and Poulet-Malassis arise as a result of his double-dealing. Frantic trip to Paris and to Honfleur in July to try to resolve the mess he has made of his literary affairs and to cadge more money out of his mother and friends. Drops off a packet of prose poems for publication in the *Revue nationale et étrangère*. Returns to the "hell" of Brussels in August, in an apocalyptic mood, medicating himself with opium, digitalis, belladonna, and quinine.

1866

Poulet-Malassis publishes *Les Épaves*, which collects the poems banned from the 1857 and 1861 editions of *Les Fleurs du mal*, as well as recent occasional verse. Health continues to decline: headaches, vomiting, vertigo. His Brussels doctor's diagnosis is "hysteria." Involves Ancelle in finding a publisher for the work he now calls *La Belgique déshabillée*, while continuing to try to bring *Le Spleen de Paris* to completion. Mid-March: collapses during a visit to the Church of Saint-Loup at Namur and is transported back to Brussels. What initially appears to be a mild stroke develops within two weeks into severe hemiplegia, characterized by partial paralysis and aphasia. In mid-April his mother arrives in Brussels to care for him. In late June she accompanies him back to Paris, where he is placed in a private clinic overlooking the Arc de Triomphe. Although lucid, he is barely capable of speech, except for the swear-word "*Crénom!*" He receives visits from Nadar, Champfleury, Banville, Leconte de Lisle, Hetzel, and other old acquaintances—among whom, Mme. Paul Meurice, who plays him excerpts from *Tannhäuser* on the piano.

1867

By mid-May he has become almost completely comatose, suffering from gangrene and bedsores. He dies in the Duval clinic on August 31, age forty-six, and is buried three days later in the Aupick family tomb in the Montparnasse cemetery.

1868

Lévy publishes the first two volumes of Baudelaire's *Oeuvres complètes*, edited by Banville and Asselineau: volume 1 contains *Les Fleurs du mal* (without the offending poems), introduced by Gautier; volume 2 is devoted to his *Salons* and selected art criticism.

1869

Asselineau publishes the first biography of Baudelaire, which contains excerpts from *Fusées* and *Mon Coeur mis à nu*, as well as sketches of his projected book on Belgium. Over the next two years, five more volumes of the *Oeuvres complètes* appear: volume 3 contains his *Art romantique* (texts on Delacroix, Wagner, and literary essays); volume 4, his *Paradis artificiels* and the first book publication of his *Petits poèmes en prose*; volumes 5 through 7, his translations of Poe.

1887

Oeuvres posthumes et correspondances inédites, edited and with a biographical introduction by Eugène Crépet, is published. Under the title *Journaux intimes* it includes the first (somewhat sanitized) printings of *Fusées, Mon Coeur mis à nu*, and selections from *La Belgique vraie*.